ARYAN INVASION THEORY AND INDIAN NATIONALISM

ARYAN INVASION THEORY
AND
INDIAN NATIONALISM

SHRIKANT G. TALAGERI

VOICE OF INDIA
NEW DELHI

First Published, 1993
Third Reprint, 2020

Fourth Reprint, 2022

ISBN 978-81-85990-02-6

Website: www.voiceofin.com

Published by Voice of India, 2/18, Ansari Road, New Delhi – 110 002.

Printed at Replika Press Pvt. Ltd.

PREFACE TO THE FIRST REPRINT

It is now ten years, almost to the month, since the first edition of this book was published, in early 1993. And much water has flown under the bridge since then — in respect of both the political aspects dealt with in Section I of this book as well as in respect of the academic Aryan homeland debate dealt with in Sections II and III.

However, I would prefer to deal with these developments in short in this preface than to make internal changes in the original book published in 1993. The reader can draw his own conclusions by comparing the two.

SECTION I

Section I of this book stands apart from the other two sections in its political nature. It was in order to keep the political debate, without pretending that it did not exist, separate from the academic debate, that my book was published in two versions: the Voice of India edition *with* the political section, entitled *Aryan Invasion Theory and Indian Nationalism*, and the Aditya Prakashan edition *without* the political section, entitled *The Aryan Invasion Theory — A Reappraisal.*

Unfortunately, this created two kinds of misunderstandings. On the one hand, there was the embarrassment of seeming to be a pretender to the authorship of two books when I had actually written only one (that was before my second book, *The Rigveda — A Historical Analysis* in 2000) — I actually met people who told me seriously that they had read "both" my books.

On the other, there was the phenomenon of academic readers being put off by the first section, and more politically-interested readers finding only that section readable.

As I said, much water has flown under the bridge since 1993, and I must make my position clear.

The three chapters in this section make three very logical points clear in a systematic manner:

1) That India has always been one civilizational entity, and its Hindu identity has been the binding force.

2) That Hinduism is as emphatically Indian and Indianising as Islam and Christianity are foreign and de-Indianising.

3) That Hinduism is not "Aryan" but "Indian", even from the Aryan invasion point of view.

If, in the course of elucidating these points (which I challenge any-one to refute) I have occasionally used avoidable and even, by hindsight, inappropriate turns of phrases (about certain individuals and political parties, or communities), well: "The moving finger writes, and having writ, moves on. Nor all thy piety nor wit can lure it back to cancel half a line, nor all thy tears wash out a word of it".

But, *then*, I was examining only one side of the coin. I find it necessary, now, to examine the other:

1) I pointed out, in Chapter 2, how Islam and Christianity can lead to foreign affiliations.

Well, today (at this time of writing), India is in the control of a regime which is umbilically affiliated to a foreign country: the U.S.A. All its socio-economic policies are devised for the benefit of that country, and all its political policies are harmonized with those of that country, as surely as the colonialist policies of the British East India Company were devised for the benefit of Great Britain and to the detriment of India and Indians.

But this regime functions in the name of Hinduism, Hindutva, Indian Nationalism and Swadeshi with as ruthless an irony as the Pig-regime of George Orwell's *Animal Farm* functioned in the name of Animalism!

As in *Animal Farm*, the regime is propped up by an army of countless slogan-shouting sheep, blindly faithful and hardworking horses, confused but compliant cows, and snarling dogs — all controlled by a range of "Hindutva" organizations (the Squealers of this Animal Farm), which otherwise make threatening noises, when elections are far off, to keep restive cadres in line, but close ranks, every-time an election approaches, and declare this to be a HINDU regime (and its opponents anti-Hindu).

All the anti-poor, anti-middle class, pro-rich, pro-NRI and pro-American policies of this elitist regime (dominated by the representatives and agents of the elitist world: ex-royalty, big business, films, sports, fashion, etc. etc. and increasingly anti-poor and virulently anti-worker) cannot prevent the Hindu masses from being brought to heel (at the time of every elections) by a variety of familiar and no-less-effective-because-repeated tactics: by visions of bogies in neighbouring countries, by the timely actions (Kargil, Godhra, and many more to come) of helpful "enemies", by Issues (temples, riots, etc) which appear at the time of elections with as unfailing a regularity as they die out immediately afterwards... all perfectly orchestrated by the Family with a Hundred Tongues — in the name of Hinduism and Hindutva.

Is this a Hindu government — under whose systematic supervision all aspects of Hindu culture and civilization are being slowly and systematically wiped out and rampant Americanisation is the norm, and under which only the most elitist or obscurantist aspects of the Hindu religion are promoted? Whose only Hindu philosophy is that of Charvaka (and America): *ṛnam kṛtvā ghṛtam pibeta* (repeated lowering of interest rates to actively discourage savings and promote the loan-and-credit culture)? Under whom casteist politics has reached new heights? Under whom the politics of vindictiveness (eg. persecution of news agencies exposing its corruption) is matched only by the politics of royal patronage (national awards for obscure singers who record the Leader's poems)? Under whom corruption and bureaucratic interference has reached unmatched proportions? Under whom people (including Hindus) are thrown out of jobs, and employment avenues completely blocked out on a war footing?

Clearly more foreign agency, anti-nationalism and injustice are possible in India in the name of Hinduism and Hindutva than in the name of Islam and Christianity or Secularism and Leftism. And more dangerous since it is cloaked in the garb of Nationalism.

2) I have depicted the Muslims as a more-or-less solid, monolithic bloc whose "foreign loyalties" and group identity lead them to "take to the streets and start vicious riots" at the drop of a pin in response to any event anywhere which affects Muslims.

The other side of the coin: today, not only can an oil-hungry America pick on one Muslim country after another to attack and destroy while fifty-odd Muslim countries stand by and watch, or even collaborate with the aggressor; but the Gujarat events can take place without causing Muslims anywhere else in India (or abroad) to raise a whimper: Muslim BJP ministers (voted to power by largely Muslim electorates) continue to support and even aggressively defend everything; Muslim Mullahs and clerics continue to join the BJP in large numbers and participate in their Iftar parties and other programmes; Muslim MPs, MLAs, etc. (even those, as in U.P., elected from parties which wooed the Muslim voters on "pseudo-secularist" and anti-BJP lines) continue to prop up BJP governments without batting an eyelid; and common Muslims go about their (as for all Indians under this regime) increasingly insecure lives as though nothing has happened.

Clearly, Money and power are greater factors than Religion. Humanity and Humanitarianism are the only casualties either way.

3) At the same time, those very forces of Islam which roused my ire in Chapter 2 have also given me occasion for reluctant respect:

In a world where bullies and masters (whether individuals, groups or nations) pick on weaker entities as targets of attack, and weaker entities crawl in submission before bullies and masters, and everything and everyone is up for sale to the highest bidder, we can also have an Osama Bin Laden who can attack an all-powerful America rather than pick on soft targets, and a Taliban which can allow itself to be wiped out rather than betray an ally.

Perhaps I have again allowed the moving finger to run away with me. In any case, politics and political entities are a depressing subject, and I will move on to sections II and III

SECTION II

Section II of the book deals with the background to the Aryan Invasion Theory, and requires no further clarification.

Dr. Rao's was the first major decipherment of the script (and the one which gave me the most personal satisfaction), and it was up to other scholars doing research on the subject to prove the correctness or incorrectness of his decipherment. However, no-one appears to have cared to take up the task as yet.

We have had a plethora of different decipherments since then, none of which, again, have been conclusively proved or disproved. I myself am not an authority on the subject.

Therefore, the last word on the subject of the Indus script is still to be said, and I can only leave it at that for the moment.

SECTION III

Section III of the book consists of my analysis and systematic refutation of the arguments in support of the Aryan Invasion Theory, and my presentation of an alternative theory more in tune with the facts: the theory of an Indian homeland.

As a basic analysis covering almost the complete gamut and range of arguments and aspects of the debate, this section will remain the foundation or stepping-stone for further research on the subject. However, in each individual aspect (represented by each chapter), there is ample scope for further detailed study and analysis, and argumentation.

This is particularly the case in respect of the chapters dealing with the literary evidence. And my analysis of the Rigveda in this book (which is primary, and consists of dealing with the arguments usually made from the text in support of the Aryan invasion theory) was carried to its logical conclusion in my second book *The Rigveda — a Historical Analysis* (Aditya Prakashan) published in 2000, and the conclusions therein will be even more conclusively reinforced in my next book (on which I am working at the moment) to be tentatively entitled *The Rigveda — Further Conclusive Evidence*.

My second book led to an offer of a "fully-paid scholarship" at Harvard University under Prof. Michael Witzel (whose writings on the subject I criticized in a full chapter in that book), with the clause that I was to be "flexible" in my views — a euphemism whose import is clear. My rejection of this offer led to a bitterly scathing, and purely personalized and un-objective, 30-odd page review of the book by Witzel on his (internet site) Electronic Journal of Vedic Studies, entitled "Westward Ho! The Incredible Wanderlust of the Ṛgvedic Tribes Exposed by S. Talageri", and a 90-odd page reply to this review from my side (available on the internet at www.bharatvani.org/general_inbox/talageri/ejvs/cover:html).

The case for the Rigvedic evidence in favour of an Indian homeland is now irrefutable, and more research can only further reinforce the case.

One basic point on which my analysis of the Rigveda in this book stands corrected is in respect of the geography of the text, and the location of the Purus. In this book, I had not yet analysed the date in the Rigveda, and I blindly accepted the general belief that the text was located in the Punjab (i.e. the Saptasindhu) region. My detailed analysis of the Rigveda in my second book shows beyond any doubt (and it fits in with all the extra-Rigvedic evidence) that the location was further to the east: in Haryana and Western U.P. This is a very fundamental correction, and my analysis of the Rigvedic and Puranic information in this book must be read with this point in mind.

All in all, the new research on the subject negates the presumptions and presuppositions on the basis of which literary analysis of the Rigveda has been carried on for the last two centuries: the only truly great Western scholar whose writings appear to presage many of our present conclusions is Prof. Edward Washburn Hopkins, Professor in Yale University (Connecticut, USA) in the late nineteenth and early twentieth centuries. I, therefore, end this preface with my respects to that great man.

AUTHOR

Dedicated to

my mother
SHAILA GANGADHAR TALAGERI
and my father
GANGADHAR SITARAM TALAGERI

FOREWORD

History of India is available in several versions — Hindu, Muslim, Christian, British, Marxist, Nehruvian. Each of these versions has created its own characrteristic politics and is, in turn, sustained by that politics.

Of these, the Hindu version alone is based on indigenous sources, literary and archaeological. The others have been floated by various imperialist ideologies that have flooded this country in the wake of foreign invasions.

The Nehruvian version which has been sold as secularist in post-independence India, and which is being proclaimed as sacrosanct, is no more than a mix of the imperialist versions. It has served as a smoke-screen for the remnants of Islamic, Christian, British, and Communist imperialisms to play their politics with impunity, indeed with self-righteous aggressiveness.

The imperialist versions of India's history differ among themselves as to what India has been, what it has to be, and what it is to be saved from. But they are all agreed that something is seriously wrong with the "native" society — *kufr* (infidelism) and *shirk* (idolatry), sin and fornication with false gods, brahminism and black magic, primitive superstition and puerile priestcraft, caste discrimination and class oppression, *sati* and infanticide, child marriage and excessive breeding, disease and destitution, Asiatic mode of production and feudalism, capitalism and servitude to American imperialism, etc.; the list is endless. They also agree that the "native" society is incapable of coming out of this morass on its own, and some ideology or agency from outside is badly needed to rescue it from its plight.

The Hindu version of India's history, on the other hand, says that Hindu civilization was the dominant civilization of the world for several millenia before the birth of Christ, the same way as Western civilization has been dominant since the nineteenth century; that Hindu presence can still be seen in the language and literature, religion and philosophy, science and technology of almost all peoples, east and west, north and south; that Hindus became complacent at some stage due to a long spell of unrivalled power and prosperity, neglected the art of warfare and border defences, and invited invaders from far and near to swarm towards their homeland; that while the earlier invaders were beaten back from India's frontiers, the later ones, who came in and caused some turmoil, were absorbed rather speedily in the socio-cultural fabric of the country; that the Islamic invaders were the first to succeed in inflicting great havoc in most parts of the country, imposing an alien rule over large areas and for long periods, and spreading on same scale a closed and inhuman ideology which was at war with whatever the Hindus had valued and preserved for ages past; that the Christian-Western imperialism intervened with equally alien regimes and ideologies at the very time when Hindus had just succeeded in breaking the stranglehold of Islamic imperialism after a long-drawn-out war of resistance followed by a swift war of liberation; and that the ills from which Hindu society had come to suffer in due course were the consequences rather than the causes of foreign invasions.

This version of India's history was vindicated by modern scholarship. Swami Dayananda, Bankim Chandra and Vivekananda confirmed it in a forceful manner. Finally, it found its full voice during the short-lived Swadeshi Movement (1905–10) led by Sri Aurobindo, Bipin Chandra Pal, and Lokamanya Tilak. Mahatma Gandhi, too, was inspired by it to a very large extent.

Unfortunately, this version suffered a setback when the Indian National Congress started wooing the Muslims in India in a vain bid to win them over to the fight for freedom against British imperialism. Hindus were told not to take too much pride in their ancient heritage, to honour Islam as a religion as good as Hinduism, and to accept the Muslim rule in medieval times as a native dispensation. The Muslims, however, remained far from satisfied by these "minor" concessions. Tampering with recorded history had failed in achieving Hindu-Muslim unity. But the misguided effort had set up an evil precedent, namely, that history could be tampered with for political purposes. That gave an opportunity to the Marxist brigade to launch their insidcous operation.

This is not the place to detail the herculean labours which the brigade has invested in re-writing the history of India from its dawn to our own times. The large-scale exercise in *suppressio vari suggestio falsi* remains incomparable except for similar exercises in the late lamented Soviet Union and her satellites. The results are there for everyone to see. What was white till recently has been painted black, and the black has been made to look pretty bright. Heroes have become villains, and vice versa. The most amazing spectacle, however, is that these merchants of the most mendacious lies insist on their version of India's history to be recognized as the only version worth teaching.

The Hindu version of India's history is coming to the fore once again, after having suffered a more or less complete eclipse during the twilight of the British Raj (1947–92). We have a long way to go before the mischief done to India's history by the Nehruvian establishment gets undone. Shrikant's present work is a significant contribution in that direction. It puts the record straight regarding the starting point of India's history, and the source of our renowned heritage.

The theory of an Aryan invasion of India was floated by Western scholars at a time when Hindus lay helpless under the heel of British imperialism, and the memories of the Muslim rule in India were still alive. It was difficult for them to conceive that Hindus could be the authors of a magnificent civilization such as the ancient texts testified. Even so, this theory was no more than a tentative hypothesis, and so it has remained till today in spite of all efforts to prove it. The situation was no different when Pandit Nehru started (1931) writing to his daughter the letters which were subsequently published as *Glimpses of World History*. In fact, supporters of the theory had started shifting their ground in view of what had been recently discovered at Harappa and Mohenjodaro.

But the scholarly debate carried no weight with Pandit Nehru. He wrote to his daughter with great aplomb, "Can you not see them [the Aryans] trekking down the mountain passes into the unknown land below?"[1] In the next letter, he went on, "It is possible that the caste system was partly based on the desire of the Aryans to keep themselves aloof from the conquered people... The very word for caste in Sanskrit is *varna*, colour. This also shows that the Aryans who came were fairer in complexion than the original inhabitants of India."[2]

Nehru retailed the same fables as history in his second book, *The Discovery of India* (1946). He had remained blissfully unaware of the acrobatics which invasionist scholars had been staging in order to accommodate inconvenient facts of the Indus Civilization in their pet theory. And it was perhaps beneath his contempt to take note of what Dr. B.R. Ambedkar had already made known on the subject.

Dr. Ambedkar had made a thorough and first-hand study of the Rigveda and the Avesta. He had examined the context and counted the frequency of the few words such as Ārya, Dāsa, Dasyu, Mṛdhravāk, Anāsā Kṛṣṇayoni, Varṇa, etc. which the invasionists had picked up from a bulky text in order to prop up their propositions. And he had said, "So far as the Rig Veda is concerned, there is not a particle of evidence suggesting the invasion of India by the Aryans from outside

[1] *Glimpses of World History*, OUP, Fourth Impression, 1987, p. 13.
[2] Ibid. pp. 24-25.

India... So far as the testimony of the Vedic literature is concerned, it is against the theory that the original home of the Aryans was outside India."[3] He had also refuted the scholars' belief that the word *varṇa* in the Veda meant skin-colour in any of the 22 places where the word had been used.[4] His conclusions at the end of the book were as follows: "1. The Vedas do not know any such race as the Aryan race; 2. There is no evidence in the Vedas of any invasion of India by the Aryan race and its having conquered the Dasas and Dasyus supposed to be the natives of India; 3. There is no evidence to show that the distinction between Aryans, Dasas and Dasyus was a racial distinction; 4. The Vedas do not support the contention that the Aryas were different in colour from the Dasas and Dasyus."[5]

These are also the conclusions drawn by Shrikant. Of course, he has covered a much larger territory, and drawn the inescapable conclusion that it was India from where the Aryans had spread to every country where Indo-European languages are spoken at present. The evidence he has marshalled from the Purāṇas in support of his conclusions is path-breaking. To the best of my knowledge—and I am no stranger to the subject—no one before him has noticed the presence and role of Puranic dynasties in the Vedic literature the way he has done. That is the most clinching part of his magnum opus.

Magnum opus because, before presenting his own arguments, he has placed before the reader all the arguments advanced by the invasionists. Next, he has examined those arguments in great detail and pointed out the flaws both as to facts and logic. Finally, he has built his own case, taking all known facts into account, and leading where straight logic is bound to lead anyone with no extra axe to grind. In short, he has not only stormed into the heart of the *cakravyuh* erected by the invasionists and regarded by them as impregnable, but has also come out of it with flying colours, although he is not much older than Abhimanyu of the Mahābhārata fame.

New Delhi **Sita Ram Goel**
10 February, 1993

[3] *Who Were the Shudras?*, first published in 1946 and reprinted in his *Speeches and Writings*, published by the Government of Maharashtra in 1990, Volume 7, p. 74.
[4] Ibid., p. 82.
[5] Ibid., p. 85.

CONTENTS

ABBREVIATIONS

ADOSS	*A Dictionary of Selected Synonyms in the Principal Indo-European Languages*, by Carl Darling Buck, University of Chicago Press, 1949.
AIHT	*Ancient Indian Historical Tradition,* by F.E. Pargiter, Motilal Banarsidas, Delhi-Varanasi-Patna, 1962.
Alphabet	*The Alphabet: A Key to the History of Mankind,* by David Diringer, Philosophical Library Inc., New York, 1948.
Aryans	*The Aryans: A Study of Indo-European Origins,* by V. Gordon Childe, Kegan, Paul, Trench, Trubner and Co. Ltd., London, 1926.
Before Columbus	*Before Columbus: Links Between the Old World and Ancient America,* by Cyrus H. Gordon, Crown Publishers, New York, 1971.
CDHR	*The Civilized Demons: The Harappans in Rigveda,* by Malati J. Shendge, Abhinav Publications, New Delhi, 1977.
CTL	*Current Trends in Linguistics,* Volume 5, *South Asian Linguistics,* edited by Thomas A. Sebeok, Mouton, the Hague, Paris.
DL	*Dravidian Linguisti: An Introduction,* by Kamil V. Zvelebil, Institute of Linguistics and Culture, Pondicherry, 1990.
EB	*Encyclopaedia Britannica,* 15th Edition (unless edition otherwise specified), Volumes 1-30.
HCIP	*History and Culture of the Indian People,* Volume I, *The Vedic Age,* edited by R.C. Majumdar.
HOR	*Hymns of the Rigveda,* Volumes I & II, by Ralph T.H. Griffith, The Chowkhamba Sanskrit Series, 4th Edition (1st edition 1889), Varanasi, 1963.
IE & IE	*Indo-European and Indo-Europeans: Papers presented at the third Indo-European Conference at the University of Pennsylvania,* April 21-23, 1966, edited by George Cardona, Henry M. Hoenigswald and Alfred Senn, University of

	Pennsylvania Press, Philadelphia, 1970.
IEP	*Indo-European Philology,* by W.B. Lockwood, Hutchinson University Library, London.
IELS	*Indo-European Language and Society,* by Emile Benveniste (tr. by Elizabeth Palmer), Faber & Faber Ltd. (first published 1969), London, 1973.
IVA	*India in the Vedic Age: A History of Aryan Expansion in India,* by P.L. Bhargava, Upper India Publishing House Pvt. Ltd. (first published 1956), Lucknow, 1971.
Karpāsa	*Karpāsa in Prehistoric India: A Chronoligical and Cultural Clue,* by K.D. Sethna, Biblia Impex Pvt. Ltd., New Delhi, 1981.
LEM	*Larousse Encyclopaedia of Mythology,* translated by Richard Aldington and Delano Ames from *Larousse Mythologie Generale*, edited by Felix Guirand, published in France by Auge, Gillon, Hollia-Larousse, Moreau et Cie, the Librairie Larousse, Batchwork Press Ltd., 1959.
LSI	*Linguistic Survey of India,* by G.A. Grierson.
MMR	*Mahabharata: Myth and Reality—Differing Views,* edited by S.P. Gupta and K.S. Ramachandran, Agam Prakashan, Delhi, 1976.
ODBL	*The Origin and Development of the Bengali Language,* Part I, by S.K. Chatterjee, George, Allen and Unwin Ltd. (first published by Calcutta University Press, 1926), London, 1970.
POIEL	*A Panorama of Indo-European Languages,* by W.B. Lockwood, Hutchinson University Library, London, 1972.
RC & IC	*The Rigvedic Culture and Indus Civilization*, by A.N. Chandra, Ratna Prakashan, Calcutta, 1980.
RVI	*Rigvedic India,* by A.C. Das, University of Calcutta, 1921.
SED	*A Sanskrit-English Dictionary,* by Sir M. Monier-Williams.
TBL	*The Burushaski Language,* Volume I, by Lt. Col. D.L.R. Lorimer, 1935.
VM	*Vedic Mythology,* by A.A. Macdonell, Indological Book House, Varanasi, 1963.

OTHER BOOKS QUOTED

1. *Arctic Home in the Vedas*, by Lokmanya Tilak
2. *The Curse of Tongues—and Some Remedies*, by Douglas Buck
3. *Decipherment of the Indus Script*, by S.R. Rao
4. *Hindutva*, by Swatantryaveer Savarkar
5. *The Loom of Language*, by Frederick Bodmer
6. *Lothal and the Indus Civilization*, by S.R. Rao
7. *Mexican Linguistics*, by T.S. Denison
8. *Muslim Separatism: Causes and Consequences*, by Sita Ram Goel
9. *Rationale of a Hindu State*, by Balraj Madhok
10. *Story of Islamic Imperialism in India*, by Sita Ram Goel
11. *The Tragic Story of Partition*, by H.V. Seshadri
12. *Understanding Islam through Hadis: Religious Faith or Fanaticism*, by Ram Swarup
13. *Writings and Speeches of Dr. Ambedkar*, Volume I
14. *Zarathustra and His Contemporaries in the Rigveda*, by Shapurji K. Hodivala

PHONETIC SYMBOLS GENERALLY USED IN THE BOOK

क्	ख्	ग्	घ्	ङ्		k	kh	g	gh	ṅ/n	
च्	छ्	ज्	झ्	ञ्		c	ch	j	jh	ñ/n	
ट्	ठ्	ड्	ढ्	ण्		ṭ	ṭh	ḍ	ḍh	ṇ	
त्	थ्	द्	ध्	न्		t	th	d	dh	n	
प्	फ्	ब्	भ्	म्		p	ph	b	bh	m	
य्	र्	ल्	व्	ळ्		y	r	l	v	ḷ	
श्	ष्	स्	ह्	क्ष्	ज्ञ्	ś	ṣ	s	h	kṣ	jñ
अ	आ	इ	ई	उ	ऊ	a	ā	i	ī	u	ū
ए	ओ		ऋ			e	o	ṛ/ri			

(sometimes "sh" is used for श् and ष्)

Dravidian sounds

ழ் ற் l l̤ ṛ

எ ஒ (short e and o) e: o:

Austric sounds

muted final consonant = sign above consonant

resultant (?) vowel = sign below vowel

Note: 1. The same word may have been written in phonetic spelling in one place, and in regular spelling in another.

2. Other spellings are as per source-books.

INTRODUCTION

History is a very potent subject. Politics can be, and very often is, based on it. A nation which forgets, or falsifies, or wilfully ignores, or glosses over the lessons of its history is a nation heading towards doom. And, conversely, when a nation is intended to be sent to its doom, a process of falsification of its history can be profitably launched.

Indian "history", as it is formulated, taught, and propagated today, has been the handiwork of Leftist "intellectuals", ever since Leftist intellectualism came into vogue. And since destruction of national identity is one of the basic tenets of Leftist ideology, it is no wonder that Indian history, as an academic subject, has been falsified on a grand scale, with the sole aim and intention of uprooting and destroying India's national identity and ethos.

VOICE OF INDIA publications have contributed a great deal towards exposing most of the fallacies and falsehoods perpetrated by Leftist historians, and their secularist fellow-travellers, in respect of medieval and post-medieval history. There is, however, one remote period of history, or prehistory, which, in spite of its remoteness, has come to acquire a major propaganda-value for Leftists and their ilk— the period of the so-called "Aryan Invasion of India".

A race of people, called the "Aryans", is supposed to have invaded India somewhere around 2000–1500 BC from the north-west. These Aryans, after centuries of warfare and bloodshed, are supposed to have destroyed, or driven southwards, or subjugated and absorbed (as lower castes) most of the natives in the north of the "subcontinent", and then themselves occupied the northern areas.

Originally formulated by European scholars, mainly for imperialistic reasons, this theory has been perfected by Indian Leftists into a powerful weapon to be used against Indian nationalism.

Two aspects of this theory must be noted. The first is that this theory is widely accepted by almost everyone, and those who do not accept it can indeed be accused of being those who do not want to accept it. The second is that this theory has the potential to undermine the rationale of Indian nationalism, at least in the minds of those who are ever-willing to rest their thinking processes, and accept whatever half-witted formulations are placed before them in a cut-and-dried manner.

GENERAL ACCEPTANCE OF THE THEORY

This theory is taught, as fact, to all Indian children in their school textbooks. Most educated Indians, long after they have left school and forgotten most of what they had studied there, continue to retain the memory that "Aryans" were some people who invaded India in ancient times, even if they do not realize the exact implications of this theory.

At one time the prestige of European scholarship was so overpowering that even some Hindu Nationalists were unable to escape its effects. Lokmanya Tilak, a staunch Hindu Nationalist, actually wrote a book, *The Arctic Home in the Vedas,* to propound his theory that the original home of the Vedic Aryans was in the Arctic region. His motives may have been (misguidedly) Hindu Nationalistic in that he sought to prove, in this way, that the Vedas were much older than postulated by European scholars. Swatantryaveer Savarkar, rightly considered by many to be the prophet of Hindu Nationalism, in his book, *Hindutva*, seems to accept the theory, hook, line and sinker. He only attempts to suggest that the Aryans did not invade India, but only immigrated into it.

The TV serial Rāmāyaṇa is accused of being partly responsible for the recent revival of "Hindu fundamentalism" in the country. The dialogues in this serial, however, show full agreement with the view, held by protagonists of the invasion theory, that the Rāmāyaṇa is an account of the expansion of the Aryans from their earlier settlements in the north into the Dravidian south. That the trend of the serial is to *glorify* the alleged expansion does not detract from the travesty, but only accentuates it.

The theory has been accepted on such a scale that any textbook or scholarly book the world over, which deals with, or refers to, India's early history, mentions the Aryan invasion of India in the second millenium BC, as if it were a natural and indisputable part of proven history.

And, so far as the common man is concerned, that is what it appears to be — a natural and indisputable part of proven history.

COROLLARIES OF THE THEORY

To the Leftist propagandists, however, the theory means much more.

It means that just as the British and the Muslim invaders came from outside, so also the Aryan invaders came from outside. Hence, Christianity, Islam and Hinduism are all equally foreign to India; or, conversely, all three are equally Indian.

Further, it means that just as Christianity and Islam were imposed on Indians by foreign invaders, so was Hinduism imposed on native Indians (Dravidians) by foreign invaders (Aryans).

For the Leftist, of course, the matter does not end there. He goes further and propounds that while the Aryans conquered India and reduced its natives to the level of lower castes within their social structure and hierarchy, in the name of Hinduism, the other invaders sought to liberate the natives from this bondage, in the name of Islam and Christianity. Hence these original natives, the "Dravidians", must reject Hinduism and align with Islam and Christianity!

In India today, the languages spoken by Indians belong to six language families:

1. Indo-European (Aryan): This includes Sanskrit, Hindi, Punjabi, Kashmiri, Sindhi, Marathi, Gujarati, Bengali, Assamese, Oriya, etc.
2. Dravidian: This includes Tamil, Malayalam, Telugu, Kannada, etc.
3. Austric: This includes the Kol-Munda languages (Santali, Savara, Gadba, etc.), the Khasi language of Meghalaya, and the Nicobarese languages.
4. Sino-Tibetan: This includes most of the languages in the Himalayas and the north-east: Ladakhi, Lepcha, Bhotia, the languages of Arunachal Pradesh, the Naga languages, Bodo, Ahom, Lushai, Meithei (Manipuri), Garo, etc.
5. Andamanese: This includes the languages of the Andaman Islands.
6. Burushaski: This consists of the Burushaski language spoken in Pak-occupied Kashmir (in Hunza, Gilgit and Nagar).

All the official languages of India belong to the first two language-families; and the four southern states have Dravidian languages as their state languages. From this, it is obvious that any attempt to strike at the unity of Indian nationalism must aim at creating an "Aryan–Dravidian" divide.

Hence the "natives" who are supposed to have borne the brunt of the "Aryan" invasion have been branded as "Dravidians".

Hence, also, the Indus Valley Civilization (IVC) sites, which were discovered in this century, were immediately branded as Dravidian sites.

And an extremely venomous political movement, ostensibly a

Dravidian movement, was launched, in the extreme south to throw off the shackles of Aryan Imperialism!

V.P. Singh, the mercifully short-termed Prime Minister of India, while launching his Mandal-*astra* to destroy Hindu Society from within by creating caste-wars, declared in Parliament that the Aryans had kept the Dravidians in subjugation for thousands of years!

BEHIND THE CURTAIN

Incidentally, the Aryan invasion theory is just one part of a larger scheme which seeks to brand India as a kind of Imperialists' paradise, into which people of different races and cultures poured in at various points of time; an area, therefore, with no native people of its own, to which no people can lay claim, and which belongs to anyone who has the power to acquire overlordship over it.

Suniti Kumar Chatterji, the eminent linguist, summarizes this view in the following words:

> "We have the advent of the following peoples in India from the outside (*no kind of man originated on the soil of India, all her human inhabitants having arrived originally from other lands...*)."[1]

He then proceeds to list these immigrants, into an originally empty India, in chronological order:

1. Negritos, "from Africa".
2. Proto-Australoids, "from the east Mediterranean area (Palestine)".
3. Early Mediterraneans (Austrics).
4. Advanced Mediterraneans (Dravidians).
5. Armenoids (Dravidians).
6. Alpines (Aryans).
7. Nordics (Vedic Aryans).
8. Mongoloids.

The sheer insolence of this detailed and specific timetable of foreign immigrations into India, can be appreciated when we consider that at the very beginning of the chapter, he admits:

> "... Lack of material has not allowed us to postulate with certainty about racial movements in ancient times, and any appraisement or reconstruction of movements of peoples in India, some four or three, *or even two thousand years ago* is bound to remain *largely hypothetical* and based on or inferred from the

[1] HCIP, pp. 142–43.

present situation only."[2]

From all these picturesque accounts, of various races making a beeline towards India from different parts of the world at different points of time, the only logical conclusion that can be drawn is, of course, that there is no such thing as "Indian" and "Foreign" in the Indian context: either everything, and everyone is Indian (or can become Indian by merely stepping within India's borders), or else nothing and no one can really be described by this term!

Needless to say, while the theory of an Aryan invasion (or immigration) is itself the result only of a long and determined effort by Western and West-oriented scholars, the other invasions (or immigrations) have not even a shred of evidence or scholarship to support them. Yet all these theories are firmly maintained as a sort of license to justify past, present and future imperialistic forays into India.

But, again, while these theories are being firmly maintained, they are being maintained only *behind the curtain*. It is only the theory of an Aryan invasion of a Dravidian India which has been, and remains, most profitable for Hindu-baiters. Hence, it is required that the Aryan invasion be played up, and a discreet veil be dropped on the earlier invasions!

LEFTIST CONSPIRACY

There are three factors which are keeping the Aryan invasion theory alive in Indian history books:

1. The weight of scholarly world opinion.
2. Intellectual lethargy on the part of the average Indian scholar.
3. The awesome propaganda power of the Left in India.

Doordarshan is today the most powerful medium in India. Millions and millions of people in remote villages, most of them unable to read the Leftist propaganda material, are able to watch the TV sets which have been set up in every corner of India. And as a result the Leftists have acquired a captive audience of many millions.

And this captive audience of millions is continuously subjected to a barrage of Leftist propaganda in the form of slanted news reports and topical discussions, "social-message" shorts between programs, and of course a never-ending supply of communist serials. Here, we may note the contents of two such serials which dwelt on the Aryan invasion of India.

[2] HCIP, p. 141.

One serial, *Amir Khusro*, devoted one entire part exclusively to the task of painstakingly explaining how the Aryans invaded India, and how this made Hinduism as foreign a religion as Islam.

Another serial, *Bharat Ek Khoj*, in its second part, graphically depicted scenes of life in a Harappan town at the time of the "Aryan invasion". The highlights were: The Harappans were firmly identified as Dravidians; the Aryans were firmly identified as uncouth, barbaric nomads, attired in outlandish costumes, and indulging in acts of hooliganism and vandalism; and the Harappans were shown referring to them, in disgust, as "lowdown foreign dogs".

Incidentally, while the "Aryans" were so graphically depicted as barbarians, foreigners and invaders, another and a later part of the serial had Jawaharlal Nehru informing the viewers that there never was such a thing as a Muslim invasion of India!

In the face of such highly motivated propaganda, aimed at destroying the very roots of Indian nationalism, there is obviously a need to tell the truth about the Aryan invasion theory.

THE AIM OF THIS BOOK

The book is divided into three sections, of which the first is distinct from the other two in that it deals with the political corollaries of the invasion theory, while the other two sections deal with the more academic or technical aspects of the invasion theory.

The first section deals with the question of Hindu Nationalism in the context of the Aryan invasion theory. *As this section makes absolutely clear, Hindu Nationalism is identical with Indian Nationalism, irrespective of whether any Aryans are supposed to have come from outside or not.*

The second section describes the basic aspects of the invasion theory as propounded by various scholars. This includes a description of the attempt by A.D. Pusalker to make a comparative study of the Puranic material, and a discussion of Dr. S.R. Rao's decipherment of the Indus script.

The third section deals with our own examination of the invasion theory. This theory is based on two centuries of misinterpretations and illogical presumptions. This section of the book demolishes the invasion theory with facts and their correct interpretations.

In addition, the third section presents incontrovertible evidence, based on the Rigveda and the Purāṇas, which proves beyond the shadow of any doubt that India is the Original Homeland of the "Aryan" or Indo-European languages.

SECTION I

COROLLARIES OF THE THEORY

One

INDIA AS A "NATION IN THE MAKING"

The very first principle of Leftist propaganda is that India is not a nation but a conglomerate of nations. Every linguistic group, at least, constitutes a separate nation. In fact, India was never one nation at any point of time in its history. The Britishers, in the course of their imperialistic drive, conquered various nations and kingdoms in a certain area; and the entire area over which they ruled came to acquire a sense of unity inspired only by a common slavery under them. This common slavery led to a common freedom movement. When the Britishers left, the entire area, ruled over by them, was divided into two major parts, India and Pakistan, each, and especially the former, consisting of many nations within itself.

The Hindu Nationalist principle, on the other hand, is that India has always been one nation since ancient times, and Hinduism has been the bond linking different parts of India to each other and binding the whole nation together.

THE LEFTIST MOTIVES

The main aim of this "multinational India" theory is to sow the seeds for the eventual breakup of India into its "constituent nations". The Leftists had played this same game in 1947 at the time of the partition of India.

The rationale behind this is that if India breaks up into small "nations", these would be easier for the Leftists to gobble up one by one. If Bengal and Kerala, for example, had become independent countries in 1947, today they would have been full-fledged, communist kingdoms.

The fact that this strategy failed to pay dividends in 1947, and that, far from gobbling up Pakistan, the Leftists were ruthlessly wiped out there, is no deterrent. It has, if anything, increased the ardour of Leftists in aligning with the forces of Islamic imperialism against Hindu Nationalism.

The deeper reason behind the Leftist sponsorship of the "multinational India" theory is that hatred and contempt for one's own nation, culture, historical ethos and identity is a fundamental feature of the Leftist mental make-up. In India, this is manifested in a psychopathic hatred and contempt for Hinduism, Hindu Nationalism and Hindu culture.

If it is accepted that India is, and always was, one nation, an elucidation of the nature of this "one nationhood" will naturally follow. And it will be found that the one bond binding India together is its Hindu religion and culture.

The main aim of the "multinational India" theory is, therefore, to deny the real, ancient, bond which binds the different parts of India together into one nation; and to replace it with an artificial, recent, bond of "composite" nationhood, which, by its very nature, would be a fragile one, unable to hold the nation together.

This theory of India's recent and "composite" nationhood, has the full support of the "secular" political leadership of India, for three reasons:

1. Indian "secularism" is basically a linear descendant of Leftist ideology, and derives its inspiration from Leftist terminology and thought categories, so that "secularism" boils down to anti-Hinduism.
2. The compulsions of India's vote-bank politics make it necessary to divide Hindu society into mutually antagonistic segments and, at the same time, to keep the Muslim vote-bank united. This can only be done by promoting the concept of a "composite" nationhood, denying India's ancient Hindu Nationhood, and following a policy of "cynical 'secularism".
3. The post-1947 political leadership of India, of whom most present-day politicians are the organisational progeny, liked the idea that the history of India, as a nation, began with themselves, and that India was a "nation in the making"—a nation of their own making. The concept of a "composite" nation taking birth and shape under their own expert guidance, was a pleasing and flattering one.

IMPLICATIONS OF A RECENT "COMPOSITE" NATIONHOOD

By accepting that India became a nation under the Britishers and the Congress, and that India's nationhood is not based on its Hindu identity, one destroys (as intended by the Leftists) the raison d'etre of India as a nation.

Take, for example, Iran, Kashmir, and Tamil Nadu. Kashmir is geographically closer to Iran than to Tamil Nadu. The people of Kashmir and Iran are Muslims, while the people of Tamil Nadu are largely Hindus. The people of Kashmir and Iran both speak languages belonging to the Indo-European family, while the people of Tamil Nadu speak a language belonging to the Dravidian family. What is it, then, which can be taken to bind Kashmir more closely to Tamil Nadu than to Iran?

Take, again, China, Manipur and Gujarat. Manipur is geographically closer to China than to Gujarat. The people of Manipur and China belong to the Mongoloid race, while the people of Gujarat belong to the Caucasoid race. The people of Manipur and China both speak languages belonging to the Sino-Tibetan family, while the people of Gujarat speak a language belonging to the Indo-European family. What is it, then, which can be taken to bind Manipur more closely to Gujarat than to China?

What is the bond which binds Kashmir, Tamil Nadu, Manipur and Gujarat to each other more closely than to, say, Iran or China? Is it only the bond of a common slavery under the Britishers, leading to a common freedom movement and subsequent common statehood? If so, it is obviously a flimsy bond, and one which is not likely to hold out against heavy odds.

Today, the major part of India consists of one kingdom ruled by one government. (The word "kingdom" is used here instead of "state", since the word "state" could cause confusion, as the term is also used for individual states within the union.) But certain parts had broken away in 1947.

Why did those parts break away in 1947? And why are different parts of India trying to break away even now?

The answer is simple. Those parts of India which broke away in 1947 had cut off their links with the religion, history, and culture of India, and established links with the religion, history, and culture of Arabia and West Asia.

Today, also, we are being taught that India is a "nation in the making" and that the religion, history, and culture of Arabia and West Asia; the religion, history and culture of Palestine and Europe; and the religion, history and culture of India; are all equally "Indian". The bond which links the parts of India together, *and keeps them distinct from other countries,* is being denigrated, denied, or diluted; and bonds, *which link parts of India, or sections of Indians, with other countries,* are being encouraged and lauded.

Only a person, whose thinking faculties have been totally deranged by Leftist and secularist propaganda, will fail to perceive that *this* is the reason why India has become a happy hunting ground for the forces of disintegration.

NATION AND KINGDOM

The Leftist concept, of India being a recent and "composite" nation, banks upon the general ignorance of the common man as to what exactly constitutes a "nation". Therefore, it is necessary to first understand the difference between a "nation" and a "kingdom", and, then, to understand how India has always constituted one nation.

A kingdom (i.e. a, more or less, sovereign state) is the area ruled over by a king, or in the modern sense, by a government of some kind.

The borders of a kingdom constantly change, and can even disappear altogether. If we take an atlas mapping out a political map of the world 5000 years ago, and then compare it with similar political maps taken after a period of every ten years right upto the present day, we will find that no two world maps are identical.

The sentimental loyalties created by a kingdom are, therefore, of a temporary and illusive nature, even if these loyalties manage, at times, to reach extremely strong proportions. They are akin to the team-loyalties and partisan loyalties which are created among students of a school in which the students are divided into teams or "houses" for the purpose of the academic year, or among workers in a factory belonging to rival trade unions, or among residents of two neighbouring buildings, or some other similar situation.

A nation, on the other hand, is distinct from a kingdom.

Balraj Madhok, in his book, *Rationale of a Hindu State,* gives several definitions of the term "nation", from which it is clear that *geographical entity* and *consciousness of nationhood* are the two basic ingredients of nationhood. The following two definitions of "nationhood" may be noted:

1. "....a *common civilization* which gives a *sense of unity* and *distinction from all foreigners* quite *apart from the bond of the state*" (Bluntschli).
2. "....a kind of fellow-feeling or mutual sympathy relating to a *definite home country.* It springs from a *common heritage*, whether of great achievement and glory or of disaster and suffering" (Prof. Hale Combe).

The description fits India to a T. India was always divided into different kingdoms, but these kingdoms had constantly been changing borders and names, and were never the basis of deep national feeling. But the people in different parts of India had always had a feeling of cultural oneness with the rest of India, and always had the subconscious urge to unite politically into one kingdom.

INDIA: A GEOGRAPHICAL ENTITY

To begin with, a glance at a geographical map of the world shows India standing out distinct from the rest of Asia. This was negatively admitted by Jinnah when he declared: "India is not one nation. It only looks that way on a map."

It "looks that way on a map" because India is a distinct geographical entity, surrounded by mountain ranges in the north, and by oceans in the south. The mountainous regions in the north, and the islands in the south-east and south-west, constitute the peripheral areas of India.

According to geologists, India was originally separate from the rest of Asia, and part of a different continent. This continent, in the course of millions of years, slowly broke apart; perhaps parts of it got sunk in the ocean; and the part that today constitutes India moved northwards and got joined to Asia. This means that India has been geographically one unit, distinct from the rest of Asia, and the world, for millions of years.

CONSCIOUSNESS OF BEING ONE NATION

Right from ancient times, there was full consciousness, both among Indians as well as among foreigners, that India was one nation, irrespective of the changing borders of the kingdoms within it.

The Viṣṇu Purāṇa states clearly:

uttaram yat samudrasya, himādreścaiva dakṣiṇam,
varṣam tad Bhāratam nāma, Bhāratī yatra santatih

(*To the north of the oceans and the south of the Himalayas lies the land of Bhārata, inhabited by Bhāratīs.*)

The entire land was therefore called Bhāratavarṣa and its inhabitants were collectively known as Bhāratī(ya)s from very ancient times, and this fact of being one nation and one people was always present in the consciousness of all Indians.

This consciousness oozes out from every pore of the entire gamut of ancient Indian literature. As Sita Ram Goel points out: "Even a dry compendium on grammar, the Aṣṭādhyāyī of Pāṇini, provides a nearly complete count of all the Janapadas in Ancient India".

Foreigners were no less definite in this regard. The ancient Iranians knew this country as "Hind" and its people as "Hindu". The Greeks pronounced the word "Hind" as "Indus" and the word "Hindu" as "Indoi". The Chinese referred to India and Indians as "Shintu". The medieval Arabs, Turks, and Europeans were also fully conscious of India being one distinct entity. The latter-day references by British Imperialists to India as a "subcontinent" in no way detracts from this awareness; in fact, it underlines this awareness and betrays an attempt at verbal jugglery.

India did not become one "nation" under the Britishers, since it was always that. A large part of India did, however, become one "kingdom" under them. But, then, even before the Britishers, a large part of India had also become one kingdom under another foreign dynasty, the Mughals.

In between these two sets of foreign rulers, a large part of India had become one kingdom under the Marathas, who had liberated it from the first of the two.

Before this, a large part of India had become one kingdom under various dynasties like the Mauryas, the Guptas and others, in the historical period itself.

The Purāṇas provide the names of various other kings and dynasties which had made the whole, or a major part, of India into one kingdom.

This urge for the entire nation to be one kingdom was always there in the national consciousness since ancient times.

As explained in detail by Sita Ram Goel:

1. The whole of India was considered to be a *cakravartī-kṣetra*, and the aim of every king was to bring the whole of India into one kingdom (under himself, of course); and there was a well-established, and well-respected, code of conduct which governed this whole process.
2. The concept of Bhāratavarṣa as one nation was the basic inspiration behind this; hence these kings never felt the need or desire to step beyond the borders of India into foreign lands to enlarge their kingdoms.
3. Whenever the vulnerable borders of the nation, in the northwest, were in danger of foreign invasion, Indian kings from far and near the borders rushed, or felt the need to rush, to its defence.

CONSCIOUSNESS OF RELIGIO-CULTURAL IDENTITY

Behind all this was the clear consciousness that India was culturally one, and distinct from all other nations—a consciousness of a special Indian religio-cultural identity. This was manifested in the innumerable Hindu pilgrim-centres dotting the whole of India from north to south and east to west; in the consciousness of the whole of India being a "holy land" (a *deva-nirmita bhūmi*); and in the regular pilgrimages by

Hindus from one corner of India to the other (regardless of the changing borders of the various kingdoms). No Hindu, on pilgrimage in another part of India, ever felt conscious of being in a foreign place.

These Hindu pilgrim-centres range from Kailash and Mansarovar in the north, to Rameshwaram in the south; and from Hingalaj (in Sindh) in the west, to Parsuram Kund (in Arunachal Pradesh) in the east. The "seven holy cities" of Hinduism include Kanchipuram in the south, Dwarka in the west, and Ujjain in Central India. The twelve Jyotirlingas include Rameshwaram in Tamil Nadu, Srisailam in Andhra, Nasik in Maharashtra, Somnath in Gujarat, and Kashi (Varanasi) in Uttar Pradesh.

The seven holy rivers of Hinduism, indeed, seem to chart out the map of the holy land. Sindhu and the (now extinct) Saraswati start in the Himalayas and move westwards and southwards into the western sea. Ganga and Yamuna also start in the Himalayas and move eastwards into the northeastern sea. Narmada starts in Central India and moves out into the western sea. Godavari starts in Western India, and moves out into the eastern sea. Kaveri winds its way through the south and moves out into the southern sea.

The Mahābhārata in its Tīrthayātrā section of the Vanaparva, gives details of the pilgrimage undertaken by the Pāṇḍavas to numerous sacred mountains, rivers, lakes and shrines all over India.

This concept of India as a holy land has persisted throughout the history of India down the ages.

Jainism originated in the north-east (in Bihar), but the majority of its followers are found in the western states (Rajasthan, Gujarat, Maharashtra), and the famous statues of Gomatteshwara are found in the south (in Karnataka).

More than a thousand years ago, Adi Shankaracharya, who was born in Kerala, established his four mathas in Badrinath in the north (U.P.), Puri in the east (Orissa), Dwarka in the west (Gujarat), and Shringeri in the south (Karnataka).

Guru Nanak was born in Punjab, but throughout his writings, he speaks of Hindustan and not of Punjab. Guru Gobind Singh appointed five disciples, calling them the *panj pyaras*, and entrusting them with the task of ensuring that Hindu Dharma prevailed everywhere. These disciples were, respectively, from Punjab and Delhi in the north, Gujarat in the west, Orissa in the east, and Karnataka in the south. The four *Takhts* of Sikhism are at Nankana Sahib (Punjab, now in Pakistan), Amritsar (Punjab), Patna (Bihar), and Nanded (Maharashtra).

One could gc on and on, giving instances of religious waves and movements which swept the nation from east, west, north and south; and of saints and holy men who travelled, on pilgrimage, to every nook and corner of this holy land.

The main point, however, is that this Hindu religious conciousness provides the only bond which has, from very ancient times, bound every part of India to every other part in a firm bond of unity and given to this country a distinct identity of its own; *and at the same time prevented any part of India from being bound to any foreign land in a similar bond.*

Denigrating, denying or diluting this bond, and advocating, instead, the "bond" of a nation, born in 1947, with a "composite" national identity consisting of an amalgam of the religions, cultures and histories of Arabia–West Asia, Palestine–Europe, and India, is nothing but a sinister conspiracy for the disintegration of India.

The concept that India was not one nation in the past is, in fact, the formula for seeing to it that India ceases to be one nation in the future.

Two

HINDUISM AS A "FOREIGN RELIGION"

The second principle of Leftist propaganda is that, whether or not India constitutes a "nation", no distinction can be made between Hinduism, on the one hand, and Islam and Christianity, on the other, using the criteria "Indian" and "Foreign". All three are equally foreign, since Hinduism was brought in by Aryan invaders, just as Islam was brought in by West Asian invaders (although, here, the Leftists will hasten to clarify that the Muslims were not really "invaders" of course), and Christianity was brought in by European invaders (and here, again, the Leftists will concur with, or at any rate, repeat, the Christian canard that it was not European invaders, but an "apostle" of Jesus Christ, who first introduced Christianity into India).

In this chapter, let us examine, once and for all, and in logical detail, the question of whether Hinduism is also a "foreign" religion, and likewise, whether Islam and Christianity can, in the alternative, be considered to be as "Indian" as Hinduism:

1. Hinduism had no founder, but every single holy man, seer and sage, and every single hero (or for that matter, villain) mentioned in every single ancient Hindu text and scripture is an Indian.

Islam was founded by Muhammad, an Arab. He was followed by four "pious" Khalifas (the first three of whom are not accepted by Shias), all of whom were Arabs. Then followed a long line of lesser Khalifas (not all of whom are accepted by all sections of Muslims, who indeed broke into different sects on the basis of the struggles for succession to the throne of Khalifa), not one of whom was an Indian.

Christianity is based on the life of Jesus Christ, a Jew from Palestine. His twelve apostles were Palestinians and Romans. Christianity was founded by Paul, a Palestinian Jew and Roman citizen.

2. The sacred language of Hinduism is Sanskrit, which even the Aryan invasion theory cannot assign to any country other than India.

The sacred language of Islam is Arabic, the language of Arabia.

Christianity, perhaps, has no such thing as a sacred language, but, if one were to be named, Hebrew (the original language of the Old Testament), or Aramaic (the language reportedly spoken by Jesus Christ), or Greek (the language which hosted the first Christian Bible, Old plus New Testament, and indeed, which gave the word "Bible"), or Latin (the liturgical language of the "Holy See", the Vatican City) would be better candidates for the post than any Indian language.

3. India is the holy land for Hindus. All Hindu pilgrim centres and holy places are situated in and around India.

Arabia is the holy land for Muslims. Their principal places of pilgrimage are Mecca and Medina in Arabia, followed by Jerusalem in Palestine (Israel), followed by a few others, notably Karbala in Iraq, all in West Asia.

Palestine is the holy land for Christians. Their principal places of pilgrimage are Nazareth, Bethlehem and Jerusalem, all in Palestine.

(If there are any places of pilgrimage for Islam or Christianity in India, it may be noted that: a) These are very minor ones as compared to the major ones in the West, more in the nature of local shrines; b) The persons commemorated by these shrines are almost invariably foreigners or converted Indians who turned against their ancestral Indian society and culture.)

4. The sacred books of all the three religions claim to have the whole world as their stage. But, in reality, they are all geographically localized.

The Hindu texts are centred in and around India.

The Quran and Hadis are centred in and around Arabia and Palestine.

The Bible is centred in and around Palestine and the Mediterranean region.

5. The heads of all Hindu religious sects are Indians. All Hindu religious centres are in India. All Hindu organisations (even those, like the Vishwa Hindu Parishad, whose names suggest an international character) are based in India, and headed and controlled by Indians.

The ultimate heads of all Muslim sects are foreigners. The major Muslim religious centres are situated in foreign lands. There are many international Islamic organisations of different kinds, but all these are based in foreign countries, and headed and controlled by foreigners.

The ultimate heads of all Christian sects are foreigners — the Pope being a prime example. The major Christian religious centres, in the form of the headquarters of each sect, are in foreign countries — that of the Catholics in the Vatican city, and those of the various Orthodox and Protestant churches, and modern fundamentalist sects, in Europe and America. The innumerable international Christian organisations are based in foreign countries and headed and controlled by foreigners.

All these points are so obvious that anyone who says that Hinduism is as foreign to India as Islam or Christianity, deserves to have his head examined.

The followers of both Islam and Christianity have full knowledge of and pride in the time and place of origin of their religions outside India, the early history of their religions outside India, the arrival of their religions into India (brought in by invaders and imperialists), and the manner in which their religions were established in India.

On the other hand, until the Aryan invasion theory was mooted by the European imperialists, no Hindu had ever suspected that any foreign connection could be attributed to his religion. Even today, with the Aryan invasion theory being instilled into every Hindu brain right from childhood, no Hindu worth his salt would accept the contention that Hinduism is of foreign origin.

Even the strongest advocate of the Aryan invasion theory cannot, in all honesty, point out any specific spot outside India to which the origin of any, *simply any,* aspect of Hinduism could be attributed.

Even if, for the purpose of this chapter, it is presumed that the "Aryans" came from outside India, and that they imposed the Hindu religion on local inhabitants (two questions which will be dealt with subsequently in this book), it will have to be admitted that there is no trace of any foreign connections in Hinduism, much less the consciousness, of any such connections, among Hindus—and least of all, any foreign loyalties, associable with such foreign connections.

The foreign nature of Islam and Christianity, as opposed to the Indian nature of Hinduism, is not restricted to the five basic points already mentioned. It has much deeper ramifications, both in respect of its effect on the attitudes and actions of the Muslim and Christian communities, in general, in India, as well as in respect of the Leftist and secularist response to these attitudes and actions. These can be examined, in brief, under four main headings.

FOREIGN ANCESTRY AND HISTORICAL PERSPECTIVE

For Indians, the various historical periods, each with its own events and personalities, are as follows:

1. The period of the Puranas and Epics.
2. The period from the age of the Buddha, through the ages of the Mauryas, Guptas and others, down to the mid-first millennium AD.
3. The early medieval period, after the arrival of Islamic invaders into India, but before Islam had become a major factor in the political arena.

4. The medieval period, representing the national struggle against Islamic imperialism.
5. The late medieval and early modern period, representing the various stages of resistance to European imperialism.
6. The relatively modern period representing the freedom movement against the British imperialists.

But, when Indians adopt Islam and Christianity, their very ancestors seem to change and their historical perspective gets transformed. History, for them, begins with Adam and Eve, the mythical first couple in both the Bible and the Quran.

For Muslims in India, the various historical periods, each with its own events and personalities, are as follows:

1. The pre-Mohammedan (Biblical) period, as described in the Quran.
2. The period of the Prophet and his first four Khalifas.
3. The early period of Islam outside India.
4. The early medieval period of Islamic invasions of India.
5. The medieval period representing imperialistic rule in various parts of India.
6. The late medieval period of Islamic crusades within India, ending with the revolt of 1857.
7. The contemporary period representing the Pakistan movement, beginning with Sir Syed Ahmed Khan and upto 1947.

According to Islam, the Ummah (the world Muslim fraternity) is more important than the national fraternity (especially if it is not a Muslim one); hence the Indian Muslim today follows three streams of historical events—the events in Muslim India, the events in Pakistan, and the events in West Asia.

For Christians, the various historical periods, each with its own events and personalities, are as follows:

1. The period of the Old Testament.
2. The period of the New Testament.
3. The early historical period of Christianity in the days of the not-yet-Christian Roman Empire.
4. The period of the Holy Roman Empire.
5. The period of the Pope's supremacy and the Protestant revolt.
6. The period of Spanish and Portuguese conquests and proselytisation by the sword.
7. The period of the British conquest of India and the planting of the missionary apparatus.

Islam requires that every Muslim invader and imperialist, right from Muhammad bin Qasim down to Ahmad Shah Abdali, be hailed as a hero; and every Muslim fanatic and iconoclast, from Muinuddin Chishti to Dudu Mian, be cherished as a saint.

Christianity requires that every "saint", "martyr" and missionary must be revered, including people like Francis Xavier, who, according to his own autobiography, and letters written by him, urged the king of Portugal to instal the Inquisition in India, and personally supervised, with a "sense of great satisfaction" (in his own words), the slaughter of thousands of Indians, the destruction of Hindu temples and idols, and the persecution of Indians who refused to convert to Christianity.

The secularist and Leftist response, to this Muslim and Christian attitude, is to falsify the whole of Indian history, and to pollute the Indian historical perspective, by belittling the pre-Muslim period of Indian history and deglorifying the national heroes who fought against the Islamic invaders and imperialists; and by whitewashing and glorifying the Islamic invaders and imperialists and the Muslim role during the freedom movement against the Britishers.

It will be noticed that while a similar process of whitewashing and glorification is extended to the religious arm of European imperialism in India (the "saints" and "martyrs"), it is not extended to the political arm of European imperialism in India, as in the case of Muslim heroes.

Thus, while the characterisation of medieval conflict in India, as a conflict between Islamic imperialists and Indian nationalists, is denied on the ground that the Islamic imperialists had some Indian mercenaries on their side, the characterisation of the freedom struggle as a conflict between European imperialists and Indian nationalists is insisted upon, in spite of the fact that the British Rule was maintained with an army of Indian stooges, so much so that in the Jallianwala Bagh massacre, the fingers which pressed the triggers were all Indian fingers.

In fact, the European imperialists are painted even blacker than they were, in order to offset the blackness of the Islamic imperialists, and to brighten the image of the Congress, which has appropriated for itself the credit for having liberated India from the Britishers.

Thus, while the prolific evidence of deliberate destruction, by Islamic invaders and imperialists, of thousands of Hindu temples is denied, the announcement, repeated at the beginning of every part of the TV-serial, *The Sword of Tipu Sultan*, tells us that the Britishers destroyed temples and mosques all over the country.

The foreign nature of Islam and Christianity, thus, makes the converted Indians detach themselves from their real ancestors, attach themselves to the ancestors of their foreign proselytisers, and adopt an alien historical perspective; and this, in turn, leads to the Leftist and secularist falsification of Indian history and distortion of the Indian historical perspective.

FOREIGN LOYALTIES AND FOREIGN CAUSES

When Indians adopt Islam, they acquire foreign loyalties which take precedence over their Indian loyalties. The three loyalties acquired by them are:

1. Indian Muslim loyalties.
2. Pakistani loyalties.
3. Pan-Islamic loyalties.

In Islam, there is a specifically stated and elaborated concept of a religious world empire, and precedence of the ties of the world Muslim Ummah over national ties (especially when the nation is not an Islamic nation), and an elaborate procedure of bringing about that world empire by a process of continuous *jihad*, until every *Dār-ul-Harb*, or *kāfir* state, is converted into a *Dār-ul-Islām*, or Islamic state.

The Indian Muslims' loyalty to Pakistan seems to catch the notice of the general Hindu public only on certain specific occasions, such as whenever there is a cricket match between India and Pakistan. Every cricket match so often ends in riots in various parts of the country due to the Muslim insistence on celebrating Pakistan's victory over India or protesting against India's victory over Pakistan. On one such occasion, there was a huge mock-funeral procession of an effigy of Syed Kirmani, then India's wicket keeper, for having caused Pakistan's defeat by some particularly difficult catches.

This loyalty to Pakistan is bold, open and shameless. In November, 1987, after cricket-riots took place in the Agripada and Kamathipura localities of Bombay, Nihal Ahmed, the leader of the opposition in the Maharashtra Legislative Assembly, sought to move an adjournment motion criticising the government for "failure to protect the Muslims". This is what *The Times of India* (11.11.87) had to report: "Moving the resolution, Mr. Nihal Ahmed... pointed out that when Pakistan lost the match, crackers were burst but nobody tried to intervene. However, when crackers were burst when the Indian team was losing the match, communalists tried to intervene and create tension..."

The insolent logic behind the above attitude must be clearly understood. It is not the attitude of a few individuals here and there. It is the basic psyche of the Indian Muslims, to which there may be some noble exceptions (Hamid Dalwai, M.C. Chagla, Abdul Hamid, Muzaffar Hussain, to name a few prominent ones). What the above attitude amounts to, in short, is: "Yes, we are loyal to Pakistan. So what? We Indian Muslims will be more loyal to Pakistan than to India. Our loyalty to Pakistan is more important than the Hindu loyalty to India. Our loyalty to Pakistan must be considered by every Hindu as being more important than his own loyalty to India. And any Hindu who refuses to concede the validity of the above points is a communalist who must be punished."

India's Leftist and secularist politicians and intellectuals are, of course, not communalists; and hence they fully concede the above points implicit in the general Muslim behaviour—the secularist politicians, with an eye on the vote-bank, and the others out of "ideological" fervour. However, they have to indulge in quite a slippery trapeze act, since they have to

1. convince the Muslims that they concede the validity of the above points, and are willing to model all their policies keeping these points in mind; and
2. at the same time, convince the Hindus who are ever-willing to be convinced that the above points are a figment of the communal Hindu imagination.

Any event in any Muslim country gives Indian Muslims the right to take to the streets and start vicious riots, all over the country, in an orgy of loot, arson and vandalism (especially vandalism of Hindu temples, shops and houses situated near Muslim areas). The event may be the arson by an Australian tourist in the Al-Aqsa mosque in far-off Jerusalem, the temporary take-over by a group of Sunni extremists of the mosque in Mecca, the execution of Zulfiqar Ali Bhutto by Zia-ul-Haq in Pakistan, or the death of Zia-ul-Haq in an aircrash.

The Leftist and secularist response to all these riots, as to every other riot started by Muslims, is the same: huge amounts of money are paid to the Muslim "victims" of the riots; action is demanded, and often taken, against police officials for "atrocities against Muslims"; conferences are held and reports published in which "Hindu communalists" are held ultimately responsible for the riots; and strident demands are made to offset the "Hindu character" of the police and paramilitary forces by largescale recruitment of Muslims.

Any and every foreign Muslim cause is, to Indian Muslims, more important than any Indian cause (as distinct from Indian Muslim cause). The story of the Khilafat Movement is a case in point. The whole sordid story may be read in detail in *The Tragic Story of Partition* by H.V. Sheshadri, and *Muslim Separatism: Causes and Consequences* by Sita Ram Goel, but the salient points may be noted here.

The Muslim leadership in India had been collaborating with the British imperialists ever since the formation of the Indian National Congress. But when the British tried to punish Turkey for waging war against them, the Indian Muslims turned against them. The Khilafat Movement was started in India, against the British and in support of the Khalifa of Turkey; and millions of Muslims, all over the country, were mobilised, on blatantly fundamentalist lines, to take up the "holy" cause.

This "cause", of the Turkish Khalifa, was not taken up by any section of Muslims outside India. The Indian Muslims who approached Arab and other Muslim leaders for their participation in the "cause", were rudely sent off with fleas in their ears.

Halfway through, the Khilafat agitation was converted into a *jihad* against Hindus. Hundreds of Hindus were slaughtered, and thousands forcibly converted to Islam, in the Moplah belt of Kerala. There was a spate of riots all over the country.

If the Khilafat agitation was ghastly and horrifying, the secularist response to it was a hundred times more ghastly and horrifying.

Mahatma Gandhi diverted the entire freedom movement in India to the cause of Khilafat. He declared that it was the 'sacred duty' of every Hindu to participate in this 'sacred cause'; and that, to him, the cause of Khilafat was more important than the cause of Indian Independence! And this at a time when the Khilafat leaders were openly proclaiming that the meanest and most sinful Muslim was superior to Mahatma Gandhi.

The Congress suppressed all reports about the atrocities perpetrated by the Moplahs against the Hindus, and Congress leaders condemned the British authorities for taking measures to quell the rioters. The Mahatma went out of his way to refer to the Moplah murderers as "my brave Moplahs", and expressed admiration for their religious fervour.

After 1947, Moplah rioters were classified as freedom fighters and made eligible for pensions paid by the government of Independent India. And every year, to this very day, the Khilafat Movement is commemorated by a massive procession, in Bombay, in which many Leftists and secularists participate along with Muslims.

Rajiv Gandhi, just before he became the Prime Minister, had participated in this annual procession (as has practically every secularist politician), and throughout the route, his jeep was followed by crowds of fanatical Muslims chanting "Rajiv Gandhi, accept Islam and become a Muslim". Pictures and news of this procession were publicized all over the country, including the government controlled TV, in order to demonstrate secularist solidarity with all Pan-Islamic causes, old and new.

Incidentally, this was around the same time as the Vishwa Hindu Parishad sponsored the Gangajal Ekatmata Yajna Rathayatra, for national integration. This grand spectacle, covering all parts of the country and with participation by crores and crores of patriotic Indians, was totally blacked out by the official news media!

Today, it is the Palestinian issue which constitutes the major Pan-Islamic "cause" occupying Indian Muslim minds. To Indian Muslims and therefore, naturally also to Indian, Leftists and secularists, the alleged occupation by Israel of Palestinian Arab land (actually the land rightfully belongs to the Jews) is a more important issue than the actual occupation of Indian land by China and Pakistan. While India has had diplomatic relations with China and Pakistan, and is constantly striving to establish friendly relations with these two countries leaving in cold storage the issue of Indian territories occupied by them, it did not have diplomatic relations with Israel until very recently, and was always ready to join, or even lead, the Islamic countries in condemning and isolating Israel. (The fact that India did establish relations with Israel is a testimony to the Big Brother's clout in the new world order, rather than to India's own sense of national interest or fairplay.)

After every Indo-Pakistan war to date, India has emerged the victor. But in response to the Pakistani loyalties of India's Muslims, India's cowardly politicians have surrendered on the conference table what India's brave soldiers had won on the battlefield.

The foreign loyalties of Indian Christians are not so open and direct as in the case of Indian Muslims. The main reasons for this are:

1. Christian countries, today, do not, either individually or en bloc, function as "Christian" countries in the same way as Muslim countries function as "Islamic" countries; nor are fundamentalist Christian principles as much at the helm of affairs in Christian countries, as are fundamentalist Islamic principles in so many Muslim countries. Christian society at large, in the modern west-

ern world, has not retained the fundamentalist fervour of the medieval ages. There are no Christian causes agitating the Christian world as there is a never-ending supply of Islamic causes.

2. Christians in India are not as many in number as the Muslims. Nor are they so violence-prone as to adopt confrontationist stands in pursuance of foreign loyalties. They have not tasted blood, as the Muslims did in 1947, and do not have a ready-made candidate for their political loyalties, as the Muslims do in the form of Pakistan.

But the truth remains that foreign loyalties of Indian Christians are no less strong than those of Indian Muslims. Every Christian church, whether Catholic, Orthodox or Protestant, and every Christian group or sect, is systematically organised in a hierarchical structure, with its headquarters situated in a foreign country (in Europe or in the USA). The Christian flock in India is more religious and devout than the dwindling Christian flock in the West, and more susceptible to the controls of its mentors abroad.

Till the end of the eighteenth century, the white man and the Christian churches were equal partners in Imperialism. But after the rise of Secularism in the modern West, the churches have lost their hold on the state, and Christianity is mainly meant for export to "third world" countries. The churches have been reduced from equal partners to employees. Thus while Indian Christians have religious loyalties towards the churches, these churches have political affiliations with Western governments. The Indian Christians, thus, have direct foreign religious loyalties and indirect foreign political affiliations.

The indirect affiliations are no less sinister, so far as India's integrity and security are concerned, as a study of the political situation in the tribal areas controlled by foreign missionaries (especially in the North-East, and in Bihar) will show. The Muslim tendency to take to the streets, in support of foreign Islamic causes, is often matched by the Christian tendency to take to the streets (though, usually, less violently) in support of foreign, and foreign controlled, missionaries and their activities.

Secularist pandering to foreign loyalties of Christians is of recent origin as compared to similar pandering to foreign loyalties of Muslims. While Muslims were being pandered to even before the days of the Khilafat agitation, similar indulgence was not shown to Indian Christians before 1947, because the Christians were, by and large, allied with the Britishers. This, perhaps, explains why Mahatma Gandhi, who had nothing but praise for even the ugliest aspects of Islam, was forthright in his criticism of the unsavoury aspects of Christianity.

After 1947, secularist politicians and intellectuals have more than made up for lost time, so far as pandering to the foreign loyalties of Christians is concerned. The flourishing conversion business carried on by foreign missionaries in every nook and corner of India (gaining separatist colours wherever possible), and the royal treatment given to the Pope, during his last visit to India, are two instances of which way the wind is blowing.

FOREIGN INTERFERENCE

The fact of there being Muslims and Christians in India, and their potential for functioning as fifth-columns, leads, naturally, to foreign interference. Every year, thousands of crores of rupees pour into India from Muslims as well as Christians abroad. This figure is not an exaggeration. When the question of foreign funds received by Muslim and Christian organisations was raised in the Lok Sabha, (as per the *Organiser* of 6.9.87): "according to figures provided by the government to the MPs... in 1984... Rs. 253.98 crores ...in 1986... Rs. 434.10 crores... P. Chidambaram, Minister of State for Home, admitted that the amounts mentioned are an underestimation of the foreign funds actually received."

The actual amounts received through several channels are several times the official figure. Consider the rise in amount, of the official figure itself, between 1984 and 1986, and one can imagine what the figure must have been for subsequent years.

The Muslim organisations receive their money from:

a. The oil-rich governments in West Asia.
b. International Islamic organisations like the World Islamic Bank.
c. Pakistani Intelligence agencies.

The Christian organisations receive their money from:

a. Western governments' contributions to missionary activities.
b. The Catholic and Protestant churches, as well as the fundamentalist Christian sects mushrooming in the West (especially the USA).
c. Contributions by the devout flock in Western countries.
d. Western intelligence agencies, and their front organisations, particularly the various foundations.

All these massive funds are received and utilised, for the following purposes:

a. Proselytisation and religious propaganda.
b. Building mosques and churches in every nook and corner of the country.
c. Buying up prime land in urban and rural areas.
d. Buying up politicians, pressmen, and government officials and setting up front organisations which masquerade as social service organisations, civil rights organisations, and so on.
e. Funding fundamentalist organisations, indoctrination activities and religious agitations.
f. Funding secessionist organisations and causes.

Need it be elaborated as to why we have continuous religious strife and turmoil in India?

The Leftist and secularist response to all this must be noted:

1. They turn a blind eye to both the funds as well as the activities carried on with these funds.

2. At the same time, they actually supplement the massive funds received by Muslim and Christian organisations from abroad, in three ways—indirect, covert, and direct:

a. *Indirect*: They save Muslim and Christian organisations plenty of expenses by themselves taking on, in the name of "secularism", "national integration", "civil rights" etc., many of the activities which these organisations would otherwise have had to take up on a larger scale. These activities include defending, whitewashing, and even glorifying these organisations and their activities; maligning and persecuting Hindu organisations; blackening Hindu religion, culture and ethos; stirring up conflicts and enmities between different sections of Hindus, etc.

b. *Covert*: Secularist government policies effectively emasculate Hindu organisations financially by having different rules for the "minorities" and the "majority". Thus, for example, temple funds are controlled by the government (and even utilised for secularist activities), but mosque and church funds are not; various land-ceiling and other acts are applicable to Hindu temple properties but not to mosque or church properties; and various tax concessions and other monetary facilities, available for Muslim and Christian institutions, are not available for Hindu institutions.

c. *Direct*: The Central and State governments contribute directly, under various account headings, and in the form of prime land, to Muslim and Christian organisations. Thus, prime land is donated to Christian missionary organisations for "charitable" activities (for example, "Pawar hands over land to Teresa in City" screams a title in *The*

Times of India, Bombay, of 13.12.88, and adds, "CM Sharad Pawar handed over a 9000 sq. m. plot at Borivli to Mother Teresa on a lease of 99 years for her missionaries of Charity") and funds are doled out under various pretexts: for repairing mosques (V.P. Singh's gift of 50 lakh rupees to the Shahi Imam of Delhi's Jama Masjid is a prominent example), for the development of Urdu, and so on.

However, foreign interference does not stop at pouring in thousands of crores of rupees annually for subversive activities. Christian governments in the West openly apply pressure on the Indian Government in the name of civil rights, human rights, and minority rights. Muslim countries do not bother to indulge in these subterfuges, and openly issue warnings to the Indian Government in the name of Islamic solidarity.

Similarly, international Muslim organisations, representing the powerful Islamic nations, and international Christian organisations, representing the powerful churches and fundamentalist sects, regularly hold meetings and conferences, and issue publications in which masterplans and superstrategies for converting India into a *Dār-ul-Islām* or Land of Christ, are openly discussed, and massive budgets allocated for the purpose.

FOREIGN CULTURE

Islam and Christianity create a process of cultural de-Indianisation. The converts, unable to change their blood and their racial features, make do with changing as much of their culture as possible.

So far as Islam is concerned, there is a very specific concept, central to the religion, which brands the culture of pre-Muslims everywhere as *Jāhilīya* (darkness) which must undergo *tablīgh* (cultural Islamisation or Arabisation). Christianity has become less blatant about it in recent years.

1. To begin with, Muslims adopt Arabic, Persian or even Turkish names. Similarly, Christians adopt Hebrew (Biblical) or European names.

2. Muslims liberally lace their speech with Arabic, Persian and Turkish words. Whenever they become the majority in any linguistic group (Kashmiri and Sindhi, for example), they drop the original Indian script and adopt the modified Arabic script; and they do the same thing whenever they reach sizable proportions among the speakers of any major language (Urdu, which is nothing but de-Indianised Hindi in the Arabic script, for example, and Punjabi as it is written in Pakistan).

Arabic and Persian replace Sanskrit, in their eyes, as their classical languages.

Christians also tend to adopt English as their mother tongue whenever possible. The state language of Nagaland is English. Christians in Goa, though they now also promote their particular dialect of Konkani, in the Roman script, flaunt English or Portuguese as their co-mother tongues.

3. In matters of dress, Muslims try to identify, as far as possible, with the Muslims of West Asia, and Christians with the Christians of the West. The typical beard, fez-cap, and costume, as worn by most Muslim men, and the *burqa*, worn by most Muslim women, present a picture which could just as well belong to Iran or Morocco.

4. The religious music of Islam (if the wailing of the *muazzin* may be called that), is West Asian. Christian church music is European music.

So far as secular (non-religious) music is concerned, Islam prohibits it; hence the music of Muslims in India is, by and large, Indian music, though there are some fundamentalist Muslims who consciously try to borrow from Arabic and Persian music.

In the case of Christians, however, European music and dance constitute their music and dance. The music may be anything from Western classical music to Western folk music to modern Western music. The moment a community becomes Christian, the guitar becomes a symbol of their musical identity. Only the language distinguishes the guitar-strumming "folk songs" of the Goan Christians from the guitar-strumming "folk songs" of Christian tribals in the Northeast. In dance also, the Indian Christian identifies with every form of Western dancing, from ballroom dances to folk dances (viz. Portuguese folk dances among Goan Christians) to modern Western dances.

5. Mosques are built in the architectural styles of West Asia, and churches in the architectural styles of Europe. As far as possible, Muslims and Christians, who can afford it, build their houses, and model their localities, in the style of houses and localities in West Asia and Europe, respectively.

Thus conversion to Islam and Christianity leads to a conscious and deliberate attempt to acquire the cultural trappings of the foreign centres of religious inspiration. This is not only in respect of names, languages and scripts, dress, music, dance, and architectural styles, but even in respect of aesthetic and philosophical concepts, and social manners and styles (from styles of greeting to styles of eating).

It must be remembered that, ultimately, every religion is rooted in the cultural and environmental ethos of its land of origin. If Hinduism uses rice, coconuts, bananas and plantain leaves, arecanuts, tulsileaves, turmeric etc. as the materials for its religious rituals, these are all Indian materials. It is inconceivable that a religion originating in, say, Finland, Mexico, or Australia, would have used those same materials in its religious rituals. This same rule applies to the entire range of customs and rituals, whether religious or secular (non-religious). If Islam visualised a Paradise with camels, datepalms, cool springs and oases, and if Christians of Northern Europe visualised a Santa Claus riding a reindeer-drawn sleigh across snowy slopes, these visualisations were rooted in the cultural ethos and natural environment of Arabia and northern Europe respectively.

When Indian Muslims and Christians identify with the cultural ethos of their respective religions, they are in fact ceasing to identify with the cultural ethos and natural environment of India, and identifying themselves with the cultural ethos and natural environment of West Asia and Palaestine-Europe respectively.

If one finds different degrees of cultural Indianness still extant among different sections of Indian Muslims and Christians in different parts of India, it is not because of Islam and Christianity, but in spite of them. It is not that these Indian Muslims and Christians have adopted or continued to retain these aspects of Indian culture, but that they have not, *as yet,* completed the full process of cultural de-Indianisation which seems to follow as a natural corollary of their religious identity.

In the case of Muslims, there are many fundamentalist organisations propagating, and in some areas, enforcing, *tablīgh*; and this cultural de-Indianisation is an accelerating process.

Some sections of Christians have made a conscious attempt to culturally Indianise certain aspects of their rituals and customs. However, these attempts have only served to highlight the fundamental nature of the cultural de-Indianisation caused by conversion, since

1. These attempts are being made by a very small section of Christians, and are being resisted or ignored by the overwhelming majority;
2. These attempts cover only some superficial aspects of culture, leaving most of the aspects, untouched,
3. Almost all these attempts are very obviously a matter of strategy, intended solely to give a boost to further conversions.

The Leftist and secularist response to this cultural de-Indianisation has been *very* positive. Indian Leftists bear a bitter, almost psychopathic hatred towards Hinduism and Indian culture. Nothing could delight the Indian Leftists more than de-Hinduisation and cultural de-Indianisation of India. Very early, in the pre-1947 days, Leftist had planted a concept called "national integration based on a composite culture" into the ideological language of the nation. Since then, this concept has been causing havoc in the realm of indigenous Indian culture.

This concept, of "national integration based on a composite culture", constitutes the very life-blood of secularist "ideology". There are three stages of this concept:

1. The first stage, the primary stage, is represented by the familiar "Hindu-Muslim-Isai" syndrome. According to this, the Arabic-West-Asian culture of Islam, the Palestinian-European culture of Christianity, and the Indian culture of Hinduism, represent the three components of our "composite" Indian culture. (The introduction of the "Sikh" as a fourth angle to this triangle, was a side-development, intended to firmly separate Sikhs from other Hindus, and bring them closer to Muslims. That this part of the conspiracy has been a roaring success needs no elaboration here.)

This first stage of the concept has been very effectively instilled into the mind of the average Hindu, through the medium of

a. Textbooks.

b. Entertainment media.

c. Political and intellectual propaganda.

Needless to say, it is only the Hindu mind which is sought to be influenced through these media. The average Muslim and Christian has his own sources of inspiration, in his religious indoctrination, and in the regular mosque, and church, congregations.

The "Amar-Akbar-Anthony" brand of film propaganda has always been an indispensable feature of our Film industry. It has served to highlight this "composite" culture, by presenting stereotypes of blatantly West-Asianised Muslims and blatantly Europeanised Christians, insisting all the time on the "Indianness" of these stereotypes.

This first stage is meant for the average man-on-the-street. This is not the place to give details of the various facets of this propaganda, since no Indian, whether or not he is willing to go alongwith it, can be unaware of it. Even the Mahabharata, on TV, began every part by flashing the name in three scripts: Indian, English and Arabic.

2. Then we come to the secondary stage. According to this, the West Asian culture of Islam is the best representative of the Pan-Indian

culture.

yahāṅ hamārā Tāj Mahal hai, aur Kutub Mīnāra hai
dūr haṭo ai duniyāwālo Hindustān hamārā hai

This was the catchy refrain in the popular patriotic film song from the pre-partition film *Kismat*.

In this second stage, the "Amar" aspect of the "composite" culture is slowly diluted and downgraded, and the "Akbar" aspect is glorified and upgraded; hence, the propaganda must, necessarily, be more subtle than the "Amar-Akbar-Anthony" brand of propaganda.

When two persons meet, in a Hindi film, and one is a Hindu and the other a Muslim, they do not greet one another with *namaste* or *Rām Rām*; nor does one say *namaste* and the other *as-salām āleykum* (nor in fact, do they refrain altogether from formal greetings); both greet each other with *ādāb arz hai* or *as-salām āleykum*. When a Hindu, in a Hindi film, is faced with some great affliction, he starts doing the rounds, turn by turn, of a temple, a mosque, and a church, but a Muslim or Christian is never shown finding it necessary to approach other shrines. These are just two of many examples—each subtle by itself, perhaps not even consciously noticed in spite of their repeated occurrence—which, in the cumulative effect, serve to create the intended psychological environment.

The entertainment media have played no mean role in carrying on this brand of propaganda. The calculated glorification of Urdu, of Lucknow *tehzīb*, of the Mughals, of *gazals* and *qawwāllīs*, etc., and the subtle ridicule of Sanskritised Hindi, has been a basic feature of the Hindi film industry. Again, this is not the place to give details of the various facets of this propaganda, which is a subject in itself.

3. The third stage is the final stage. This is the highest and most refined stage of all. At this stage, every aspect of India's mainstream culture, which existed in India prior to the arrival of Islamic culture from West Asia, represents "communalism".

Thus, it is perfectly secular for Indian politicians to don *fez* caps, visit mosques, perform *namāz* to clicking cameras, etc. But it is "communal", for them to visit temples, or bow down before Hindu holy men, or to wave *ārti*, or break coconuts while inaugurating a function, since the customs of visiting temples, bowing before holy men, waving *ārti*, and breaking coconuts, all existed in India before the arrival of Islam from West Asia.

This last, and ultimate stage of "secularism" and "national integration based on a composite culture", can be comprehended only by the ideologically advanced sections of Indians — the Leftists.

When the Rāmāyaṇa was being shown as a serial on TV, Leftist and progressive artists, led by doughty warriors like A.K. Hangal and Dina Pathak, organised a march in Bombay to protest against this "communal" act of Doordarshan (Rāma being a pre-Islamic Indian hero, any serial on him would obviously be a "communal" one). Addressing a rally at the conclusion of the march, Dina Pathak bitterly castigated Doordarshan for showing another "communal" item on its network—a report of the archaeological discovery, by Dr. S.R. Rao, of the remains of ancient Dwarka, under the sea, off the coast of Gujarat (Dwarka, having sunk under the sea long before the birth of Islam, any report on it would obviously be a "communal" one). Need we say more?

THREE

HINDUISM AS AN "ARYAN" RELIGION AND THE "ARYANS" AS FOREIGNERS

The third principle of Leftist propaganda is that, whether or not Hinduism can be shown to be a "foreign" religion, the Aryans were certainly foreign invaders; and Hinduism was their religion, which they forcibly imposed on the indigenous Dravidians.

Based on this, the Leftists have two pieces of advice to give—the first, to a section of Hindus, and the second, to Hindus as a whole:

1. The "Dravidians" (that is, the people speaking Dravidian languages today; as well as the lower castes and tribals among the Aryan-language speakers, who were also originally "Dravidians") must reject this legacy of a religion imposed upon them by their enemies.
2. Hindu must stop carping at the proselytisation activities of Islam and Christianity, and harping on the tolerance of Hinduism.

HINDUISM AS AN "ARYAN" RELIGION

For the purpose of this chapter, let us put aside the question of whether any "Aryans" did or did not invade India (which question will be dealt with in the third section of this book), and let us examine whether, *as per the Aryan invasion theory itself*, Hinduism is an "Aryan" religion.

Hinduism has generally been accepted, by protagonists of the theory, as a fusion of the "Aryan" and the "Dravidian" religions. Suniti Kumar Chatterji has listed some of the features of Hinduism, which are supposed to be of "pre-Aryan" origin (mainly "Dravidian", sometimes "Austric").[1]

As a study of the material, presented therein, will show, almost every aspect of Hinduism as we know it today, certainly every feature central to the religion, is supposed to be of "pre-Aryan" origin.

The "Aryans" are supposed to be "worshippers of the elements" (fire, air, water, sky). The ritual worship of fire, in the form of *yajña*, is supposed to be the "Aryan" form of worship.

1. *The entire system of idol-worship*, which today forms the very essence of popular Hinduism, is supposed to be of "pre-Aryan" origin.

[1] HCIP, Chapter 8.

Thus, the worship of consecrated idols is of "pre-Aryan" origin, whether of

a. the *liṅgam*; or
b. "rude blocks of stone" with eyes painted on them; or
c. roughly, or finely, carved, or cast, images of stone, metal or some other material.

The concept of *grihadevatās* and *grāmdevatās* (family deities and village deities) is of "pre-Aryan" origin.

The entire process of idol-worship is of "pre-Aryan" origin:

a. treating the idols as living beings; bathing, dressing and feeding them, putting them to sleep, etc.
b. performing *pūjā* by offering flowers, water, and fruits, bananas, coconuts, clothes and ornaments to the idols;
c. performing *ārati* by waving lights in front of the idols;
d. performing music and dance before the idols;
e. partaking of *prasāda*, of food offered to the idols.

The entire system of idol-temples and pilgrim-centres, with sacred tanks and bathing-*ghāṭs,* and of temple festivals, with palanquins and chariots, is of "pre-Aryan" origin.

2. The use of sandalpaste, turmeric, and vermilion (*sindūr*), for smearing on the idols, and on the foreheads of worshippers, is of "pre-Aryan" origin.

From this, it follows that two very fundamental outward symbols of Hinduism today, are also of "pre-Aryan" origin:

a. The *tilak* marks (of whatever material) on the forehead.
b. The sacred saffron colour, and, by implication, also the saffron flag.

3. The idea of soul, and the concept of transmigration of souls, and rebirth, is supposed to be of "pre-Aryan" origin. This concept forms a very fundamental aspect of Hindu philosophy, and is the one concept accepted by all the schools of Hindu philosophy (except the *cārvaka* and other *nāstika* schools of thought), including the Buddhist and the Jain schools of thought.

4. The enumeration of the days by the phases of the moon, the *tithis,* is also supposed to be of "pre-Aryan" origin. The importance of the *pañcāṅga* (the annual calendar based on the *tithis),* in ritualistic Hinduism, can never be underestimated.

5. Zoomorphic aspects of Hinduism are also supposed to be of "pre-Aryan" origin. These cover;

a. The worship of certain animals, birds and reptiles;

b. The concept of God coming down to earth in the form of zoomorphic *avatāras* (Narasiṁha, Kūrma, Matsya, Varāha; and, incidentally, the very concept of God coming down to earth in the form of *avatāras* is itself of "pre-Aryan" origin).

c. The concept of every God and Goddess having a "vehicle" (Viṣṇu's Garuḍa, Gaṇeśa's mouse, Kārtikeya's peacock, Śiva's bull, Durgā's lion, etc).

6. Of all the Hindu Gods and Goddesses, Brahmā, Viṣṇu, and Śiva constitute the trinity. From another angle, Śiva, Viṣṇu, and Śakti (the Mother Goddess, also called Umā, Durgā, Ambā, Pārvatī, etc) constitute a trinity, since all Hindu sects are broadly classified into Śaiva, Vaiṣṇava, and Śākta. Gaṇeśa is the God whom it is considered necessary to invoke before any other God. Kriṣṇa is probably the single most popular God among the Hindu masses.

Of these, Brahmā — the only God who is very little worshipped, having hardly one or two known temples devoted to him in the whole of India — is presumably the only "Aryan" God. All the others are supposed to be either wholly or partially "Dravidian".

Śiva, Śakti, Gaṇeśa are all supposed to be wholly "Dravidian".

Viṣṇu is "partly Aryan, a form of the Sun God, and partly at least the deity is of Dravidian affinity as a Sky-God whose colour was of the blue sky. (cf. Tamil *viṇ* 'sky' and the Middle IA or Prakrit form of Viṣṇu, which was Viṇhu, Veṇhu)."[2]

Kriṣṇa also "represents, partly at least, a Dravidian God of Youth, who has later been identified with Viṣṇu as an incarnation of his."[3]

Kārtikeya and Hanumāna are also of "pre-Aryan" origin.

7. The legends and stories in the Purāṇas represent the rich ethos of Hindu tradition. "Myths and legends of Gods and Heroes current among the Austrics and Dravidians, long antedating the period of Aryan advent in India (c. 1500 BC) survived the Aryan impact... (were) rendered into the Aryan languages... and it is these myths and legends of Gods, kings and sages, which we largely find in the Purāṇas ... (these) can be properly understood as cases of rendering in the Aryan's language of pre-Aryan material."[4]

In addition to all the above, there are many minor mythological and philosophical concepts, and socio-religious rituals (for example, the concept of the "evil eye", and rituals for its removal) which are

[2] HCIP, p. 160.
[3] HCIP, p. 161.
[4] HCIP, p. 165.

supposed to be of "pre-Aryan" origin. Haṭhayoga and Āyurveda are also supposed to be " pre-Aryan" in origin.

To all this, one may add two more aspects, referred to in the previous chapter:

1. Hinduism has several sacred cities and many sacred shrines, rivers, mountains, lakes and tanks, all of which are located in India. It is obvious that the "Aryans" could not have brought these along with them. Therefore, these must have been sacred to the "pre-Aryans" as well.

2. Hinduism uses a very wide range of materia botanica (coconuts, bananas, rice, sandalwood, turmeric, etc.), in its rituals and ceremonies, not one of which is alleged to have been brought in by the "Aryans" from outside. Therefore, these materials must have been used in those very rituals by the "pre-Aryans" as well.

After all this, how much remains, of Hinduism, which can be classified as "Aryan"? According to the Aryan invasion theory itself, Hinduism is practically a "pre-Aryan", and more specifically, a "Dravidian" religion adopted by the "Aryans".

DRAVIDIANS: HINDUISM VS. ISLAM AND CHRISTIANITY

A certain section of die-hard Leftists in the extreme south had decided, well before 1947, to make political and ideological capital out of the very first premise of the Aryan invasion theory, namely, that Aryans invaded India and drove the Dravidians south. Starting under the name "Justice Party", this section floated the "Dravida Kaḻagam" (DK), claiming to represent a movement of, by, and for, the "Dravidians", to liberate them from "Aryan dominance". This philosophy today constitutes the dominant political current in Tamil Nadu, with the DMK and the AIADMK, linear descendants of the DK, dominating the political scene. Hatred for Brahmins, Sanskrit, Hindi, and Hinduism, forms the main plank of this "Dravidian Movement". Moreover, this movement has always entered into an alliance with Islam and Christianity, and against Hinduism.

This political philosophy is now being propagated on a war footing, all over India, by a grand alliance of fundamentalist Islamic and Christian forces, and rabid Leftists of every kind.

"Dravidians" all over India are being exhorted to throw off the shackles of "Aryan imperialism" as represented by Hinduism, and to align with Islam and Christianity. The term, "Dravidian", is supposed to include all tribals, and all Aryan-language speaking lower castes!

It is true that there has been exploitation and oppression of certain sections of Hindus by certain other sections of Hindus, but that really has little to do with Hinduism, and certainly nothing whatsoever to do with the "Aryan-Dravidian" question.

Let us, therefore, examine the contention that "Dravidians" (that is, sections of Hindus, branded as "Dravidians", in opposition to other sections, branded as "Aryans") must reject Hinduism, as an "Aryan" imposition on them, and align with Islam and Christianity, since their greater affinity lies with Islam and Christianity.

Firstly, it has already been demonstrated that, as per the Aryan invasion theory itself, almost all the fundamental features of Hinduism are supposed to be "pre-Aryan" (and specifically "Dravidian"). So, even if there happen to be some other features of Hinduism which are "Aryan" (the "Aryan" features ultimately boil down to the Sanskrit language and the Vedic texts, Vedic rituals, and Vedic gods, sages and personalities), there is still no logical reason, whatsoever, why "Dravidians" should be expected to feel a greater affinity towards totally alien religions like Islam and Christianity, than towards Hinduism, or even towards the particular "Aryan" features of Hinduism.

Secondly, a study of the fundamental features which differentiate Hinduism from Islam and Christianity, particularly features which arouse the animosity of Muslim and Christian theologians, proves very instructive. It shows that it is the "Dravidian" features of Hinduism, towards which the theologies of Islam and Christianity harbour the greatest hatred.

The differences between Hinduism, on the one hand, and Islam and Christianity, on the other, fall into three categories:

1. Geography-based differences.
2. Social-system-based differences.
3. Religious-concept-based differences.

Geography-based differences

These have been elaborated in the previous chapter. It is inconceivable that any genuine "Dravidian" movement should consider itself closer to Islam and Christianity, than to Hinduism, on any of the points which constitute the geography-based differences.

The reason why Hindu Nationalists identify with Hinduism, rather than with Islam and Christianity, and why anti-national elements (like the Leftists) identify with Islam and Christianity rather than with Hinduism, is precisely because Hinduism is Indian, and Islam and Christianity are foreign.

The "Aryan" elements in Hinduism (the Sanskrit language and the Vedic texts) fall in this category. Muslim and Christian theologians may well resent the Vedic texts, as they would resent the religious texts of any religion other than their own, including each other's religious texts; but the Vedic texts are not the objects of their strongest religious ire. The Sanskrit language also, although they (especially the Muslims, who have a foreign "sacred language" of their own) might resent it being considered a sacred language, is not a major object of their religious ire.

There is no reason at all why any "Dravidian" movement should resent the Vedic texts or the Sanskrit language. The Vedic texts are just Hindu texts from the Punjab, just as there are various other Hindu texts from various other parts of India (including Tamil texts from Tamil Nadu). Their importance lies in their being the *oldest* Hindu texts extant, and in their being in the oldest extant form of Sanskrit, the sacred language of Hinduism. If the sole objection of the "Dravidian" movement to Hinduism is that Sanskrit (another Indian language) is the sacred language of Hinduism (a religion, which, as per the Aryan invasion theory itself, is practically a "Dravidian" one), this unreasonable objection totally exposes the movement.

Social-system-based differences

The basic difference, in this category, lies in the Indian caste-system which is not found in Islam and Christianity outside India.

The caste system (whatever may have been its original form, and whatever role it may be alleged to have played in preserving Hindu society through the vicissitudes of foreign invasions) is, in its nastier aspects, the bane of Hinduism and Indian society. This system, however, is a social system, and is not really a central aspect of Hinduism, although vested interests down the centuries have strived, with great success, to identify it with Hinduism.

It is a feature, of Hindu society, which every genuine Hindu, and Hindu Nationalist organisation (like the RSS), has sought to wipe out, or at least, to neutralise; and which every Leftist and secularist politician and intellectual, and Muslim and Christian force, has tried to strengthen and perpetuate with the full, conscious or unconscious, cooperation of the vested interests among the various castes.

That the Hindu who belongs to an oppressed section should resent his oppressors is natural. But that he should resent and turn against the religion, culture and national ethos of his oppressors, which also happen to be his own religion, culture and national ethos, is ridiculous. It is like a man, oppressed by his brother, resenting and turning against his own mother, who is also being oppressed by the brother, simply because she also happens to be the mother of his oppressor. The unsavoury aspects of Islam and Christianity are intrinsic to those religions, since the very founders of the two religions (Muhammad and "St." Paul respectively) had instilled those aspects into them. However, Hinduism has no founder. Hinduism is not a religion in the same sense as Islam and Christianity. It is in fact the religious personification of India's cultural ethos, and any evils, introduced into it in the course of time by perverted persons or vested interests who may have happened to be Hindus, cannot be considered intrinsic to Hinduism.

And the caste system certainly does not have anything to do with any "Aryan-Dravidian" divide. Today Tamil Nadu is one of the states leading in atrocities on the lower castes and tribals, and the perpetrators of these atrocities also belong to castes which are considered hardcore "Dravidian" castes.

Muslim and Christian theologians have nothing against the caste system. To them, in fact, it is a treasury of weapons and tools — weapons to attack Hinduism, and tools to prise out sections of Hindus into their own folds. Only a knave would claim, and a fool believe, that Islam and Christianity are morally concerned about the injustices of the caste system. Caste prejudice is notoriously as strong among Christian converts as among their Hindu counterparts.

As for Islam, consider the attitude of Shah Waliullah (18th century), one of the very topmost interpreters of true Islam, as recorded by S.A.A. Rizwi in his, *Shah Wali-Allah and His Times*, 1980: "The proselytisation of Shah Wali-Allah only included the leaders of the Hindu community. The low class of the infidels, according to him, were to be left alone to work in the fields and for paying jiziya. They, like beasts of burden and agricultural livestock, were to be kept in abject misery and despair."

Religious-concept-based Differences

These are basically four in number:

a. Semitic exclusivism vs. Hindu universalism.
b. Semitic non-vegetarianism vs. Hindu vegetarianism
c. Semitic iconoclasm vs. Hindu idol-worship.
d. Semitic belief in single-life vs. Hindu belief in multiple lives.

a. *Exclusivism vs. Universalism*: The basic difference between Semitic religions and Hinduism is that Semitic religions are exclusivist, while Hinduism is universalist.

Islam declares that there is only one God, Allah, represented by his Last (and greatest) prophet, Muhammad. Belief in Muhammad as the only spokesman of the only God, Allah, is the only path to salvation. All other paths lead to damnation.

Christianity declares that there is only one God — Jehovah — represented by his "only-begotten son" — Jesus Christ. Belief in Jesus Christ as the only begotten son of the only God, Jehovah, is the only path to salvation. All other paths lead to damnation.

Hinduism, on the other hand, allows that all paths if followed sincerely lead to salvation. (A full analysis of this contrast between Semitic religions and Hinduism is given by Ram Swarup in *Hinduism vis-à-vis Christianity and Islam*, and by Sita Ram Goel in *Defence of Hindu Society*.)

Islam and Christianity inherited their exclusivist base from their parent, Judaism. But they added a revolutionary new ingredient to it, viz. Proselytisation: the sacred duty of thrusting "salvation" down the throat of every single human being unfortunate enough to be traversing any of the various "paths to damnation". The proselytising zeal of Islam and Christianity, down the ages, has resulted in death and destruction for millions of people, hundreds of religions, cultures and civilizations, and a major part of the world's cultural heritage.

As per the Aryan invasion theory itself, universalism was a basic feature of the belief-system of both the "Aryans" as well as the "Dravidians". And the exclusivist Semitic zeal of Islam and Christianity has no respect for the religious concepts of any other section of humanity: neither "Aryan" nor "Dravidian" nor Sinitic, nor African, nor Red Indian, nor Australian aboriginal, nor pagan European, nor any other.

There is, therefore, no conceivable reason whatsoever why "Dravidians" should be expected to feel closer to Islam and Christianity on the basis of this very fundamental religious attitude (exclusivist vs. universalist), than to Hinduism. This fact will become very much clearer when we consider the next three religious concepts.

These three concepts constitute those features of Hinduism which (and especially the last two) arouse the deepest hatred and ire of Semitic theologies, and all of them, as per the Aryan invasion theory itself, are very definitely "Dravidian" and equally definitely not "Aryan".

b. *Non-Vegetarianism vs. Vegetarianism*: Non-vegetarianism is a basic feature of Semitic religions. While Christianity did not retain the Judaic system of ritualistic slaughter of animals, Islam not only retained it, but even made it compulsory. However, so far as vegetarianism is concerned, the concept is as alien to Christianity as it is to Judaism and Islam. Islam, in fact, specifically prohibits vegetarianism (*Sahih Muslim,* hadīs 3236) alongwith celibacy and physical auserity. And both Islam and Christianity require that a convert from another religion be compelled to eat the flesh of the particular animal prohibited by his earlier religion, in order to set the seal on his conversion. (For this, also, Islam provides specific precedents, as, for example, an incident quoted from *Tabqāt-i-ibn Sa'd* by Ram Swarup in *Understanding Islam through Hadis* p. 191).

Hinduism, on the other hand (including its major sects like Buddhism, Jainism and Sikhism, and barring only some minor sects and cults) considers vegetarianism to be a major virtue.

The "Aryans", however, are supposed to have been non-vegetarians. The Leftists are never tired of declaring that the "Vedic Aryans" were meat-eaters and even beef-eaters. Vegetarianism was introduced as an ethical reform by Buddha and Mahavir, and has been an intrinsic part of Hindu ethics ever since. But as per the Aryan invasion theory itself, vegetarianism was an important concept among "pre-Aryan Dravidians".

The concept of vegetarianism has deeper connotations. It is based on a basic respect and reverence for all forms of life. Along with the zoomorphic aspects of Hinduism, and the concept of transmigration of souls into animals and plants, it represent a practical manifestation of the basic Hindu philosophy of Pantheism, which is anathema to Semitic religions. These religions believe in a man-centred creation, devoid of inherent divinity, with the plant and animal kingdoms, in fact the whole of nature, created by God for use and exploitation by man.

c. *Iconoclasm vs. Idol-worship*: Iconoclasm is another basic feature of Islam and Christianity. In both religions (as in Judaism) Polytheism and idol-worship constitute the most cardinal of sins, any and every sin can be forgiven by God (i.e. Allah or Jehovah) but not these two. Idol-worship constitutes the most blatant form of Polytheism, so far as Semitic religions are concerned, and (inspite of the Catholic icons of Jesus, Mary and various saints and angels, the Protestant Cross and the Muslim Kaaba, all of which are also idols of a kind) both Islam and Christianity extol iconoclasm and condemn idol-worship. And each of the two has an encyclopaedic history of iconoclastic activities.

Hinduism, on the other hand (and this includes Mahayana Buddhism and Jainism), is an unashamedly idol-worshipping religion. This includes also the Sikhism of the Gurus, although the present-day semiticisation brought about by "Sikh" scholars and extremists (earlier, under British directions, and now under Pakistani directions)would appear to indicate otherwise.

The "Aryans", however, are supposed to have been not only non-idol-worshippers, but actually against idol-worship. Witness the iconoclastic stance (which only just stops short of actual idol-breaking in the Semitic style) of certain sections of the Arya Samaj, today, which have allowed the Aryan invasion theorists to dictate their ideas of "Aryan" religion and culture. (In the popular TV serial, *Buniyād*, which relates the story of Hindu refugees from Pakistan, the Arya-Samajist heroine, Lajwanti, is full of praise for the beauties of Islam, but she frowns heavily on the hero, Haveliram, for being willing, in spite of his being a convert to the Arya Samaj, to attend a Satyanarayana Puja, at his own parents' house).

As per the Aryan invasion theory itself, the entire system of idol-worship in Hinduism, in all its different dimensions, is "Dravidian" in origin.

d. *Belief in Single Life vs. Belief in Multiple Lives*: Islam and Christianity believe in one single life, followed by a state of coma, until the *Yaum-ul-Ākhir*, the last day of *Qayamat*, the Day of Judgement. On this day, God (Allah or Jehovah) will raise all the souls from their state of coma, and dispatch them either to an eternal heaven (to enjoy endless joys and pleasures forever) or an eternal hell (to suffer endless pain and tortures forever), depending upon the deeds of the soul during its one single life.

Hinduism, on the other hand, believes in transmigration of souls and repeated rebirth, each birth depending upon the sum total of deeds in previous lives, until each soul achieves liberation from the cycle of birth and death. There are different opinions, among different schools of Hindu philosophy, about the precise nature, procedure, mechanism, and other details of this repeated rebirth and ultimate liberation, but the basic concept is common to all schools of Hindu thought (including the Buddhist and Jain), except certain *nāstika* schools.

It is difficult to say which of the two prospects is more attractive: the prospect of an eternal heaven after a single life on this earth, or the prospect of ultimate liberation for all souls; and which is more frightening and terrible: the prospect of an eternal hell after a single life on this earth, or the prospect of repeated rebirths and indefinite number of lives on this earth.

Any comparison of the two concepts, however, is rendered superfluous by the fact that the Islamic-Christian concept is inextricably interwoven with the exclusivist concept: the only "sin" which ultimately leads to eternal hell is the "sin" of not being a believer; the soul of the believer, whatever be the magnitude of his sins, reaches eternal heaven.

However, the Vedic Aryans are not supposed to have had any particular or strong beliefs about life after death and certainly no ideas of rebirth. As per the Aryan invasion theory itself, belief in transmigration of souls and rebirth is "Dravidian" and "Austric" in origin.

In short, those features of Hinduism (most notably idol-worship, zoomorphy, vegetarianism, rebirth and transmigration, ultimate liberation for all, etc.) which contrast most sharply with the most fundamental Semitic dogmas and which, therefore, arouse the most vitriolic and righteous ire of Islam and Christianity, are supposed to be specifically "Dravidian" and definitely "non-Aryan". What is one to make, therefore, of a "Dravidian" movement which aligns with Islam and Christianity against Hinduism, and whose activists go around breaking idols and desecrating Hindu temples; and, incidentally, whose ideologues brand all Brahmins, even Tamil Brahmins, as descendants of "Aryan imperialists", but perform *Rāvaṇalīlā*, to counter the traditional *Rāmālīlā* of the north, and claim Rāvaṇa (whom every single ancient text is unanimous in describing as a Brahmin) as a Tamil hero who resisted "Aryan imperialism"?

Clearly, these "Dravidian" movements have nothing to do with any "Dravidians" or with anything "Dravidian". They are nothing but anti-Hindu Leftist "movements" functioning as fronts for Islamic and Christian fundamentalist forces.

THE "ARYANS" AS FOREIGNERS

Whether Hinduism is "foreign" or not, and whether Hinduism is "Aryan" or not, the last-ditch stand of anti-Hindu Leftist propagandists will be that the Aryans were certainly foreigners (assuming, that is, that they will be honest enough to admit themselves wrong on the two earlier counts).

This is the common stand of those who are, deliberately or naturally, prone to half-baked reasoning. Syed Shahabuddin's *Muslim India* (27.3.89) declares: "They (Aryans) don't belong to India and hence, don't love India. They are foreigners, the enemy within. As Aryans, they are also India's first foreigners. If Muslims and Christians are foreigners, and must get out of India, as India's first foreigners, the Aryans are duty bound to get out first."

To begin with (leaving aside the mystery as to how *Muslim India* arrived at the conclusion that "Aryans", whoever they are in the present context, "don't love India"), let alone "Aryans" but even Muslims and Christians are not "foreigners" in India. Muslim and Christian fundamentalists may identify wholly with their foreign brethren, and some Muslims may even gloat at the idea that they are the descendants of Islamic heroes who "conquered and ruled" a land teeming with of *kāfirs*, the fact remains that they are all Indians, as much as the Hindus (including the "Aryans"). At a certain point of time, their ancestors were the more helpless among the Hindus who were forcibly converted to Islam.

Secondly, who exactly *are* the Aryans in India today? As per the Aryan invasion theory itself, the overwhelming majority of people in India today are Dravidians, and there are no "pure Aryans" left. If one presumes, along with Hitler (who was, after all, the high priest of the concept of the "pure Aryan race") that the "typical" German or Scandinavian, with blue eyes, blonde hair and extremely fair skin, constitutes the model of the "pure Aryan", how many communities are there in India today which can claim closer resemblance to Germans or Scandinavians than to other Indian communities in general?

Finally, in historic times there were invasions of India by Persians, Greeks, Scythians, Kushans and Huns. Many of the invaders stayed in India and got integrated into the population. Today some anthropologist may manage to dig out material and claim that some community, or the other, constitutes the descendants of one, or the other, of those invaders. But who would treat such a claim, even if it were proved beyond any doubt, as the basis for branding that community as a "foreign" community?

Indian society and culture have been known for their capacity for synthesis and assimilation, and every single foreign community entering India, right from ancient times, has been completely absorbed into the Indian identity. This happened in the case of the Persians, Greeks, Scythians, Kushans and Huns. And according to the Aryan invasion theory itself, this happened in the case of the "Aryans" as well.

The point is not, therefore, that Muslims and Christians are "foreigners". The point is that Islam and Christianity are foreign, and this point has been dealt with in detail in the previous chapter. The point is that while Hinduism Indianises foreigners, Islam and Christianity foreignise or de-Indianise Indians.

Hindu nationalism has nothing to do with any childish, petty and ridiculous idea of dividing Indians into "outsiders" and "insiders" on the basis of whether or not their ancestors, actually or supposedly, came from outside. Hindu Nationalism believes only in identifying the de-Indianising elements, as opposed to the Indianising ones, and doing whatever has to be done in the matter.

Even if it is assumed that a group of people, called "Aryans", invaded, or immigrated into, India in ancient times, and (while in all other respects their submergence into the national Hindu identity was as total as that of the Scythians and Huns, etc.) contributed the Vedic heritage, and, immeasurably more important, the Sanskrit language (and, thereby, also the subsequent Indo-Aryan languages); even these two elements in Hinduism, allegedly imported by the incoming "Aryans" from outside, cannot be construed as de-Indianising elements in any sense of the term, since (as pointed out, in detail, in the previous chapter) they have left no trace, if ever there was any, of any link, much less the consciousness of any link, much less any loyalties associated with such a link, to any place outside India.

The Aryan invasion theory, therefore, stands bereft and shorn of all its Leftist corollaries.

But is the basic theory itself, namely, that groups of people, who may be called "Aryans", entered India from outside, bringing alongwith them, if nothing else, at least the Sanskrit language (and therefore, the subsequent Indo-Aryan languages), at all valid? Did, indeed, any "Aryans" ever invade, or even immigrate into India from outside? Shorn of its Leftist and anti-Hindu corollaries, this becomes a purely academic question with no present-day political implications.

This academic question will be dealt with in the next two sections of this book.

SECTION II

THE ARYAN INVASION THEORY

Four

TRADITIONAL HISTORY

The earliest beginnings of Indian civilization, as we know it today, are shrouded in obscurity or controversy. This is because the traditional version of these beginnings, as contained in the Purāṇas, and the modern version of them, as contained in the Aryan invasion theory, contradict each other sharply.

"The scene of traditional history," as Pusalker puts it, "opens in India" and it comprises "the whole of Northern India extending in the east upto Orissa."[1] On the other hand, modern historians start dating Indian historical events from the hypothetical "Aryan invasion" of Northwest India around 1500 BC.

This situation is particularly peculiar since in the case of no other civilization, ancient or modern, is the concept of an "external" origin of the basic ethos of that nation made so much of, or given so much significance. The ancient Egyptians had a traditional belief that their ancestors had migrated to Egypt from some place far to the east of Egypt. Yet, no one would seriously consider the idea of discussing the Egyptian civilization of the Pharoahs and the pyramids, so peculiarly native to that land, as being of "foreign" extraction.

In the case of India, however, even in the face of a traditional history which shows "total absence of extraterritorial memory,"[2] the theory of a tumultuous foreign invasion is not only postulated, but is also treated as the very root of Indian civilization as we know it today.

The traditional version of Indian history is contained in the Purāṇas, which are 18 in number, the Upapurāṇas, which are also 18 in number, and in the Epics; as also in various other minor Purāṇas not included in the classification. Historical material is also derived, or sought to be derived, from other ancient Sanskrit texts.

The 18 Purāṇas are the Brahma, Brahmāṇḍa, Brahmavaivarta, Mārkaṇḍeya, Bhaviṣya, Vāmana, Viṣṇu, Bhāgavata, Nārada, Padma Garuḍa, Varāha, Śiva, Liṅga, Skanda, Agni, Matsya, and Kūrma.

The Upapurāṇas are the Ādi, Nṛsiṁha, Vāyu, Śivadharma, Naṇdikeśvara, Uṣanah, Kapila, Durvāsa, Bṛhannāradīya, Varuṇa, Śvāmba, Kālika, Māheśvara, Devī Bhāgavata, Vaśiṣṭha, Pārāśara, and Sūrya.

[1] HCIP, p. 311.
[2] HCIP, p. 206.

The Epics are, of course, the Rāmāyaṇa and the Mahābhārata.

The other ancient civilizations (Egyptian, Mesopotamian, Chinese) have left evidence, in the form of inscriptions and other written records, of various kings and dynasties which ruled them for thousands of years before the Christian era. In the case of India, however, failure to accord history its rightful place has resulted in a paucity of such evidence. In the first place, knowledge was kept alive for thousands of years in oral form, and the written records used perishable materials, which have not survived. Hence, the earliest written records, now available, are of comparatively later dates.

And even when written records, on non-perishable materials, came to be maintained, little importance was given to history. As Monier-Williams points out, in his introduction to his Sanskrit dictionary, "Scarcely a subject can be named, *with the single exception of historiography,* not furnishing a greater number of texts, and commentaries, or commentaries on commentaries than any other language of the ancient world."[3]

Hence, the Purāṇas do not appear to be pure historical texts. They deal mainly with the creation and dissolution of the universe; the activities of Gods, demons and sages; and the histories of kings, kingdoms and royal dynasties. They are, therefore, a rich mixture of religion, mythology and history. In addition, a study of the extant Purāṇas shows that there have been repeated redactions and revisions of the texts, and plenty of insertions and interpolations.

So far as their historical value is concerned, opinions vary, and range from total rejection to absolute blind faith. However, modern historians agree that the Purāṇas are the only source of India's traditional history, and that all ancient historical traditions have a hard core of genuine historical material in them, which cannot be dismissed outright.

A discussion of the precise details given in the Purāṇas would be irrelevant to the topic with which we are concerned here. The basic point which needs to be noted is that the Purāṇas do not contain even the faintest inkling or the slightest consciousness of any foreign connections which could be ascribed to its heroes (the Gods, kings and sages), or to the ancestors, however remote, of these heroes. The Purāṇas know only India; and it is only at later stages that mention is made of Greeks, Romans, and other foreigners. They could, indeed, be

[3] SED, Introduction, p. xxi.

accused of having an Indocentric view of the universe.

Thus, we have two contradictory versions of India's history.

But the basic fact, which cannot be ignored, is that the traditional version is the only version which was known in India from time immemorial, till the Aryan invasion theory was mooted by Europeans in the 18th century. Before this Aryan invasion theory was mooted, no one, in India or anywhere else, had ever thought of the possibility that the ancient Indians could be classified as "Aryans" and "pre-Aryans", and that those classified as "Aryans" could be supposed to have come from somewhere outside India and taken over the land from the "pre-Aryans". This theory is, therefore, purely a product of the 19th century. The background of this theory, and the evidence cited and arguments made in support of this theory, will be given in the next two chapters.

These two versions of Indian history have been supplemented, in this century, by two other factors: the comparative study of traditional material (which has corroborated the traditional views), and the discovery of the Indus Civilization, and analysis of its implications (which has been made to corroborate the Aryan invasion theory).

Finally, we have the decipherment of the Indus script by Dr. S.R. Rao, and its implications.

We undertake, in this book, a radical reappraisal of the Aryan invasion theory, based on comparative linguistics and mythology, and on the actual evidence of the Vedic and Puranic texts.

FIVE

BACKGROUND OF THE THEORY

In ancient historical times, the contacts between Europe and India were limited to contacts between Greeks and Romans on the one hand, and Indians on the other. The Greek invasion of India, under Alexander, affected only a small part of India and for only a short period of time. After that, for many centuries, there were no contacts between the two.

In the interim, many changes had taken place in Europe: the Romans had become Christians, and had forcibly thrust Christianity on the rest of Europe; then the Roman empire had broken up, and various countries of Europe had come into prominence; then had followed the tumultuous history of medieval Europe in which the Catholic Church, and later also the various Protestant churches, played no mean role.

The Arabs, meanwhile, had become the traders between India and Europe, transferring Indian goods like cotton, spices and sandalwood to Europe. But with the rise of Islam, and the subsequent bitter wars and crusades between Muslims and Christians, relations between the Arabs and the Europeans worsened. Finally, the Muslims captured Constantinople in Turkey, stopped transferring Indian goods to Europe, and prevented the Europeans from availing of any land route leading to India (most of the routes passing through Muslim controlled territory).

The Europeans started the quest for a sea-route to India which would not compel them to have to pass through Muslim controlled waters or face Muslim pirates. This quest changed the history of the world: the Europeans "discovered" America and Australia (to the lasting misfortune of the natives of these continents) as well as till-then unexplored parts of Africa; and even petty European countries soon acquired world-wide empires.

The Europeans had started out as traders, but the traders were soon followed by flocks of missionaries, empire-builders and scholars, in that order—all these four categories of imperialists coordinating their activities with each other.

The Europeans, in the course of their international adventures, came into contact with all kinds of linguistic and racial groups all over the world. However, in India, they came across a phenomenon which intrigued them. Although India was separated from Europe by a great distance, and this distance covered a number of areas where strange languages were spoken, some of the Indian languages seemed to bear an uncanny resemblance to some of the European languages— a resemblance which was not shared by the more familiar languages (Turkish, Arabic, etc.) which separated Europe and India.

To begin with, the Europeans came into contact with India's rich Sanskrit literature. At this point itself, it was noticed that many Sanskrit words seemed to bear a close resemblance to Greek and Latin words. Subsequently, a study of Sanskrit grammatical works revolutionised European linguistic perceptions. European grammatical studies (derived from the grammatical norms of Greek and Latin) were of a rudimentary and functional nature, dealing with nouns, verbs, tenses, and so on. Sanskrit grammarians, on the other hand, had developed grammar and linguistics into a science. The Europeans were wonder-struck by the depth of linguistic analysis achieved by Pāṇini and his successors, and even more intrigued to find that the linguistic rules and verbal roots, derived by Pāṇini, seemed to apply particularly well to Latin and Greek.

Filippo Sessetti was the first to declare in 1583 that Sanskrit appeared to bear some relationship with many of the principal languages of Europe. Much later, in 1786, Sir William Jones established that Sanskrit and most European languages had a common origin. The study of Sanskrit grammar had given rise to linguistics as a science in Europe as well, and Sir William Jones laid the foundations of Comparative Philology (Comparative Linguistics) and of the concept of language families. Ever since, most of the languages of the world have been classified into language families, each language family being a group of all the languages which can be shown to have a common origin, or which appear to be related to each other.

THE LINGUISTIC FACTS

Today, 19 families of languages are generally recognized. The "Aryan" or Indo-European family of languages was the first to be recognized as such, and it is the one which has been the subject of the deepest study and analysis.

The Indo-European family tree is divided into 9 living branches. The languages belonging to the first 4 branches (given hereunder) are called "Kentum" languages, and those belonging to the other 5 branches are called "Satem" languages.

This twofold division is based on the fact that many common words, which are represented by a K-sound in Kentum languages, are represented by a S/Sh-sound in Satem languages.

The 9 branches are as follows:

1. *Germanic*: (Northern) Icelandic, Norwegian, Danish, Swedish; (Western) German, Dutch, Flemish, Yiddish, Frisian, English; (Eastern, now extinct) Gothic.
2. *Celtic*: (Goidelic) Irish, Scots-Gaelic, Manx. (Brythonic) Welsh, Cornish, Breton.
3. *Italic*: (Ancient) Latin; (Modern Romance) French, Spanish, Portuguese, Catalan, Italian, Rumanian, Sardinian.
4. *Hellenic*: Ancient Greek, Modern Greek.
5. *Illyrian*: Albanian
6. *Baltic*: Lithuanian, Latvian, (extinct) Prussian.
7. *Slavonic*: Russian, Byelorussian, Ukrainian, Polish, Czech, Slovak, Slovene, Serbian, Bulgarian, Serbocroat, (extinct) Old Church Slavonic.
8. *Thraco-Phrygian*: Armenian.
9. *Indo-Iranian*: (Iranian) Persian, Pashtu, Kurdish, Baluchi, Tadzhik, Ossetic, (extinct) Avestan; (Dardic/Paisaca) Kashmiri, Shina, Chitrali, Pashai, Kalasha, Gawarbati, etc.; (Indo-Aryan) Sanskrit, Pali, Ardhamagadhi, etc.; (Modern Indo-Aryan) Assamese, Bengali, Oriya, Sindhi, Punjabi, Nepali, Sinhalese, Gujarati, Marathi, Konkani, Bhili; (various dialects of Hindi): Rajasthani, Maithili, Bhojpuri, Magadhi, Avadhi, Bagheli, Braj, etc.

The 19 families of languages, into which the languages of the world are divided, are as follows:

1. *Indo-European*: as detailed above.
2. *Dravidian*: Tamil, Malayalam, Telugu, Kannada, Tulu, Brahui, Oraon, etc.
3. *Uralo-Altaic*: Finnish, Hungarian, Turkish, Mongolian, Manchu, Japanese, Korean, etc.
4. *Semito-Hamitic*: Arabic, Hebrew, Amharic, etc.
5. *Sino-Tibetan*: Chinese, Tibetan, Thai, Burmese, Naga languages, Lepcha, Manipuri, Bodo, Ahom, etc.
6. *Austro-Asiatic/Austric*: Santali, Nicobarese, Khasi, Khmer, Vietnamese, etc.
7. *Austronesian*: Malay, Javanese, Malagasy, Tagalog, Fijian, Hawaiian, etc.
8. *Niger-Congo*: African languages like Swahili, Mende, Zulu, Yoruba, Fulani, etc.

9. *Sudanic*: African languages like Kanuri, Nubian, etc.
10. *Khoisan*: African languages like Bushman, Hottentot, etc.
11. *Caucasian*: Georgian, Abkhaz, etc.
12. *Paleo-Eskimo*: Eskimo, Chukchee, etc.
13. *Amerindian Superfamily*: All American Indian languages like Maya, Nahuati, Cree, Cherokee, Quechua, Guarani, Navajo, etc.
14. *Australian*: The aboriginal languages of Australia.
15. *Papuan*: The tribal languages of Papua–New Guinea.
16. *Andamanese*: The languages of the Andaman Islands.
17. *Basque*: The lone Basque language of Northern Spain.
18. *Burushaski*: The lone Burushaski language spoken in Pak-occupied Kashmir.
19. *Ainu*: The lone Ainu language of Northern Hokkaido in Japan.

The Indo-European family of languages is a linguistic fact. It is not only that this family has been more deeply studied, and for a far longer period, than any other. The relationship will be obvious to any layman who goes through any comparative dictionary or grammar of the Indo-European languages. But is an Indo-European or "Aryan" race an ethnic fact?

The accompanying charts show the numerals one-to-ten in some representative Indo-European languages, as well as in some representative languages from the other language families (except Papuan). The numerals in the Indo-European languages of Europe and the Indo-European languages of India may be compared with each other as well as with the non Indo European languages of India (Dravidian, Burushaski, Andamanese, and some Sino-Tibetan and Austric languages) and the non-Indo-European languages of Europe (Basque, Georgian, Finnish, Hungarian, Turkish, Maltese).

LANGUAGE AND RACE

When the European scholars, following Sir William Jones' declaration of the linguistic relationship between various Indian and European languages, started studying the languages, and evolved the concept of language family, they originally named it the "Aryan" family of languages, based on the word *Ārya* used by the ancient Indians and Iranians, which these scholars decided was the racial name applied to themselves by the ancient Indians and Iranians. The family was even then named "Indo-European" by some scholars, and even "Indo-Germanic" by German scholars.

Chart 1
Indo-European (Aryan)

	German	Irish	Latin	Greek	Albanian	Lithuanian	Russian	Armenian	Persian	Sanskrit
1.	ein	aon	unus	hẽis	nje	vienas	od'in	mi	yak	eka
2.	zwei	dā	duo	duo	dy	du	dva	ergou	dū	dvā
3.	drei	trī	tres	treĩs	tre	trys	tr'i	erek	si	trī
4.	vier	ceathair	quattuor	téssares	katër	keturi	č'etur'e	čors	čahār	catur
5.	fünf	cūig	quinque	pénte	pesë	penki	pyat'	hinq	panj	panca
6.	sechs	sē	sex	héx	gjashtë	šeši	š'est'	vets	šiš	ṣaṭ
7.	sieben	seacht	septem	heptá	shtatë	septyni	s'em'	eothu	haft	sapta
8.	acht	ocht	octo	októ	tetë	aštuoni	vos'em'	outhu	hašt	aṣṭa
9.	neun	naoi	novem	ennéa	nënd	devyni	d'evyat'	inu	nuh	nava
10.	zehn	deich	decem	déka	dhjetë	dešimt	d'esyat'	dasu	dah	daśa

Chart 2

	Dravidian			Austric					Andamanese		
	Tamil	Kannada	Telugu	Santali	Savara	Shompeng Nicobarese	Khasi	Vietnamese	Biada	Bojigiab	Onge
1.	vonṛu	vondu	vokaṭi	mit	bo	heng	wei	mot	ōbatul	lungī	yuwoiya
2.	iraṇḍu	yeraḍu	reṇḍu	bāreā	bagu	au	ār	hai	ikpaurda	īrpōl	nīnāgā
3.	mūnṛu	mūru	mūḍu	peyā	yagi	luge	lāi	ba	(No Numerals beyond 2)		
4.	nāngu	nālku	nālugu	pōneā	unji	fuat	sāw	bon			
5.	aindu	aidu	ayidu	mārẽ	molloi	taing	san	nam			
6.	āṛu	āru	āru	turūi	tuḍru	lagau	hinrīw	sau			
7.	yēḻu	yēḻu	yēḍu	ēāe	gulji	aing	hinniew	bay			
8.	yeṭṭu	yeṇṭu	yenimidi	irāl	tamji	towe	phrā	tam			
9.	vonbadu	vombattu	tommidi	are	tinji	lungi	khündāi	chin			
10.	pattu	hattu	padi	gel	galji	teya	šiphew	muoi			

Chart 3

	Sino-Tibetan						Burushaski	Semitic			
	Tengima (Naga-land)	Abor-miri (Aruna chala)	Lepcha (Sikkim)	Ahom (Assam)	Thai	Tibetan	Buru-shaski	Arabic	Hebrew	Amharic	Maltese
1.	po	ā-ka	kāt	lüng	hnïng	gchig	han	wāḥīd	äḥād	and	wiehed
2.	kenna	ānyī-ka	ñat	shang	song	gnyis	ālto	īt̲h̲nan	shnayim	hulat	tnejn
3.	se	ā-ūm-ka	sām	shām	sām	gsum	usko	t̲h̲alāt̲h̲at	shloshāh	sost	tlieta
4.	dā	āpī-ka	falī	shi	sī	bzhi	wālto	arba'at	arba'āh	arāt	erbgha
5.	pangu	ānga-ka	fango	hā	hā	lnga	tsundo	khamsat	khamssāh	amst	hamsa
6.	suru	ākheng-ka	tarak	ruk	hok	drug	mīšīndo	sittat	shishāh	sadst	sitta
7.	thenā	kīnit-ka	kakyak	chit	chet	bdun	talo	sab'at	shiv'āh	sabāt	sebgha
8.	thethā	pinyī-ka	kaku	pit	bpet	brgyad	āltambo	t̲h̲amāniyat	shmōnāh	samnt	tmienja
9.	tekwü	kanāng-ka	kakyōt	kau	ko	dgu	hunčo	tis'at	tish'āh	zatañ	disgha
10.	kerr	ē-ing-ka	katī	ship	sip	bchu	tōrumo	'asharat	äsārāh	asr	ghaxra

Chart 4

	Uralo-Altaic					Basque	Caucasian	Austronesian		Ainu	Australian
	Finnish	Hungarian	Turkish	Mongolian	Manchu	Basque	Georgian	Malay	Hawaiian	Ainu	Kamilaroi
1.	yksi	egy	bir	nigen	emu	bat	erthi	satu	akahi	shine	mal
2.	kaksi	kettö	ikī	khoyar	juwe	biga	ori	dua	alua	tu	bular
3.	kolme	három	üç	gorban	ilan	hidur	sami	tiga	akolu	re	guliba
4.	neljä	négy	dört	durben	duin	laur	othkhi	empat	aha	ine	bular-bular
5.	viisi	öt	beş	tabon	sunju	bortz	khouthi	lima	alima	ashikne	bular-guliba
6.	kuusi	hat	alti	jirgogan	ninggun	sei	ekhwsi	enam	aono	iwan	guliba-guliba
7.	seitsemän	het	yedi	dologan	nadan	zazpi	shwidi	tujoh	ahiku	arwan	(no numerals
8.	kahdeksan	nyolcz	śekiz	naiman	jakūn	zortzi	rwa	dlapan	awalu	tupesan	beyond 6)
9.	yhdeksän	kilencz	dokuz	yisun	uyun	bederatzi	tskhra	sembilan	aiwa	shinepesan	
10.	kymmenen	tĭz	on	arban	juwan	hamar	athi	spuloh	umi	wan	

Chart 5

	Sudanic		Niger-Congo	Khoisan	Amerindian		Super-family		Paleo-Eskimo
	Kanuri	Masai	Wolof	Namagua -Hottento	Azetc (Nahuatl)	Maya	Tonkawa	Navajo	Eskimo
1.	tilo	nabu	ben	ckui	ce	hun	wē'icbax	dalai	attausuk
2.	ndi	ari	nī-ar	ckam	ome	ca	gedai	naki	maggook
3.	yasg ə	üni	nī-at	qnona	yey	ox	med'ic	txa	pingashoot
4.	degə	ungwun	nī-anit	haka	naui	can	cigid	di	sittamut
5.	ugu	miet	jiū-rum	kore	macuilli	ho	gacgwa	ašdla	tedlemut
6.	arasg ə	elle	jiū-rum-rum-ben	qnani	chicace	uac	cikwālau	hastxa	pingashoorooktoot
7.	tulur	nabishäna	jiū-rum-nī-ar	hû	chicome	uuc	cikye'ecdau	tsotsed	pingashoorooktoot attausuglo
8.	wusg ə	issiet	jiū-rum-nī-at	xkhaisi	chicuey	uaxac	cigidyē'ec	tsebi	sittamaurooktoot
9.	ləgar	endörroi	jiū-rum-nī-anit	goisi	chicanaui	bolon	cikwē'ic-xw'ela	naastai	tedlemulo sittamulo
10.	megu	tomon	fūk	disi	matlactli	lahun	cikbax	nezna	tedlemaurooktoot

All the Indo-European languages were systematically studied, and a hypothetical parent of all the known Indo-European languages was linguistically reconstructed. This artificially reconstructed parent Indo-European language was called "proto-Aryan" or "proto-Indo-European".

Meanwhile, early in this century, manuscripts and inscriptions were found in two different places, where Indo-European languages are not spoken today, showing evidence of the existence of now extinct Indo-European languages in the past. In West Asia (Northern Iraq, Syria, and Turkey), evidence was found of the Hittite and Mitanni people of the 2nd millennium BC ; and their languages turned out to be Indo-European languages. In Sinkiang (Chinese Turkestan), evidence was found of the Tocharian people of the late 1st millennium AD; and their language also turned out to be Indo-European.

These discoveries, and the study of the Hittite, Mitanni and Tocharian languages, gave new and significant material to the scholars in comparing the different languages and reconstructing the hypothetical "Proto-Indo-European" tongue.

From the very beginning, these scholars had derived two conclusions from this linguistic fact:

1. That the different peoples speaking Indo-European languages today must have originally constituted one single "Aryan" or "Indo-European" race.
2. That this race must have originally lived in one common homeland, from which different groups of people, set out in different directions at different points of time, and settled down in their present habitats.

The first proposition failed to convince, in the face of the wide racial difference between, for example, a typical Scandinavian and a typical Indian, and, indeed, even between different groups of people within Europe itself.

However, this racial diversity was very easily explained as being a result of racial mixture between the "original Aryans" (or Indo-Europeans) and the local people in the different areas to which these Aryans migrated, accompanied by the adoption, by these local people, of the Indo-European speech. Most scholars are agreed on this hypothesis, which is, indeed, the only logical explanation for the widely differing peoples speaking the related Indo-European languages.

But the question now arose as to which people, if any, from among the present-day speakers of Indo-European languages, represented the "purest" (i.e. least mixed with other races) descendants of these "original Aryans". German scholars firmly declared that the Germans and Scandinavians were the "purest Aryans"; and that the original Aryans were tall, dolichocephalic, blonde and blue-eyed Nordics who migrated eastwards and southwards from their original homeland in northern Europe (Germany and Scandinavia).

This theory, however, had no basis, and was never seriously accepted by scholars outside Germany. In fact, all scholars are now agreed that northern Europe could not have been the original homeland of the Indo-Europeans. The point is worth noting only because of the havoc created, not only in Europe but all over the world, by the German preoccupation with "racial purity" and the "original Aryan race". This preoccupation became an obsession with most German scholars, and became a mania under Hitler and the Nazis, the results of which are too well-known to be repeated here.

One result of the racial theory of the Nazis, which may be noted, was that the word "Aryan" became taboo in western scholastic circles; and it was decided that "Indo-European" was the only correct word to use for the family—the word "Aryan" to be used, if at all, only in respect of the Indo-Iranian branch.

It is now generally agreed that, logically, there must have been an original area where the Proto-Indo-European language was originally spoken, and from where this language was spread far and wide, either by diffusion of speech or by emigration of small groups of people to different areas. But, that there is no rational way, whatsoever, in which one could identify the racial features of these Proto-Indo-Europeans, much less characterise any present-day people as being "purer" Indo-Europeans, on racial grounds, than any other.

THE ORIGINAL HOMELAND

The only point of controversy which remained was, therefore, the precise geographical location of this "original Indo-European homeland". In the very beginning, the European scholars had felt that India was the most likely candidate; but, for various reasons, this view was abandoned. In the course of countless speculations on this point, different places have been sought to be identified as the original homeland, some of the main candidates being North India, Tibet, Central Asia, West Asia, Central Europe, Northern Europe, the Arctic region, and so on. However, the version which was finally accepted was that South Russia was the "original homeland".

In the case of the Indo-Iranian languages, a secondary, or interim, homeland was also proposed in Central Asia. Linguistic studies showed that a physical split, between the Indo-Iranian languages on the one hand and all the other branches on the other, must have taken place at an earlier date than any other split and dispersion. Also, certain common features in the Vedic and Iranian religions indicated that the Vedic people and the Iranians must have lived together for a considerable period of time after splitting away from the other Indo-Europeans. Central Asia, between South Russia and Indo-Irania, was therefore accepted as this interim "Indo-Iranian homeland".

To sum up the matter, it was accepted that the Indo-Aryans:

1. Originated, and lived together with the other Indo-Europeans, in South Russia.
2. Migrated from South Russia to Central Asia, alongwith the Iranians, and lived together there with them for a considerable period of time.
3. Split from the Iranians, and migrated towards the south-west, invading India in the 2nd millennium BC.

SIX

THE ARGUMENTS AND EVIDENCE

A formidable case has been built up in support of the Aryan invasion theory. These arguments may be noted in some detail:

Arguments against an Indian homeland theory, based on present-day distribution of Languages.

a. Geographical Distribution of Modern Languages.

Evidence pointing to South Russia as the Original Homeland

b. Indo-Europeans in West Asia.
c. South Russia and the Kurgan Culture.
d. Historical Links with Uralic and Semitic.
e. Chronological and Geographical Timetable, and the Indo-Iranian Homeland.

Arguments based on the Study of Sanskrit

f. The Cerebrals in Vedic Sanskrit.
g. Austric and Dravidian Words in Sanskrit.
h. Vedic Sanskrit vs. Later Indo-Aryan.

Evidence based on Ethnic Studies

i. Racial Evidence.

Arguments based on Ancient Texts

j. Evidence in Sanskrit Texts.

GEOGRAPHICAL DISTRIBUTION OF MODERN LANGUAGES

These arguments cover three factors:

i. The present distribution of Indo-European languages.
ii. The location of the Lithuanian language.
iii. The location of the Brahui language.

The Present Distribution of Indo-European Languages

There are nine living branches of Indo-European languages, and, of these, eight (if we include Armenia in Europe) are basically restricted to Europe. Only one branch is found in India. And even this branch is not restricted to India: the Kurdish language is spoken right upto Northern Iraq and South-east Turkey.

Moreover, the original proto-Indo-European language is believed to have first split up into two distinct groups of dialects, the Kentum dialects and the Satem dialects, which later evolved into the present-day branches and languages. All the present-day Kentum branches are restricted to Europe, and the Satem languages are also found there in strength (four of the five branches being restricted to Europe).

According to B.K. Ghosh, the "obviously most important empiric fact about the known Indo-European languages" is that "quite a large number of them are crowded together within the comparatively small space of Europe, covering practically the whole of that continent, whereas outside Europe...are found only scattered members of (that speech family)".

Also, "the strongest single argument against the Indian home hypothesis (is)... the fact that the whole of South India, and some parts of North India too, are to this day non-Aryan in speech,...(since) it may be reasonably argued that had India been the original home of the Aryans, they would have certainly tried fully to Aryanise the whole of this subcontinent before crossing the frontier barriers in quest of adventure".

He concludes, therefore, that "the geographical distribution of the idioms of the Indo-European speech family does suggest that the original home of the Indo-Europeans is to be sought in Europe rather than Asia."[1]

The Location of the Lithuanian Language

Philologists, by comparing the different widely-scattered Indo-European languages of the present day, have artificially reconstructed a "proto-Indo-European" language (a hypothetical reconstruction of the original parent language).

According to Ghosh, "of all the living Indo-European languages of the present-day, it is Lithuanian, and not Sanskrit (even if considered a living language) or any of its daughter dialects, that has kept closest to the basic idiom reconstructed by comparative philology."[2]

Hence, since the Lithuanian language is "certainly the most archaic" Indo-European language, and it is spoken in Lithuania in Europe, to the north-east of Germany and the north-west of South Russia, Ghosh concludes that the original homeland must be somewhere in that vicinity, because "the Indo-European original home could not have been very far removed from Lithuania..."

[1] HCIP, p. 202.
[2] Ibid.

The Location of the Brahui Language

The Dravidian languages in India are concentrated in the South, where they reign supreme. Some tribal languages are spoken in East-Central India, in small scattered groups in Orissa, South Bihar, South-West Bengal and East Madhya Pradesh. However, there is one Dravidian language which stands geographically isolated from all the others. This is the Brahui language spoken in a part of Baluchistan.

According to Ghosh, "the existence of a Dravidian speech-pocket (Brahui) in Baluchistan clearly suggests that the whole or at least a considerable part of India was originally non-Aryan in speech."

All these "fundamental facts", Ghosh concludes, "make a strong prima facie case against the theory that India was the original home of the Aryans."[3]

INDO-EUROPEANS IN WEST ASIA

The earliest recorded and dated evidence of an Indo-European language is not in India or in Europe, but in West Asia. As Childe picturesquely puts it, "Aryan peoples first emerge from the gloom of prehistory on the northern borders of the Fertile Crescent of the Ancient East. The oldest Aryan names and words that have come down to us are inscribed upon cuneiform tablets from Babylonia, Egypt and Cappadocia."[4]

The existence of these Indo-European languages in ancient West Asia became known only at the beginning of this century. Innumerable manuscripts and inscriptions were found, which, when deciphered, provided the knowledge that Indo-European languages (now extinct) were spoken in West Asia in the 2nd millennium BC. These manuscripts and inscriptions provided the earliest datable material evidence of the existence of Indo-European languages anywhere in the world.

However, this fact failed to facilitate any theory of an original Indo-European homeland in West Asia, since, ironically enough, these same records also showed that these Indo-European speakers were not natives of West Asia, but invaders from outside.

West Asia is a region which is represented by detailed written records from the end of the 4th millennium BC, and there is no evidence of any Indo-European name or language or people before 1950 BC, when the Indo-European speaking Hittites invaded and conquered the Semitic-speaking Assyrians in Cappadocia (in present-day Turkey). By

[3] HCIP, pp. 207–08.
[4] Aryans, p. 16.

1000 BC, these Indo-Europeans, of whom three distinct groups are recorded, had disappeared without a trace, having been completely absorbed into the Semitic linguistic and cultural stream of West Asia. (The ancient Egyptians as well as the ancient Babylonians spoke Semitic languages.)

These three distinct groups of Indo-European speakers appeared in West Asia at different points of time:

1. The Hittites, around 1950 BC (as invaders in Cappadocia).
2. The Kassites, around 1760 BC (as invaders in Babylon).
3. The Mitanni, around 1400 BC (as ruling clans in Mesopotamia, Syria and Palestine).

Since the Indo-European identity of these languages is known only through records of the 2nd millennium BC, the linguistic substance of these records must be noted.

The Kassites: The Kassites have left hardly any records of their language. Soon after taking over Babylon, they abandoned their original language and adopted the Semitic language and culture of the Babylonians. Their claim to "Aryanhood" rests on the information that they worshipped *Šuriaš* and *Maruttaš* (identified as *Sūrya* and *Maruta*), and had names like *Indabugaš* (identified as *Indra + bhaga)*, and are believed to have referred to their gods as *bugaš (bhaga)*. Also, according to Childe, "these Kassites introduced the use of the horse for driving chariots into the ancient East,"[5] and the horse, according to him, is a "peculiarly Aryan quadruped"[6] and "indeed the Aryan animal par excellence."[7]

The Mitanni: The Mitanni also abandoned, though more gradually, their original language, and adopted the local language and culture. However, they have left behind the following evidence of being speakers of an Indo-European language:

1. Clay tablets, of the 15th century BC, discovered at El Amarna in Egypt, recorded the names of Mitanni kings ruling in Syria at that time. These names are distinctly Indo-Iranian: *Artatama, Artamanya, Šauššatar, Šutarna, Šubandu, Dušratta, Šuwardata* and *Yašdata.*
2. Later on, in Boghaz-Köi, in Asia Minor, there are extant records of treaties between the Hittite king Shubbiluliuma and the Mitanni king Mattiuza. These treaties refer to the Mitanni Gods *Mi-*

[5] Aryans, p. 18
[6] Aryans, p. 183.
[7] Aryans, p. 83.

it-ra, In-da-ra, U-ru-w-na and *Na-sha-at-tī-ya* (the Vedic Gods *Mitra, Indra, Varuṇa* and *Nāsatyas).*

3. An extant manual of chariot-racing composed by a Mitanni author named Kikkuli, in the Hittite language, mentions the Mitanni numerals *aeka, tera, panza* and *satta* (one, three, five and seven), and phrases like *aeka-vartana* (one round).

According to Ghosh, not only did the Mitanni language provide "the earliest indubitable trace of a definitely characterised Indo-Iranian language of the Indo-European family", but it was "an archaic Indo-Iranian dialect which was not yet fully characterised either as Indo-Aryan or as Iranian."[8]

The Hittites: The language of the Hittites is the one recorded in the greatest detail.

The Hittites have been known as a historical people since ancient times, and are referred to not only in Egyptian and other records, but also in the Old Testament of the Bible. However, little was known about their linguistic identity until the beginning of this century, when innumerable Hittite documents were found at Boghaz-Köi in Turkey. The documents were deciphered in 1917, and the discovery that the Hittites spoke an unknown Indo-European language electrified the academic world.

Detailed study of the Hittite documents and manuscripts, written in the Babylonian cuneiform script, showed that the Hittite language constituted a distinct branch of Indo-European languages (unlike the Mitanni language, which belonged to the Indo-Iranian branch). Later, it was discovered that the Hittites spoke distinct dialects, only one of which is now referred to specifically as "Hittites", the others being referred to as Luwian, Palaic, Lydian, Lycian, etc. All these dialects together are known as "Anatolian", since the main area of settlement of all these Hittite peoples was in Anatolia (Turkey).

The study of the Anatolian dialects, as recorded in various documents, has been of great help to philologists in the reconstruction of the proto-Indo-European language, by helping to clarify certain points, which had remained unexplained by the other living branches and languages, such as the presence of "laryngeal" consonants in proto-Indo-European.

Thus, we have the three groups of speakers of Indo-European languages, all of whom can be dated, on material evidence (of documents

[8] HCIP, p. 206.

and inscriptions), at an earlier date in West Asia than any other speakers of Indo-European languages anywhere else in the world. And yet, all these groups are recorded as invaders who appeared in West Asia from outside in the 2nd millennium BC. How does this help to locate the original Indo-European homeland, beyond showing that it does not lie in West Asia?

The facts are interpreted as indicating that the original Indo-European homeland must have been located in South Russia, since, as pointed out by Ghosh, the earliest of these Indo-Europeans, the Hittites, "could not have come from very far, for the earliest theatre of Indo-European historical activity could not have been too distant from the Indo-European original home."[9]

Both the Hittites and the Kassites invaded from the north. The Hittites, moreover, appeared "not in Western, but in Central and Eastern Asia minor."[10] Therefore, they could not have come from India and Iran in the south-east, or from Europe in the north-west, but from the north-east, that is, from South Russia, across the Caucasus mountains to the north and north-east of Central and Eastern Asia Minor. The fact that the Kassites introduced the use of the horse for drawing chariots into West Asia also indicates the same direction, since the horse, according to Childe, was domesticated "in Transcaucasia"[11] to the immediate south of South Russia.

As for the Mitanni, the nature of their language shows, according to Ghosh, that they represented a group which had split from the main body of Indo-Iranians before that main body split into Indo-Aryans and Iranians. "The apparently simultaneous beginning of Vedic culture in India and the appearance of Aryan princes in Mesopotamia (Mitanni), Syria and Palestine about the middle of the second millennium BC" shows, according to him, that the Indo-Iranians spread out into two directions and "advanced not only into India, but also spread westward from their common home that was situated probably in the Pamir region (Meyer) or in Russian Turkestan (Herzfeld)".[12]

Thus, the first appearance of Indo-Europeans in West Asia is interpreted as evidence of an Indo-European original homeland in South Russia.

[9] HCIP, p. 206.
[10] HCIP, p. 207.
[11] Aryans, p. 190.
[12] HCIP, p. 206.

SOUTH RUSSIA AND THE KURGAN CULTURE

An archaeologically identified material culture of South Russia, named the Kurgan culture, was postulated, and has now since long been generally accepted as the material culture of the proto-Indo-Europeans.

This conclusion was arrived at, according to Warren Cowgill in the *Encyclopaedia Britannica*, by a procedure involving three steps: linguistic reckoning, archaeological identification, and linguistic-paleontological confirmation.

Firstly, philologists, by using a method of linguistic reckoning described as "dead reckoning", arrived at 3000 BC as the most likely date at which the original proto-Indo-European language must have started splitting.

Secondly, archaeologists, by locating a material culture in Eurasia whose time-frame and geographical area of expansion and fragmentation fitted in with the above time-frame and with the later and present-day geographical area of Indo-European languages, identified the Kurgan material culture of South Russia as the proto-Indo-European material culture.

(The Kurgan culture is also known as the "red-ochre-grave" culture. This archaeologically identified culture derives its name, according to Childe, from the fact that its remains are "derived almost exclusively from graves containing contracted skeletons covered with red-ochre (ochre-graves) and surmounted by a mound or Kurgan".[13])

Thirdly, linguistic paleontologists, by comparing the archaeologically reconstructed Kurgan culture with the linguistically reconstructed proto-Indo-European culture, confirmed the above identification.

(Paleontology is a science which, according to Childe, "attempts to reconstruct the environment of the still undivided Aryan culture by taking the words and names which occur in a plurality of the separate Indo-European languages. The objects and concepts denoted by these words are therefore the objects and concepts familiar to the ancestors of the Indo-European peoples. The sum of such corresponding terms would then depict the culture of the original undivided Indo-Europeans."[14])

This entire procedure, by which the Kurgan culture of South Russia was identified as the proto-Indo-European culture, as described by Warren Cowgill in the *Encyclopaedia Britannica*, may be quoted in full:

[13] Aryans, p. 183.
[14] Aryans, p. 79.

"Linguists have not found a reliable and precise way to determine from linguistic evidence alone the date at which any set of related languages must have begun diverging. The best that can be done is to estimate the degree of difference between the languages in question, taking into account all that is known about them, and then compare this estimate with the estimated degrees of differences within families of languages—such as the Romance family—whose actual time of divergence is approximately known. Using this sort of 'dead reckoning' it can be said that the earliest attested Indo-European languages—Anatolian, Indo-Iranian and Greek—are different enough that the parent language must have split into several distinct languages well before 2000 BC, but similar enough that the first split into separate languages is not likely to have been much earlier than 3000 BC, and may have been somewhat later.

"For further progress, the linguistic findings must be correlated with those of archaeologists and paleontologists to see if there was a population group within Eurasia that was relatively small and homogeneous before 3000 BC and that underwent considerable expansion and fragmentation beginning about 3000 BC—give or take a few centuries — such that some of its fragments can be ancestral to components of the cultures of the speakers of the various recorded Indo-European languages. The culture of this population group in the centuries around 3000 BC must also correspond to what can be inferred for proto-Indo-European from the linguistic data.

"At present, the archaeological evidence seems to find such a group in the Kurgan culture of the South Russian steppe, east of the Dnepr (Dnieper) river, north of the Caucasus and west of the Urals. According to the Lithuanian-American archaeologist Marija Gimbutas, in *Indo-European and Indo-Europeans* (1970), this culture began spreading west c. 4000–3500 BC (Kurgan II) and began occupying a really wide area stretching from eastern Central Europe to northern Iran c. 3500–3000 BC (Kurgan III). Allowing a few centuries for the speech of widely separated bands to diverge to the point of becoming distinct languages, this agrees tolerably well with the data suggested by the linguistic evidence for break-up of the parent language."[15]

The evidence, pointing to South Russia and the Kurgan culture as the original homeland and parent culture of the proto-Indo-Europeans, may be classified under three heads:

[15] EB, Vol. 9, p. 436.

1. The Archaeological Evidence;
2. The Mesopotamian Connection;
3. The Evidence of the Horse.

The Archaeological Evidence

Marija Gimbutas, in her paper, "*Proto-Indo-European culture: The Kurgan culture during the fifth, fourth and third millennia BC*",[16] presented at the third Indo-European Conference at the University of Pennsylvania in 1966, gives a detailed archaeological description of the Kurgan material culture.

Finally, she sums up the evidence in a conclusive statement, which may be noted here in full:

"CONCLUSION: Kurgan elements in economy, habitation patterns, social structure, and religion *fully agree* with the common words in Indo-European languages which have been used by linguists for the hypothetical reconstruction of the mother culture.

"A. Ecology and Economy: Floral and faunal remains from the early Kurgan period which extends from the middle of the fifth millennium to the start of the fourth, show a splendid coincidence. In the list of trees are the following: oak, birch, fir, elder, elm, ash, aspen, willow and beech. In the list of wild animals there are aurochs, elk, boar, wild horse, bear, wolf, fox, beaver, squirrel and badger. There were also snakes and frogs. All these remains indicate forested conditions and a damper and warmer climate in the Pontic steppe area than at the present time. All domesticated animals — sheep, ox, steer, cow or cattle, pig and horse—are evidenced. Cattle and horse raising was the principal economic activity. This agrees well with the linguistic reconstruction: agriculture coupled with stock breeding. Grain or seed (*sēmn) is attested. The wooden ard {from the root *ar(ā)} was probably used universally. They reaped (*kerpō) their harvests, wool and flax were known.

"B. Technology: The Kurgan people were using objects made from pure or arsenical copper from the fourth millennium onward (a copper and tin alloy was not known to them, hence they were not acquainted with bronze). It is not surprising that there is no one proto-Indo-European word for 'metallurgy'. Metal could have been borrowed first from the Balkano-Danubian area via the Cucuteni-Tripolyte and the Dnieper-Donets cultures and in the third millennium BC, from the Near East

[16] IE & IE, pp. 155–98.

{*roudhos could well be derived from the Sumerian urud(u)}. The usage of vehicles *well agrees* with the existence of the root *vegh in many Indo-European languages, as well as with words for wheel, axle, pole, lynch-pin and nave. Common words for boat, rudder and oar indicate the use of boats. The latter are not proven archaeologically because wooden objects require special conditions for preservation, but it can be surmised that the Kurgan people used their rivers for navigation, and that from the beginning of their expansion they navigated in the Black Sea and also in the Aegean, Mediterranean and Adriatic seas. Both language and archaeology show that the Kurgan people were fairly mobile.

"C. Social Structure: The presence of hill forts (Greek pólis, Lithuanian pilis, Sanskrit pur-as) with royal houses or palaces and living quarters for the ruling class, and of small villages in the vicinity of the tribal centre, *conforms with the linguistic evidence* which indicates that early Indo-European society was divided into castes, the warrior nobility and laboring. This stratified society is *proved* by the earliest Greek, Hittite, Indo-Iranian and Roman sources. Studies in proto-Indo-European kinship have shown that proto-Indo-European culture had patriarchal, patrilocal families that probably lived in small houses or huts. Villages were small and presumably exogamous. Both internal and external evidence for patriliny is excellent. The whole system seems to be typical of the patrilineate in its most highly developed form. Archaeological data does not contradict this reconstruction; on the contrary it supports it.

"D. Religion: Elements in the religion of the Kurgan people suggest the existence of a thundergod, sun, fire, horse, bull, wolf, dog, bear and snake cults, very strong belief in life after death, frequently practised animal and human sacrifices, and not highly developed ceremonialism. No real sanctuaries have ever been found; they probably had open sanctuaries. Although the archaeological reconstruction cannot be complete, the data available *splendidly agree* with the ancient elements of Indo-European mythology reconstructed on the basis of comparative mythology and linguistics."[17]

The Mesopotamian Connection

According to Childe, the South Russian homeland theory is also proved by the fact that three reconstructed proto-Indo-European words

[17] IE & IE, pp. 190–91.

**roudhos* (copper), **ester* (star) and **peleku* (axe) are believed to be derived from Mesopotamian words: Sumerian *urudu*, Sumero-Akkadian *Ishtar*, and Assyrian *pilakku;* and at the same time, the Kurgan people are believed to have received copper and the battle-axe and the Goddess Ishtar from Mesopotamia:

"Metal reached the steppe from the Mesopotamian region and we find that one Indo-European word for copper is derived from the Sumerian. The Aryan word for axe was borrowed from the same direction. Not only are the copper axes from South Russia obviously allied to types in use by the Sumerians from the IVth millennium BC, but one grave at Maikop on the Kuban contained a battle-axe shaped like a hoe with the blade at right angles to the shaft...This weapon was unquestionably an import from Mesopotamia since the type is not met elsewhere outside the Tigris–Euphrates valley where it was in use from about 3500 BC to 1100 BC. Moreover, clay figurines of naked women are found, although extremely rarely, in ochre graves; these bear a distinct likeness to models of the Goddess *Ishtar* found at Assur and elsewhere in Mesopotamia...This divine name is concealed in the Indo-European word for star, **ester*, and the ideogram for Ishtar in Babylonian was precisely a star. The connections with Mesopotamia postulated by philology for the Indo-Europeans are proved to have been a reality among the early nomads of South Russia."[18]

The Evidence of the Horse

The horse is generally believed to have been domesticated by the "Aryans". K.D. Sethna also refers to "the domesticated horse, the typical Aryan animal".[19]

Childe refers to it as "that peculiarly Aryan quadruped, the horse".[20] According to him: "the Aryans had domesticated the horse, which they named 'the swift one'. The horse is indeed the Aryan animal par excellence in the early history of Mesopotamia, in the Veda, and in Homer; in Iran, Darius boasts of having made his land 'rich in horses' ('*uvāspa*) even before he mentions 'rich in men' ('*uvamartīya)*. The words also seem to have had an Indo-European faminine (*aśvā, equa, aszwà*) and Feist notes how often Aryan personal names, in India, Iran, Greece and Gaul, contain 'horse' as an element."[21]

[18] Aryans, pp. 185–86.
[19] Karpāsa, p. 13.
[20] Aryans, p. 183.
[21] Aryans, p. 83.

There are cognate words for the horse in the oldest versions of almost every single branch of Indo-European languages. The importance of the *aśvamedha*, the horse-sacrifice, in Vedic ritual is well-known. Quite a few mythical animals in Greek mythology are associated with the horse: the one-horned horse, the unicorn; the winged horse, Pegasus; and the half-man half-horse, the Centaur. All these facts show that the close association of the ancient Indo-Europeans with the horse is undeniable.

If the horse was domesticated by the ancient Indo-Europeans, then the area of domestication of the horse would indicate the area of origin of the Indo-Europeans.

The horse, according to Childe, was domesticated "in Transcaucasia",[22] that is, to the immediate south of South Russia. In any case, "the horse, indeed, would seem to limit the possible regions (of the original homeland) to countries lying north of the Eurasiatic mountain axis; south of that, the horse was a latecomer...while the typical draft animal was the ass for which there is no (common) Indo-European name".[23]

HISTORICAL LINKS WITH URALIC AND SEMITIC

Indo-European languages bear several striking points of similarity with Finno-Ugrian (Uralic) languages on the one hand, and with Semitic languages on the other; and while these admittedly do not indicate any "organic or genetic" relationships, they do appear to indicate "historical" relationships of mutual influence in very early times.

According to Cowgill, Indo-European and Finno-Ugrian languages have "strong resemblances in a number of basic words or word parts, including personal, demonstrative, interrogative and relative pronouns, personal endings of verbs, the accusative case-ending *-m*, and such words as those for 'water' and 'name'; typologically, the families are fairly similar (e.g. both have many suffixes, but few or no prefixes or infixes)".[24]

Ghosh points out that "similarities between Indo-European and Finno-Ugrian are so striking that they cannot be brushed aside as cases of mere fortuitous coincidence....the conclusion in any case is irresistible that Indo-Europeans and Finno-Ugrian had influenced each other in very early times. The original seat of the Finno-Ugrians was...in Central Russia."[25]

[22] Aryans, p. 190.
[23] Aryans, p. 88.
[24] EB, Vol. 9, p. 436.
[25] HCIP, p. 211.

As for similarities between Indo-European and Semitic languages, Ghosh points out the similarity in "endings of nominative, accusative and genitive singular; in certain elements of dual and plural formation, and in nominative and accusative singular of the pronominal flexion."[26]

He, therefore, concludes that "it is no longer possible to deny that there must have been at least historical contact of some sort between early Indo-European and early Semitic. This is important, for if the primitive Indo-Europeans had on the one hand contact with the Finno-Ugrians of Central Russia, and on the other with the Semites, then the region that naturally detaches itself as the possible Indo-European cradle land is no doubt South Russia, especially as Indo-Finnic relations were decidedly more intimate."[27]

CHRONOLOGICAL AND GEOGRAPHICAL TIME-TABLE AND LOCATION OF THE INDO-IRANIAN HOMELAND

Moving backwards in time from the Rigveda, a chronological and geographical timetable has been prepared to chalk out the journey of the Indo-Aryans from the "original Indo-European homeland", and from the "Indo-Iranian common homeland" to the Punjab region. The two important factors in this are the date of the Rigveda and the location of the Indo-Iranian homeland.

This timetable, as charted out by Ghosh, is given below:

The Date of the Rigveda: Ghosh declares 1000 BC to be the date of the Rigveda: "from a purely linguistic point of view, the Rigveda in its present form cannot be dated much earlier than 1000 BC."[28]

This was the date assigned to it by Max Müller. However, Ghosh also arrives at the same date by using a method of linguistic reckoning, (the "dead reckoning" method already illustrated). By comparing the languages of the Rigveda, the Avestan Gāthās, the Old Persian inscriptions of the Achaemenid emperors of Iran, and Ulfilas' Gothic Bible with Old English and Old High German, he demonstrates that "from general linguistic considerations, we get for the Rigvedic language as known to us, an approximate date of 1000 BC."[29]

He also declares 1500 BC to be the almost precise date for the beginnings of the Vedic Age in India, since, on the one hand, "the culture represented by it (i.e. the Rigveda)...can hardly be pushed back

[26] HCIP, pp. 211–12.
[27] HCIP, p. 212.
[28] HCIP, p. 203.
[29] HCIP, p. 204.

considerably before 1500 BC"[30], and on the other "it is quite impossible to assign for the beginnings of the Vedic Age—and of the specific Indo-Aryan culture beginning therewith—any date later than 1500 BC."[31]

The Location of the Indo-Iranian Homeland: Ghosh declares the Indo-Iranian common homeland to have been situated in Central Asia, "probably in the Pamir region...or in Russian Turkestan."[32]

Since the Indo-Iranians are supposed to have come from the north, and since they are supposed to have dispersed from their common home in two different directions, Central Asia, to the north of both the Punjab region as well as Iran and equidistant from the two, (and, in addition, an erstwhile candidate for the original Indo-European homeland as well), fits the bill.

The Location of the Original Indo-European Homeland: Ghosh finally arrives at South Russia as the Original Indo-European homeland. His argument is as follows:

"The date 1950 BC, practically certain for the Hittite invasion of Asia Minor, is of great importance for Indo-European prehistory, for the Indo-Iranians too should have reached their common home...about that time...now if the oldest known Indo-European tribes, the Hittites and the Indo-Iranians appear about the same time (c. 2000 BC) in Cappadocia and Central Asia respectively, it will be reasonable to conclude that the original home whence both the Hittites and the Indo-Iranians came was more or less equidistant from Cappadocia and Central Asia. Hence follows that neither India nor Central or Western Europe could have been the original Indo-European home."[33]

And the place, "equidistant from Cappadocia and Cental Asia" (and, in addition, from Lithuania as well), is of course South Russia.

THE CEREBRALS IN VEDIC SANSKRIT

Indo-Aryan languages have cerebral sounds (ṭ, ṭh, ḍ, ḍh, ṇ, ḷ) as distinct from dental sounds (t, th, d, dh, n, l). This distinction between cerebrals and dentals is found in Indo-Aryan languages right from the language of the Rigveda.

The distinction between cerebrals and dentals is found in both the Kol-Munda as well as the Dravidian languages. However, it is not

[30] HCIP, p. 204.
[31] HCIP, p. 205.
[32] HCIP, p. 206.
[33] Ibid.

found in any of the Indo-European languages outside India, not even in the Iranian languages. Those languages, by and large, have alveolar sounds, which are pronounced in between dentals and cerebrals.

This leads to two conclusions:

1. The distinction between cerebrals and dentals is not a feature of Indo-European languages.
2. This distinction is a characteristic feature of Dravidian languages.

This further leads to two final conclusions:

1. The cerebral sounds found in Indo-Aryan languages constitute a phonological feature borrowed from the Dravidian languages. Hence, the Dravidian languages must have been spoken in the Punjab region at the time of the Rigveda or prior to it.
2. The Indo-European languages outside India do not have these cerebral sounds. Hence their ancestral forms, including that of the Iranian languages, never came into contact with Dravidian languages. Hence, these ancestral forms can never have been spoken in India. Hence India cannot be the original homeland.

As Ghosh puts it, "the cerebral sounds of Sanskrit which sharply distinguish it from all the other Indo-European speech families, including Iranian, are best explained as the result of Austric and Dravidian influence on the language of the incoming Aryans."[34]

AUSTRIC AND DRAVIDIAN WORDS IN SANSKRIT

The vocabulary of the Indo-Aryan languages, right from the time of the Rigveda, shows that the names for many of the plants and animals, which are native to India, have been borrowed from Austric (Kol-Munda) and Dravidian languages.

S.K. Chatterji gives the following Sanskrit names borrowed from Austric: the words for banana *(kadalī, kandalī)*, coconut *(nārikela)*, betel *(tāmbūla)*, brinjal or eggplant *(vāṭingaṇa)*, pumpkin *(alābu)*, lime *(nimbuka)*, roseapple *(jambu)*, cotton *(karpāsa, karpaṭa)*, silk-cotton *(śālmalī, śimbalī)*, domestic fowl *(kurkuṭa, kṛkavāka)*, elephant *(gaja, mātaṅga)* and peacock (*mrok* in the Atharvaveda).[35]

He also gives the following examples of Sanskrit names borrowed from Dravidian: the words for monkey *(kapi, markaṭa)*, rice *(vrīhi, taṇḍula)*, peacock *(mayūra)*, rhinoceros *(khaḍgī)* and sesame *(tila)*.[36]

[34] HCIP, p. 202.
[35] HCIP, p. 150.
[36] ODBL, p. 42.

The implication of these words is obvious: the "Aryans" entered India from outside, and therefore they were unacquainted with most of the plants and animals native to India and the east, and had no names for them in their own language. Hence, they borrowed the local (Austric and Dravidian) names for these plants and animals.

VEDIC SANSKRIT VS. LATER INDO-ARYAN

Indo-Aryan languages, from the time of the "Aryan invasion" in 1500 BC, are chronologically classified into three periods. The details are given by S.K. Chatterji:[37]

1. *Old Indo-Aryan Period (OIA):* 1500 – 600 BC. This includes Vedic Sanskrit and Classical Sanskrit.

2. *Middle Indo-Aryan Period (MIA):* 600 BC – AD 1000. This is divided into four stages:

a. Early stage: 600 – 200 BC. This includes Aśokan Prakrit and Pali.

b. Transitional stage: 200 BC – AD 200. This includes the Prakrits of the earlier Kharoshti and Brahmi inscriptions.

c. Second MIA stage: AD 200 – 600. This includes the Dramatic Prakrits like Śauraseni, Mahārāṣṭrī, Māgadhī and Ardhamāgadhī.

d. Third MIA stage: AD 600 – 1000. This includes the Apabhraṁśas.

3. *New Indo-Aryan Period (NIA):* AD 1000 onwards. This includes all the present-day Indo-Aryan languages along with their oldest known distinct forms.

There is a vast sea of difference between Vedic Sanskrit and the New Indo-Aryan languages—phonological, morphological, syntactical, grammatical, semantical and lexical. Chatterji[38] details the linguistic characteristics of the languages of each of the above periods and stages.

At the same time, there are "the most fundamental agreements" between the New Indo-Aryan languages and the Dravidian languages, in phonology, morphology, syntax, grammar and semantics; and Chatterji[39] details many of these affinities between Aryan and Dravidian languages in India. These affinities are very obviously a result of Dravidian influence on the Indo-Aryan languages. These fundamental agreements are so striking that, in many respects, "Indian Dravidiandom and

[37] ODBL, pp. 17–20.
[38] Ibid.
[39] ODBL, pp. 170–78.

Aryandom are one",[40] to the extent that in syntax, for example, "a sentence in a Dravidian language like Tamil or Kannada becomes ordinarily good Bengali or Hindi by substituting Bengali or Hindi equivalents for the Dravidian words and forms, without modifying the word-order, but the same thing is not possible in rendering a Persian or English sentence into a NIA language."[41]

Moreover, this convergence of the linguistic structures of Indo-Aryan and Dravidian languages is not confined only to the New Indo-Aryan languages. It is found right from the early Middle Indo-Aryan stage, and even the Classical Sanskrit stage. As Chatterji points out, "the syntactical arrangement of a Tamil sentence is in many respects similar to that of an ordinary Sanskrit sentence."[42]

Vedic Sanskrit, however, stands apart. Hence, according to Chatterji, "the theory of an Aryan invasion of India is borne out by....the character of the Vedic speech, which in its habits differentiates itself from later Indo-Aryan and associates itself with Greek and others in preserving a pure Indo-European structure."[43]

In short, the association of the linguistic structure of Rigvedic with that of Greek and other ancient Indo-European languages outside India, contrasted with the association of the linguistic structure of later Indo-Aryan languages with that of the Dravidian languages, is best explained as the progressive influence of the Dravidian languages on the speech of people who originally came from outside.

RACIAL EVIDENCE

The concept of an "Aryan race" is not considered to be a proper one. Even Max Müller had discounted the idea of there being an actual race of "Aryans", or, at any rate, the idea of identifying such a hypothetical Aryan race with any particular section of the present-day speakers of Indo-European languages. After the racist orgy indulged in by the Nazis, the concept has become even more taboo.

However, many scholars believe that the concept of an Aryan race cannot be totally dispensed with, particularly when dealing with ancient Indo-European history. Chatterji, for example, avers that "race is not, of course, synonymous with language, but....a connexion between the two is justified."[44]

[40] ODBL, p. 177.
[41] Ibid.
[42] Ibid.
[43] ODBL, pp. 26–27.
[44] HCIP, p. 141.

Bhargava is much more forthright in his insistence on "Aryans" being, or having been within historical memory, a race: "According to Max Müller, 'Aryan in scientific language is utterly inapplicable to race. It means language and nothing but language' (*Collected Works*, Vol. X, p. 90). It should, however, be remembered that the word *Ārya* of which the word Aryans is an anglicized form, is used in the Rigveda as the name of a people and not as that of a language. The corresponding word in the Avesta, viz. *Airya*, also means a people and not a language. Whatever meaning may be given to the word Aryan, the fact remains that the original word from which it is derived meant a people or a race and not a language."[45]

German scholars, by and large, believe that this original "Aryan race" was a Nordic one, as typified by the typical German or Scandinavian. While some prominent German scholars, notably Max Müller, disagreed violently with this idea; some notable non-German scholars like Childe[46] also agreed with it.

B.S. Guha, Director of the Anthropological Survey of India, who classified the races of India in 1944, also declared the "Vedic Aryans" to have been "Nordics". According to him, as quoted approvingly by S.K. Chatterji, the original Aryans were "tall, fair-skinned, yellow or golden-haired and blue-eyed.... (but) owing to miscegenation and to climatic conditions, the complexion of the body and the colour of the hair have been modified or eliminated by natural selection to light-brown or brown and to black (for the hair and the eyes), although light-eyed people are not uncommon among the Nordic longheads in India, scattered as they are all over the country".[47]

Further, "Nordic elements are strong in some parts of the northwest frontier of India, particularly along the Swat, the Panjkora, the Kunar and the Chitral rivers, and in the South of the Hindu Kush range. In the Punjab and Rajputana and in the Upper Ganges Valley, Nordic elements are present (although more and more mixed with other racial elements as we proceed further to the east), particularly among the higher castes or groups; among certain sections elsewhere in India, the Nordic type predominates, e.g. among the Chitpavan Brahmans of the Maratha country."[48]

That the "Vedic Aryans" were Nordics who were racially distinct

[45] IVA, p. 1, footnote.
[46] Aryans, Ch. 7 "North European Cradle".
[47] HCIP, p. 144–45.
[48] Ibid.

from the native "non-Aryans" is proved by the fact that the Rigveda refers to its heroes and composers, the Āryas, as *śvitnya*[49] (white), and at the same time, refers to their enemies, the Dāsas and Dasyus, "by whom are undoubtedly meant the aborigines of this country"[50], as *kṛṣṇatvac*[51] (black-skinned) and *kṛṣṇayoni*[52] (black species).

Even today, "the theory of an Aryan invasion of India", according to Chatterji, "is borne out by the wide difference in racial type between the South Indian Dravidians and the North-west Indians"[53] (i.e. the typical Kashmiri, Punjabi or Sindhi).

EVIDENCE IN SANSKRIT TEXTS

Sanskrit texts have been interpreted as giving plenty of evidence, albeit indirect, of the Aryan invasion.

The Rigveda is the earliest extant Sanskrit text, and the entire geographical knowledge of the Rigveda is confined to the north-western parts of India from "the south of the Hindu Kush range"[54] to an area "not...much further into the interior beyond the frontiers of the Punjab and Rajputana." This proves that "by the time the Rigveda was composed, the Aryans had not penetrated much further into the interior"[55] beyond these frontiers.

And "the general outlook upon life as presented by the Vedic poems", according to S.K. Chatterji, "is that of a warlike and conquering people establishing themselves in a country previously inhabited by another people."[56]

The Vedic literature, as well as the Purāṇas, are interpreted as giving details of the "Aryan" expansion into India from their first settlements in the north-west. A.D. Pusalker[57] devotes an entire chapter to describing "the geographical background of the Aryan conquest of India *as described in the Purāṇas*."[58] This "traditional account of the Aryan expansion", according to him, "enables us to trace the progress of Aryan advance"[59] in India.

[49] Rigveda, I, 100, 18.
[50] IVA, p. 47.
[51] Rigveda, I, 130, 8; IX, 41, 1.
[52] Rigveda, II, 20, 7.
[53] *ODBL*, pp. 26–27.
[54] IVA, p. 49.
[55] HCIP, p. 312.
[56] ODBL, pp. 26–27.
[57] HCIP, Ch.14.
[58] HCIP, pp. 311–12.
[59] Ibid.

P.L. Bhargava devotes an entire book to describing "the glorious epoch when the people who called themselves Aryas colonized one district after another of the country",[60] and "spread further and further...(and) inspite of the tough resistance of the aboriginal tribes, colonized the whole of North India and a considerable part of the Deccan."[61] The book is a detailed study of the traditional accounts contained in the Purāṇas.

The evidence of Sanskrit literature is classifiable under three categories:

1. Positive evidence
2. Negative evidence
3. Cultural evidence

Positive Evidence: All the positive evidence in the Sanskrit texts rests almost solely on the basic identification of certain peoples, mentioned in these texts, as "non-Aryans", and specifically as Dravidians and Austrics. These are the *Dāsas* and *Dasyus* mentioned in the Rigveda and part of the later Vedic literature, and the *Asuras, Dānavas* and *Daityas* mentioned in the later Vedic literature and the Purāṇas.

The Rigvedic hymns frequently refer to the enemies of the composers of the hymns. These enemies, referred to as Dāsas and Dasyus, are reviled, criticized, cursed and condemned in the Rigveda. The Dasyus are referred to "as black-skinned (*kṛṣṇatvac)*[62] and perhaps snubnosed (*anās*)[63] and of hostile speech (*mṛdravāc)*".[64] According to Bhargava, "the authors of the Rigveda themselves have sharply distinguished the Aryas from the Dāsas by whom are undoubtedly meant the aborigines of this country,"[65] and "one of the proudest tasks of Aryan kings was to eradicate these predatory Dasyus, a fact indicated by names like Trasadasyu and Dasyavevṛka"[66] (i.e. terror-to-the-Dasyus and wolf-to-the-Dasyus).

The post-Rigvedic literature constantly refers to the wars and enmity between the Devas and the Asuras. According to Pusalker, "Asuras, Daityas, Dānavas and Nāgas denoted people of different cultures in various stages of civilization ranging from the rude, aboriginal, uncivilized tribes to the semi-civilized races, offering strong resistance

[60] IVA, Introd., p.1.
[61] IVA, p. 56.
[62] Rigveda, I, 130, 8; IX, 41, 1.
[63] Rigveda, V, 29, 10.
[64] IVA, p. 209.
[65] IVA, p. 47.
[66] IVA, p. 56.

to the spread of Aryan culture."[67]

All the other positive evidence follows as a natural corollary to this basic identification of Dāsas/Dasyus and Asuras/Dānavas/Daityas as non-Aryan aboriginals. Thus, for example, the Devas are interpreted by some to be an Aryan tribe, and Indra a tribal chieftain. Indra is referred to in the Rigveda as *Purandara* (destroyer of forts), and some hymns describe Indra bursting open the clouds with his thunderbolt and letting loose the stored waters. He is, therefore, identified as an Aryan chieftain who led his gang of marauding Aryans in attacks on Dravidian fortresses, and who destroyed the dams and bunds built on the rivers by the Dravidians.

The Rāmāyaṇa and the Mahābhārata are also interpreted as accounts of Aryan expansion and colonization, and Pusalker tells us that "Rāma and Kriṣṇa may not unreasonably be regarded as true types of Aryan heroes who were pioneers in the spread of Aryan culture and colonization all over India."[68]

Negative Evidence: The Rigveda contains many omissions which are regarded as significant. For example: there is no reference to South India; there is no mention of rice; there is no reference to the tiger, the Indian animal par excellence, but lions are repeatedly and prominently mentioned; and elephants are referred to as *mrigahastin*, as if they were a novelty. All these things indicate that the composers of the Rigvedic hymns were new to India and were not fully familiar or intimate with the different native features of this land.

Cultural Evidence: S.K. Chatterji derives evidence of an Aryan invasion from one more aspect: "The theory of an Aryan invasion is borne out by...the totally different form of culture and ideas presented by the Rigveda on the one hand and the oldest Tamil poems on the other—poems which, according to competent authority, represented the Dravidian spirit at its purest and most ancient form."[69]

All these different arguments and pieces of evidence put together present a very strong and formidable case in support of the Aryan invasion theory.

[67] HCIP, p. 303.
[68] HCIP, p. 315.
[69] ODBL, pp. 26–27, footnotes.

SEVEN

COMPARATIVE STUDY OF TRADITIONAL MATERIAL

In modern times, it is accepted that "traditional history" all over the world has usually a hard core of actual historical material when all the mythological trappings are cleared away. Traditional history is, therefore, studied in comparison with established historical information, with material from other independent traditional sources, and on the basis of certain accepted statistical norms.

The traditional history contained in the Purāṇas has been subjected to just such a study; and the conclusions arrived at are very significant. It must be kept in mind that the study or analysis presented in this chapter represents mainly the views of A.D. Pusalker. We will, in the later chapters on the Purāṇas, undertake a more logical, valid and authentic analysis of the Puranic material. In this chapter, let us examine Pusalker's conclusions.

These conclusions may not corroborate the traditional views in precisely the manner that a devout Hindu would wish; but the one thing they definitely do is to prove the hard core of historical material in the traditional views contained in the Purāṇas, and to put paid to the theory of an Aryan invasion in the 2nd millennium BC, and the alleged consequent disruption of the ethnic composition in Northern India and establishment of new foreign dynasties.

The Purāṇas, like all traditional histories, have their rich quota of mythology and exaggeration. Also, there are some minor contradictions in the details given in different Purāṇas, and so also any number of interpolations, insertions and changes affected in the course of time, before the Purāṇas were written down in the form in which they have finally come down to us today.

However, the historical core of the Purāṇas can be confirmed by subjecting the Puranic material to a comparative study.

The information given in the Purāṇas can be divided into four eras on the basis of degrees of broad agreement among scholars:

1. The post-Buddha Era (6th century BC, or so, onwards).
2. The post-Mahābhārata Era (mid-2nd millennium BC to 6th century BC).
3. The post-Manu-Vaivasvata Era (3100 BC, or so, to mid-2nd millennium BC).

4. The pre-Manu-Vaivasvata Era (before 3100 BC)

The main aspect of the Purāṇas, which is taken into consideration for the purpose of extraction of historical material, is the enumeration of kings and dynasties. For this purpose, also, various exaggerations have to be weeded out: for example, the periods of rule, of kings who are supposed to have ruled for hundreds and thousands of years, certainly cannot be regarded as authentic historical details.

The Post-Buddha Era (6th century BC, onwards): For the post-Buddha period, from the 6th century BC, onwards, the Puranic material is supplemented by the following independent sources:

1. Buddhist and Jain historians and the details provided in the historical works written by them. (It must be kept in mind that a keen sense of history was never a strong point among ancient Indians, and until the *Rājataraṅgiṇī* of Kalhaṇa in the 11th century AD, which dealt with the history of Kashmir, there was really no serious attempt at systematic writing of history. Nevertheless, the works of the Buddhists and Jains are of great significance, since they provide the first sources of historical writing in India outside the Puranic traditions.)

2. The writings of Greek historians (who referred to India very often in their writings, especially after the abortive attempt, by Alexander, to conquer India).

By cross-reference with these sources, the Purāṇas are admitted to contain genuine historical material, and are still used in reconstructing dynastic history from Bimbisāra onwards.

But for the period before this, the Purāṇas are still considered unreliable, merely and purely because of the absence of similar independent sources for the purpose of cross-reference.

However, by subjecting the Puranic material, pertaining to the pre-Buddha period, to a comparative study, the general veracity of the dynastic lists upto around 3100 BC can be confirmed. The chronology indicated by this method may not be acceptable to most orthodox Hindus, but it seems to fit the facts reasonably well.

The Post-Mahābhārata Era (mid-2nd millennium BC, to 6th century BC): The date of the Mahābhārata war has always been a subject of controversy. It has been variously dated at around 3100 BC, 1500 BC, and even 800 BC (This last dating is often by that section of "historians" who add the proviso: "if the war ever took place, that is").

The Mahābhārata war is supposed to have heralded the advent of the Kaliyuga and the Kaliyuga is believed to have started in 3102 BC. This is the date generally accepted in orthodox Hindu tradition, and

Āryabhaṭa, in the 5th century AD, was the first to fix this date as the starting-point of the Kaliyuga.

However, today, it is generally accepted that the Mahābhārata war took place in the mid-2nd millennium BC (around 1500 BC).

This is based on the following points:

1. The various Purāṇas state that a period of 1015 to 1050 years had elapsed between the birth of Parīkṣita (Arjuna's grandson who was born during the 18-day Mahābhārata war) and the coronation of Mahāpadma Nanda (of the Nanda dynasty). Elsewhere, again, they state that 10 *nakṣatras* (each *nakṣatra* being equivalent to a hundred years) had elapsed between the two events.

Now, Mahāpadma Nanda's coronation date has been confirmed, *through Greek records,* as 378 BC or 382 BC. Adding 1015 or 1050 years to this, we get a date in the 15th century BC.

2. This date, according to A.D. Pusalker,[1] is also confirmed by a consideration of the *vaṁśāvali* which gives a successive list of Gurus or teachers in chronological order.

3. The eminent astronomers, S.B. Roy and K.C. Verma, have demonstrated[2] that the astronomical details, mentioned in the Mahābhārata, at the time of the war, indicate that it took place in the 15th century BC.

4. The recent archaeological discovery of underwater Dwarka, and excavations at the site, by the "Marine Archaeology" unit of the National Institute of Oceanography, Goa, led by the eminent archaeologist Dr. S.R. Rao, has provided a major archaeological landmark in the dating of the Mahābhārata.

According to the Mahābhārata, Śrī Kṛṣna's Dwarka was submerged by the sea some years after the Mahābhārata war. The pottery found at the excavated underwater site has been dated by the latest, and most accurate, scientific method known as the "thermo-luminescence" or TL dating method; and the dates arrived at fall in the mid-2nd millennium BC.

Therefore, the date of the Mahābhārata now stands confirmed as the 15th century BC.

The Post-Manu-Vaivasvata Era (3100 BC to mid-2nd millennium BC): The Purāṇas also refer to another important historical event: the Great Flood. Manu Vaivasvata is supposed to be a king who ruled at the time of this great flood (this "Manu Vaivasvata" is not to be confused with the Manu of Manusmṛiti fame).

[1] HCIP, Ch. 14.
[2] MMR, pp. 93–125.

A great flood is known to have occurred in ancient times, as there are legends about such a flood in almost every part of the world. A comparison of the chronology of the flood as per the Purāṇas, with the chronology of the flood as per a totally foreign source, proves very instructive:

1. A study of the different Purāṇas shows that, according to them, 95 dynastic generations (generations of kings) are supposed to have ruled in the period between the flood and the Mahābhārata war.

The Purāṇas mention the number of years of the rule by many of these kings, but, as already pointed out, these figures sometimes run into hundreds and thousands, and cannot be considered reliable.

However, there is an accepted statistical method by which one can reasonably arrive at the total number of years, roughly, covered by a certain number of dynastic generations. It is accepted that some kings may have a long reign, and some may have a very short reign. But when a very long period of time is considered, it has been found that the average rule of each dynastic generation boils down to a standard figure.

In the case of oriental dynasties, the figure has been worked out at 18 years per dynastic generation.

Applying this figure to 95 generations, we arrive at the conclusion that, statistically, a period of $95 \times 18 = 1710$ years had elapsed between the flood and the Mahābhārata war.

If we take 1400 BC, as the rough date of the Mahābhārata war, the flood must have occurred roughly in 3110 BC. Even if we take any other date in the mid-2nd millennium BC, as the date of the Mahābhārata war, the rough date of the flood will fall in the same vicinity (that is, towards the close of the 4th millennium BC).

2. In the Purāṇas, as well as in many other ancient texts, one finds many references to astronomical details which indicate a date somewhere around 3100 BC. This shows that this date heralded an event which was regarded as significant by ancient Indians.

It is on the basis of these astronomical details that Āryabhaṭa, in the 5th century AD, had concluded that the significant event heralded by this date was probably the advent of the Kaliyuga.

But, in the light of the above evidence, it is certainly more likely that the event heralded by this date, 3102 BC as computed by Āryabhaṭa, was really the start of the reign of Manu Vaivasvata after the flood.

3. The flood is recorded in most mythologies of the world. How-

ever, it is only from Mesopotamian records (according to A.D. Pusalker) that the date of the flood has been confirmed; and it has been confirmed at around 3100 BC.

From all this, we arrive at the following rough dates:

1. Mahābhārata war (around 1500 BC).
2. Manu Vaivasvata (around 3100 BC).

And these dates are based on:

1. Details given in the Purāṇas, and the Mahābhārata, regarding: a) the number of years separating the Mahābhārata war from the coronation of Mahāpadma Nanda; b) the number of generations separating Manu Vaivasvata (and the flood) from the Mahābhārata war; c) the astronomical position at the time of the Mahābhārata war.
2. Greek records regarding the date of coronation of Mahāpadma Nanda.
3. Mesopotamian records regarding the date of the flood.
4. Accepted statistical norms for computing the period covered by a large number of dynastic generations.

Thus, the historical core, in the Puranic material on the dynasties ruling between Manu Vaivasvata and the Mahābhārata war, stands confirmed.

The Pre-Manu-Vaivasvata Era (before 3100 BC): The Purāṇas continue to give names of kings who ruled before the flood. Are these names to be accepted as containing a historical core, as in the case of the lists of kings who ruled after the flood? Or are they to be rejected outright, purely and simply because we have, as yet, no foreign sources to attempt a comparative study of these lists? It would be logical to presume that the Puranic lists, which are broadly confirmed upto a certain point of time by comparison with independent sources, cannot totally cease to be valid beyond that point of time merely because there are no similar independent sources for comparison.

From all this, one fact stands out: The Purāṇas contain lists of Indian dynasties and kings in a continuous line going beyond 3100 BC, and these lists stand broadly confirmed upto 3100 BC or so, and prior to that point, the Purāṇas indicate a greater antiquity.

How does this tally with the Aryan invasion theory, according to which "Aryans" from outside invaded India around 1500 BC, displaced the existing native dynasties and peoples, and changed the entire ethnic-demographic composition of northern India?

The protagonists of the Aryan invasion theory either ignore or reject the dynastic lists contained in the Purāṇas, or else they try to squeeze the lists into the short span of time following the alleged Aryan invasion of India in the mid-2nd millennium BC.

A.D. Pusalker[3] outlines the substance of the comparative study of traditional material, as detailed above, and thus more or less accepts the chronological details emerging from this comparative study. But he rejects the geographical details given in the Purāṇas, since the Purāṇas open the scene of traditional history in "the territory comprising the whole of northern India extending in the east upto Orissa."[4]

His reason for rejecting the geographical details is that the Rigveda, which is dated at 1000 BC, shows, according to him, that at the time of its composition "the Aryans had not penetrated much further into the interior beyond the frontiers of the Punjab and Rajputana", and hence the testimony of the Rigveda "is decidedly fatal to the geographical views assumed in the Purāṇas."[5]

The validity of this kind of logic will be discussed in a later chapter. Here it is sufficient to note that the Puranic lists cannot be logically rejected. There are two other ways in which protagonists of the Aryan invasion theory, who do not outright reject the dynastic lists, try to explain them away:

1. These lists are explained as pertaining to Dravidian kings who ruled North India before the "Aryan invasion". The Aryans adopted these traditional lists as their own, "Aryanised" the names of the kings and dynasties, and linked their own subsequent kings and dynasties to these earlier Dravidian ones.
2. These lists are, alternately, explained as pertaining to Aryan kings and tribal chieftains who ruled in the original Indo-European homeland and the common Indo-Iranian homeland. The Aryans retained strong traditional memories of these dynastic lists, Indianised the localities of these kings and dynasties after settling down in India, and linked their subsequent kings and dynasties to these earlier ones.

Both these explanations are, however, based on very determined wishful thinking. Neither of them can explain how these dynastic lists are supposed to have passed through such traumatic transfers of allegiance (of race and language, in the first case, and geography in the second).

[3] HCIP, Ch.14 "Traditional History from the Earliest Times".
[4] HCIP, p. 311.
[5] HCIP, p. 312.

Moreover, the dynastic lists cannot be pertaining to Dravidian kings and dynasties adopted by the "invading Aryans", since the very idea of such a mass conversion of Dravidian names of kings and dynasties into "Aryan" ones is inconceivable. Moreover, Vivasvata, the father of Manu Vaivasvata, is remembered as an ancestral king in Iranian tradition as well — as "Vivanhant". In fact, the Iranian tradition seems to have preserved a vague and garbled version of the original tradition: while Indian tradition mention two distinct Vivasvatas, one being the father of Yama, and the other being the father of Manu; Iranian tradition confuses the two, and associates Yima, son of Vivanhant, with the flood.

Nor can the dynastic lists be pertaining to kings and dynasties in any "homeland" outside India, since:

1. The Purāṇas are unambiguous in placing the kings and dynasties squarely within India, and give no evidence of any foreign associations.
2. The Iranian traditions are equally unambiguous in placing Vivanhant, well outside Iran, as being an ancestral king in their original homeland, which they call *Airyana Vaejo* or *Eranvej*.
3. There is no other place, anywhere else in the world, which has any tradition of ever having been ruled by any of the kings and dynasties named in the Purāṇas.

EIGHT

DISCOVERY OF THE INDUS CIVILIZATION

Archaeological remains are considered to be of prime importance in the study of ancient history. In fact, the main objection against Indian historical tradition is that appropriate archaeological remains have yet to be found to confirm it.

Till the beginning of this century, indeed, it was maintained that Indian history could not be very much older than the Buddha, since no significant archaeological remains had been discovered older than the 3rd or 4th century BC. But the discovery of the Indus civilization in this century transformed this idea of the antiquity of Indian civilization.

In 1875 itself, Sir Alexander Cunningham had first reported certain ruins, in Harappa in West Punjab, and the finding of terracotta and copper seals with strange letters on them. However, he thought that the ruins probably represented a medieval town of Mughal times or an older town of the Buddhist period. So the significance of the discovery was not appreciated at that time.

It was in 1922 that Rakhaldas Bannerjee, the then Superintendent of the Western Circle of the Archaeological Survey of India, excavated similar ruins in Mohenjo-daro in Sind. When it was found that this ruined city dated back to the 3rd millennium BC, and that its beginnings went back into the 4th, and even the 5th millennium BC, in its earlier formative stages, the discovery sent shock waves in archaeological and historical circles.

Since then, hundreds of such sites have been found, the most important being Lothal in Gujarat and Kalibangan and Dholavira in Rajasthan. Many more very important sites are unexcavable now, since they lie buried in the very heart of important cities like Chandigarh. The entire culture represented by these sites is collectively known as the Indus Civilization, or Indus Valley Civilization, or Harappan Civilization.

Details of this civilization, and of the many fields in which it was far ahead of the other contemporary civilizations of Mesopotamia and Egypt, may be read in any history textbook pertaining to this period. What is relevant here is the historical interpretation given to this civilization: it was decided that this civilization represented the "Pre-Aryan" civilization of India which was destroyed by the Aryan invaders. There were four main factors which facilitated this interpretation:

1. It had already been decided that the Aryans had invaded India in the 2nd millennium BC, and a whole elaborate theory had been built up on this point. The Indus Civilization, in its early formative stages, went back to the 5th millennium BC. Therefore, it had to represent a pre-Aryan civilization.
2. It had been decided that the Aryan invasion, and the destruction of the original Dravidian Civilization, took place in the 2nd millennium BC. The Indus Civilization fitted perfectly into this timeframe. The decline of the Indus towns started in the 2nd millennium BC, and indeed, these towns seemed to come to an abrupt end at various points of time in this millennium, and the civilization appeared to have disappeared after that. A few corpses, with axe-injuries on the head, were found in one of the cities, confirming the invasion theory.
3. It was asserted that the urban culture of the Harappans, as understood from the excavations, and the pastoral culture of the Vedic Aryans, as understood from the Rigveda, are "as different as chalk and cheese." Therefore, the two cultures could not have pertained to the same people.
4. It had been decided that, of the Hindu trinity, Śiva was a "Dravidian" God, while Brahmā and Viṣṇu were "Aryan" Gods, (though, according to S.K. Chatterji, Viṣṇu was also "partly at least....of Dravidian affinity as a Sky-God"[1]). Among other things, the Puranic story of Śiva first declining to attend, univited, the *yajña* organised by his father-in-law, Dakṣa—and, indeed, Dakṣa's refusal to invite him to his *yajña*, or even to accept him as a son-in-law—and then disrupting the *yajña* alongwith his wild retinue, is interpreted as indicating that Śiva originally represented a culture inimical to the culture of Vedic rituals.

Chatterji[2] derives the name Śiva from Tamil *Civa* (to redden, to become angry) and the name Śambhu from Tamil *Cembu* (copper, the red metal), and points out that Śiva is also described in Sanskrit as *nīlalohita* (the red God with the blue throat), thereby showing the Dravidian origin of the God.

The famous Paśupati seals of the Indus Valley Civilization depict a figure, surrounded by various animals, which can be none other than that of Śiva, since many of the attributes, specifically ascribed to Śiva

[1] HCIP, p. 160.
[2] HCIP, p. 162.

in later Hindu texts, are found depicted on these seals.

B.K. Ghosh points out: "The cult of Śiva-Paśupati (=Rudra) was borrowed by the Vedic Aryans from the Mohenjo-daro culture. Now, it is hardly an accident that precisely this Rudra—and no other deity—is regarded in Vedic cult and religion as an apotropaeic God of aversion—to be feared but not adored. Offerings to all other Gods are sacrificed into the fire, but those to Rudra and his followers (Rudriyas) are simply deposited at cross-roads or various forbidding places."[3]

This identification of Śiva as a Dravidian God, and also as a Harappan God, "proved" the identity of the Dravidians and the Harappans, and the Dravidian authorship of the Indus Civilization.

The discovery of the Indus Civilization, thus, "confirmed" the Aryan invasion theory.

[3] HCIP, p. 203.

NINE

DECIPHERMENT OF THE INDUS SCRIPT

The discovery of the Indus Civilization by archaeologists took the academically recognised history of India 3000 years back from the days of Aśoka, and about half that number of years back from the postulated period of the Aryan invasion.

But the linguistic identity of the Indus people became a major subject of controversy. The major sites of the Indus Civilization cover roughly the same regions (more or less the north-west of India, i.e. present-day Pakistan) as the Rigveda testifies for its composers. As Sethna puts it, "the Rigveda no less than the Harappa culture flourished in the Indus Valley."[1] Hence, while protagonists of the invasion theory classified the Indus Civilization as "Dravidian", others classified it as "Aryan".

The identification of the language spoken by the Indus people is therefore of very crucial significance for Indian history. If they spoke a Dravidian language, it would certainly corroborate the Aryan invasion theory according to which a Dravidian civilization in the north was destroyed by invading Aryans. If, however, they spoke an Indo-European language, it would certainly demolish the invasion theory, since the Indus Civilization is archaeologically dated more than a millennium and a half — almost two millenniums—before the alleged date (1500 BC) of the invasion, and its roots go even further back by more than a millennium.

But the main problem in identifying the language of the Indus people was that they did not leave behind documents and inscriptions in their language. The only things, in this connection, excavated by archaeologists from the Indus sites were thousands of small seals (used for stamping purposes) made of steatite, terracotta or copper, depicting figures of human beings and animals, and bearing short inscriptions of a few letters each, in an unknown script which has been simply called the Indus or Harappan script.

The decipherment of this unknown script therefore became the crucial factor in the linguistic identification of the Indus people.

EARLIER ATTEMPTS AT DECIPHERMENT

The major obstacle in deciphering the script was the inadequacy of

[1] Karpāsa, p. 41.

the available material. The script was an absolutely unknown one, it was not found anywhere in conjunction with another known script (in the form of a bilingual inscription), and the inscriptions on the seals were nowhere of any greater length than a few letters each.

The situation may be compared with that of the Egyptian hieroglyphic script. This script was not deciphered till the beginning of the 19th century, although attempts were being made since 1556. In 1779, during Napoleon's conquest of Egypt, a large stone slab was found, containing a priestly decree drawn up in honour of Ptolemy V Epiphanes. This decree was in the form of a long inscription containing the same message in two languages and three scripts (the Egyptian language in the hieroglyphic and demotic scripts, and the Greek language in the Greek script). This stone slab, named the Rosetta Stone, was transported back to France, where it was dated to 197 BC, and studied in great detail by French scholars. Finally, in 1822, the French Egyptologist, Jean Francois Champollion, published a study of the hieroglyphic script which set in motion the process of its full decipherment.

The decipherment of the hieroglyphic script became possible because, to begin with, lengthy inscriptions in the script were available anyway; and further, a bilingual inscription was found juxtaposing the unknown hieroglyphic script with the known Greek language and script. On the other hand, all the Indus inscriptions are short, containing a few letters each in which both the language and the script are unknown; and no bilingual inscription has been found.

Nevertheless, many attempts were made to decipher the Indus script, by individual scholars like Langdon, Hunter, Hrozny, Mahadevan and others, and by teams of Finnish and Soviet scholars. All these attempts, however, met with failure. The main reason for this failure was that the whole exercise of attempted decipherment was based on arbitrary and whimsical methods. Moreover, these scholars set out on the exercise with two preconceived notions: first, that the script could not be an alphabetic one, and could only be a pictographic-ideographic one; and second, that the language of the inscriptions was a Dravidian one (or, in the case of some Indian scholars, that it was Sanskrit).

A pictographic-ideographic script is one in which the letters do not represent sounds, they represent words. Most of the ancient scripts were pictographic-ideographic: the Egyptian hieroglyphic script, the Babylonian cuneiform script, the Mayan glyphic script, the ancient Chinese script (which is the only pictographic-ideographic script still in active use), and primitive scripts like the pictographic systems of the pre-Columbian Americans (Red Indians) and others.

In a pictographic script, every object is represented by its pictorial form: a picture of the sun represents the sun, a picture of the moon represents the moon, etc. In time, the pictures may become so highly stylised, as in the Chinese script, that the letter may not be immediately identifiable as a picture. But pictures cannot represent complicated objects, subtle distinctions between different objects, abstract concepts, grammatical ideas, and so on; and the pictographic script has to develop highly complicated techniques to express all these words.

In Chinese, for example, the letter representing the sun and the letter representing the moon, taken together, form the letter representing the adjective "bright". The letter representing mouth and the letter representing bird, taken together, form the letter representing the verb "sing". The letter representing woman, reduplicated, forms the letter representing the abstract noun "quarrel".

日 sun	月 moon	明 bright
女 woman	奻 quarrel	
口 mouth	鳥 bird	鳴 sing

The different letters on the Indus seals total up to around four to five hundred letters. The scholars attempting to decipher the script decided that with so many letters, the script could not be an alphabet: it had to be a pictographic-ideographic script.

Having taken two arbitrary steps, in presuming the script to be a pictographic-ideographic one, and in presuming the language to be Dravidian, the scholars then proceeded to set out on a spree of reckless and whimsical interpretations: each individual letter of the Indus script was taken up and arbitrarily presumed to stand for a particular object or concept; then the letter was "read" by giving it the sound-value of the particular present-day Tamil or general Dravidian word which was arbitrarily presumed to be the one word, out of many, which best expressed that object or concept; then that letter, on different seals, was variously read with different arbitrary variations of that sound-value, each variation being again arbitrarily connected up with other similar present-day Tamil or general Dravidian words or word-parts.

Using these arbitrary and whimsical methods, it is not very surprising that these scholars came up with a hundred different, even diametrically opposite, "readings" for any single seal, and ended up tying themselves up into knots and convincing no one but themselves and their committed admirers.

S.R. RAO'S DECIPHERMENT OF THE SCRIPT

However, Dr. S.R. Rao, the eminent archaeologist, decided to be less speculative in his method. He refused to presume the identity of the Indus language to be either Aryan or Dravidian, and preferred to await the results, if any, to decide its identity.

He noticed two basic facts about the Indus script which had not caught the attention of the earlier scholars. Firstly, he noticed that of the 400 to 500 letters found on the seals, some letters seemed to be basic letters, while most of the other letters seemed to be those same basic letters with some additional signs attached to them. Secondly, he noticed that the script was not, as generally believed, absolutely uniform over the entire period of the Indus Civilization. Those seals, which were later in time, seemed to have less complicated letters, thereby indicating an evolution.

He, therefore, gathered together all the data on the different inscriptions and classified them periodwise. He also separated the basic letters from those with additional signs, and arrived at a small number of basic letters.

Then, he decided to examine, without prejudice, those scripts and alphabets of the world which were closest, in time, to the Indus script, to see whether those scripts or alphabets could give any clue as to the sound-values which could be assigned to these basic letters.

The oldest extant inscription of the Indian Brahmi script dated to around 450 BC or so, while the Indus sites excavated dated down to the mid-2nd millennium BC, leaving a gap of a thousand years.

However, in West Asia, the South Arabic and Old Aramaic alphabets had come into prominence by the beginning of the 1st millennium BC, and the Ahiram Sarcophagus (1300 BC) and Gezer potsherd (1600 BC) provided the earlier stages of these West Asian scripts. And here Dr. Rao struck gold. He found that many of the basic letters of the Indus script bore resemblance to the letters of these two West Asian alphabets.

He decided to assign to each Indus basic letter the same sound-value as the West Asian letter which closely resembled it. After assigning these values to the Indus letters, he proceeded to try to read the inscriptions on the Indus seals. The language that emerged turned out to be an "Aryan" one.

The above is a rather simplistic narration of the procedure adopted by Dr. Rao, which is given in detail in the two relevant books by him.[2]

[2] *Lothal and the Indus Civilization* and *The Decipherment of the Indus Script.*

Among the many words yielded by Dr. Rao's decipherment are the numerals *aeka, tra, chatuś, panta, happta/sapta, daśa dvadaśa* and *śata*, (1,3,4,5,7,10,12 and 100) and the names of Vedic personalities like *Atri, Kaśyapa, Gara, Manu, Śara, Trita, Dakṣa, Druhu, Kaśu*, etc.

While the direct connection between the late Indus script (1600 BC) and the Brahmi script could not be definitely established earlier, more and more inscriptions have been found all over the country in the last few years, dating 1000 BC, 700 BC, and so on, which have bridged the gap between the two. Now it is evident that the Brahmi script evolved directly from the Indus script.

ACCEPTANCE OF THE DECIPHERMENT

Dr. S.R. Rao, who has deciphered the Indus script, is no ordinary scholar. He was formerly head of the Archaeological Survery of India (ASI), and then Scientist Emeritus, Principal Investigator, Marine Archaeological Project of the National Institute of Oceanography, Goa, He is also a member of the prestigious National Committee of the International Union of the History and Philosophy of Science, and represented India at the XV International Congress of the History of Science at Edinburgh (1977). He is also the writer of many books and articles.

As an archaeologist since 1948, Dr. Rao is the discoverer and excavator of more than fifty Indus sites, including Lothal, Rangpur and Bhagatrav in Gujarat and Daimabad in Maharashtra, neolithic sites like Paiyampalli and Hunur in Karnataka, and early historical sites like Amreli in Gujarat, Kanheri in Maharashtra, Chandrapura in Goa, Kaveripatnam in Tamil Nadu, and Aihole and Pattadakal in Karnataka, as well as the submerged ports in Udyawar in Karnataka and Dwarka in Gujarat. The most important of these are, of course, Lothal (which is the third most important Indus site after Harappa and Mohenjo-daro, and which brought to light, among other things, the oldest artificial port in the world) and Dwarka, which gave the very first major archaeological confirmation of the historicity of the Mahābhārata.

The decipherment of the Indus script by Dr. Rao is being increasingly accepted all over the world. Some of the prominent people and institutions who have accepted the decipherment according to Dr. Rao are:

1. Prof. S.H. Ritti (President, Epigraphical Society of India).
2. Prof. P.B. Desai (President, Indian History Congress, Epigraphy Section, and Head, Department of Ancient History, Culture and Archaeology, Karnataka University).

3. Prof. K.D. Bajpai (Chairman, Epigraphical Society of India; President, Archaeological Survey of India; former Professor of Archaeology, Sagar University).
4. Dr. B.C. Chhabra (President, First Epigraphical Congress; retired Joint-Director-General of Archaeology; Government Epigraphist for India).
5. Prof. Ajaya Mitra Shastri (Head, Department of Ancient Indian History, Culture and Archaeology, Nagpur University).
6. Dr. David Diringer (Founder-Director of the Alphabet Museum, Cambridge and Tel Aviv).
7. Prof. W.W. de Grummond (Florida State University, USA).
8. Prof. F.N. Souza.
9. Dr. Katscher.
10. Prof. Mrs. Anleu Kammenhuber (Munich University, West Germany).
11. The American Journal of Oriental Studies (in a review).
12. University of California, Berkeley (which announced the acceptance of the decipherment in September, 1986).

The decipherment is being increasingly accepted by more and more scholars all over the world. However, the acceptance of the decipherment by the late Dr. David Diringer, mentioned above, is particularly noteworthy. Dr. Diringer is considered one of the leading authorities on scripts and alphabets, and his voluminous book[3] on the subject is considered something of a magnum opus.

Dr. Diringer, in his above book, had this to say about the Aryan invasion: "The immigration of Aryan tribes into India is now attributed to the second half of the second millennium BC."[4] About the Brahmi script being descended from the Indus script, he forcefully rejected any such idea: "The Indian alphabet is in no respect an independent invention of the people of India ... the idea ... was derived from Western Asia beyond any reasonable doubt,"[5] and "all historical and cultural evidence is best coordinated by the theory which considers the early Aramaic alphabet as the prototype of the Brahmi script"[6]; and he referred contemptuously to "Indian scholars who patriotically consider the Brahmi as the descendant of an indigenous prehistoric script..."[7]

[3] Alphabet.
[4] Alphabet, p. 333.
[5] Alphabet, p. 337.
[6] Alphabet, p. 336.
[7] Alphabet, p. 328.

Dr. Diringer's acceptance of Dr. Rao's decipherment, which goes against all the views expressed by him in his magnum opus, is therefore all the more important.

SIGNIFICANCE OF THE DECIPHERMENT

Quite apart from the Aryan angle, the decipherment of the Indus script by Dr. Rao is of great significance for Indian culture in another way: it proves that the South Arabic and Old Aramaic alphabets of West Asia, as well as the Indian Brahmi, are all derived from the Indus script. Between themselves, these three alphabets are the ancestors of every single alphabet and script in use in the world today with the sole exception of the Chinese script (and the Japanese Katakana and Hiragana syllabaries which borrow their shapes at least from the simplest Chinese letters).

This means that India's contributions to the world include not only the zero-based decimal system, without which modern scientific progress would have been impossible, but also the Alphabet, without which, also, progress would have been very greatly hampered indeed.

Dr. Rao's decipherment has demolished the Aryan invasion theory. However, while the identification of the language as an Aryan one is beyond any doubt, a subsidiary and subjective interpretation that Dr. Rao puts on his own decipherment is *not:* Dr. Rao interprets the language and culture of the Indus people as "pre-Vedic", apparently unwilling or reluctant to tamper with the sacred cow of the accepted date of the Rigveda (1000 BC).

But, Dr. Rao's interpretation is untenable. Even fully recorded and documented languages cannot be dated merely on their linguistic style; the Indus language, as deciphered by him, has certainly proved to be an Aryan one, but the deciphered language certainly cannot be subjectable to interpretation in respect of its age vis-a-vis the language of the Rigveda. And, as will be demonstrated later in this book, the Indus civilization is very definitely post-Vedic.

The fact, nevertheless, remains that Dr. Rao's decipherment has proved the Indus language to be an Aryan one. B.K. Ghosh,[8] a staunch protagonist of the Aryan invasion theory, before giving all the arguments in support of the theory and countering all the arguments against it, makes it clear that "could it be proved that the language of the prehistoric Mohenjo-daro was Sanskrit or Proto-Sanskrit, then indeed it might have been possible to argue that in spite of all evidence to the

[8] HCIP, Ch.10 "The Aryan Problem".

contrary India was the original home of the Aryans; for there is no evidence of an Aryan race or language previous to the age of the Mohenjo-daro culture."[9]

But Ghosh, even while conceding that an "Aryan homeland" in India would be proved by a decipherment of the Indus script showing the language to have been an Indo-European one, refers to "all evidence to the contrary" — that is, evidence in support of the Aryan invasion theory, and in opposition to an Indian homeland theory. This evidence has already been detailed in a previous chapter[10] of this section.

Let us therefore examine this "evidence".

[9] HCIP, pp. 202-03.
[10] Ch. 6.

SECTION III

THE INVASION THEORY EXAMINED

TEN

GEOGRAPHICAL DISTRIBUTION OF MODERN LANGUAGES

The evidence, based on the present-day distribution of languages is rather argumentative in nature. Let us examine the various arguments.

DISTRIBUTION OF BRANCHES OF THE INDO-EUROPEAN FAMILY

Of the nine present-day branches of Indo-European languages, eight are restricted to Europe and its peripheral areas, and even the ninth branch (Indo-Iranian) is not restricted to India, but is spoken right upto northern Iraq and south-eastern Turkey (viz. the Kurdish language). But any conclusion derived from these bare figures (eight versus less than one) would be very deceptive.

The Indo-Iranian branch is not just "one among nine" branches. It is a branch which is admitted to constitute, all by itself, *one out of two* groups of Indo-European languages, with all the eight other present-day branches together constituting the other group. It is believed that the original speakers of proto-Indo-European, after it had developed Kentum and Satem dialects, separated into two groups: one group consisting of the Indo-Iranians, and the other group consisting of speakers of all the other dialects (which later developed into the other eight branches).

Thus, Childe points out, "many philologists since Flick have only accepted as belonging to the parent speech, words found in Indo-Iranian on the one hand, and a European language on the other".[1]

According to Ghosh,[2] Wilhelm Brandenstein, who sought to locate the original Indo-European homeland by using a method called "applied semasiology", was also compelled to classify as "early Indo-European" those words which are found in *both* Indo-Iranian as well as in one or the other of the other branches; and as "later Indo-European" those words which are found *only* in Indo-Iranian, or in all or some of the other branches but *not* in Indo-Iranian.

Further, it is accepted that after the first split or separation between the Indo-Iranians on the one hand, and the speakers of the other Indo-European dialects (which later became the other eight branches) on the other, there was a second split or separation between the Indo-Aryans

[1] Aryans, p. 79.
[2] HCIP, pp. 210–11.

on the one hand and the Iranians on the other.

These facts are not in the least inconsistent with the idea that India was the original home of the Indo-European languages; that the major body of the speakers of the other Indo-European dialects moved away to the north-west after the first split, any remnants who may have remained behind getting absorbed into the Indo-Iranian speech branch in the course of time; and that later, after a considerable period of time, there was the second split, after which the Iranians moved westwards.

GENERAL DISTRIBUTION OF LANGUAGES

The very idea of considering the present-day distribution of Indo-European languages as making "a strong prima facie case against the theory that India was the original home of the Aryans"[3] is indicative of the bias involved. For in the case of no other language group is the present-day distribution of languages treated as a clinching argument.

About the Dravidian languages, for example, it could likewise be pointed out that a large number of them are crowded together within the comparatively small space of South India, whereas outside South India, instead of a compact body of speakers of that speech family, we find only scattered members of it; and that the geographical distribution of the idioms of the Dravidian speech family does suggest that the original home of the Dravidians is to be sought in South India rather than elsewhere.

But this logic is not applied in the case of Dravidian languages. Not only is it presumed that the Dravidians came to South India from North India, but it is further presumed that they came to North India, as Chatterji puts it, "from their original homeland in the islands of the Aegean and the tracts of mainland along the Aegean Sea—Greece and Asia Minor"[4]; from a place, in short, where not only there is no Dravidian language spoken today, but where there is not the slightest evidence of any Dravidian language ever having been spoken at any point of time even in the remotest past. Without the slightest evidence, and based on a few weak and far-fetched arguments, it is not only maintained that the Dravidians came to India from outside, but even the specific spot from which they came is specified.

The arguments based on the present-day concentration and distribution of Indo-European languages may therefore be safely dismissed as superfluous.

[3] HCIP, p. 202.
[4] HCIP, p. 158.

DISTRIBUTION OF SATEM AND KENTUM LANGUAGES

Of the nine living branches of Indo-European languages, all the four Kentum branches are restricted to Europe. The original proto-Indo-European language is believed to have split into Satem and Kentum dialects, even before the physical split between the speakers of Indo-Iranian, on the one hand, and the speakers of all the other dialects, on the other. The absence of Kentum languages outside Europe was therefore taken to be evidence that the original homeland was situated within Europe.

However, written documents dating from the 7th century AD to the 10th century AD, in the Brahmi script, were unearthed early in this century from Chinese Turkestan (Sinkiang, to the north of Kashmir); and the language contained in these documents was found to be an unknown and extinct Indo-European language, not belonging to any of the present-day branches but constituting *a Kentum branch* by itself. This language was named Tokharian.

Suniti Kumar Chatterji tries to explain away the presence of a Kentum language within the eastern area as "an ethnic and linguistic problem, *a likely explanation* of which is that it is due to the migration of a western Indo-European tribe into the east *in some unknown epoch*".[5]

However, Childe grudgingly admits: "the simplest explanation of the presence of a Centum language in Central Asia would be to regard it as the last survivor of an original Asiatic Aryan stock. To identify a wandering of Aryans across Turkestan from Europe in a relatively late prehistoric period is frankly difficult."[6]

Most significant is Ghosh's admission: "Tocharian, like Hittite, has been characterised as a distinct dialect *even before the Satem-Centum split had taken place*."[7]

While even staunch supporters of the northern-Europe-cum-South-Russia-homeland theory, like Childe, are compelled to admit that it is "frankly difficult" to speculate a Tokharian migration from the direction of Europe, the direction from which the Tokharians received their religion and culture is not a matter of speculation: the Tokharian documents are Buddhistic works in the Brahmi script; and some of the documents are bilingual with Sanskrit comprising the second language.

In addition, we have the evidence of the Bangani language spoken

[5] ODBL, p. 24.
[6] Aryans, pp. 95–96.
[7] HCIP, p. 207.

in the Bangan area in the northwest of Garhwal (Uttar Pradesh), which has been found to have preserved in its vocabulary and grammar archaisms that belong to Vedic Sanskrit, and even beyond that to an earlier stage.

Dr. C.P. Zoller, an eminent German linguist, after years of research, has discovered that much simplified Bangani, which he describes as "being part of the so-called Kentum branch of the Indo-European family of languages", can be divided into three historical layers. "The youngest and most extensive layer," he says, "is where Bangani shares many similarities with the Indo-Aryan languages of Himachal Pradesh and Garhwal. The second one is an older layer of Sanskrit words where one can observe a strikingly high number of words that belong to the oldest stages of Sanskrit, the Sanskrit of the Vedas. The third and the oldest layer in Bangani is formed by words that have no connection with Sanskrit but with the Kentum branch of Indo-European languages."[8]

Therefore, far from ruling out the possibility of an Indian homeland, a study of the Satem-Kentum division will indicate that it took place in and around the Himalayan region.

NON-ARYANISED HOMELAND AND ADVENTUROUS ARYANS

Ghosh considers "the fact that the whole of South India, and some parts of North India too, are to this day non-Aryan in speech" to be "the strongest single argument against the Indian home hypothesis", since it is "reasonably argued that had India been the original home of the Aryans, they would have certainly tried fully to Aryanise the whole of this subcontinent before crossing the frontier barriers in quest of adventure."[9]

Many scholars[10] seem to find it necessary to counter this "reasonable" argument with equally "reasonable" explanations. But is the case "against the Indian home hypothesis" so flimsy that this should be its "strongest single argument"?

The "reasonable" argument starts out with the unreasonable presumption that the "Aryans" set out from their original homeland, with missionary zeal, for the specific purpose of linguistically "Aryanising" the world. Even the Sanskrit phrase "*kṛṇvanto viśvamāryam*" ("let us ennoble the world"; or at its worst interpretation, "let us convert the

[8] *The Times of India*, 14/6/87, "Bangani older than Sanskrit".
[9] HCIP, p. 202.
[10] Karpāsa, pp. 59–61.

world to our Vedic cult", but surely not "let us linguistically Indo-Europeanise the world"!) cannot be twisted around to mean such a thing; and if it is, then to Indians must go the dubious credit of being the world's first linguistic missionaries, and to India the credit of being the Indo-European homeland. After all, Catholic and Protestant missionaries from Germany did not wait to first convert the whole of Germany to Catholicism or Protestantism, before setting out to convert heathens.

Let us apply the same "reasonable" argument to the English language.

English is more or less the lingua franca in the British Isles (as it is in many parts of the world where it is not even the mother tongue of the majority), but we find Irish spoken in the Republic of Eire and also in Northern Ireland, Welsh spoken in Wales, and some Scots Gaelic in Scotland. Two centuries ago, we also had Cornish in Cornwall and Manx on the Isle of Man.

At the same time, English is spoken in major parts of North America, as well as in Australia and New Zealand; and in large tracts of these continents, tracts much larger in area than the whole of the British Isles put together, English is practically the only language spoken.

Can we consider this the "strongest single argument" against England being the home of the English language, since, if it had been, the English people would have certainly tried fully to Anglicise the whole of the British Isles before crossing the frontier barriers in quest of adventure? Or, conversely, that America or Australia must be the home of the English language?

If the same "reasonable" argument is applied to South Russia, then that area is also left with no leg to stand on, for the Indo-European languages of South Russia (Slavonic; and Armenian to the South) are even today situated in a sea of languages belonging to the Uralo-Altaic and Caucasian families.

THE LOCATION OF THE LITHUANIAN LANGUAGE

Lithuanian, according to Ghosh, is "certainly the most archaic" [11] of all Indo-European languages today, and hence "the Indo-European original home could not have been very far removed from Lithuania."[12]

It may be noted that Lithuania itself is not claimed to be the original homeland, since, except for the claims of the Lithuanian language to be an archaic one, Lithuania does not fulfil any other real or alleged

[11] HCIP, p. 207.
[12] HCIP, p. 208.

criterion. It is merely claimed that the original homeland must be close to Lithuania, and since Lithuania is situated to the north-east of Germany and the north-west of Russia, this is used for the purpose of bolstering the claims of South Russia, or of northern Europe.

And yet, no one can claim any particularly archaic character for even the oldest attested languages in and around South Russia (Slavonic, Armenian) or northern Europe (Germanic). Ghosh himself admits, after pointing out that "the oldest attested Indo-European language of Europe, namely Greek, is frankly an import from outside,"[13] that "the other European languages of the same family (other than Greek and Lithuanian) need not be discussed for a solution of the Aryan problem from the linguistic point of view, for they are all *violent variations of the original Indo-European, particularly Germanic and Celtic.*"[14]

Let us examine the validity of the Lithuanian claims to being the most archaic of Indo-European languages. It will become apparent that the only reason why its archaic nature is stressed at all is because it is a *living* language. As W.B. Lockwood puts it, Lithuanian "combines an exceptionally archaic structure with the rich documentation of a living language."[15]

But this archaic character of Lithuanian is not necessarily an indication that the Indo-European homeland is close to Lithuania. It is in fact, an indication of the conservative nature of the Lithuanians. Ghosh himself quotes the following counter-argument: "A language remains archaic even when the persons using it are unprogressive, or if they remain in a locality where no fusion is possible with races speaking other languages, or if they develop a highly refined technique for preserving and using archaic forms. The first two conditions are probably responsible for the archaic character of Lithuanian."[16]

Is Lithuanian the most archaic Indo-European language? Ghosh certainly asserts that "it is Lithuanian, and not Sanskrit...that has kept closest to the basic idiom reconstructed by comparative philology".[17] These Indian scholars, who so gloatingly quote the Lithuanian argument, must keep in mind that the Lithuanian argument was thought up by European scholars only in order to counter a similar argument made

[13] Ibid.
[14] Ibid.
[15] IEP, p. 125.
[16] HCIP, pp. 216–17.
[17] HCIP, p. 202.

in respect of Sanskrit and India. Bhargava relates the whole story as follows: "Some European scholars sharply reacted to the generally accepted belief that the original home of the Aryans lay somewhere in Asia. One of the earliest of these was Latham.... He urged firstly that Lithuanian is closely related to Sanskrit and no less archaic, and so if the original home of the Aryans can be claimed to be somewhere in Asia on the ground of the archaic nature of Sanskrit, it can as well be claimed to have been somewhere in Europe on the ground of the archaic nature of Lithuanian."[18]

Let us compare the archaic nature of Sanskrit with that of Lithuanian, and see which of the two languages is more archaic. The archaisms may be compared under two headings:

1. Archaisms in vocabulary.
2. Archaisms in general linguistic structure.

Archaisms in Vocabulary

In respect of vocabulary, there is no doubt whatsoever that it is Sanskrit, and not Lithuanian, which has "kept closest to the basic idiom reconstructed by comparative philology."

Childe,[19] at the end of his chapter on *Primitive Aryan Culture Reconstructed by Linguistic Palaeontology,* gives a list of 72 basic cognate words in different Indo-European languages. Of the 72 words given, Sanskrit has 70 cognates, Greek 48, Teutonic (Germanic) 46, Latin 40, Lithuanian 39, Celtic 25, Armenian 15 and Tocharian 8. The position of Lithuanian vis-a-vis Sanskrit is self-evident; especially when it is considered that Childe has counted the entire Baltic and Slavonic branches under the heading "Lithuanian", and the actual Lithuanian words are only 20, old Slavonic words are 16, Old Prussian words are 2, and there is one Lettian word.

It can, of course, be argued that there are so many cognate words in Sanskrit, as compared to the other languages, purely and simply because the very criterion adopted for classifying cognate words as "belonging to the parent speech" is that they must be "found in Indo-Iranian on the one hand, and a European language on the other."[20]

However, it must be noted that this criterion has been adopted and accepted, not by scholars who can be accused of being biased in favour of an Indian homeland, but by scholars, like Childe, who are staunch

[18] IVA, p. 43.
[19] Aryans, Ch. 4, appendix, pp. 91–93.
[20] Aryans, p. 79.

supporters of the South Russia homeland theory. The adoption of this criterion is itself tantamount to an open acceptance of the fact that Sanskrit has a greater number, than any other language, of what Brandenstein called "early Indo-European words", and that Sanskrit vocabulary is therefore the closest to that of proto-Indo-European.

The study of Sanskrit vocabulary is indeed a fascinating subject. The vocabulary is so rich that there are many different words for every single object or concept. Thus, for example, water is *udaka/udan*, *vāri*, *jala*, *ambhas/ambu*, *āpa*, *salila*, *pānīya*, *nīra*, etc., to name just some of the commonest words. All these words are of obvious or demonstrable Indo-European etymology (the word *nīra*, which is alleged to be borrowed from Dravidian, has its cognate in Greek[21] *neró*, from *nīrón*).

A study of the Sanskrit lexicon shows that it contains the largest number of proto-Indo-European roots and words, in their primary sense as well as in the form of secondary derivatives. And an overwhelmingly greater number of words, in various Indo-European languages belonging to different branches, have cognates in Sanskrit roots and words than in the roots and words of any other branch—often the etymology of words in different languages can be derived only from a consideration of Sanskrit roots and words. To continue the example of words for water: Buck[22] points out that the Sanskrit word *vāri* supplies the etymology of Avestan *vār* and Old Norse *ūr*, both meaning rain, Avestan *vairi* and Lithuanian *jurēs*, both meaning lake/sea, and Greek *ōuron* and Latin *ūrina*, both meaning urine (i.e. "make water"); the word *āpa* supplies the etymology of Lithuanian *ūpe* and Irish *abann*, both meaning river; the word *jala* supplies the etymology of German *quelle*, meaning spring; and the word *ambhas/ambu* supplies the etymology of Greek *ómbres* and Latin *imber*, both meaning rainstorm.

So far as the actual words for water are concerned, the word *āpa* is cognate to Persian *āb;* the word *vāri* is cognate to Tocharian *war/wär*; and the word *udan/udaka* is congnate to all the other Indo-European words (except the Latin-Romance and some Celtic words), including English *water*, Umbrian (an extinct Italic language) *utur*, Irish *uisce*, Ancient Greek *hýdōr*, Lithuanian *vanduo*, Slavonic *voda*, Albanian *ujē*, and Hittite *watar*. The modern Sinhalese word is *watura*.

Although not mentioned by Buck, the word *salila* (also *sala*) is undoubtedly cognate to words like salt and saliva; and the two words for water in European languages which are not cognate to direct San-

[21] ADOSS, p. 35.
[22] ADOSS, pp. 34–35.

skrit words for water also have their cognates in Sanskrit: Latin *aqua* has its cognate in Sanskrit *ākhāt*, meaning pond or bay; and Irish *dobur* has its cognate in Sanskrit *dabhra*, meaning ocean.

Ghosh himself quotes the following counter-argument by K.M. Munshi: "The Vedic Sanskrit has the largest number of vocables in the Aryan languages. These are preserved in the languages of the Sanskritic family in different parts of India, even when there has been inter-racial contact for centuries. On the other hand, if the pre-Vedic Aryan language was spoken in different parts of Europe and Asia where the Aryans had settled before coming to India, how is it that only a few vocables are left in the present-day speech of these parts, while the largest number of them is found in the distant places of ultimate settlement and racial admixture in India? On the contrary, this disparity can easily be explained if the pre-Vedic was the language of the homeland of Aryans, and the other Aryan languages came into existence as a result of contact between migrating Aryans and non-Aryan elements outside India and Persia."[23]

Therefore, even if one were to presume that Lithuanian is the language which has "kept closest" to the reconstructed parent language in general linguistic structure, it is Sanskrit which has kept closest to proto-Indo-European in vocabulary; and the question, therefore, is whether it is archaic linguistic structure or archaic vocabulary which is a better criterion for postulating the location of the original homeland.

An examination of the facts will show that, as a general rule, the language of a migrating group may retain many of its original structural and formal features, even when these features may have been lost or evolved away in the language still spoken in its original area; but it is much more likely to lose or replace a substantial part of its original vocabulary (though it may retain many telltale archaic words) as compared to the language still spoken back home.

Warren Cowgill points out that this was the case with most ancient Indo-European languages: "In prehistoric times, most branches of Indo-European were carried into territories presumably or certainly occupied by speakers of non-Indo-European languages...it is reasonable to suppose that these languages had some effect on the speech of the newcomers. For the lexicon, this is indeed demonstrable in Hittite and Greek, at least. It is *much less clear*, however, that these non-Indo-European languages affected significantly the sounds and grammar of

[23] HCIP, p. 216.

the Indo-European languages that replaced them."[24] Similarly in the case of the modern languages: "When Indo-European languages have been carried within historical times into areas occupied by speakers of other languages, they have generally taken over a number of loan-words ...however, there has been very little effect on sounds and grammar."[25]

Therefore, it is obvious that it is the archaic vocabulary of Sanskrit, rather than the allegedly archaic general linguistic structure of Lithuanian, which is a better pointer to the location of the original homeland.

But is Lithuanian anyway more archaic than Sanskrit even in general linguistic structure?

Archaisms in General Linguistic Structure

Declension: According to the *Encyclopaedia Britannica*,[26] Lithuanian "has preserved many archaic features from the ancient proto-Indo-European, among these are the use of forms for the dual number in both nouns and verbs, and in Old Lithuanian, the locative plural ending—su".

This archaism of Lithuanian, the "use of forms for the dual number in both nouns and verbs", is indeed a remarkable one. As W.B. Lockwood points out, the dual number had declined even in Greek and Latin: "Greek preserved a second and third person dual, but Latin had lost the number entirely." But, just before this, Lockwood points out that the dual number "was fully developed, as seen in Sanskrit, but had declined in the other classical languages."[27]

That Lithuanian has (or, at least, "*some* Lithuanian dialects"[28] have) retained the dual number to this day, when no modern Indo-Aryan language has done so, and when other European languages, even in ancient times, had done so only partially (if at all), is certainly a tribute to the fact that Lithuanian has preserved an archaic structure: it is the *only* actively spoken language to preserve the dual number. But that does not make it more archaic than Sanskrit.

Lockwood points out that the Vedic language, with its "three genders, three numbers and eight cases", presents "the fullest representation of the Indo-European system";[29] and that "the abundance of its

[24] EB, Vol. 9, p. 438.
[25] EB, Vol. 9, p. 438.
[26] EB, Micropedia, Vol. 6, p. 265.
[27] IEP, p. 110.
[28] EB, Vol. 2, p. 663.
[29] POIEL, p. 215.

records and the archaic nature of the language give Vedic an *unsurpassed importance.*"[30]

Proto-Indo-European, as reconstructed by philologists, had three genders (masculine, feminine and neuter); three numbers (singular, dual and plural); and eight cases (nominative, accusative, genitive, dative, vocative, ablative, locative and instrumental). Vedic retained *all* the three genders, three numbers and eight cases. Ancient Greek retained the three genders and three numbers, but only five cases (having lost the ablative, locative and instrumental cases). Lithuanian retained the three numbers, but only two genders and seven cases (having lost the neuter gender and the ablative case). Obviously, Sanskrit here is more archaic than Lithuanian.

Phonology: Proto-Indo-European had three accents: acute *(udātta)*, grave (*anudātta*) and circumflex *(svarita)*. All the three archaic Indo-European languages: Vedic Sanskrit, Greek and Lithuanian, preserved these three accents.

About Lithuanian, Lockwood points out that it is "particularly conservative in these matters. It not only preserves the free accent of the parent tongue, but by distinguishing acute and circumflex intonation, it reflects, albeit in somewhat changed form, an ancient Indo-European principle."[31]

Here again, the retention of the distinction between acute and circumflex accents to this day is certainly creditable testimony to its archaic character, since not only has no other modern European language preserved the three accents, but in India the three accents of Vedic Sanskrit are not found even in later Classical Sanskrit.

However, the following point must be noted: Proto-Indo-European, as reconstructed by philologists, had a free pitch-accent, and Lockwood[32] points out that Vedic also had a free pitch-accent.

Ancient Greek had a pitch-accent, but it was not a free accent. Lockwood points out that "the accent was not completely free, as it could not occur further back than the third syllable from the end."[33]

Lithuanian had a free accent, but it was not a pitch-accent. Lockwood points out that "the accent is predominantly one of stress."[34]

Hence, Vedic is obviously more archaic than Lithuanian in this

[30] POIEL, p. 195.
[31] IEP, p. 125.
[32] IEP, p. 85.
[33] Ibid.
[34] IEP, p. 125.

respect also. Moreover, it must be noted that while the three-accent system was lost even in later Classical Sanskrit, it is still found in the Konkani language (spoken at present on the West Coast but originating in Kashmir) — how far the three accents of Konkani correspond to the three accents of Vedic and proto-Indo-European can be a matter for study, but Konkani also undoubtedly "reflects, albeit in somewhat changed form, an ancient Indo-European principle."

Lockwood[35] also points out that proto-Indo-European had four series of occlusive consonants: unvoiced unaspirated (p, t, k), voiced unaspirated (b, d, g), unvoiced aspirated (ph, th, kh) and voiced aspirated (bh, dh, gh).

According to Lockwood, Sanskrit is the only language which preserved all the four series of occlusive consonants in the same original form as in proto-Indo-European. Ancient Greek preserved the first two series, and Germanic preserved none of them in the original form. Again, it is obvious that Sanskrit is the most archaic Indo-European language.

Conjugation: The verbal system of any language occupies a central and primary position in the study of the language. The verbal system of proto-Indo-European is supposed to have been extremely complicated and irregular.

Speaking about the verbal systems of the three classical languages, Lockwood points out that "the high degree of regularity obtaining in the Latin verbal system stands in contrast to the chaotic diversity of the Indo-European ancestor. Greek and Sanskrit represent an intermediary stage: this is why there are so few completely regular verbs in these languages. It is the irregular and defective verb which *best reflects the prehistoric background.*"[36]

In respect of Lithuanian, however, Lockwood points out that "the Indo-European verbal system has been *considerably reshaped.*"[37]

In the matter of comparison of adjectives also, "Lithuanian is remarkable in having entirely regularised the forms of comparison."[38]

Again, it is clearly Sanskrit, and not Lithuanian, which is closest to proto-Indo-European.

Morphology: Morphology is that branch of philology which deals with inflexion and word-formation. There are generally three morpho-

[35] IEP, pp. 86-87ff.
[36] IEP, p. 109.
[37] IEP, p. 131.
[38] IEP, p. 130.

logical types: inflexion, agglutination and isolation. Languages are, in fact, classified according to their morphological methods; Indo-European and Semitic languages are classified as inflexional; Dravidian and Uralo-Altaic languages are classified as agglutinative; Sino-Tibetan languages are classified as isolating. This, of course, is a broad classification, and individual languages classify differently. Many modern Indo-European languages have become extremely analytical, especially English and Persian, and can even be classified as agglutinative-isolating. However, proto-Indo-European, as well as all the older, and many of the modern, languages are inflexional.

S.K. Chatterji admits that "the morphology of Vedic is as luxuriant as it can be, and it *retains most faithfully* the inflections of primitive Indo-European."[39]

Sir M. Monier-Williams is even more specific. In the introduction to his Sanskrit dictionary, he explains the difference between the form of inflexion found in Semitic languages and the form of inflexion found in Indo-European languages, by comparing examples from Arabic and Sanskrit, and declares: "Sanskrit, *the faithful guardian of old Indo-European forms*, exhibits these remarkable properties *better than any other member of the Aryan line of speech.*"[40]

From all this, it is clear that it is Sanskrit, and not Lithuanian, which is closest to the reconstructed proto-Indo-European in respect of both vocabulary as well as general linguistic form and structure. If archaism is a pointer to the original homeland, then India is undoubtedly the homeland indicated.

THE LOCATION OF THE BRAHUI LANGUAGE

The presence of the isolated Brahui language in Baluchistan is taken as evidence "that the whole or at least a considerable part of India was originally non-Aryan in speech."[41]

Basically, the presence of the Brahuis in the north-west is taken as evidence of two things:

1. That the Dravidians preceded the Aryans as invaders from the north-west.
2. That the Aryans followed them from the north-west and drove them southwards, the Brahuis being the last remnants.

However, G.A. Grierson, a supporter of the Aryan invasion theory,

[39] ODBL, p. 38.
[40] SED, Introduction, p. xiii.
[41] HCIP, p. 202.

rejects the first of the two above contentions: "The fact that one tribe, not of the 'Dravidian' physical type, but speaking a language certainly belonging to the Dravidian linguistic family, the Brahuis, is found in the extreme north-west of India has been adduced by Bishop Caldwell and others as indicating that the speakers of proto-Dravidian, like the Aryans, must have entered India from the north-west, but the facts are equally consistent with an assumption that they form the survivors of the vanguard of a national movement from the east or from the south of India."[42] As he reiterates, "it is uncertain whether it is the advance guard or the rearguard of a Dravidian migration."[43]

And all the facts go to show that Grierson is right in speculating that the Brahuis are the survivors of the advance guard of a Dravidian migration from the south: the fact that all the other Dravidian languages are concentrated in the south; the fact that no Dravidian language is spoken, or is known ever to have been spoken, outside India; the fact that the "Dravidians" in the south not only have no traditions of migrating southwards from the north, but have active traditions of an ancient civilization and empire in South India extending much farther south into an area now believed to be sunk under the seas; and the fact that certain Dravidian speaking tribes in north India (for example the Kurukh/Oraon tribes of Bihar, according to K.D. Sethna[44]) have traditions of migrating northwards from the south.

Incidentally, in pointing out that the Brahuis could well be the survivors of the advance guard of a Dravidian migration from the south, and in pointing out elsewhere that there is "no information to show that the Dravidians are not the original inhabitants of the south"[45], Grierson unwittingly discounts the idea of Aryans occupying an originally Dravidian area in north India.

And there is one very fundamental fact which Aryan invasion theorists find it convenient to ignore: the Brahuis are linguistically Dravidians, but in racial features they are identical with their neighbours in north-west India. As Grierson puts it: "the Brahuis do not belong to the Dravidian race, but are anthropologically Eranians."[46]

How is this to be explained? Protagonists of the invasion theory usually try to get away with asserting the "evidence" of the Brahui

[42] LSI, Vol. 1, p. 81.
[43] LSI, Vol. 1, p. 82.
[44] Karpāsa, p. 116.
[45] LSI, Vol.4, Introduction, p. 5.
[46] Ibid.

language without explaining the racial counter-evidence; and when unable to get away with it, they offer any one of two alternate theories according to which the Brahuis were originally supposed to have been either invading Aryans or local Dravidians.

An examination of these two theories, however, will show them to be untenable; the real explanation is that the Brahuis were originally Dravidian immigrants from the south.

The Brahuis as Invading Aryans: According to this theory, the Brahuis, being identical with their Aryan-speaking neighbours, were originally Aryans. They were a section of the invading Aryans who adopted the language of the original natives.

This explanation is untenable. There are, of course, innumerable cases of invaders adopting the language and culture of the invaded people — the Kassites and Mitanni in West Asia, and the Greek, Persian, Scythian, Hun and Mongol invaders in India, for example. But in every such case, the invaders were a small group of people who merged into the teeming masses of native people, and adopted the highly developed native language (and culture) whilst living amidst a sea of speakers of that native language.

In this case, however, we are asked to believe that a group among the invaders (Aryans) abandoned their own language and adopted a primitive variety of the local (Dravidian) language, even whilst living amidst a sea of speakers of their own original (Aryan) language, and in circumstances which have left no trace of any native (Dravidian) race anywhere in the neighbourhood! No such case is known anywhere in the world, and the theory is obviously far-fetched.

The Brahuis as Local Dravidians: According to this theory, the Brahuis, being linguistically Dravidians, were originally native Dravidians. They were a section of the natives who remained behind (after the rest of their people were slaughtered or driven southwards) and preserved their linguistic identity, but due to racial intermixing with the Aryan invaders over the millenniums, became racially identical with them.

This theory is more popular with the invasion theorists, but is just as untenable as the first one. There are, of course, innumerable cases of the invaded people being swamped by the language and culture of the invaders — the Australian aborigines, New Zealand islanders, American Indians, etc. vis-a-vis the white European colonialists. But nowhere is there any evidence of a native race which has so completely merged into the racial identity of the invaders as to be racially indistinguishable from them, and has yet retained its linguistic identity. In every case, the natives have either remained relatively distinct groups by language, race and culture; or else have adopted the language or culture, or both, of the invaders, while remaining racially distinct; or have got merged into the invaders in all respects, forming a hybrid race, or a mosaic of hybrid races.

In this case, however, we are asked to believe that a group among the natives (Dravidians) got so intermixed with the invaders (Aryans) as to lose every single trace of their original racial features and to become racially identical with the invaders, but yet retained their distinct native (Dravidian) language and linguistic identity, while living amidst a sea of speakers of the invaders' (Aryan) language. While not impossible, it is extremely improbable, and again, no such case is known anywhere in the world.

The Brahuis as Dravidian Immigrants: The most likely and logical explanation, therefore, is that the Brahuis are the survivors of a group of Dravidian immigrants from the south who retained their linguistic identity although their racial identity got completely submerged into that of the native Aryan-speaking population.

Now, it may seem that this explanation relies on the same premise as the second theory outlined above (which treats the Brahuis as local Dravidians)—viz. that a small Dravidian-speaking group got racially submerged into an Aryan-speaking population while retaining its linguistic identity.

But, there are two major and crucial differences:

1. The local-Dravidians theory asks us to believe firstly that there was originally a Dravidian (i.e. South Indian like) race in Baluchistan—which is not attested by any known facts—and further asks us to believe that this entire race disappearred without a trace, thereby further straining the credibility.

The Dravidian-immigrants theory, on the other hand, places the particular "Aryan" (i.e. Baluchi) race and language and the Dravidian (i.e. South Indian like) race and language in the very same areas where their present, and earliest known, presence attests them to have been spoken; and does not ask us to believe that an entire (and unproved) race disappeared without a trace.

2. The local-Dravidians theory presumes a situation which is not precedented by any similar case anywhere else in the world.

The Dravidian-immigrants theory, on the other hand, is precedented by many similar cases all over the world, where a group of immigrants got so racially intermixed with the local population that they became practically indistinguishable from the local people, but managed to preserve their linguistic and cultural identity. The most prominent example is that of Jews, who became so greatly integrated into the local populations of different parts of Asia and Europe, and even Africa, in the course of two millenniums, that they became, in many cases, almost indistinguishable from the local peoples, but managed to retain their cultural (religious) and linguistic (at least in religious matters) identity.

Therefore, the Brahuis are obviously the descendants of a Dravidian-speaking community which migrated to the north-west and settled down there among the local Aryan-speaking population, in ancient times. The fact that the north-west region was a bustling commercial centre of international trade during the heyday of the Indus Valley Civilization in the third and second millenniums BC, provides the context in which such a migration must have taken place.

Therefore, the presence of an Iranian-like race of Dravidian-language speakers in Baluchistan is best explained by a theory which places the "Aryan"-language speakers and Dravidian-language speakers, in ancient times, in very much the same areas presently occupied by them.

ELEVEN

INDO-EUROPEANS IN WEST ASIA

The earliest recorded evidence of the existence of Indo-Europeans anywhere in the world is in West Asia, and not in India or Europe.

But ironically, the very factor which certifies the presence of Indo-Europeans in West Asia at an earlier date than in any other area, also certifies the fact of these Indo-Europeans being outsiders in West Asia. As Childe puts it, "these first historic Aryans appear as late intruders in a region illumined by the light of written documents from the end of the 4th millennium BC."[1]

But although West Asia is therefore very definitely not the original homeland of the Indo-Europeans, the fact that Indo-European presence is first recorded there certainly makes it inevitable that some clue or the other as to the location of the original homeland should be expected to be found among these Indo-Europeans of West Asia.

The clue that protagonists of the invasion theory derive is that since "Aryan peoples first emerge from the gloom of prehistory on the northern borders of the fertile Crescent"[2] (that is, ancient West Asia), and moreover "not in Western, but in Central and Eastern Asia Minor",[3] the direction indicated is the Caucasus Mountains lying between South Russia and West Asia. And they "could not have come from very far, for the earliest theatre of Indo-European historical activity could not have been too distant from the Indo-European original home."[4] Hence, the original home indicated is South Russia.

But is that indeed the logical conclusion to be derived from the evidence of the Indo-Europeans in West Asia? Let us examine the evidence of each of the three distinct groups of West Asian Indo-Europeans, starting with the Kassites, who furnish the weakest evidence of the three.

THE KASSITES

The Kassites invaded and conquered Babylon in 1760 BC, and ruled till almost 1170 BC; but they have left no records whatsoever of their language, since they immediately abandoned their own language

[1] Aryans, p. 16.
[2] Ibid.
[3] HCIP, p. 207.
[4] HCIP, p. 206.

and adopted the language and culture of the Babylonians.

At the same time the Kassites are recorded as having been worshippers of *Šuriaš* and *Maruttaš* (identified with *Sūrya* and *Maruta*) and having names like *Indabugaš* (identified with *Indra + bhaga*), and are believed to have referred to their Gods as *bugaš (bhaga);* and they are recorded as having introduced that "peculiarly Aryan quadruped", the horse, for driving chariots, into West Asia.

But contrast this with what Childe has to comment upon the Kassites. "As a whole, they were not Aryans. Though they adopted the Babylonian language and culture, the local scribes have recorded the Kassite names for god, star, heaven, wind, man, foot, etc.; not one of these is in the least Indo-European. Moreover, the majority of the personal names of the period....suggest rather a relationship, between the Kassites and the Asianic folk to the north-west.[4a] Childe, therefore, concludes that the Kassites may have been non-Aryan people led by "Aryan princes", which accounts for the few Aryan names recorded.

Whether the Kassites, before adopting the language and culture of Babylon, were full-fledged Indo-European speakers, or only their ruling clan consisted of "Aryan princes" as alleged by Childe, the material is inadequate to facilitate any conclusion; but the one fact that clearly stands out is that the words identified as Indo-European are all pure Rigvedic names of Gods: *Sūrya, Maruta, Indra* and *Bhaga;* and the word *Bhaga,* in its form *Bhagavān*[5], is even today a common Indian word for God. Any clue that can be derived from these words can lead only, and *only*, towards India.

THE HITTITES

The Hittites are mentioned in the Old Testament of the Bible, and were therefore known to have been an ancient people of West Asia, but nothing was known of their linguistic identity until the numerous Hittite texts were discovered in Boghaz-köi, in Turkey, at the turn of the century. These texts were deciphered in 1917, and it was only then that the Indo-European identity of the language came to be known.

However, the following observations of Childe must be noted. "(The Hittite language) cannot be accepted without qualification as Aryan. The deviations in the inflection are puzzlingly numerous....the very Indo-European looking endings of the verbal stem are not quite strictly 'personal', but seem sometimes to be used indifferently to de-

[4a] Aryans, p. 16.
[5] Rigveda, 5.46.6.

note the first or third person, the singular or plural...several of the supposedly Indo-European verbal terminations have parallels in non-Indo-European languages, Vannic and even Sumerian. Again, *the number of Indo-European words and stems identified in the vocabulary is but small.* Finally, the syntax remains essentially un-Aryan, for the structure is 'incorporation' as in the Asianic tongues."[6]

Childe further points out: "Now if these documents dated from the 14th century AD, few would hesitate to declare that they were written in an Indo-European language and explain the discrepancies as due to the familiar phenomenon of decay, assimilation of forms, and foreign borrowing. But the texts from Boghaz-keui are many centuries older than the earliest written memorials of Sanskrit or Greek. Yet their language diverges from the hypothetical original Aryan tongue far more than Greek or Sanskrit differs from the parent speech or one another. It is a fact impossible to believe that a truly Indo-European language would look so odd in the 14th century before our era."[7]

Moreover, "the names of the Hittite kings—Hattusil, Dudhalia, Mursil, Mutallu—do not look in the least Aryan. Again no Hittite deities have Aryan names.... Again, the dynastic lists are said to take the dynasty, with the same non-Aryan names, back to 1900 BC, if not earlier."[7a]

From all this, Childe postutates that the Hittite language was most probably an artificial language, created for literary and administrative purpose by a basically non-Indo-European people, in which "Aryan elements, words and terminations might be borrowed to express concepts and relations unknown to the more primitive Asianic dialects which constitute the substratum of the language. In the same way, a whole mass of Babylonian terms have been incorporated."[8]

All this was written by Childe in 1926, not long after the decipherment of the Hittite texts. Since then, the Hittite language (in all its forms) has been studied in great detail, and philologists generally agree that it is an Indo-European language. In fact, many new points have been sought to be adduced from the Hittite language in reconstructing some aspects of the proto-Indo-European language and culture, and while many of these conclusions are disputed and dubious, the Indo-European identity of Hittite is not now generally disputed.

[6] Aryans, pp. 22-23.
[7] Ibid.
[7a] Ibid.
[8] Aryans, p. 23.

However, the points made by Childe are not totally invalid. The Hittite language is indeed so different from other Indo-European languages that a school of American philologists went so far as to postulate that Hittite was not a branch of Indo-European, but a distinct subfamily of its own; that is, that there was a hypothetical language, proto-Indo-Hittite, which developed into two hypothetical lanuguages, proto-Hittite (the ancestor of Hittite) and proto-Indo-European (the ancestor of all the other Indo-European languages). This theory, however, has now been rejected, and it is now accepted that Hittite constitutes just one more extinct branch of Indo-European languages.

But even today, philologists have to admit that Hittite has a large percentage of non-Indo-European words in its vocabulary, a particularly astonishing and inexplicable fact considering that the Hittite documents are the oldest extant Indo-European documents. Philologist H.J. Houwinkten Cate, in the *Encyclopaedia Britannica*, admits: "It has often been remarked—and not without reason—that although the grammar of the Anatolian languages would be recognizably Indo-European, the vocabulary would be less so. This is usually attributed to the deeply penetrating influences exercised by strange surroundings not only while the Anatolians were 'en route', but also after their arrival in Anatolia."[9]

The facts are very clear: the Hittites, while en route to Anatolia, where they made their first appearance in Cappadocia in 1960 BC, had travelled long distances through "strange surroundings" which exercised "deeply penetrating influences" on their language.

How do these facts fit in with B.K. Ghosh's claim that the Hittites "could not have come from very far, for the earliest theatre of Indo-European historical activity could not have been too distant from the Indo-European original home"?[10]

In fact, far from showing that the Hittites could not have come from distant Europe or India, but must have come from nearby South Russia, the facts actually show that the Hittites *must* have come from a distant region after long journeys through "strange surroundings", and this conclusively proves that the original homeland *could not possibly have been in so nearby a place as South Russia* across the Caucasus mountains, but must have been in either Europe or India. Their long travels through different regions, before they arrived at the northern side of the Caucasus mountains, from where they swooped into Cappadocia, are not marked by records of their presence in these different

[9] EB, Vol. 1, p. 834.
[10] HCIP, p. 206.

regions, purely and simply because none of these regions was "illumined by the light of written documents", as was West Asia "from the end of the 4th millennium BC."[11]

But was it from Europe, or from India, that the Hittites set out on their long travels? The very name of the Hittite people—*Khatti,* as they are called in the oldest documents—furnishes a clue. Even a rabid Leftist like D.D. Kosambi cannot refrain from pointing out that "the word *Khatti* which means Hittite may possibly be connected with Sanskrit *Kshatriya* and Pali *Khattiyo*".[12]

The *Larousse Encyclopaedia of Mythology* points out that nothing is known about the original Indo-European Gods of the Hittites, with the sole exception of one God, *Inar,* whom the encyclopaedia actually describes as "a God who had *come from India* with the Indo-European Hittites".[13] *Inar* is very obviously the Rigvedic God Indra.

The Hittites, therefore, were obviously emigrants from India, who appeared in Cappadocia from across the Caucasus mountains after centuries of wanderings in North Asia.

THE MITANNI

The Mitanni are the only people, of the three, whose language is clearly affiliated to a known and living branch of Indo-European languages—the Indo-Iranian branch. The Mitanni also, like the Kassites, had abandoned their language and adopted the language and culture of the local Semitic people; but they left distinct evidence in the form of their numerals and their divine and personal names.

Since the language of the Mitanni was so obviously Indo-Iranian, it became necessary to try and incorporate the presence of the Mitanni in West Asia in the 15th century BC into the chronological and geographical timetable of the hypothetical Aryan invasion of India. Hence it was originally postulated that "the Indo-Iranians, already as a specifically characterised Indo-European tribe, entered Asia from Europe over the Caucasus, and after occupying Iran pushed on further to the Punjab".[14]

However, this contention was a bit too thick to swallow, even for staunch protagonists of the Aryan invasion theory. This is not the place to discuss the date of the Rigveda and the location of the Indo-Iranian

[11] Aryan, p. 16.

[12] *The Culture and Civilization of Ancient India* (Routledge and Kegal Paul, London, 1965), p. 77, quoted in Karpāsa, p. 71.

[13] LEM, p. 85.

[14] HCIP, p. 205.

homeland, both of which will be discussed in a later chapter.[15] Here it is sufficient to note that even a staunch protagonist of the invasion theory, like B.K. Ghosh, admits that the Rigveda cannot be dated later than 1000 BC. He also admits that it is "*quite impossible* to assign for the beginnings of the Vedic Age—and of the *specific Indo-Aryan culture* beginning therewith—*any date later than 1500 BC*"[16], and that (as per his theory and dates) "the Indo-Aryans had become *completely Indianised* when the Rigvedic culture started on its course as a *distinct product of the Indian soil* about 1500 BC."[17]

So even Ghosh finds the contention, that the Mitanni were proto-Indo-Iranians en route to Iran and the Punjab, too thick to swallow. As he points out: "If the forefathers of the Vedic Aryans were still in Cappadocia in the 14th century BC on their march towards India, there would be no time left for them to forget all their previous history before giving the final form to the Rigvedic hymns not later than 1000 BC."[18]

Therefore, an attempt was made to explain the Mitanni presence in West Asia in a way which would not upset the chronological timetable of the hypothetical invasion of India, by postulating that the proto-Indo-Iranians in their common home in Central Asia spread out in two directions: an undifferentiated proto-Indo-Iranian group (the Mitanni) first spreading westwards into West Asia and later the distinctive Indo-Iranians branching out eastwards and southwards into India and Iran. This, according to Ghosh, explains "the apparently simultaneous beginning of Vedic culture in India and the appearance of Aryan princes (Mitanni) in Mesopotamia, Syria and Palestine about the middle of the second millennium BC."[19]

But both these hypotheses, the one accepted by Ghosh as well as the one rejected by him, are based on one basic premise that the language of the Mitanni was "an archaic Indo-Iranian dialect which was not yet fully characterised either as Indo-Aryan or as Iranian".[20]

Is this basic premise valid? A close look at the Mitanni numerals and the divine and personal names shows that the language of the Mitanni was clearly and definitely Indo-Aryan as opposed to Iranian. Childe, referring to the Mitanni evidence, points out: "These numerals and divine and personal names are the oldest specimens of any Aryan

[15] Ch. 14.
[16] HCIP, p. 205.
[17] HCIP, p. 206.
[18] HCIP, p. 204.
[19] HCIP, p. 206.
[20] Ibid.

speech which we possess. The forms deserve special attention. They are already quite distinctly Satem forms; in fact *they are very nearly pure Indic.* Certainly they are much more nearly akin to Sanskrit than to any of the Iranian dialects that later constituted the western wing of the Indo-Iranian family. Thus among the deities *Nāsatya* is the Sanskrit form as opposed to the Zend *Ṇaoṇhaitya,* and all the four gods are prominent in the oldest Veda, while in the Iranian Avesta they have been degraded to secondary rank (*Mithra*), converted into demons (*Indra*) or renamed (*Varuṇa = Ahura Mazda*). The numerals are distinctly Indic, not Iranian; *aika* is identical with the Sanskrit *eka,* while 'one' in Zend is *aeva.* So the 's' is preserved in *Satta,* where it became 'h' in Iranian (*hapta*), and the exact form is found, not indeed in Sanskrit, but in the Prakrits which were supposed to be *post-Vedic.* Even the personal names look Indic rather than Iranian. Thus *Biridaświa** has been plausibly compared with the Sanskrit *Bṛhadaśva* (owning a great horse). If this be right, the second element *aświa,* horse, is in contrast to the Iranian form *aspa* seen in Old Persian and Zend."[21]

Thus, all the numerals and all the divine names and almost all the personal names of the Mitanni are distinctly Indo-Aryan and equally distinctly non-Iranian. The word *vartana* (round) found attached to the Mitanni numerals in Kikkuli's Hittite manual of chariot-racing is also obviously the Sanskrit word *āvartana.* The Mitanni people, or at any rate, the ruling warrior clans among them, were known as *Maryanni,* which, as Childe points out "has suggested comparison with the Sanskrit *māryā,* youngmen, heroes"[22] (*Maryā* is found in the Rigveda[23]), a meaning curiously akin to that of the Hittite name *Khatti,* both suggesting the emigration of warrior groups from India.

The only Iranian element in the Mitanni make-up is the prefix *Arta-* in a few names like *Artamanya* and *Artatama,* as in Persian names like *Artaxerxes,* which is not known in Indo-Aryan. However, this does not indicate an Iranian, as opposed to Indo-Aryan element. The prefix *Arta-* is in fact the Sanskrit *Ṛta,* which appears as *Arta-* in Mitanni since, as Keith points out, "in Mitanni script it was impossible to reproduce *Ṛta* correctly".[24]

Certainly, the only explanation of the Mitanni presence in West Asia in the 15th century BC can be that they migrated from the Punjab.

[21] Aryans, p.19. *The name Dušratta is also obviously the name Daśaratha.

[22] Ibid.

[23] Rigveda, 3.54.13 and 5.59.6

[24] *The Early History of the Indo-Iranians,* R.G. Bhandarkar Commemoration Volume, (Poona, 1917), p. 90.

Even Ghosh, with his criterion of the Aryan invasion theory and the latest possible datings, admits that "the Indo-Aryans had become completely Indianised...about 1500 BC".[25] So if the Mitanni are to be presumed to have separated from the proto-Indo-Iranian group in Central Asia, they should be presumed to have left Central Asia at least a few centuries prior to 1500 BC.

And simple logic will show that this cannot be so; the Mitanni cannot have left Central Asia centuries before 1500 BC, wandered around in obscurity for hundreds of years, and then made their appearance in West Asia just before 1400 BC; and have yet maintained a language and religion which was not only purely Indo-Iranian, but purely Indo-Aryan and Vedic.

The evidence is very clear: The Rigvedic people were very obviously a settled and flourishing people in the Punjab region. Even Ghosh admits them to have been "completely Indianised" in 1500 BC. In fact, the Purāṇas and Epics actually talk about groups of people migrating out of India from the northwest and establishing kingdoms outside. Bhargava refers to "the testimony of a number of Purāṇas according to which Druhyu princes, after ruling in Gandhāra for some generations, spread out into the Mleccha countries to the north beyond India and founded countries there".[26] The Mahābhārata also refers to groups of warriors setting out for the west—the Mahābhārata, it may be noted, is now dated in the 15th century BC.

On the other hand, the Mitanni suddenly appear in the 15th century BC, clearly and obviously outsiders in West Asia; and their culture is clearly that of the Vedas, which, in the words of Ghosh, is "a distinct product of the Indian soil".[27] And they are certainly not transporters and transplanters of this culture, but people who, having moved *away* from this culture-area, are shedding their culture and getting assimilated into the local culture of West Asia.

To sum up, therefore, the evidence of all the three groups of West Asian Indo-Europeans—whether the Šuriaš, Maruttaš and Bugaš worshipping Kassites, the Khatti (Hittites), or the purely Vedic Mitanni—points inexorably away from South Russia and towards India. And the clinching evidence is that the *only* common factor in these three groups is the Vedic God Indra — Hittite Inar, Kassite Inda-bugaš and Mitanni Indara.

[25] HCIP, p. 206.
[26] IVA, p. 56.
[27] HCIP, p. 206.

Twelve

SOUTH RUSSIA AND THE KURGAN CULTURE

South Russia has been identified as the original Indo-European homeland; and this is claimed to be final on the basis of the "Kurgan" material culture unearthed by archaeologists in a major area stretching from Central Asia to Eastern and Central Europe. According to the scholars, the archaeological reconstruction of the Kurgan culture coincides perfectly with the linguistic-paleontological reconstruction of the proto-Indo-European culture.

The process, by which the Kurgan culture has been identified as the proto-Indo-European culture, has been given, in some detail, earlier.[1] A seemingly impregnable case has been built up on the basis of this Kurgan culture. However, an objective examination of the facts explodes this claim, and shows the extent to which *any* facts can be made to appear to "prove" *any* hypothesis by an entrenched and predetermined scholarship.

The main issue is, of course, the validity of the equation sought to be established between the archaeological reconstruction of the Kurgan culture and the linguistic-paleontological reconstruction of the proto-Indo-European culture.

But, before that, let us examine the validity of the basic presumptions and the general criteria and logic used in determining the location, in time and space, of the proto-culture.

VALIDITY OF BASIC PRESUMPTIONS

The basic presumptions used in determining the location in time and space of the proto-culture, and for zeroing in on the Kurgan culture, are:

1. That the date of the first split of proto-Indo-European into distinct dialects, and their period of expansion and fragmentation, can be determined by a method of "dead reckoning".
2. That any material culture in Eurasia (the entire region to the north of the Asiatic mountain-chain, whose fringes touch northern Iran and Eastern Europe), which occupies a central location in the region and which can be seen spreading all over the region somewhere around this determined time, must represent the culture of the proto-Indo-Europeans.

[1] Ch. 6.

Validity of the Dead-Reckoning Method

This method of dead-reckoning is an extremely arbitrary, subjective, and even whimsical, method of trying to determine the degree of change taking place in a language in a given period, or the period taken for a given degree of change to take place in a language.

The rate of change in a language cannot be so conveniently, if at all, quantified and compared, since there are umpteen factors operating on any language; and neither is it possible for all such factors to be listed and their effects quantified, nor is any one factor likely to have the same degree of effect on two different languages, or even on any one language at two different points of time.

Therefore, trying to estimate the point of time of split, expansion and fragmentation of ancient languages, based on some particular known model, as is sought to be done here, is not a very valid exercise,[2] except as a strictly academic one.

And, in fact, this is admitted even by those who use this method. But even then, by using this method, it is decided that the Indo-European languages started splitting and separating around 3000 BC; and on this basis, the Kurgan culture is identified as a culture which could fit into this time-frame—"give or take a few centuries"[3], and "allowing a few centuries" for this, that and the other.

Validity of Material Culture as Evidence

The attempt to try and identify the original Indo-European homeland, and the dispersal of the Indo-European languages, on the basis of material culture, is not a valid one on many counts.

1. Eurasia, to the north of the Asiatic mountain chain, is one huge expanse of land. That any material innovation which took place in any one part should have spread over large parts of Eurasia is but natural. Any material culture spreading all over Eurasia would, perhaps, naturally touch the fringes of Northern Iran and Eastern Europe. Therefore, treating such a material culture on this count as automatically representing the proto-Indo-European culture is not warranted. It amounts to starting out with the precondition that the original home *must* be somewhere in Eurasia.

Among other things, such a culture may well represent the culture of the proto-speakers of the Uralo-Altaic languages, which *are*, in fact, spread out over the expanse of Eurasia.

[2] See also Chs. 14 and 17.
[3] Warren Cowgill, EB, Vol. 9, p. 436.

2. In any case, material culture cannot indicate linguistic identity.

The identity of the Hittite language as an Indo-European language, for example, came as a distinct shock to scholars all over the world, who had heard of the Hittites from the Old Testament of the Bible, but never suspected them to be Indo-Europeans. And indeed, even the most detailed archaeological discoveries on the material culture of the Hittites, if they had failed to yield any records indicating their language, would have left the scholars as much in the dark as before about the Indo-European identity of the Hittites.

But the people of the Kurgan material culture are sought to be proclaimed not only as Indo-European, but as *the* original Indo-Europeans, *in the total absence of even the slightest bit of evidence about the language spoken by them.*

In the absence of actual evidence about the language spoken by them, their identification as proto-Indo-Europeans would have had some justification if the excavated culture had proved to be so startlingly and unmistakably identical with the linguistically reconstructed proto-Indo-European culture as to *itself raise* such a speculation. But here, it was *first* decided that the Kurgan culture must be proto-Indo-European, and *then* attempts were made to compare and identify it with the linguistically reconstructed proto-Indo-European culture.

Even then, if the two cultures could have been shown to tally perfectly, the identification would have had some justification. But (as will be seen presently), the "identification" is a forced one, and made only by taking some general common points, which could pertain to almost any major civilization, and by ignoring basic differences; and it is totally unconvincing, except to those who are grimly determined to be convinced, or those who do not notice contradictions and are overwhelmed by the mass onslaught of archaeological details supplied.

3. One material culture does not indicate one linguistic identity; and the spread of a particular material culture cannot be taken as indicating the spread of a particular language family.

Material-culture areas are very often spread over areas with linguistic and racial diversity; and related languages can often fall in different material-culture areas; as was the case with the American ("Red") Indians at the time of the European invasion and colonisation of America.

This fact is admitted by S.K. Chatterji also, in a different context, when he points out: "In Chota-Nagpur, in spite of diversity of language, the Dravidian-speaking Oraons and the Austric (Kol)-speaking Mundas are within the field of a common culture and in Central Europe, the Indo-European speaking Germans and Slavs, in spite of their pronounced linguistic diversity although within the same family, and the entirely distinct Finno-Ugrian speaking Magyars, share a common type of economic and cultural life. The same observation can be made about the Indo-European speaking Armenians and Ossetes, the Uralo-Altaic speaking Azerbaijanis and the Caucasic Georgians and others in the Caucasus region."[4]

So how can a particular material culture, whose linguistic identity is not known, be identified as the material culture of a single linguistic group, and that group the proto-Indo-European one; and how can the spread of this material culture be interpreted as the spread of this particular linguistic group?

The study of archaeological artifacts involves the study of material remains: physical (like bones, etc.) and cultural (like excavated dwellings and habitations, and burial sites; and material objects like pottery, tools, weapons, and others). The use of material objects can spread from one area to another without it necessarily following that a particular language group, believed to be originally using those material objects, is also spreading in the wake of the objects.

And alternately, a language or language-family can spread from one area to another without it being necessary that archaeological remains should be found of a material culture spreading in its wake.

4. Moreover, is even the alleged spread of this material culture identified as proto-Indo-European, an archaeological fact?

Pottery is usually considered a major archaeological criterion in tracing out the spread of material cultures. S.P. Gupta, for example, in a different context, insists that a "one ware, one people" equation is correct, "because in the absence of anthropological and linguistic data, what criterion may we evolve to identify a homogeneous group of people? For pre-literate cultures, pottery has been accepted as the common denominator, howsoever apologetically it might have been done."[5]

Even while preaching a presumptuous equation between material culture and people (race), S.P. Gupta takes pottery as the common denominator for identifying a common material culture. However, pottery is clearly not a factor taken into account by the protagonists of the Kurgan material culture. Marija Gimbutas describes the pottery of the Kurgan culture as "crude and unpainted; clay was mixed with crushed

[4] HCIP, pp. 145-46.
[5] MMR, Introduction, p. 49.

shells and sand."[6] And this, she speculatively seeks to connect up with a distinctly different pottery-type in northern Iran: "The appearance of the Gray Ware culture in northern Iran in the period synchronous with the Early Dynastic Period of Mesopotamia (c. 3000–2370 BC) and the displacement of the older culture in the tells of northern Iran (Hissar II, Tureng Tepe, Shah Tepe) *was probably* in connection with the movements of the Kurgan people."[7]

5. And even after this speculative linking-up of different material cultures in a presumptuous chain of "Kurgan expansion", neither Gimbutas nor any other archaeologist can link up the Kurgan culture to any material culture excavated in India, let alone one which can be declared to be the material culture of the Vedic Aryans.

And least of all can any archaeologist demonstrate simultaneous link-ups of the Kurgan culture through different chains of connectable material cultures, let alone through the spread of one single material culture, to the material cultures of the earliest known Indo-European peoples: the Hittites, the Vedic Aryans and the Greeks.

And in India, there is not even one material culture which could be identified as the proto-Aryan or Vedic material culture. K.D. Sethna[8] quotes three arch-advocates of the Aryan invasion theory who admit the fact. Sir Mortimer Wheeler acknowledges: "It is best to admit that no proto-Aryan material culture has yet been identified in India[9]"; T. Burrow also admits that "the Aryan invasion of India....cannot yet be traced archaeologically[10]"; and George R. Dales points out that the Aryans in India "have not yet been identified archaeologically."[11]

These circumstances totally disprove the idea that material culture, identifiable from archaeological excavations, can be a criterion for tracing out the origin and spread of "Aryans" from their original homeland. Chatterji, for example, speaks of "the parallel cases of Persian, Greek and Italic Indo-European cultures"[12] (parallel to the Vedic culture, that is); but the description of the so-called expansion of Kurgan culture, given by Gimbutas and other Kurgan enthusiasts, certainly does not make it appear that "parallel cases" of culture could possibly be the

[6] IE & IE, p. 164.

[7] IE & IE, p. 181.

[8] Karpāsa, pp. 7-8.

[9] *Early India and Pakistan* (Bombay, 1959), p. 126.

[10] "The Early Aryans", *A Cultural History of India*, edited by A. L. Basham (Clarendon Press, Oxford, 1975), p. 21.

[11] "The Decline of the Harappans", *Scientific American* (New York), May, 1966, p. 95.

[12] ODBL, p. 27.

result of the different presumable chains of expansion—the chain of presumed Indo-Iranian expansion itself, to take one example, flounders in the realm of speculative "probabilities" even in the case of the material culture "in the tells of northern Iran" even at so remote (as per the chronology of the Aryan invasion of India) a period as 3000 BC.

The culture of the Rigveda, as per the studies of comparative philologists, represents the oldest and hoariest, even the most primitive, from among the different oldest Indo-European cultures known: and it has the greatest number of mutual correspondences with the other cultures, even more than the other cultures have with each other. Thus, a greater number of correspondences can be found between the Vedic culture on the one hand, and the ancient Greek or the ancient Celtic or the ancient Germanic or the ancient Lithuanian cultures on the other, than can be found between any two of these European cultures (except where there are clear cases of borrowing and historical influence).

Hence no material culture *(if material culture is to be taken as a criterion)* which does not show a direct and indisputable link with the Indo-Aryan culture, and specifically with the Rigvedic culture of Punjab, can legitimately be claimed to be the proto-Indo-European material culture.

GENERAL LINGUISTIC PALEONTOLOGY

Linguistic paleontology, as already explained,[13] "attempts to reconstruct the environment of the undivided Aryan culture" by taking the words and names which are common to far flung Indo-European languages and treating the objects and concepts denoted by these words and names as being the objects and concepts familiar to the proto-Indo-Europeans in their original homeland.

Since the Kurgan culture is identified as the proto-Indo-European culture on the ground that it "corresponds to what can be inferred for proto-Indo-European (culture) from the linguistic data", let us examine the effectiveness of linguistic paleontology as a major criterion in identifying any material culture as proto-Indo-European.

To begin with, Warren Cowgill admits that "only a small fraction of the vocabulary can be traced back to words that can confidently be asserted to have existed in the parent language with approximately their present meaning. The same is true, albeit in a lesser degree, even for the oldest recorded Indo-European languages."[14]

[13] Ch. 6.
[14] EB, Vol. 9, p. 438.

It is true that even this "small fraction of the vocabulary" can form the subject of exciting linguistic research and analysis, and the source of fascinating, if often speculative, information—a fact to which generations of linguists, and volumes of comparative linguistic research and analysis, can testify—but only an extremely motivated person could claim to discern a particular geographical location as being indicated in all this linguistic material.

For the most part, the common words deal with verbs, adjectives, adverbs, pronouns, and the like; and with nouns having to do with daily life, family and social relationships, some rituals and beliefs, and so on. Thus, for example, the fact that Sanskrit *pitar, mātar, bhrātar, svasar, sūnu* and *duhitar* have direct cognates in English "father, mother, brother, sister, son and daughter" is a very interesting piece of information: it shows clearly that the two languages are related, and that the parent language had words for these social relationships, but it is not very illuminating as to the geographical location of that parent language.

On a higher level, several common words have been interpreted as indicating the degree or level of social organisation and technology of the parent Indo-European culture. But even here, neither is the picture of the society, thus conjured up, either complete or convincing; nor is it convincingly, or even reasonably, identifiable with one particular known ancient society more than with any other.

The only nouns or words which *could* specifically point to some particular geographical location could be the common names for animals and plants. But even this evidence could be very deceptive. To take a very extreme hypothetical example, if the Indo-European languages had had a common name for the kangaroo, it would certainly have indicated that Australia was the original homeland of the Indo-Europeans.

But, even in this hypothetical example, would the Indo-Europeans have continued to have a word for the kangaroo, after staying for millenniums in the area spread out from India to Europe, where no kangaroos are found? And even if they had retained such a word, using it as the name for some other animal found in their new area by a process of transfer-application, how could the word now be identified as originally having been applied to the kangaroo? This would be possible only if the Indo-Europeans retained graphic traditional memories of the physical description of the kangaroo, stressing its particular peculiarities; in which case, when the medieval Europeans invaded Australia, they would have discovered that the animal described in their ancient texts or traditions was found there, and that it was known by a name similar to the one used in those texts or traditions. That would have provided a strong argument for an Australian homeland.

However, the Indo-European languages do not provide such a simple and direct method of locating the original homeland. They have common words for dog, horse, cow/ox/bull/cattle, sheep, goat, goose/swan, boar/pig, owl, crow, mouse, fly, snake, wolf, bear, otter and fox; and besides a common word for "tree" (there is no common word for "animal" or "bird"), common words have been suggested for a few species of trees like the birch, pine and oak.

None of these animals or plants are locally restricted to any particular part of the present Indo-European speaking belt stretching from India to Western Europe. They are found, and are known to have been found as far back as historical records show, almost all over this entire belt, and there is no logical way in which these words can be cited to pinpoint a particular geographical region as the original homeland.

And nor can the *absence* of common words for certain other animals and plants be utilised, negatively, to eliminate the candidature of those areas where such other animals and plants are found. The proto-Indo-Europeans are supposed to have been a pastoral people, but there is no common word for milk. In spite of a common word for honey, there is no common word for bee. It is impossible that the proto-Indo-Europeans in their original homeland could have been acquainted with only a handful of plants and trees, and yet the number of common words for plants and trees is not more than a handful. Therefore absence of common words for any particular animal or plant cannot be given much importance.

In short, linguistic paleontology is not an ideal method for locating the original homeland.

THE ARCHAEOLOGICAL EVIDENCE

Does the archaeological reconstruction of the Kurgan culture, for what it is worth, tally with the linguistic reconstruction of proto-Indo-European culture?

Archaeologist Marija Gimbutas certainly seems to think so. After giving detailed descriptions[15] of the different features of the Kurgan culture, she concludes her paper with a summation[16] beginning with:

[15] IE & IE, pp. 155–90.
[16] See Ch. 6.

"Kurgan elements in economy, habitation patterns, social structure and religion *fully agree* with the common words in Indo-European languages which have been used by linguists for the hypothetical reconstruction of the mother culture."[17]

The summation continues with repeated assertions about the close identity of the archaeological reconstruction of the Kurgan culture with the linguistic reconstruction of the proto-Indo-European culture: "splendid coincidence... agrees well with the linguistic reconstruction... conforms with the linguistic evidence... is proved by the earliest sources... splendidly agree..." and so on.

Let us examine Gimbutas' claims under the same headings (ecology and economy, technology, social structure, and religion) used by her in her summation.

It will be seen that the archaeological reconstruction of the Kurgan culture not only does not *fully agree* with the linguistic reconstruction of Indo-European culture on any point, but any "agreements" pertain only to a few minor points which would show "agreement" with almost *any* other culture or civilization, and there are even sharp disagreements on some major points.

Ecology and Economy

Do the elements of ecology and economy of the Kurgan people agree with the linguistically reconstructed ecology and economy of the proto-Indo-Europeans?

1. Gimbutas claims that the "floral and faunal remains from the early Kurgan period...show a splendid coincidence."[18] She names nine trees and basically eleven animals (wild and domesticated). But, all these trees and animals are found in most parts of the Indo-European belt stretching from north India to western Europe; and floral and faunal remains from most of these parts would show an equally "splendid coincidence."

Even then, there are no common words (which, as pointed out by Childe, means "words found in Indo-Iranian on the one hand, and a European language on the other"[19]) for many of the trees, and for four of the eleven animals named by Gimbutas. There are no common words for the beaver, badger, squirrel and deer (elk). The deer, it may be noted, is among the most commonly found animals in the Kurgan

[17] IE & IE, p. 190.
[18] Ibid.
[19] Aryans, p. 79.

remains. Another animal named by Gimbutas, the bear, has common words in many languages—(Sanskrit *ṛkṣa*, Greek *arctos*, Latin *ursus*, Irish *art* and Cornish *ors*), but curiously not in the Slavonic languages closest to South Russia (all the Slavonic words, e.g. Russian *medvědĭ*, mean "eater of honey").

According to Gimbutas[20] herself, the lion is commonly found (alongwith the deer and bull) in the shape of carved figurines in the Kurgan tombs. But linguists have concluded, from the absence of any common word for the lion, that the lion was not known to the undivided Indo-Europeans.

Does all this show a "splendid coincidence"?

2. Gimbutas also claims that "Grain or seed (**sēmn*) is attested. The wooden ard (from the root **ar(ā)*) was probably used universally. They reaped (**kerpō*) their harvests. Wool and flax were known",[21] and that "this agrees well with the linguistic reconstruction: agriculture coupled with cattle breeding." But a "grain or seed" was known to most of the civilizations of ancient times, and the people of all the ancient civilizations reaped their harvests, and used the wooden ard, and wool and flax (linen). How does the Kurgan culture show any particular coincidence with the reconstructed proto-Indo-European culture, and why should these things connect up to the proto-Indo-European words (**semn, ar(ā), kerpō*)?

According to Childe[22], there is a common word for "plough" (Sanskrit *vṛka*, Greek *eúlaka)*. This would indicate that agriculture was an important proto Indo-European occupation. However, in the Kurgan culture, according to Gimbutas, "agriculture was practised but not highly developed...a triangular sandstone...found in the *upper* layer of the Mikhajlovka settlement *may* have been used as a ploughshare....in *Denmark,* plough marks have been observed under a burrow of Kurgan type."[23]

Compare this meagre and vague evidence of Kurgan agricultural occupation at a late date with the highly developed agriculture in other cultures (for example, the Indus, Egyptian, Mesopotamian and Chinese cultures). Clearly, the "splendid coincidence" does not extend to agriculture.

3. Earlier, Gimbutas also points out that "the presence of bone or

[20] IE & IE, p. 172.
[21] IE & IE, p. 190.
[22] Aryans, p. 92.
[23] IE & IE, p. 161.

antler harpoons, points, fish-hooks and fishbones in Kurgan villages indicates that fishing was an important means of subsistence."[24]

And here we find a major point which not only does not show a "splendid coincidence", but in fact contrasts sharply with the linguistic reconstruction of proto-Indo-European culture. The Indo-European languages do not have a common word for "fish". Childe also points out: "fishing is never mentioned either in the Veda or the Avesta, and the repugnance felt by the Homeric Greeks for a fish diet is notorious,"[25] and also: "it is notorious that early Aryans, even in a maritime region, eschewed a fish diet."[26]

Now, the bit about fishing not being mentioned in the Veda may not be correct. Bhargava[27] gives many specific references from the Rigveda to show that the Rigvedic people were fully acquainted with seas, fishes and fishing. But the fact remains that there is no common word for fishes and fishing in Indo-European languages, and this factor has led linguists to the conclusion that fishing was not commonly known to the proto-Indo-Europeans. In fact, Childe,[28] himself a supporter of the Northern-Europe-cum-South-Russia homeland theory, points out that the commonness of fishing and maritime activities in Northern Europe is held as a factor going against the candidature of Northern Europe as the original homeland.

Now it is quite possible that linguistic paleontology is wrong or inadequate in this matter (the inadequacies of linguistic paleontology have already been pointed out) and that fishes and fishing were indeed commonly known to the proto-Indo-Europeans. But that is a surmise which must be drawn *against* the evidence of linguistic paleontology rather than in "splendid coincidence" with it.

Technology

Do the elements of Kurgan technology show full agreement with the linguistically reconstructed technology of the proto-Indo-Europeans?

1. According to Gimbutas, "the Kurgan people were using objects made from pure or arsenical copper from the fourth millennium BC."[29] But so were almost all the civilizations of the Old World. Gimbutas

[24] IE & IE, p. 160.
[25] Aryans, p. 84.
[26] Aryans, p. 167.
[27] IVA, pp. 70-77.
[28] Aryans, Ch. 4.
[29] IE & IE, p. 190.

also tells us that "in late Kurgan times, flat shaft holed axes appeared, which alongwith dagger points and awls, were made on the spot. *The existence of local metallurgy is proven by nozzles and crucibles.*"[30] But linguists have always claimed that Indo-European languages had a common word for metal, but no common words for metallurgy and metallurgical terms; and that this was to be construed as indicating that the proto-Indo-Europeans did not have metallurgical knowledge but imported their metal goods from elsewhere. Gimbutas herself refers to this linguistic reconstruction when she points out that "there is no one proto-Indo-European word for metallurgy."[30a]

2. Gimbutas claims that "the usage of vehicles well agrees with the existence of the root **vegh* in many Indo-European languages, as well as with words for wheel, axle, pole, lynch-pin and nave."[31]

But why should the mere fact that vehicles were used in the Kurgan culture connect up to the common words for vehicle, wheel, axle, pole, lynch-pin and nave in the Indo-European languages? Vehicles are not found only in the Kurgan culture; they were used in every other Old World culture, whether that of Egypt, Mesopotamia or the Indus Valley.

Moreover, it is the horse-driven chariots of the "Aryans" that are made much of. The Aryans are supposed to have "introduced the use of the horse for driving chariots into the Ancient East".[32] In this context, the following observation by Gimbutas about the Kurgan culture may be noted: "There is no indication that horses were used for traction. Most probably oxen were used for this purpose."[33]

3. In the matter of boats, Gimbutas goes one step further in presumptuousness. She tells us: "common words for boat, rudder and oar indicate the use of boats. The latter are not proved archaeologically because wooden objects require special conditions for preservation, but it can be surmised that the Kurgan people used their rivers for navigation."

Boats and ships were known to most Old World civilizations. In the case of our own Indus Civilization, we have the oldest discovered docks in the world at Lothal, and "the representation on a seal of a mastless ship, with a central cabin and a steersman seated at the rudder

[30] IE & IE, p. 163.
[30a] IE & IE, p. 190.
[31] IE & IE, p. 191.
[32] Aryans, p. 18.
[33] IE & IE, p. 161.

indicates that the people of the Indus Valley were acquainted with maritime vessels."[34] Hence any evidence of boats in the Kurgan remains would not have represented any particular "agreement" between the Kurgan culture and the proto-Indo-European culture.

But here, in fact, in the *absence* of evidence of boats in the Kurgan remains, it is "surmised" (though doubtless with perfect truth) that the Kurgan people used boats; and we are asked to treat this as one more "agreement."

Social Structure

Does the social structure of the Kurgan society, such as is claimed to have been surmised from the Kurgan remains, show "full agreement" with the social structure of the proto-Indo-European society?

1. On the grounds that Kurgan settlements had "hill-forts...with royal houses or palaces and living quarters for the ruling class, and...small villages in the vicinity of the tribal centre", Gimbutas concludes that the people were "divided into castes, the warrior nobility and labouring."[35] Except for the suggestive use of the word "castes" to hint at a connection with India (castes being a peculiarly Indian phenomenon), her conclusion is reasonably fair.

But then, she goes one step further and connects this with proto-Indo-European society on the ground that "this stratified society is proved by the earliest Greek, Hittite, Indo-Iranian and Roman sources" and that it "conforms with linguistic evidence" of the Indo-European languages.

Emile Benveniste[36] has tried to prove that the Greek language and literature give evidence of a three-fold and four-fold division of society, akin to the four castes of Hinduism, and that this common system had its roots in the social structure of proto-Indo-European society; but the evidence (quite apart from the fact that the caste system in India is supposed to be "post-Rigvedic") is far from convincing.

But, even presuming that the Greeks also had a *four-fold* division of society like the Hindus, how does it follow that the presumed *two-fold* division of Kurgan society "conforms with the linguistic evidence" of this presumed *four-fold* division of proto-Indo-European society?

In a similar situation, A.D. Pusalker (surprisingly, since he is no opponent of the Aryan invasion theory) suggests an equally presumptu-

[34] HCIP, p. 179.
[35] IE & IE , p. 191.
[36] IELS, Ch. 2.

ous equation: "The remains unearthed at Mohenjodaro demonstrate the existence of different sections of people who may be grouped into four main classes, the learned class, the warriors, the traders and artisans, and finally manual labourers, corresponding roughly to the four varnas of the Vedic period."[37] The saving grace of Pusalker's equation is that the number and nature of the divisions that he presumes to discern in the Mohenjodaro remains at least corresponds to the number and nature of the divisions "of the Vedic period" with which he seeks to draw a connection.

The mere fact that Kurgan society was "stratified", and that all the earliest known Indo-European societies were also "stratified", does not prove anything since every single society— ancient, medieval or modern, and Indo-European or non-Indo-European—has been, and is "stratified" in some way or the other.

2. Further, according to Gimbutas, "the burial rites indicate not only social differences, but also man's dominant role in society".[38] This, according to her "conforms with the linguistic evidence" of Indo-European languages, since "studies in proto-Indo-European kinship have shown that proto-Indo-European culture had patriarchal, patrilocal families that probably lived in small houses or huts. Villages were small and probably exogamous...the whole system seems to be typical of the patrilineate in its most highly developed form."[39]

But anyone going through the Old Testament will find that it also depicts "the patrilineate in its most highly developed form". In fact, the overwhelming majority of cultures and civilizations were male-dominated, so that can hardly be a criterion for identifying the Kurgan culture as proto-Indo-European.

Religion

Does the description of the Kurgan religion, as gleaned and surmised from the archaeological remains, fully agree with the hypothetically reconstructed religion of the proto-Indo-Europeans?

1. Gimbutas claims that "although the archaeological reconstruction of religion cannot be complete, the data available *splendidly agree* with the ancient elements of Indo-European mythology reconstructed on the basis of comparative mythology and linguistics".[40]

[37] HCIP, p. 179.
[38] IE & IE, p. 169.
[39] IE & IE, p. 191.
[40] Ibid.

The ancient elements of Indo-European mythology as reconstructed by comparative mythology and linguistics are not very numerous: the ancient Indo-Europeans are supposed to have basically worshipped the Earth as a Mother Goddess (Sanskrit *Pṛthivī)* and the Sky as a Father-Sky God (Sanskrit *Dyaus Pitar*, Greek *Zēus Páter*, Latin *Jupiter)*. They are also believed to have worshipped Dawn as a Goddess (Sanskrit *Uṣas*, Greek *Ēos*, Latin *Aurora*); as well as a pair of youthful Twin-Gods (Sanskrit *Aśvinau*, Greek *Dioskoūroi*, and the twin-sons of the Lettic God) who are divine horsemen and who rescue people from the ocean; and a Rain-God (Sanskrit *Parjanya* and Lithuanian *Perkunas)*. Another major God (Sanskrit *Varuṇa*, Teutonic *Woden*, Greek *Ouranos*) has also been identified. And the Gods are generally believed to have been identified with light (Sanskrit *Devas*, Lithuanian *Devas*, Latin *Deus*, Greek *Theos*). Beyond the identification of these common Gods, hardly any common mythology as such has been identified.

But not even the most presumptuous scholar has been able to claim that the Kurgan remains have yielded any evidence of a Father-Sky God, a pair of divine Twin-Gods or a Goddess of the Dawn; much less claim that the Kurgan Gods (of whom nothing is known) were generally identified with Light. And Gimbutas herself fails to cite a single instance of the "splendid agreement" in mythology claimed by her.

2. Earlier, in giving more detailed descriptions of the religion of the Kurgan people, Gimbutas writes: "From graves, we know that these people had very strong beliefs about life after death, which had to continue in the same way as life on earth. Therefore graves imitated houses, and the dead needed their weapons, tools, pots, ornaments and even vehicles."[41]

The above description could fit many other prominent civilizations much better than it fits any of the known ancient Indo-European civilizations. The Egyptian civilization, with its pyramid-tombs, could well be the one being described by Gimbutas. Certainly, the oldest known Indo-European religions, of the Rigvedic people and the Greeks, did not have graves which imitated houses.

Moreover, it is often claimed that the original "Aryans" did *not* have "very strong beliefs about life after death." In fact, S.K. Chatterji[42] insists that "notions of future life (survival of the soul after death...)" are "proto-Australoid" as opposed to "Aryan" elements in Hinduism.

[41] IE & IE, p. 170.
[42] HCIP, p. 150.

3. And here we come to a very basic point on which Kurgan "religion" clashes very sharply with the evidence of all the oldest-known Indo-European cultures: the Kurgan people buried their dead while all the oldest known Indo-Europeans (Hindus, Greeks, Romans, Hittites, etc.) cremated their dead.

The burial mound is a very fundamental feature of the Kurgan culture. As Childe points out, the Kurgan remains are "derived almost exclusively from graves containing contracted skeletons covered with red-ochre (ochre-graves) and surmounted by a mound or Kurgan."[43] The very culture derives its name from these burial mounds.

Childe, while describing the attempt by an earlier scholar, F. de Michelis, to trace the internal migrations of Indo-Europeans within Europe on the basis of the evidence of cremation, admits that "de Michelis' thesis achieves the finest cultural synthesis among all Aryan peoples yet found. It gives a distribution of a cultural peculiarity which harmonizes exceptionally well with the distribution of Indo-European languages." In fact, Childe tries to bring the alleged Aryan invasion of India into the picture by adding: "In Asia, the Aryan Hindus practised cremation, and we know now that in the Indus Valley the rite superseded the older practice of inhumation."[44]

(Incidentally, this last bit constitutes a distortion of the facts. A.D. Pusalker states that "three forms of burial have been found at Mohenjodaro, viz. complete burials, fractional burials and post-cremation burials". About complete burials, he states: "All these burials appear, on stratigraphical evidence, to *relate to the declining years* of Mohenjodaro", whereas "post-cremation burials have been discovered... *distributed among strata of all periods.*"[45] This conforms with the Vedic practice, in which, according to A.A. Macdonell, "cremation was the usual way for the dead—besides the bones and ashes of adults, only young children and ascetics were buried."[46] The third form of burial found at Mohenjodaro, fractional burial, "represents a collection of some bones after the exposure of the body to wild beasts and birds."[46a] The exposure of the body to wild beasts and birds has survived among the Iranians, i.e. Zoroastrians.)

But Childe probably realizes the threat to the Kurgan claims posed by the acceptance of cremation as a proto-Indo-European custom, for

[43] Aryans, p. 183.
[44] Aryans, p. 145.
[45] HCIP, p. 189.
[46] VM, p. 165.
[46a] HCIP, p. 189.

he hastens to disclaim de Michelis' thesis on the ground that "it can neither be shown that all Aryans cremated, nor that all cremationists were Aryans"[47], and that "cremation is not universally attested among the earliest Aryan peoples while it is sometimes practised by non-Aryans."[48]

These weak disclaimers notwithstanding, it is obvious that cremation must have been the general practice among the original Indo-Europeans, and this fact heavily discounts the claims of the Kurgan culture.

4. In her summation,[49] Gimbutas refers to the "existence of a thunder god" in the religion of the Kurgan people, and counts it among the elements in the Kurgan religion which "splendidly agree" with the elements in the proto-Indo-European religion.

This "thunder-god" is described earlier by Gimbutas, when she describes the Kurgan graves "topped with a stone stela. The stela was primitively carved in a human shape and on some of them male attributes were indicated. The figure held an axe or a mace in one hand...the stela *may have* portrayed a male divinity, *probably* a thunder god".[50]

From *probably,* it seems to become *positively* a thunder god by the time Gimbutas reaches her summation. And having decided that the "male divinity" was a "thunder god", she identifies it as Indo-European, inspite of the fact that no Indo-European Thunder-God, armed with "an axe or a mace", is known to be used as a topping on graves.

5. In her description of the Kurgan religion, Gimbutas points out that "bull, stag and lion figurines are known from royal tombs of the third millennium BC",[51] evidently inferring bull, stag and lion cults.

If this is meant to be another point of "splendid agreement" with the reconstructed Indo-European religion, it is a dismal failure. To begin with, there is no known major cult involving stag-worship among any section of Indo-Europeans, although such cults are common among the Red Indians of America.

The worship of the bull and the lion is found in Hinduism, where the bull and the lion are the vehicles of Śiva and Pārvatī respectively. But worship of these two animals is found in most of the ancient cultures of Asia; and moreover, protagonists of the Aryan invasion theory have classified it as a "Dravidian" contribution to Hinduism. S.K. Chat-

[47] Aryans, p. 148.
[48] Aryans, p. 149.
[49] IE & IE, p. 191.
[50] IE & IE, p. 170.
[51] IE & IE, p. 172.

terji (while expounding his favourite theory of the "migration" of Dravidians to India from their "original homeland") claims: "The Dravidians brought to India from their original homeland... the great Asianic Mother Goddess and Father God, the former having as her symbol or vehicle the lion, the latter the bull."[52]

But the bull and lion cults are not found in the Indo-European cultures of Europe. In Greek mythology, bull worship of a kind is a feature of the pre-Hellenic (pre-Indo-European) Aegean or Minoan culture (as evidenced by the myth of the Minotaur) and this has been confirmed by archaeologists. (In fact, it is this factor which leads hopeful scholars to identify the bull and the lion in Hinduism as "Dravidian", and then connect it up with an "original homeland" of the Dravidians "in the islands of the Aegean and the tracts of the mainland along the Aegean Sea—Greece and Asia Minor."[53])

6. Earlier, Gimbutas points out a distinctive characteristic of the Kurgan religion: "The presence of a male divinity or divinities contrasts sharply with the pre-eminence of various symbolic female figurines in the Anatolian, Aegean and Balkan cultures prior to the Kurgan expansion."[54]

If this is true, then it contrasts equally sharply with "the ancient elements of Indo-European mythology reconstructed on the basis of comparative mythology and linguistics." Gimbutas is obviously under the impression that the reconstructed proto-Indo-European religion depicts male Gods in opposition to the female Goddesses of other cultures, but the case is quite the opposite. Let us examine the evidence of the two cultures whose mythology has been recorded from the earliest times and in the greatest detail, viz. the Hindu and the Greek.

In Hinduism, the Mother-Goddess (Durgā, Ambā, etc.) reigns supreme. As Lakṣmī, she is the Goddess of wealth; as Sarasvatī, she is the Goddess of knowledge and virtues; and as Pārvatī, her most representative form, she is the Goddess of energy and power. The Trinity of Gods is thus matched by a Trinity of Goddesses, and nowhere (except in later Vaiṣṇava traditions, where Lakṣmī is perpetually seated at the feet of a reclining Viṣṇu, pressing his feet) is she shown in a degraded position or as being inferior to the male Gods. In her proper form as Durgā, Ambā or Ādimāyā, she is *the* greatest of the Gods and Goddesses, the ultimate Power supplicated to by all the other Gods; and nowhere is she

[52] HCIP, p. 158.
[53] Ibid.
[54] IE & IE, p. 171.

shown as the suppliant.

And for those who classify Hinduism as consisting of "Aryan" and "non-Aryan" elements, and the prominence given to the Mother-Goddess as being one of those "non-Aryan" elements, the Rigvedic facts noted by K.D. Sethna[55] may be pointed out: the Father-Sky God Dyaus and the Mother-Earth Goddess Pṛthivī are acknowledged by comparative mythologists to be the oldest. The two are always mentioned together, and are worshipped in six hymns. However, while Dyaus is never lauded alone in any hymn, Pṛthivī alone is invoked in one short hymn[56] of three stanzas, and thus, as Sethna puts it, "the Mother-Goddess has, by however thin a margin, an edge over the Father God".[57] Also, as Aditi (meaning "boundlessness"), she is acknowledged to be the mother of all the Gods, and is described as follows: "She is the heaven, she is the atmosphere, she is the mother; she is the father, son, all gods, and the whole world; she is creation and birth."[58] Amazingly, even Dyaus is referred to in twenty passages as feminine.[59]

Also, the Rigvedic hymns described as "perhaps *the oldest* and certainly the most beautiful" (by B.K. Ghosh, an advocate of the Aryan invasion theory) are the Dawn hymns pertaining to Uṣas who is hailed as "O radiant one...O bountiful Goddess."[60]

In Greek tradition also we have the twelve great Gods and Goddesses on Olympus, of whom six are Gods (Zeus, Poseidon, Hephaestus, Hermes, Ares and Apollo) and six are Goddesses (Hera, Athene, Artemis, Hestia, Aphrodite and Demeter). And going back to the roots, we get the following picture of Greek mythology as described in the *Larousse Encyclopaedia of Mythology:*

"In the beginning, Hesiod says, there was Chaos, vast and dark. Then appeared Gaea, the deep-breasted earth. ...The Chaos of Hessiod ...simply designates open space... a pure cosmic principle devoid of God-like characteristics.... The only divinity with well-defined features is Gaea, the earth. According to Hessiod, it seems likely that Gaea, from whom all things issued, had been the great deity of the primitive Greeks...the Mother-Goddess. This is again confirmed by the Homeric hymn in which the poet says: 'I shall sing of Gaea, universal mother, firmly founded, *the oldest of divinities*'...(Gaea) was thus at one time

[55] Karpāsa pp. 33-35.
[56] Rigveda, V. 84.
[57] Karpāsa, p. 33.
[58] Rigveda, I.89.10.
[59] VM, p. 22.
[60] Rigveda, I.48.1.

the supreme Goddess whose majesty was acknowledged not only by men but by the Gods themselves."[61]

About the Gods and Goddesses of the Hittites, little is known, since, as the *Larousse Encyclopaedia of Mythology* points out, the Hittites adopted deities from various peoples: from the "indigenous" peoples (Irbitiga, Kalhisapi, Teteshapi, Wasezzel), the Luwians (Santa, Tarhunza, Wandu), the Hurrians (Teshup, Hepat), and the Babylonians and Assyrians (their names represented by ideograms, hence unreadable). The original deities of the Hittites, if any, are also represented by ideograms, and are therefore not readable, except for one God Inar (=Indra), whom the encyclopaedia describes as "a God who had *come from India* with the Indo-European Hittites."[62]

But from what little has been gleaned about the original mythology of the Hittites: "At the head of the pantheon can be distinguished the *divine couple,* symbolising vital forces.... certain feminine deities seem to play a *preponderant* role."[63]

Going on to another Indo-European mythology, the Celtic mythology, we find the Celts worshipping two main Gods, the Dagda (also called Eochaid Ollathair, or "Father of all") and Lug, and two main Goddesses, Danu (also called Anu or Brigit) and Macha. And, "the Gods of the Celts....perhaps complemented the functions of the Goddesses, who in their turn appear to have retained the concept of the Mother-Goddess which had evolved in much earlier times....the Gods of the Celts in Ireland are frequently called the *People of the Goddess Danu.*"[64]

All the evidence of comparative mythology and linguistics thus shows that the Mother-Goddess was the oldest and highest divinity of the Indo-Europeans; and the fact that the Kurgan people exclusively worshipped "a male divinity" or divinities, "contrasts sharply" (in Gimbutas' own words) with this reconstruction.

7. Gimbutas also has the following comments to make about the religion of the Kurgan people:

"Animal bones show the importance of cults and indicate sacrifices...human sacrifice is evidenced by the disposal of separate human bones in pits close to the grave, in some cases mixed with animal bones."[65]

[61] LEM, pp. 89-92.
[62] LEM, p. 85.
[63] Ibid.
[64] LEM, p. 239.
[65] IE & IE, p. 170.

"The abundance of ochre, charcoal and ashes in the graves indicates the ritual significance of fire and of the red colour of ochre."[66]

"No real sanctuaries have ever been found; they probably had open sanctuaries."[67]

If all these above details are supposed to "splendidly agree" with the details of any known religion, it would be the religion depicted in the Book of Genesis (*Bereshith* in Hebrew) of the Old Testament, more than any known Indo-European religion. The ancient Hebrews worshipped their *exclusively Male God Jehovah* with animal sacrifices in open sanctuaries, in the light of flaming torches.

8. Gimbutas also refers to the evidence of "sun, fire, horse, bull, wolf, dog, boar and snake cults"[68] among the Kurgan people. It is not quite clear as to how exactly Gimbutas infers the existence of these various cults among the Kurgan people, but, since she does, it may be pointed out that these cults also do not "splendidly agree" with the reconstructed Indo-European religion.

Sun-worship is found among most of the ancient cultures and civilizations all over the world. Even the Egyptians had a major God, Ra, who represented the Sun. So far as worship of fire is concerned, the only evidence of fire-worship in the Kurgan settlements seems to be "the abundance of ochre, charcoal and ashes", which really indicates nothing: fire has always been used by all cultures (candles and lamps, torches, incense, sacrificial fires, and so on), and cannot be cited as evidence of any special link between two hypothetically reconstructed religions.

Worship of animals is found all over the world in different cultures, and the animals worshipped would naturally be from among the animals prominent in the particular area. Yet, curiously enough, the wolf and the dog are not known to have been prominently worshipped in any Indo-European society, although both are found all over the Indo-European speaking area and have common names in the far-flung languages. Although an extremely wide range of animals is worshipped in Hinduism, the wolf and the dog do not figure among them.

Snake worship is found only among the Hindus, and protagonists of the invasion theory have firmly determined that it is a "non-Aryan" element in Hinduism. S.K. Chatterji proclaims: "The worship of the Nāgas or serpentine deities...would appear to have come from the

[66] IE & IE, p. 174.
[67] IE & IE, p. 191.
[68] Ibid.

proto-Australoids."[69] Macdonell also declares that "serpent-worship...was probably due rather to the influence of the aborigines. For on the one hand, there is no trace of it in the Rigveda, and on the other it has been found prevailing very widely among the non-Aryan Indians."[70]

Worship of the bull is also found only among the Hindus, and even here the bull is superseded in importance and sacredness by the cow. In the cultures of Europe also, the cow occupies an important position: in Teutonic mythology, the Mother-Goddess giving birth to all creation is pictured as a cow. But there is no evidence that the cow was worshipped by the Kurgan people.

The boar does occur in Indian mythology, as the Varāhavatāra (an incarnation of Viṣṇu), and in the Rigveda,[71] Rudra is described as a boar (and also as a bull). The horse of course figures, in different ways, in the mythology of the Greeks and Hindus. But there is no particular way in which the hypothetical presence of the horse and boar as cult objects in the Kurgan religion can be construed as evidence of the Kurgan culture being the proto-Indo-European culture.

From all the details given, it is obvious that the Kurgan material culture can by no means be identified as the proto-culture of the Indo-European people. Only a highly motivated, or at any rate prejudiced and predetermined, scholarship could make and maintain such an "identification."

THE MESOPOTAMIAN CONNECTION

The Indo-European words for copper, star, and axe (reconstructed proto-Indo-European words **roudhos*, **ester* and **peleku* respectively) are believed to be linguistically derived from Mesopotamian words (*urudu*, *ishtar* and *pilakku* respectively); and the actual objects (copper, the Babylonian Goddess Ishtar, and the battle-axe respectively) are archaeologically proved to have been borrowed from Mesopotamia by the Kurgan people. This, according to Childe, proves that the Kurgan people were the proto-Indo-Europeans, since "the connections with Mesopotamia postulated by philology for the Indo-Europeans are proved to have been a reality among the early nomads of South Russia."[72]

[69] HCIP, p. 163.
[70] VM, p. 153.
[71] Rigveda, I.114.5.
[72] Aryans, p. 186.

However, an examination of the three words shows that only one of them (the word for "axe") can perhaps ultimately be derived from Mesopotamia, and the circumstances of the derivation rule out any possibility of any connection with the Kurgan culture or with South Russia. Let us examine each of the three cases.

Copper

The cognate Indo-European words for "copper" are Sanskrit *lohita/rohita*, Latin *raudus*, Old Norse *raudi* and Old Slavic *ruda*, from which the proto-Indo-European word **roudhos* has been reconstructed. However:

1. The word **roudhos* is derived from the proto-Indo-European root word **reudh*, meaning "red". Carl D. Buck[73] correctly derives it from this root.

2. The common words for copper were not the **roudhos*-forms: the oldest words in Sanskrit and Latin are *ayas* (Avestan *ayah*) and *aes* respectively. The oldest attested European language, Greek, has a totally different word, *khalkós*, borrowed from a non-Indo-European source. All the later European languages by and large have words similar to the English word "copper" (derived from the name of Cyprus, which was a main supplier of the metal), and most of the Indian languages have words derived from Sanskrit *tāmra*, also meaning "red".

In fact, the **roudhos*-based words mentioned above are so unimportant that Buck does not mention a single one of them other than the Sanskrit form, which also he mentions as *loha/lohāyasa/lohitāyasa*, clearly meaning "*red* metal." As pointed out by K.D. Sethna[74], the word *ayas* must have originally meant "copper"; later it came to mean "brass", and the two words *lohāyasa* or *lohitāyasa* (for copper) and *śyāmāyasa* or *kṛṣṇāyasa* (for bronze) were coined; and later still, the word *lohāyasa* was transferred to "iron", and the word *tāmra* came to be used for "copper."

The reconstructed proto-Indo-European word **roudhos* therefore has nothing to do with the Sumerian word *urudu*.

Star

Almost all the branches of Indo-European languages have cognate words[75] for "star": Sanskrit *tārā* or *star-*, Avestan *star-*, Hittite *astiras*,

[73] ADOSS, pp. 611-12.
[74] Karpāsa, pp. 48-49.
[75] ADOSS, p. 56.

Tocharian(A) *śreñ*, Greek *astēr*, Latin *stella* or *astrum*, Welsh *ser*, Gothic *stairnō* and Armenian *astl*. A proto-Indo-European word **ester* has been reconstructed from these words. However:

1. The word **ester* is derived from the proto-Indo-European root word **ster* (Sanskrit root *stṛ-*) meaning "spread out." Carl D. Buck not only derives it correctly from this root, but he specifically mentions and dismisses the Akkadian word *Ishtar* as a "less likely source of the word."[76] This derivation is further confirmed by the other Sanskrit word *nakṣatra (nak*, "night" + *stṛ*, "spread out, cover, envelop").

2. A star is a very common object, for which even the most primitive languages, which for example lack words for numerals above two or three, have a name. Among Indo-European languages, practically all the branches, including the extinct Hittite and Tocharian branches, have forms of the same common word (the very curious exceptions being those very branches, Slavonic and Baltic, closest to South Russia: for example, Russian *zvezda* and Lithuanian *žvaigžde*). To presume that the proto-Indo-Europeans borrowed the common, and almost only, word for "star" from the Akkadian (Babylonian) language would be to presume either that they did not have their own word for it, or that the proto-Indo-European language borrowed so heavily from the Akkadian language as to displace a major part of its original vocabulary right down to the commonest words such as the word for "star". The first proposition is as obviously absurd as the second one is obviously untrue.

3. There is no evidence at all, in any Indo-European culture, of the worship of a Star-Goddess; much less of a Star-Goddess named Ishtar. The closest one gets to a star-divinity is the Aśvini twins (Greek Dioskoûroi) who are supposed to represent either the morning star and evening star respectively, or else the twin-star constellation Gemini. It must be remembered that the only point which brings the Kurgan culture into this picture is that clay figurines have been found in South Russia which, according to Childe, "bear a distinct likeness to models of the Goddess Ishtar found at Assur and elsewhere in Mesopotamia."[77]

The reconstructed proto-Indo-European word **ester* therefore has nothing to do with the name of the Akkadian Goddess Ishtar.

Axe

There are only two words in Indo-European languages, Sanskrit

[76] Ibid.
[77] Aryans, pp. 185-86.

paraśu and Greek *pelekus*, which are believed to be derived from the Mesopotamian words for "axe" (Akkadian *pilakku*, Sumerian *balag*); and a proto-Indo-European word **peleku* has been postulated for them. Of the three suggested words, this is the only one for which a case of Mesopotamian origin is possible, since unlike the other two words (**roudhos* and **ester*), no derivation has been suggested for this word from any Indo-European root. However:

1. The word is attested in only two languages, Sanskrit and Greek. Even the Iranian section of the Indo-Iranian branch does not attest this word, the Avestan word for "axe" being *taša*. As both ancient India and ancient Greece had close contacts with West Asia, it is perfectly possible that both Sanskrit and Greek independently borrowed the word from Mesopotamia, well after the dispersal of the Indo-Europeans from their original homeland—whatever the location of that homeland. Even Childe, who insists on the Kurgan connection in the first place, admits: "it may be that Hindus and Hellenes each borrowed independently such a word as *pilakku*."[78]

Moreover, both Sanskrit and Greek had other words for "axe" (*kuṭhāra* and *axine* respectively); therefore if there was any borrowing from Mesopotamia, it was restricted to one of the names for an axe, or perhaps for a variety of axe.

2. If any axe can be shown to have spread outwards from South Russia, it is the South Russian battle-axe (as distinct from a tool-axe) which can archaeologically be shown to have spread all over Siberia and northern and central Europe. Childe, in fact, describes these battle-axes as "the most peculiarly European objects"[79] and as being "genuinely European."[80] He points out that "the characteristic attribute and symbol of the Nordic cultures...was the perforated battle-axe. Now the genesis of this very peculiar weapon can be explained in South Russia better than anywhere else."[81] Childe[82] traces out in detail the spread of these battle-axes in northern and central Europe, and emphasises their importance in the cultures of these regions.

And yet, the languages of northern and central Europe, which can be shown to have acquired their battle-axes from South Russia, do not show the faintest trace of the word *pilakku;* whereas India and Greece,

[78] Aryans, p. 87.
[79] Aryans, p. 66.
[80] Aryans, p. 143.
[81] Aryans, p. 188.
[82] Aryans, Ch. 6-7.

which cannot be shown to have derived any axe from South Russia, have words which can be alleged to be derived from the Akkadian word.

3. The axe in ancient India and Greece was not a battle-axe, but a tool-axe. Childe himself admits that in the Rigveda "axes of copper are mentioned, but as tools, not weapons".[83] The axe is mainly mentioned[84] as a tool of the God Tvaṣṭṛ, who is the Divine Craftsman of the Rigveda. If the word *paraśu* is today best known as a weapon in the hands of Paraśurāma, it is particularly due to its rarity as a weapon in his hands (like the use of the plough as a weapon by Balarāma).

Similarly, Carl D. Buck points out, about the battle-axe in Europe: "it was not a usual weapon of the Greeks....or the Romans, but an important one among the Celtic and Germanic tribes."[85]

4. The battle-axe of South Russia, which spread all over northern and central Europe, may itself not have been an axe borrowed from Mesopotamia. According to Gimbutas, "one of the most typical Kurgan tools which appears in graves and settlements was a hammer-hoe made of elk-antler. This could be a prototype of the later battle-axe made of stone and metal."[86]

From all this, it is obvious that the Indian and Greek words for "axe", even if borrowed from Mesopotamia, give no evidence whatsoever of any connection with South Russia, much less any evidence of the South Russian Kurgan people being the proto-Indo-Europeans.

THE EVIDENCE OF THE HORSE

The horse is considered to be "the typical Aryan animal"[87] and a "peculiarly Aryan quadruped."[88] The horse is particularly associated with Indo-Europeans for three reasons. Firstly, the Kassites are believed to have "introduced the use of the horse for driving chariots into the Ancient East"[89] (i.e. ancient West Asia). Secondly, there are cognate words for horse in the oldest versions of almost all the branches of Indo-European languages. Thirdly, the horse occupies a very prominent place in the mythology and religion of the earliest Indo-Europeans (the Vedic Aryans, the Persians, the Greeks).

[83] Aryans, p. 22.
[84] Rigveda, VIII, 29.3.
[85] ADOSS, p. 1386.
[86] IE & IE, p. 160.
[87] Karpāsa, p. 13.
[88] Aryans, p. 183.
[89] Aryans, p. 18.

From these three facts, two conclusions are drawn. First: that "the Aryans had domesticated the horse."[90] Second: that since the horse was domesticated "in Transcaucasia"[91] and since, in any case, the horse was native to "countries lying north of the Eurasiatic mountain axis", and "south of that the horse was a latecomer"[92], the "Aryans" must originally have lived in South Russia.

However, these conclusions are not in the least warranted by the facts. Even if the horse was indeed domesticated in South Russia or "Transcaucasia", it had spread over the whole of northern Asia in very ancient times. The horse is a very major part of the life, religion and mythology of the Uralo-Altaic peoples, and most of the northern Sino-Tibetan peoples, as well. Therefore, the horse could have been very well known to the proto-Indo-Europeans in their original homeland before their dispersal from it (which is really the only thing indicated by the facts), without the horse necessarily being a native of that homeland, or they themselves being its domesticators.

Keeping this in mind, let us examine the facts to see what they indicate.

1. A.D. Pusalker, referring to E.J.H. Mackay's interpretation of the model horse found in a very early stratum at Mohenjodaro, points out: "Dr. Mackay takes the model animal...to represent a horse, and has conjectured that the Indus Valley people probably knew the horse at about *2500 BC at the latest.* The finds of saddles in some of the lowest strata at Mohenjodaro, and the representations of the horse in the Indus Valley art seem to prove that the horse was known."[93]

If A.D. Pusalker, a staunch supporter of the Aryan invasion theory, can admit that the horse was common in Sind in "about 2500 BC at the latest" (and this fact is further substantiated by K.D. Sethna[94]), it is obvious that the horse must have been common in northern Punjab much earlier, and in Kashmir and the northern Himalayan and trans-Himalayan region even very much earlier still. That full-fledged archaeological evidence has not yet been found is no objection, since not a single trace of the Rigvedic culture itself, whose existence is not doubted by anyone, has yet been found.

If the area in which the Indo-Europeans started splitting into Satem

[90] Aryans, p. 83.
[91] Aryans, p. 190.
[92] Aryans, p. 88.
[93] HCIP, p. 194.
[94] Karpāsa, p. 13-15.

and Kentum groups, and large sections started moving westwards (Europe and Cappadocia) and northwards (Chinese Turkestan), was in Kashmir and the northern Himalayas, the horse would certainly have been very well known to the proto-Indo-Europeans before their split and dispersal (and may even have been the catalyst leading to their westward migration).

2. A study of the common word for "horse" in Indo-European languages also indicates the same location (i.e. northernmost India). The cognate words are Sanskrit *aśva*, Avestan *aspa*, Old Lithuanian *ešva* or *ašva*, Illyrian *ikkos*, Ancient Greek *hippos*, Latin *equus*, Old Irish *ech*, Gothic *aihwa* and Old English *eoh*. From these, a proto-Indo-European word **ekwo* has been reconstructed.

Of all these cognate words, the Sanskrit word *aśva* in the Rigveda is the earliest attested one. Moreover, even in the Rigveda itself, *aśva* is already just *one* of the words for "horse". The others are *arvant*, *haya*, *vājin* and *sapti*. The oldest actual recorded specimen of an Indo-European word is in the Mitanni inscription giving the name *Birīdašva (Bṛhadaśva)*; and the Mitanni, as already explained,[95] were migrants from the Punjab region.

But these cognate words gave way to other words in almost all the branches. Thus modern Greek has *àlogos* instead of a derivative of the original Ancient Greek *hippos;* modern Romance languages have derivatives of Latin *caballus* (e.g. French *cheval*) rather than of *equus;* and almost all modern Indo-Aryan languages have derivatives of a later Sanskrit word *ghoṭaka* rather than of *aśva*. But even today, the word has survived, in its original meaning of "horse", in only two modern Indo-European languages: Persian *asp* and Sinhalese *asuwa* (both Indo-European languages concentred around India).

And while this common Indo-European word for "horse" is attested in an area concentred in and around India, and *only in this area*, from the very earliest known times to the present day, the Slavonic branch of Indo-European languages, which is spoken in and around South Russia, is ironically the only branch which does not attest this common word at all even in the very earliest languages.

3. The Kassites are believed to have "introduced the use of the horse for driving chariots"[96] into West Asia. Does the evidence of the Kassites indicate South Russia or India? A close look at the facts shows that the evidence points away from South Russia and towards India

[95] Ch. 11.
[96] Aryans, p. 18.

Firstly, the Kassites were worshippers of Šuriaš, Maruttaš and Indaš Secondly, even Marija Gimbutas, the arch-advocate of South Russia, admits about the Kurgan culture that "there is no evidence that horses were used for traction. Most probably oxen were used for this purpose."[97]

4. A linguistic analysis of the common Indo-European word for "horse", in its reconstructed form **ekwo*, appears to indicate that the proto-Indo-Europeans in their original homeland *could* have been introduced to both the horse itself as well as its name by some other people, rather than having themselves been its domesticators. According to Carl D. Buck, the word **ekwo* has a "root connection wholly obscure"[98], a circumstance which is often used by linguists to brand words (especially in Sanskrit) as "non-Aryan".

5. At the same time, a linguistic comparison of the words for "horse" in the Dravidian and Kol-Munda languages shows that the horse must have been known in India from very ancient times indeed; and both linguistics and archaeology disprove the idea that any so-called "Aryan invaders" introduced the horse to the "non-Aryans".

Sanskrit has many words for the horse: *aśva, arvant* or *arvvā, haya, vājin, sapti, turaṅga, kilvī, pracelaka* and *ghoṭaka,* to name the most prominent among them. And yet, the Dravidian languages show no trace of having borrowed any of these words; they have their own words. Tamil, for example, has the words *kudirai, parī* and *mā*. (Significantly, the word *mā* primarily means both "horse" as well as simply "animal", and in a secondary meaning it also means "elephant". This shows the close association of the horse and the "non-Aryan" Dravidian-language speakers.)

The Kol-Munda (Austric) languages use words which are very obviously borrowed from modern Indo-Aryan derivatives of the word *ghoṭaka,* but that is simply because these languages today are, anyway, heavily loaded with lexical borrowings from Sanskrit and New Indo-Aryan languages. The Santali and Mundari languages, however, have preserved the original Kol-Munda word *sādom.*

Not only has no linguist ever claimed that the Dravidian and Kol-Munda words for "horse" are borrowed from "Aryan" words, but in fact some linguists have even sought to establish that Sanskrit *ghotaka,* from which all the modern Indo-Aryan words are derived, is borrowed from the Kol-Munda languages!

[97] IE & IE, p. 161.
[98] ADOSS, p. 167.

The *Encyclopaedia Britannica*, in the course of a description of Indian archaeological finds, makes the following incidental observation: "Curiously, however, it is precisely in those regions that used iron, *and were associated with the horse*, that the Indo-Aryan languages did not spread. Even today, these are the regions of the Dravidian language group."[99]

From all this, it is clear that the close association of the Indo-Europeans with the horse does not show any connection with South Russia, but in fact shows connections with India.

The well-orchestrated attempt to identify South Russia and the Kurgan culture with the original Indo-European homeland and the proto-Indo-European culture respectively is very clearly an attempt to fit a square peg into a round hole.

[99] EB, Vol.9, p. 348.

THIRTEEN

HISTORICAL LINKS WITH URALIC AND SEMITIC

Indo-European languages are supposed to have several points of similarity with the Finno-Ugrian section of Uralic languages on the one hand, and the Semitic languages on the other. This is construed as evidence that the primitive Indo-Europeans must have had close contacts with the Finno-Ugrians as well as the Semites.

The conclusion drawn from this is that the primitive Indo-Europeans must have lived in a region situated between the original area of the Finno-Ugrians (which, according to Ghosh, was Central Russia) and that of the Semites (West Asia). This region could only be South Russia.

Let us examine the two cases, and see whether these conclusions are justified.

SEMITIC AND INDO-EUROPEAN

The alleged similarities with Semitic, consisting of "endings of nominative, accusative and genitive singular, certain elements of dual and plural formation and nominal and accusative singular of the pronominal flexion"[1], and perhaps a few items of vocabulary, do not boil down to much, and are not really considered to be of much importance. Warren Cowgill admits: "*If* Indo-European is related to other language families, e.g. to Hamito-Semitic (Afro-Asiatic) or Caucasian...*the number of cogent similarities is much smaller*."[2]

In fact, these similarities are important *only* in conjunction with the alleged similarities between Indo-European and Finno-Ugrian. As Ghosh puts it: "There must have been *at least historical contact of some sort* between early Indo-European and early Semitic. This is important, for if the primitive Indo-Europeans had on the one hand contact with the Finno-Ugrians of Central Russia and on the other with the Semites, then...the Indo-European cradle-land is no doubt South Russia, especially as *Indo-Finnic relations were decidedly more intimate*."[3]

Ghosh is certainly right on one point: the similarities are undoubt-

[1] HCIP, p. 211-12.
[2] EB, Vol. 9, p. 437.
[3] HCIP, p. 212.

edly a result of historical contact. But this historical contact has nothing to do with South Russia. There is plenty of archaeological evidence of trade and cultural contacts between ancient Semitic West Asia and the Indus Valley Civilization. Later, we have the Indo-European Hittites, Kassites and Mitanni in West Asia. Later still, there is plenty of literary evidence of trade and cultural relations between the Semites (the Hebrews, the Arabs and the Egyptians and Ethiopians) and the Indo-Europeans (Greeks, Romans and ancient Hindus). Even the Old Testament of the Bible gives evidence of trade and cultural relations with Greece on the one hand, and India on the other. All this, it must be noted, is in the centuries BC.

A parallel case is offered by that of the Nahuatl language of the pre-Columbian Aztec civilization of Mexico. T.S. Denison, in his various books (combined together under the title, *Mexican Linguistics*) showed that there was a very large number of correspondences between the Nahuatl language on the one hand, and the Classical Indo-European languages (Sanskrit, Greek and Latin) on the other, and claimed that the Aztecs were "the primitive Aryans of America." (Incidentally, Bhikkhu Chaman Lal, in his book, *Hindu America,* conclusively proved that the ancient Mexicans were culturally indebted to India, and his findings were accepted by the Government and the National Museum of Mexico.)

The American archaeologist-linguist, Cyrus H. Gordon, while rightly rejecting[4] Denison's view that Nahuatl was an "Aryan" language, has demonstrated that the linguistic evidence shown by Denison was an indication of linguistic influence due to historical contact rather than genetic relationship.

Moreover, Gordon brings the Semitic languages also into the picture. In one chapter[5] of his book, he gives examples of Greek, Latin, Sanskrit and Semitic words in Nahuatl. He demonstrates similarities[6] in the conjugation of the Nahuatl verb, and the conjugation of the Greek verb as well as the Hebrew verb. He demonstrates that the second and third person singular verbal prefixes, *ti-* and *ye-* respectively, in Nahuatl are paralleled by the second and third person singular verbal prefixes, *ti/te-* and *yi/ye-* respectively, in Hebrew.

He further identifies Mexico with the *Tarshish* mentioned in the Old Testament, and treats various references to *Tarshish* in the Old

[4] Before Columbus, p. 203, Note No. 120.
[5] Before Columbus, Ch. 7.
[6] Before Columbus, pp. 202-03, Note No. 119.

Testament as evidence of Mexican relations with the Greeks (Genesis 10:4), the Persians (Esther 1:14) and the Benjaminite Israelites (1 Chronicles 7:10).

If such distant contacts between the Mexicans and the Semites/ Indo-Europeans at such a comparatively late date (involving the Greeks and the Hebrews), and contacts which require to be demonstrated and proved, could result in so many and close linguistic correspondences, the much older and closer contacts between the Semites and the Indo-Europeans, contacts abundantly attested by archaeology and literature, could very easily result in the alleged similarities, without hypothetical contacts having to be postulated with South Russia.

URALIC AND INDO-EUROPEAN

The similarities between the Finno-Ugrian and Indo-European languages, consisting of "strong resemblances in a number of basic words or word parts, including personal, demonstrative, interrogative and relative pronouns, personal endings of verbs, the accusative case-ending *-m*, and such words as those for 'water' and 'name' "[7], are considered as evidence that "Indo-Finnic relations were decidedly more intimate."[8]

Let us examine this evidence.

1. The similarities are restricted to the Finno-Ugrian *section* of the Uralic *bra*nch of the Uralo-Altaic family of languages. They are not found even in the Samoyed languages which are closely allied to the Finno-Ugrian languages. As Robert T. Harms points out: "Finno-Ugrian dialects borrowed numerous terms from very early dialects of Indo-European. *These are lacking in the Samoyed languages.*"[9]

Hence the historical relations between Indo-European and Finno-Ugrian languages cannot be claimed to have been established at so early a date as to warrant the postulation of neighbouring or contiguous homelands. The Finno-Ugrian languages are found spoken within the Indo-European area from the earliest known times. Hence the similarities could have been acquired at any point of time after the Indo-European languages had spread out over this area.

2. The similarities are the result of a one-way borrowing. All the similar words in the two families have proved to be Indo-European words borrowed by the Finno-Ugrian languages. Attempts have been made to brand *one* word as being a Finno-Ugrian word borrowed by

[7] EB, Vol. 9, p. 436.
[8] HCIP, p. 212.
[9] EB, Vol. 18, p. 1027.

proto-Indo-European: the proto-Indo-European word **medhu*, "honey" or "mead", reconstructed from Sanskrit *madhu*, Old Slavonic *medŭ*, Lithuanian *medus*, Tocharian *mit*, Irish *miodh* or *mil*, Greek *mèli*, Latin *mel*, Gothic *midus*, Armenian *melr*, Albanian *mjall* (Finnish *mete*, Hungarian *mez*).

However, Childe rejects this idea; "It is in any case certain that the Finno-Ugrians borrowed many words from Indo-European languages ...*Indo-European borrowings from Finnish*, of which **medhu* has been cited as an example, *are unproven*."[10] And in fact, the *Encyclopaedia Britannica*[11] clearly mentions **medhu* as an *Indo-European* word borrowed by *Finno-Ugrian*.

It is not only in vocabulary that Indo-European borrowings from Finno-Ugrian are unproven. Cowgill points out that "Influence of non-Indo-European languages on the sounds and grammar of proto-Indo-European are not demonstrable, partly because there is no direct evidence about the languages that were in contact with Indo-European before 3000 BC."[12]

There are, of course, local borrowings by individual Scandinavian or East European languages from Finnish or Hungarian, but these are obviously latter-day borrowings. There are no features peculiar to Indo-Iranian languages which can be traced back to a Finno-Ugrians origin. *That* would have been evidence of a sort, since any Finno-Ugrian influence on Indo-Iranian languages could only have been in the prehistoric past.

Hence, the similarities are obviously a result of borrowing by Finno-Ugrian from Indo-European at a date *after* the rest of the Indo-Europeans had parted from the Indo-Iranians and occupied their present habitats.

3. In any case, this method, of trying to locate the original homeland on the basis of similarities with other language families, is a very speculative one. Innumerable claims have been made linking different groups of languages to each other; and often the claims have been not merely of "historical contact in early times", but of organic or genetic relationship. And if we examine two prominent claims, both concerning the Finno-Ugrian languages, the similarities between the Indo-European and Finno-Ugrian languages can in fact be given a totally different interpretation.

[10] Aryans, pp. 89-90.
[11] EB, Vol. 18, p. 1027.
[12] EB, Vol. 9, p. 438.

The Hungarian scholar, William Hevesy, presented a strongly argued case linking the Austric (Kol-Munda) languages of India with the Finno-Ugrian languages. "According to Hevesy, Munda or Kol belongs to the Finno-Ugrian speech group... Hevesy bases his views on certain points of agreement between the Kol speeches on the one hand and the Finno-Ugrian speeches on the other." But Hevesy's claims, according to S.K. Chatterji, have neither been confirmed, nor effectively refuted by any other scholar, since it would be exceedingly rare to find "a competent linguistician who is equally at home in Kol and in Finno-Ugrian."[13]

And, according to Kamil V. Zvelebil in the *Encyclopaedia Britannica*: "The Dravidian languages have remained an isolated family until now...the most promising and plausible hypothesis is that of a linguistic relationship with the Uralic (Hungarian, Finnish) and Altaic (Turkish, Mongol) language groups."[14]

If claims, on the basis of similarities, can be made even of organic or genetic relationship of the Finno-Ugrian languages with the Austric languages on the one hand and the Dravidian languages on the other, these similarities may be presumed to be at least the result of "historical contact in early times".

So, to use the logic employed by the advocates of South Russia: if the primitive Finno-Ugrian had, on the one hand, contact with the Indo-Europeans, and on the other with the Kol-Munda people, and also with the Dravidians, then the Finno-Ugrian cradleland is no doubt India.

Therefore, the similarities between Indo-European and Finno-Ugrian certainly do not show South Russia to be the original Aryan homeland.

4. Moreover, this method of locating the original homeland can cut both ways. A very much stronger case can be built up showing that the Indo-European homeland lies in India, on the basis of similarities with another language family. This case is much stronger because

a. The basic points of similarity are found in the two families in their entirety (unlike the alleged similarities of the Indo-European family with only the Finno-Ugrian section of the Uralic branch of the Uralo-Altaic family, or with only the Semitic branch of the Semito-Hamitic family).
b. The similarities cannot be attributed to latter-day borrowings, since the two families are not spoken in common (like Finno-

[13] HCIP, pp. 152-53.
[14] EB, Vol. 5, p. 989.

Ugrian and Indo-European) or contiguous (like Semitic and Indo-European) areas.

c. Inspite of the non-contiguous distribution of the two families, there *are* hypotheses—and separate hypotheses—which suggest a common homeland for both of them.

This other language-family is the Austronesian family of languages.

THE AUSTRONESIAN CONNECTION

Isidore Dyen, in his paper *The Case of the Austronesian Languages*,[15] presented at the 3rd Indo-European Conference at the University of Pennsylvania, 1966, has made out a case showing the similarities between many basic words reconstructed in the proto-Indo-European and proto-Austronesian languages.

1. He gives a list of many words showing similarities between the two families:

Among the numerals are the very first four. Proto-Indo-European **sem*, **dwōu*/**dwai*, **tri*, and **qʷetʷor* and proto-Austronesian **esa*, **dewha*, **telu* and **pati*/**epati* (Malay *sa*/*satu*, *dua*, *tiga* and *epat*. Tocharian *sas*/*se*, "one". Rumanian *patru*, "four". Welsh *pedwar*, "four").

Among the personal pronouns are the words for "I, we, you, he/she/it, (demonstrative) this/he". Proto-Indo-European **eĝh*, **n̊sme*, **yu*, **eyo*/**eya* and **to*/**eno*. Proto-Austronesian **aku*, (Tagalog) *Ka-mi*, (Tagalog) *ka-yo*, **ia* and **itu*/**inu*.

Among other basic words are the words for "water" and "land". Proto-Indo-European **wer* and **ter-s*. Proto-Austronesian **wair* and **darat* (Sanskrit *vāri* and *dharā*/*dharatī*).

Dyen gives many more such words, and adds that "the number of comparisons could be increased at least slightly, perhaps even substantially, without a severe loss of quality."[16]

2. The Indo-European languages are spoken from India westwards. The Austronesian languages are spoken from Malaysia eastwards: Indonesia, Philippines, and most of the islands in the eastern Indian Ocean and the Pacific Ocean, including New Zealand, Hawaii, Fiji, etc., except for an isolated migrant group in Malagasy off the coast of Africa.

Moreover, these Austronesian languages have occupied a major

[15] IE & IE, pp. 431-40.

[16] IE & IE, p. 439.

stretch of their present habitat since thousands of years. According to the *Encyclopaedia Britannica*: "Estimates indicate that diversification of Austronesian languages began around 4000 to 5000 years ago in the New Hebrides, in New Caledonia and in the Solomons, and earlier still in the region of New Guinea."[17]

Hence, if a historical relationship existed between Indo-European and Austronesian, it must have been at a remote period, since the common words are common to the entire range of the two families.

3. Isidore Dyen, it must be noted, is not drawing a comparison between Indo-European and Austronesian in order to buttress any pet theory of his own, of a common homeland for the two families. In fact, he points out at the very outset that the hypothesis of similarities proposed by him is not, so far as he knows, supported by any evidence of a common homeland:

"The hypothesis to be dealt with is not favoured by considerations of the distribution of the two families...The probable homelands of the respective families appear to be very distant; that of the Indo-European is probably in Europe, whereas that of the Austronesian is no farther west than the longitude of the Malay Peninsula in any reasonable hypothesis, and has been placed considerably farther east in at least one hypothesis. The hypothesis suggested by linguistic evidence is not thus facilitated by a single homeland hypothesis."[18]

In short, not only is Dyen *not* prejudiced in favour of a single homeland hypothesis, he is in fact prejudiced by his preconceived notions as to the Indo-European homeland being " probably in Europe" and the Austronesian homeland being "no farther west than the longitude of the Malay Peninsula", and inclined to allow these preconceived notions to override what he describes as "the hypothesis suggested by linguistic evidence."

But, inspite of this inclination, Dyen ends his thesis on a note of doubt: "I must confess that I am impressed with the extent to which I have been successful in gathering matchings between the reconstruction of the two families. Granted that thus far I have not wavered in my steadfast belief in the likelihood that an Austronesian–Indo-European relationship cannot be demonstrated, should I waver now?"[19]

The above is, of course, an attempt by Dyen to end his thesis on a rhetorical note; but the fact remains that Dyen *has* indeed, in his thesis,

[17] EB, Vol. 2, p. 486.
[18] IE & IE, p. 431.
[19] IE & IE, pp. 439-40.

made an *unmotivated* presentation of linguistic facts whose logical interpretation runs counter to what he believes to be the actual case, and that the linguistic facts are impressive.

The facts are even more impressive if looked upon as indicating a historical relationship in very ancient times leading to mutual influence in the formative stage, than as indicating an organic or genetic relationship.

4. The only objection Dyen has against the logical interpretation of what he admits to be the "linguistic evidence" is that so far as he knows, or so far as his preconceived notions will allow him to accept, "the hypothesis suggested by linguistic evidence is not facilitated by a single homeland hypothesis."

However, his objection is totally unfounded. There are hypotheses which suggest a common homeland for the two families, that common homeland being India. So far as Indo-European languages are concerned, a hypothesis of an Indian homeland has been in the running ever since the concept of an original Indo-European homeland was first thought of.

And, as for the Austronesian languages, here is what S.K. Chatterji has to say on the subject—S.K. Chatterji, an ardent advocate of the Aryan invasion theory, and a person who certainly cannot be accused of being a supporter of an Indian homeland theory or of any idea which would facilitate such a theory: "It seems that India was the centre from which the Austric race spread into the lands and islands of the east and Pacific."[20] And again, "The Austric speech...in its original form (as the ultimate source of both the Austro-Asiatic and *the Austronesian* branches) could very well have been characterised within India."[21]

The similarities between the Indo-European and Austronesian families therefore indicate that India was the original Indo-European homeland.

THE NUMERAL "ONE"

As we have seen, the similarities with Finno-Ugrian can be turned around to show that India was the original homeland; and similarities with Austronesian also show the same thing. Let us take one more example, the Indo-European words for the very first numeral "one", and see what it indicates.

The majority of Indo-European languages have words for "one"

[20] HCIP, p. 153.
[21] HCIP, p. 148.

which are derived from two reconstructed proto-Indo-European words: **oi-no* and **oi-ko*, which are prominent in the non-Indo-Iranian and the Indo-Iranian branches respectively (as already explained, these are the two divisions suggested by linguists for identifying "early Indo-European" words). Thus the word **oi-no* is not represented in the Indo-Iranian languages at all, and the word **oi-ko* is not represented in the non-Indo-Iranian languages at all.

Now there is one language which has forms comparable to both **oi-no* and **oi-ko*, and this is the non-Indo-European language Burushaski spoken in northern (Pak-occupied) Kashmir. Burushaski "one" = *hin* (or *han*) and *hik*. Does this, perhaps, indicate the location of the area where the non-Indo-Iranian branches split away from the Indo-Iranian branch?

There are some Indo-European words for "one" which are not derived from either **oi-no* or **oi-ko*. But almost all of these are connected with the Sanskrit words *sama* and *eva*, both of which mean "same". Thus Tocharian A to the north of Kashmir has *sas* (masculine) and *säm* (feminine). (Tocharian B has a common *se*.) The Greek *heis* (masculine) is obviously cognate to the Tocharian. Avestan to the west of India had *aeva* and Old Persian had *aiwa;* and some modern Iranian languages have *eva*-forms—and so does a modern Dardic language Bashgali, which has *ev* (although many modern Iranian and most modern Dardic languages, including modern Persian *yak* and Kashmiri *akh*, have the normal **oi-ko*-forms). Thus all the evidence seems to point towards Kashmir.

But there are still two major words which cannot be satisfactorily explained: Greek *mía* (neuter) and the sole Armenian word *mi*. Compare the Austric (Kol-Munda) words for "one": Santali *mit*, Mundari *miť/mīať*, Korku *mīa*, Kharia *moi*, Savara *mi*, Juang *min*, Gadaba *mui-rō*. Could the Greek and Armenian words be derivatives of the Austric words? The Austric words are certainly the original, for a cognate word *môt* is attested by the Austric Vietnamese language.

Thus, by trying to locate the original homeland in South Russia on the basis of similarities with other families, protagonists of South Russia only succeed in opening up a Pandora's box of similarity-theories which prove India to be the original homeland.

FOURTEEN

CHRONOLOGICAL AND GEOGRAPHICAL TIMETABLE AND THE INDO-IRANIAN HOMELAND

The chronological and geographical timetable of the Aryan invasion of India is as follows:

1. The Indo-Iranians separated from the other Indo-Europeans, and from their original homeland, and came and settled in Central Asia around 2000 BC.
2. After staying together for a considerable period of time in Central Asia, the Indo-Aryans and the Iranians separated from each other and moved into the Punjab and Iran respectively, and the distinctive Vedic culture started developing in the Punjab around 1500 BC.
3. The Rigveda, the earliest of the Vedic texts, was composed around 1000 BC.

Let us examine the above contentions on the following counts:

1. The Date of the Rigveda.
2. The location of the Indo-Iranian homeland.
3. The location of the original Indo-European homeland.

THE DATE OF THE RIGVEDA

The Rigveda was originally dated at 1000 BC by Max Müller, and ever since then the date has been treated as sacrosanct by the invasion theorists, almost as if this was the date written in the Rigveda itself.

A fact determinedly ignored by them is that Max Müller himself, when faced with criticism on this point, was compelled to take back his words. K.C. Verma[1] quotes the following admissions by Max Müller:

"I need hardly say that I agree with almost every word of my critics. I have repeatedly dwelt on the entirely hypothetical character of the dates I ventured to assign to the first three periods of Vedic literature. All I have claimed for them has been that *they are minimum dates.*"[2]

"If now we ask how we can fix the date of these three periods, it is quite clear that *we cannot fix a terminum a quo*, whether the Vedic hymns were composed 1000 or 2000 or 3000 years BC, no power on earth will ever determine."[3]

[1] MMR, pp. 99-100.
[2] Preface to the text of Rigveda, Vol. 4, p. xiii.
[3] Collected Works, Vol. II, p. 91.

As K.C. Verma points out: "All attempts to date the Vedic literature on linguistic grounds have failed miserably for the simple reason that (a) the conclusions of comparative philology are often speculative and (b) no-one has yet succeeded in showing how much change should take place in a language in a given period. The only safe method is astronomical."[4]

Even A.D. Pusalker, a staunch supporter of the invasion theory, is compelled to admit that "the presumed age of the Rigveda is really no barrier to the Aryan authorship of the Indus culture (if other evidence proves that hypothesis) for...that age is not known with even an approximate degree of certainty."[5]

But protagonists of the Aryan invasion theory are not deterred by the constraints of linguistics and logic. Bulldozing past all these obstacles, they still manage to arrive at the magical date of 1000 BC. The following arguments by B.K. Ghosh may be taken as an example:

"From a purely linguistic point of view, the Rigveda in its present form cannot be dated much earlier than 1000 BC. The language of the Rigveda is certainly no more different from that of the Avestan Gāthās than is Old English from Old High German, and therefore they must be assigned to approximately the same age; and the relation between the language of the Gāthās and that of the Old Persian inscriptions of the sixth century BC cannot be better visualised than by comparing the former with Gothic and the latter with Old High German. Now if the inscriptions of the Achaemenid emperors of Iran were composed in Old High German, what would be the date assigned to Ulfilas' Gothic Bible? Surely something like 1000 BC. This then would be the approximate date of the Gāthās of Avesta...with which the Rigveda in its present form must have been more or less contemporaneous. Thus from general linguistic considerations we get for the Rigvedic language, as known to us, an approximate date of 1000 BC."[6]

The logic used by Ghosh is astounding, to say the least. Using a peculiar kind of linguistic arithmetic known only to himself, Ghosh manages to quantify linguistic relationships and linguistic changes, and to derive linguistic and chronological equations out of them.

He first quantifies the linguistic relationship between the language of the Rigveda and the language of the Gāthās. Then he quantifies the linguistic relationship between Old English and Old High German. He

[4] MMR, p. 99.
[5] HCIP, p. 194.
[6] HCIP, pp. 203-04.

finds these two linguistic quantities equal to each other, thereby giving a linguistic equation. From this, he derives a chronological equation: Since Old English is contemporaneous with Old High German, therefore the language of the Rigveda must be contemporaneous with the language of the Gāthās.

Further, he quantifies the linguistic change from Gothic to Old High German. Then, he quantifies the linguistic change from the language of the Gāthās to the language of the Old Persian inscriptions of the 6th century BC. He finds these two linguistic quantities equal to each other, thereby giving a linguistic equation. From this, he derives a chronological equation: Since Gothic is roughly 400 to 500 years older than Old High German, therefore the language of the Gāthās must be 400 to 500 years older than the language of the Old Persian inscriptions of the 6th century BC.

Combining the two above chronological equations Ghosh derives 1000 BC as the date of the Gāthās, and therefore of the Rigveda.

The incredibly arbitrary and utterly whimsical nature of the above procedure will be obvious to anyone. The faultiness of his logic becomes even more clear if we examine[7] the present state of linguistic development of the two languages, English and German, chosen by Ghosh to illustrate his equations.

It is only by using whimsical criteria of this sort that the Rigveda can be dated to 1000 BC, the date which Max Müller has admitted to be the *minimum date*, i.e. the date than which the Rigveda may be thousands of years earlier, but not an year later.

The more substantial evidence, however, suggests that the composition of the earliest hymns of the Rigveda started around 4500 BC, if not slightly earlier. Let us examine this evidence:

1. The Astronomical evidence proves that the earliest Rigvedic compositions date from the fifth millennium BC.

K.C. Verma, points out that Lokmanya Tilak and Hermann Jacobi "established that the Vedic period commences in 4500 BC, and that the bulk of the hymns of the Rigveda were composed between 3500 BC and 2500 BC, when vernal equinox was in the Orion (4500–3500 BC) and later receded (3500–2500 BC) to Rohinī; the Krittikā period during which the existing Brāhmanas and Upanisads were composed extended from 2500–800 BC. They have been supported on independent grounds by P.C. Sengupta, *Ancient Indian Chronology*, 1947, pp. 60–115 (he has also shown on pp. 101 ff. that the solar eclipse in Rigveda V.

[7] See Ch. 17.

40.5–9 took place on July 26, 3928 BC and the beginnings of the Brāhmaṇa literature is to be traced back to 3500 BC)..."[8] He adds: "No one, to the best of my knowledge, has so far been able to refute the arguments advanced by these scholars."[9]

A few attempts to find fault with their arguments have been answered in full detail by other eminent astronomers like B.V. Kameshwara Aiyar,[10] Gorakh Prasad[11] and N.N. Law.[12] Astronomy, it must be remembered, is a precise science, not to be confused with astrology; and the astronomical observations in the Rigveda, and in other Vedic and Puranic texts, are the best and most reliable evidence in dating these texts, or at least in dating the "core" or the earlier sections of these texts. As K.C. Verma points out: "The only safe method is astronomical."[13]

According to Verma,[14] Mary Agnes Clerk, in the *Encyclopaedia Britannica*[15] in speaking about a late Rigvedic passage, admits "that the Krittikā passage could not have been composed later than 1800 BC and it harks back to 2300 BC". The Sanskrit texts are full of such passages containing astronomical observations and statements.

Some scholars have tried to brand the astronomical statements given in the Vedic literature, the Purāṇas and the Epics as fabrications based on astronomical back calculations. However, not only does this attitude show a firm refusal to accept facts, and a willingness to attribute sinister motives to the ancient Indians (notably, a tendency to deliberately doctor their texts with fabricated astronomical statements in order to befool future astronomers); but it also presumes the ancient Indians to have been aware of certain particular astronomical techniques required in order to carry out such fabrications. According to K.C. Verma, "it has been proved beyond doubt that before the discoveries of Newton, Liebnitz, La Place, La Grange, etc., *back calculations could not have been made;* (hence) they (the astronomical statements) are based on observational astronomy."[16]

The noted astronomer, physicist and mathematician John Playfair,

[8] MMR, p. 99, footnotes.
[9] MMR, pp. 100-01.
[10] *Journal of the Mythic Society*, Vol. XII, 1921-22, pp. 171-93, 223-49, 357-66.
[11] *Journal of Bihar and Orissa Res. Soc.*, XXI, 1935, pp. 120-36.
[12] *Age of the Rigveda*, 1965, pp. 1-160.
[13] MMR, p. 99.
[14] MMR, p. 99, footnotes.
[15] EB, 11th Edition, Vol. 28, pp. 995-96, *Zodiac*.
[16] MMR, p. 124.

in the *Edinburgh Review*, 1790, reproduced by Dharampal[17], shows that the Indian Zodiac originated in 4300 BC, and rejects any idea of the astronomical statements in the Sanskrit texts being fabrications.

2. K.D. Sethna[18] proves conclusively, on the evidence of the use of cotton in north-west India, that the Rigveda preceded the Harappan Culture in the Indus Valley.

"The Rigveda no less than the Harappa culture, flourished in the Indus Valley."[19] The Rigveda does not mention cotton even once; and unlike some other things which may happen to have not been mentioned in the Rigveda just by chance, but are plentifully mentioned in other post-Rigvedic texts, cotton is not mentioned in *any* of the earlier Vedic texts: "none of the three other Vedas, none of the numerous Brāhmaṇas and Āraṇyakas, none of the early principal Upanishads contain the word *karpāsa*."[20] It is mentioned for the first time in the early Sūtras.

It is not as if these texts do not contain references to cloth or clothes: "The Vedic literature from the Rigveda down to the Sūtra period contains numerous references to weavers, the art of weaving, the weaver's shuttle, wearing of clothes like turbans, shirts, etc., soiled garments and washermen."[21] The texts also contain very frequent references to wool (*sāmulya* and *ūrṇā*) and to a cloth made from the bark of the *tripā* or *triparṇa* tree (*tārpya).*

Cotton (*karpāsa)*, is mentioned for the first time in the earliest Sūtras, and silk (*kauśeya*) is mentioned for the first time in the Vāsiṣṭha Dharmasutra, which is considered to be a rather late Sūtra. Archaeologically, cotton is first attested in the Indus sites around 2500 BC, and silk is first attested in Nevasa around 1250 BC. This fits in perfectly with the astronomical dating of the Sūtras (2500–600 BC) by Tilak and Jakobi.

This proves that the age of the four Vedas, the Brāhmaṇas and Āraṇyakas and the early principal Upaniṣads preceded the age of the Indus culture. K.D. Sethna[22] further confirms this by demonstrating how the culture of the Rigveda gradually developed into the culture of the Indus Civilization.

[17] *Indian Science and Technology in the Eighteenth Century* (Impex India, Delhi, 1971), pp. 9-69, specifically p. 63.

[18] Karpāsa, pp. 18-39.

[19] Karpāsa, p. 41.

[20] Karpāsa, p. 24.

[21] Karpāsa, p. 19.

[22] Karpāsa, pp. 40-63.

3. Sethna[23] also proves, from a totally different angle, that the Sūtras were contemporaneous with the Indus culture, by collating references in the Sumerian texts with references in the Sūtra and post-Sūtra literature.

Cuneiform texts from Mesopotamia, inscribed on clay tablets, dated 2350–1700 BC, frequently mention a far-away kingdom called Meluhha (pronounced *Melukkha* or *Milukkha*) with which the Sumerians carried on regular trade. It has now been accepted that Meluhha was none other than the Indus region during Harappan times. The evidence for this is very clear.

Archaeological evidence shows that Mesopotamia had close trade relations with the Harappan region from the second half of the third millennium BC, and that the trade slowly diminished until it petered out in the first quarter of the second millennium BC; the Mesopotamian clay tablets show an identical trade relationship between Mesopotamia and Meluhha. The Harappan region is the easternmost region with which archaeology connects the Mesopotamians; Meluhha was supposed to be the most distant kingdom with which the Mesopotamians had trade, and was moreover supposed to be the last of a series of three kingdoms named Dilmun, Makan and Meluhha; and Dilmun and Makan have now been accepted as being the names for Bahrain and the Trucial-Oman-cum-Southeast-Iranian-coast region respectively.

The products of Meluhha, mentioned in the Mesopotamian texts, were gold, ivory and precious woods, copper, lapis lazuli and peacocks (called *dha-ja-musen*). The peacock is a native only of India; copper and gold were plentifully used by the Indus people as also lapis lazuli, which in fact was found only in Afghanistan, and ivory-carving was a major Indus handicraft ("a couple of pieces of ivory work from Meluhha—a comb and two human-headed bulls mounted on a pedestal supported by wheels—were found in a grave of the Akkad period of Kish. Ivory combs and model oxen mounted on wheels as well as human-headed animal figurines are familiar Indus articles"[24]). Moreover, the Old Testament, in a later age, mentions more or less these same items (ivory, peacocks, sandalwood) as imports from India.

The identity of the Indus culture with the Meluhha of the Mesopotamian texts is therefore certain.

Coming to Indian sources, the Rigveda is centred wholly in and around the Indus Valley (more or less modern Pakistan). If the Rigve-

[23] Karpāsa, pp. 64-98.
[24] Karpāsa, p. 79.

dic "Aryans" had been invaders who attacked and destroyed the last remnants of the Indus Civilization in the mid-second millennium BC, the Rigveda should have given indication of the name "Melukkha" or some comparable word, and even if it were the pre-Rigvedic "Aryans", who had done the destroying, some memory of the name should have survived: it must be remembered that while the Rigveda shows either ignorance or reticence about many parts of India and all the areas outside India, there is no reticence at all in its descriptions of the Saptasindhu region.

However, the word is mentioned for the first time in the *post-Rigvedic* Vedic literature. In this literature, the epicentre of Vedic culture has shifted eastwards from the Saptasindhu region to Āryāvarta, the Ganga-Yamuna doab region.

The Śatapatha Brāhmaṇa (III.2.1,24) first refers to the Indus people as *mleccha* (from the verb *mlec*, meaning "to speak indistinctly", derived from the Sanskrit root *mlic*), and gives an example of their corrupted speech. The Vedic people, thus, appear to have harboured contempt for the Indus people, who succeeded them as inhabitants of the Saptasindhu.

However, it is only in the Sūtras that we find this contempt, for the contemporary people of the Saptasindhu, turning into active aversion. The exact reason for this hostility will be made clear in later chapters.[25] Here, let us only examine the identity of the *mlecchas* mentioned in the Sūtras. Although the term came to mean any foreigner in later times, in the Sūtras it referred to specific peoples.

The oldest example, the Gautama Dharmasūtra (IX.17) refers to *Mlecchadeśa*. Another early Sūtra, the Baudhāyana Dharmasūtra (I.1.2, 14-15), refers to kingdoms that are of mixed origin ("corrupted" nature), and insists that anyone who visits these kingdoms needs purification. The kingdoms named include "all the post-Harappa culture sites outside the Ganges Valley", including Āraṭṭa=Punjab, Sindhu=Sind, Sauvīra=the Multan region, and Saurashtra. A later Sūtra, the Viṣṇu Dharmasūtra (84.1-2), practically bans all visits to any *mleccha* kingdom except on a pilgrimage.

Even the late Manusmriti (II.17-23) is very specific in its definition of *Mlecchadeśa* as the land "comprising the territory from the Sutluj to the Kabul in the north and to the Dravida country in the south".[26] As the Manusmṛiti, though a late text, has recorded the narrowest orthodoxies

[25] Ch. 19, 21, 23.
[26] Karpāsa, p. 65.

of the Sūtra period, the geographical definition given in that text may safely be accepted as the original orthodox definition of that word.

And this definition clearly delineates the area of the Indus Civilization. The term Dravida in orthodox tradition does not refer to the Dravidian languages. The term *pañca*-Dravida refers to the Brahmins of present-day Tamil Nadu, Kerala, Andhra, Karnataka, Maharashtra and Gujarat: so the phrase "to the Dravida country in the south" obviously defines Gujarat as the southern limit of *Mlecchadeśa* proper.

The Prakrit forms of the word *mleccha*, as attested in the earliest Buddhist texts, are *melakha* (in the Aṅguttara Nikāya) and *milakkha* (in the Dīgha Nikāya, III.264). Compare these words with *Meluhha* (pronounced *Melukkha* or *Milukkha*) of the Mesopotamian texts.

Obviously, therefore, the Mlecchadeśa so prominently featuring in the Sūtras is the same as the Meluhha so prominently featuring in the Mesopotamian texts dated 2350–1700 BC. This confirms the astronomical dating of the earliest Sūtras at 2500 BC, which, as already pointed out, is also confirmed by the archaeological and literary evidence of cotton.

Therefore, the entire pre-Sūtra literature (going backwards in time, the early principal Upaniṣads, the Āraṇyakas, the Brāhmaṇas, the other three Veda Saṁhitās, and the Rigveda Saṁhitā, in that order) clearly goes back beyond 2500 BC.

4. Although not so chronologically specific as the evidence already cited, there is other evidence which points to the antiquity of the Rigveda.

Firstly, K.C. Verma cites the following evidence: "Gurdip Singh ('The Indus Valley Culture' in *Archaeology and Physical Anthropology* in *Oceania*, Vol. VI, No.2, July 1971, pp. 177-189)... has shown that NW India....became arid in ^{14}C date 1800 BC (which becomes 2100 BC when MASCA correction is applied). Thus it is reasonable to hold that Sarasvati, river par excellence of the Rigveda, dried up in the period 2100–2000 BC, and hence many Vedic works which praise the splendour of that river must antedate this period."[27]

Secondly, the *Inar* (Indra)-worshipping Hittites, whom the *Larousse Encyclopaedia of Mythology* instinctively describes as having "come from India"[28] and who invaded Cappadocia in 1950 BC, and were obviously far travellers from their original land (the Vedic northwest), prove that the Rigveda far antedates this period. The bulk of the

[27] MMR, p. 101, footnote.
[28] LEM, p. 85.

Rigvedic hymns may therefore be dated, as done by Tilak and Jacobi on astronomical grounds, mainly between 3500–2500 BC, with the earliest hymns going back to 4500 BC and the latest hymns coming down to perhaps the latest date at which the Rigveda was standardised.

THE LOCATION OF THE INDO-IRANIAN HOMELAND

The concept of an Indo-Iranian homeland is based on the fact that it is not only in respect of linguistic affinity that the Vedic Aryans and the Gathaic Iranians can be grouped closely together, but in respect of cultural and religious affinity as well. As Ghosh points out, "A specific Indo-Iranian culture and religion...may be reconstructed at least partially, by comparing the Veda and the Avesta"[29] and this presupposes not only that the Indo-Aryans and Iranians must have had a common home not shared by the other Indo-Europeans, but also that "the Indo-Iranians must have passed a long time in their....common home."[30]

That the Vedic "Aryans" and the Iranians shared a common homeland and culture for a long period before they separated from each other is therefore an unavoidable hypothesis. But where was this common homeland located?

Protagonists of the Aryan invasion theory declare this common homeland to have been in Central Asia "in the Pamir region or in Russian Turkestan."[31]

However, Max Müller puts the true state of affairs in a nutshell: "The Zoroastrians were a colony from Northern India. They had been together for a time with the people whose sacred songs have been preserved to us in the Veda. A schism took place and the Zoroastrians migrated westward to Arachosia and Persia."[32]

While the contention that the common homeland was in Central Asia is nothing but wishful thinking, the contention that the Iranians and Vedic people shared a common homeland and culture in the Punjab region is borne out by solid evidence:

1. The Indian traditions, in the Rigveda and in later Sanskrit texts, give no indications whatsoever that the Vedic people had entered the Punjab region from outside. On the other hand, the Iranian traditions clearly state that their ancestors came to Iran from outside.

A.L. Basham, even while expounding the Aryan invasion theory,

[29] HCIP, p. 218.
[30] Ibid.
[31] HCIP, p. 206.
[32] *Science of Language*, Vol. 2, p. 279.

admits: "Direct testimony to the assumed fact is lacking, and no tradition of an early home beyond the frontier survives in India."[33]

B.K. Ghosh also admits that there is a "total absence of extra-territorial memory in the Rigveda"[34] and that "it really cannot be proved that the Vedic Aryans retained any memory of their extra-Indian associations".[35]

Ghosh further contrasts this with the Iranian traditions: "The Iranians had retained a distinct memory of the Indo-Iranian common home (Erānvēj) in their mythology, but the Indo-Aryans....have nothing to say on the point."[36]

The natural conclusion one would derive from this is that the Vedic Aryans retained no memories of extra-Indian associations for the simple reason that there *were* no extra-Indian associations of which they could retain extraterritorial memories; and that the common homeland that the Iranians remembered was probably situated in the only homeland known to the Rigveda—the Punjab region.

2. The Iranian traditions, in any case, leave no scope for doubts on this issue. Bhargava points out: "The evidence of the Avesta makes it clear that sections of these Aryans in course of time left Sapta Sindhu and settled in Iran. The first chapter of the Vendidad or the handbook of the Parsees enumerates sixteen holy lands created by Ahura Mazda which were later rendered unfit for the residence of man (i.e. the ancestors of the Iranians) on account of different things created by Angra Mainyu, the evil spirit of the Avesta... The first of these lands was of course *Airyana Vaejo* which was abandoned by the ancestors of the Iranians because of severe winter and snow; of the others, one was *Hapta Hindu,* i.e. *Saptasindhu.* This is clearest proof that the Aryan ancestors of the Iranians were once part and parcel of the Aryans of Sapta Sindhu before they finally settled in Iran. Excessive heat created in this region by Angra Mainyu was, according to the testimony of the Vendidad, the reason why the ancestors of the Iranians left this country."[37]

3. The Hapta Hindu mentioned in the Vendidad is obviously the Saptasindhu (the Punjab region), and the first land, "abandoned by the ancestors of the Iranians because of severe winter and snow" before

[33] *The Oxford History of India*, 3rd edition, p. 53.
[34] HCIP, p. 206
[35] HCIP, p. 204.
[36] HCIP, p. 219.
[37] IVA, pp. 50-51.

they came to the Saptasindhu region and settled down among the Vedic people, is obviously Kashmir.

Even today the Dardic languages of the Kashmir region share many features of the Iranian languages, to the extent that many linguists classify them as holding "an intermediate position between Iranian and Indian".[38] And the Bashgali language still uses the word *ev* for "one" (Avestan *aeva*, Old Persian *aiwa*, but modern Persian *yak*).

4. The *soma* plant *(haoma* in the Avesta) was the main libation offered in the rituals of both the Rigveda and the Avesta. Today no one really has any idea of the exact identity of the *soma* plant, and it is known only from the texts.

While the Avesta merely mentions that the plant grew on a certain mountain, the Rigveda[39] clearly states that it is a plant growing only, or originally, on the Mūjavat mountain in the north of Punjab. This fact is confirmed by the Vājasaneyī Saṁhitā,[40] the Āpastamba Śrautasūtra,[41] Yāska's Nirukta,[42] and various other texts and commentaries.

This confirms that the common home of the Vedic people and the Iranians was in the Punjab.

5. A comparison of the post-Rigvedic Vedic culture and the Iranian culture shows that the Iranian culture is also post-Rigvedic. This means that the Iranians migrated to Iran from the Punjab, since the Rigvedic culture is definitely native to the Punjab and has no "extra-Indian associations" or "extraterritorial memory". Even B.K. Ghosh refers to the "distinctively Indian Rigvedic culture"[43], and calls it "a distinct product of the Indian soil."[44]

P.L. Bhargava gives many specific examples to show that the original Gods of the Rigveda are found in the Avesta in drastically changed forms, thereby showing the Avesta to be post-Rigvedic. He also points out that the thread ceremony, which is unknown to the Rigveda, is common to both the later Vedic traditions as well as the Iranian traditions; and that the theory of transmigration, which also is unknown to the Rigveda, is strongly present in both the later Vedic scriptures as well as in the Hoshang and the Nama Mihabad of the Iranians. According to him, "all these are strong proof that the separation

[38] ODBL, p. 26.
[39] Rigveda, 10.34.1.
[40] Vājasaneyī Saṁhitā, 3.61.
[41] Āpastamba Śrautasūtra, 12.5.11.
[42] Nirukta, 9.8.
[43] HCIP, p. 219.
[44] HCIP, p. 206.

of the Iranians and the Indians took place after the completion of the bulk of the Rigveda."[45]

The earlier Rigvedic hymns contain many references to the God *Dyaus* or *Dyaus Pitar* (also found in the Greek and Latin traditions as *Zeus* or *Zeus Pater* and *Jupiter* respectively) who is not found in later Vedic traditions or in the Iranian traditions. Thus, while the Rigveda goes back to the proto-Indo-European era, the Iranian traditions fall in line with the post-Rigvedic Indian traditions. Again, the Rigveda refers to its Gods as both *Deva* and *Asura*; while the later Vedic traditions have converted the term *Asura* into a term for demons, and the Iranian traditions have converted the term *Deva* into a term for demons. This indicates that the original Rigvedic people split into two conflicting groups at a later stage.

The detailed evidence about the location of the Indo-Iranian homeland in India will be taken up in our analysis of the Vedas and the Purāṇas.

THE LOCATION OF THE ORIGINAL INDO-EUROPEAN HOMELAND

B.K. Ghosh, who charts out the chronological and geographical timetable[46] of the Aryan invasion of India by moving backwards in time from the Rigveda, manages to "locate" the Indo-European homeland in South Russia by his method.

But, as pointed out, he bases his table on two extremely incorrect propositions:

1. He dates the Rigveda at 1000 BC; and, as we have seen, the earliest hymns of the Rigveda can be dated to the fifth-fourth millenniums BC.
2. He postulates Central Asia as the common Indo-Iranian homeland; and, as we have seen, this homeland can only be located in the Punjab region.

Even after starting out with the two incorrect propositions, Ghosh takes two more arbitrary and whimsical steps:

1. He decides that the Indo-Iranians "arrived" in their Central Asian "homeland" in around 2000 BC.
2. He further decides that, since the Indo-Iranians arrived in Central Asia "about the same time (c. 2000 BC)" as the Hittites are known to have arrived in Cappadocia in Turkey, "it will be reasonable to conclude that the original home whence both the Hit-

[45] IVA, p. 55.
[46] HCIP, pp. 203-06.

tites and the Indo-Iranians came was more or less equidistant from Cappadocia and Central Asia."[47]

Let us examine the peculiar logic used by Ghosh

1. To begin with, Ghosh arbitrarily takes 1000 BC (the "minimum date" as per Max Müller) as the date of the Rigveda. Then he arbitrarily decides on the almost exact figure of 500 years (obviously a minimum period) as the period for "the beginnings of the Vedic Age—and of the specific Indo-Aryan culture beginning therewith", thus arriving at 1500 BC. Then he arbitrarily takes another period of 500 years (another minimum period) for "the dispersal of the Indo-Iranians from their original home" and for their "reaching the common homeland in Central Asia", thus arriving at 2000 BC.

The arbitrariness of the datings and periods is of course calculated so as to make the Indo-Iranians "appear" in Central Asia "about the same time" as the Hittites appeared in Cappadocia. And for this purpose, not only does Ghosh invent his own dates and periods, but he violates his own chronological conception of the common homeland.

For, in a different context, Ghosh tells us that "the Indo-Iranians must have passed a long time in their....common home, for here grew up a specific Indo-Iranian religion and culture that may be reconstructed at least partially by comparing the Veda with the Avesta".[48]

Then, again, he tells us that the Indo-Aryans had "become completely Indianized when the Rigvedic culture started on its course as a distinct product of the Indian soil about 1500 BC".

Is it then logical to assert that the Indo-Iranians left their "original home" (South Russia) about 2000 BC, arrived in Central Asia, "passed a long time in their...common home" there, had a conflict and split from each other, the Indo-Aryan section of them arrived in India, "became completely Indianized", and commenced the Rigvedic culture in India about 1500 BC, *having lost all memories of their extra-Indian associations*—all in the course of 500 years?

Further, in the event of this incredible chain of events having so taken place, is it logical that it could be possible to reconstruct a "specific Indo-Iranian culture and religion", even partially, "by comparing the Veda with the Avesta", with both the Rigveda and the Avesta being dated at 1000 BC, 500 years after the events?

Yet he uses such predetermined and arbitrary methods as a basis for postulating an Aryan invasion of India.

[47] HCIP, p. 206.
[48] HCIP, p. 218.

2. After having the Indo-Iranians "appearing" in Central Asia "about the same time" as the Hittites appeared in Cappadocia, Ghosh proceeds to conclude that the original homeland therefore lay in South Russia.

If Ghosh uses a peculiar linguistic arithmetic, known only to himself, in arriving at 1000 BC as the date of the Rigveda, he uses an equally peculiar geographical geometry in arriving at South Russia as the original homeland. For this purpose, he probably uses a schoolboy's atlas and a schoolboy's compass-box.

First, having dated both the Rigveda and the Avesta at a common date, 1000 BC, he uses his atlas and compass-box to mark out the "common" place from which the authors of the Rigveda and the Avesta must have come—viz, Central Asia, more or less equidistant from the Punjab and Iran.

Then, having put the "arrival" of the Indo-Iranians in Central Asia and the arrival of the Hittites in Cappadocia at a common date, 2000 BC or so, he uses his atlas and compass-box to mark out the "common" place from which both of them must have come—viz. South Russia, "more or less equidistant from Cappadocia and Central Asia".[49]

This, in short, is the brilliant way in which Ghosh charts out the chronological and geographical timetable of the "Aryan invasion of India" and the location of the "original homeland", moving backwards in time and space from the Rigveda in the Punjab region. The arbitrary and fluid logic employed, and the grim predetermination exhibited in the employment of this kind of logic, is self-evident.

It is only by using this kind of whimsical logic that the hoary Vedic culture can be squeezed into the chronological ambits of "Aryan" history outside India so as to facilitate the concept of a South Russian homeland and reject the concept of an Indian homeland.

THE ORIGINAL HOMELAND IN INDIA

The most logical interpretation of the evidence and the facts, is that the original homeland of the Indo-European languages lay in India. It would be an exercise in sheer guesswork to try and chart out a chronological timetable of the spread of Indo-European languages from India to their later and present-day habitats, until exact datable evidence of the same is found. However, the following scenario may be postulated.

The original Indo-European language, which we will here call "proto-proto-Indo-European" to distinguish it from the hypothetical

[49]HCIP, p. 206.

language (proto-Indo-European) reconstructed by European linguists, was spoken in interior North India; but in very ancient times it had spread out and covered a large area extending to Afghanistan, and had developed a number of dialects, which may be classified as follows:

1. *Outer Indo-European dialects*: Spoken in Afghanistan and northern Kashmir and the adjoining north Himalayan region.
2. *Central Indo-European dialects*: Spoken in what we may call the "Punjab region" and in southern Kashmir.
3. *Inner Indo-European dialects*: Spoken in the expanse of northern India from the Gangetic region to Maharashtra and from Punjab to Orissa and Bengal.

The Outer Indo-European region developed a rich concentration of dialects; and the first major migration took place with a major section of them moving out northwards and westwards towards Europe. The Outer dialects were thus the ancestral forms of the European languages. The migration of the Outer Indo-European speakers may have taken place in two waves, as we shall see later (in Chapter 21).

Those (speakers of the Outer dialects) who remained behind got absorbed into the speech of the Central dialects. That some of the speakers of the Outer dialects may have retained their original speech is proved by the evidence of the Tokharian language of Chinese Turkestan (late 1st millennium AD) to the north of the Kashmir region, and perhaps by sundry other evidence (such as that of the Bangani language of the Garhwal region, already referred to earlier).

The proto-Indo-European language reconstructed by philologists is therefore a close approximation of the proto-Outer-Indo-European language, with the additional factors of Rigvedic and Iranian having been taken into consideration in its reconstruction. The area indicated by the paleontological study of this language is therefore the Kashmir region.

The Central Indo-European dialects, which had contacts with both the Outer and Inner dialects had developed into northern and southern groups; the northern groups were occupants of Kashmir. A body of speakers of these northern dialects (finding, as per the evidence of the Avesta, the northern winters unbearable) moved southwards into the Punjab region, and formed part of the Rigvedic culture which had developed there. Later, conflicts developed, and this section moved out westwards to Arachosia and Persia, as pointed out by Max Müller.

The Inner Indo-European dialects, meanwhile, had undergone a process of development in conjunction with the other language families of the mainland.

As the Rigvedic culture became rapidly accepted all over India a hybrid but refined language (Classical Sanskrit) was developed by the Indian grammarians, coordinating the Central dialect of the Rigveda with the Inner dialects spoken by the masses over the major part of North India. Gradually, by a process which is not quite clear even to linguists, the Inner dialects superseded Classical Sanskrit as a literary medium. Today, all the languages of India (with the exception of the Dardic languages, which include Kashmiri) are descendants of the Inner dialects, though highly influenced by Vedic and Classical Sanskrit. The Inner dialects have even superseded the Central dialects in the region of the Rigveda.

However, the full and correct picture of the earliest history of the Indo-Europeans will become clear only when we analyse the contents of the Vedas and the Purāṇas.

FIFTEEN

THE CEREBRALS IN VEDIC SANSKRIT

The distinction between cerebral (also known as retroflex, cacuminal or post-alveolar) sounds and dental (also known as pre-alveolar) sounds in Indo-Aryan languages right from the language of the Rigveda is regarded as evidence of the Aryan invasion of India, since this distinction is found in the Dravidian and Austric languages of India, but is not found in any of the Indo-European languages outside India—not even in the Iranian languages.

The logic is that these cerebral sounds must be originally Dravidian or Austric sounds borrowed by the Indo-Aryan languages; and the fact that these sounds are not found in the Indo-European languages outside India proves that those languages must never have come into contact with the Dravidian and Austric languages, and this further proves that India could not possibly be the original homeland.

The main contention, of course, is that the cerebral sounds were originally Dravidian, or even Austric, sounds borrowed by Indo-Aryan languages. Let us examine this contention, keeping in mind the fact that cerebrals are today found in four language families spoken in India: Austric, Dravidian, Burushaski, and Indo-Aryan.

CEREBRALS AS ORIGINALLY AUSTRIC SOUNDS

Ghosh describes the cerebrals as "the result of Austric and Dravidian influence on the language of the incoming Aryans."[1]

However, Norman H. Zide, the acknowledged authority on the Kol-Munda languages, reaches a totally different conclusion: "Proto-Munda, as various scholars of the Indian linguistic area have noted, probably had no retroflex series, since in Sora and some dialects of Korku there is no retroflex/dental opposition. This has proved true of the proto-languages. *All the other languages have borrowed the retroflexion feature from Indo-Aryan.*"[2]

The Austric languages therefore cannot be the original source of the cerebral sounds.

CEREBRALS AS ORIGINALLY DRAVIDIAN SOUNDS

It is the Dravidian languages which are most often cited as the

[1] HCIP, p. 202.
[2] CTL, Vol. 5, p. 423.

original source of the cerebral sounds. Even G.A. Grierson, when he declares that it is "quite possible that the Indo-Aryan cerebrals have been developed quite independently", follows this up immediately with: "The cerebral letters, however, form an essential part of Dravidian phonology, and it therefore seems probable that Dravidian influence has been at work, and at least given strength to a tendency which can, it is true, have taken its origin among the Aryans themselves."[3]

Are the cerebral sounds such an "essential part of Dravidian phonology" as to warrant such a presumption? The two following facts seem to show otherwise:

1. There are five sets of consonantal stops in the Dravidian languages (as in the Indo-Aryan languages): *k c, ṭ, t, p.* Of these, four can occur in two positions in a word: in the initial position and in the medial position. The only consonantal stop, *the odd man out,* which *cannot* occur in the medial position in a word, is the cerebral consonantal stop *ṭ*.

This probably indicates that the proto-Dravidian speakers found it difficult to pronounce the cerebral consonantal stop without the aid of a preceding vowel (just as many people find it difficult to pronounce certain unfamiliar initial consonantal clusters without a similar aid, and therefore pronounce the English word "school" as "ischool" or the Sanskrit word *strī* as *istrī*); and it very definitely *does* indicate that the cerebral consonantal stop was *not* as integral a part of the proto-Dravidian phonological system as the other four consonantal stops (the velar *k*, the palatal-affricate *c*, the dental *t*, and the bilabial *p).*

2. The largest number of cerebral sounds is found *not* in proto-Dravidian or any modern Dravidian language, but *in a totally unrelated language spoken at the extremely opposite corner of India:* the Burushaski language spoken in Pak-occupied Kashmir.

While proto-Dravidian had four cerebrals (*ṭ, ṇ, ḷ, ḻ*), the Burushaski language[4] has seven cerebrals or post-alveolars (ç̣, j̣, ỵ, ṭ, ḍ, ṣ, ẓ̌) distinct from the pre-alveolar forms of the same sounds.

The Burushaski language also deprives the proto-Dravidian language of its claim to having a unique cerebral sound not found in non-Dravidian languages—a claim which could have carried a little weight in giving a Dravidian origin to the cerebral sounds in general. This is the cerebral *ḻ*, which today is confined to the Tamil-Malayalam belt and is not found even in Telugu and Kannada. It is, however, found in

[3] LSI, Vol. 4, p. 279.
[4] TBL, Vol. 1, p. 6.

Burushaski, as the cerebral *y*, about which D.L.R. Lorimer writes: "Its identification as a 'cerebral *y* ' is tentative. From different people I recorded it variously as peculiar kinds of *r, l, ž* and sometimes as a hiatus or 'hamza'."[5] In a similar fashion, Kamil Zvelebil, in writing about the Dravidian cerebral *ḻ*, points out that it (he transcribes it as *ṛ*) is "also symbolized *ẓ*, *ṛ*, or *ḻ*, and *zh* in broad transcription."[6]

Therefore, it is obvious that the cerebrals are neither so fundamental or well-integrated a feature of the Dravidian languages, nor so unique or peculiar to them, as to warrant the automatic presumption that these sounds must have originated in the Dravidian languages.

CEREBRALS AS ORIGINALLY BURUSHASKI SOUNDS

Can the cerebrals be of Burushaski origin? The line-up of Burushaski cerebrals is certainly impressive. Rigvedic Sanskrit has one cerebral consonant in excess of proto-Dravidian (the consonant *ṣ*), and proto-Dravidian has one cerebral consonant in excess of Rigvedic Sanskrit, (the consonant *ḻ*); but Burushaski has both of them. Proto-Dravidian has one palatal-affricate *c*, while Rigvedic Sanskrit has two distinct palatals *c* and *j* in a single form (that is, not differentiated into dentals and cerebrals); but Burushaski has pre-alveolar and post-alveolar forms for both the consonants *c* and *j*. Finally, neither Rigvedic Sanskrit nor proto-Dravidian has the consonant *ž* (pronounced like the letter "s" in the English word "vision") in any form; but Burushaski has it in both forms, pre-alveolar and post-alveolar.

However, any claims of a Burushaski origin for the cerebral sounds is rendered doubtful by the following facts:

1. Burushaski does not have cerebral forms of the basic consonants *l* and *n*.
2. The cerebral sounds in the Burushaski language have been recorded at a very late date. The book[7] by D.L.R. Lorimer in 1935 represented one of the earliest attempts, and perhaps the only detailed one, to analyse the phonological structure of the language.
3. The distinction between the dental (pre-alveolar) and cerebral (post-alveolar) sounds in Burushaski is not very marked. Lorimer makes this point very clear: "There are two series: one produced with the tip of the tongue in a *relatively* advanced, and

[5] TBL, Vol.1, p. 6.
[6] DL, p. 7.
[7] TBL.

> the other with the top of the tongue in a *relatively* retracted, position. The latter...it is a common practice to call such sounds 'cerebrals', but I do not think they are cerebrals according to the Sanskritists' definition of the term. On the whole I think that the post-alveolar nature of the sounds is less marked in Burushaski than in Shina... when writing Burushaski, my informants appear to have consistently differentiated *ḍ* and *ṭ* from *d* and *t*... They did not attempt to distinguish the other post-alveolar sounds, except at my specific request."[8]

Shina is the Dardic language spoken closest to Burushaski, and when one considers the fact that according to G.A. Grierson "a noteworthy feature of the Dardic languages is the confusion between cerebral and dental letters"[9], it is clear that the confusion in Burushaski is even more marked.

Thus, while the proto-Dravidian language seems to show that it was originally unfamiliar with cerebral sounds, by exhibiting a seeming inability to pronounce them in the initial position in words; the Burushaski language seems to show the same thing in a different way, by exhibiting a failure to distinguish sharply and clearly between cerebrals and dentals.

CEREBRALS AS ORIGINALLY INDO-ARYAN SOUNDS

All the evidence points to the conclusion that the cerebral sounds originated in the Indo-Aryan languages:

1. Cerebral sounds as distinct from dental sounds are first attested in Rigvedic Sanskrit. The bulk of the hymns of the Rigveda, as pointed out in detail in the previous chapter, can be dated 3500-2500 BC; but even if we take the "minimum date", and accept, along with B.K. Ghosh, that "we get for the Rigvedic language, as known to us, an approximate date of 1000 BC"[10], even then the existence of cerebrals as distinct from dentals will have to be accepted as being attested in the language of the Rigveda nearly a thousand years earlier than the earliest attested evidence of its presence in any Dravidian language known to us.
2. The cerebral consonants are found sharply and clearly distinct from the dental consonants, and in a full set of four distinct phonemes (unvoiced *ṭ*, unvoiced aspirate *ṭh*, voiced *ḍ*, voiced

[8] TBL, pp. 6-7.
[9] LSI, Vol. 8, pt. 2, p. 243.
[10] HCIP, p. 204.

aspirate *ḍh*) alongwith the nasal *ṇ*. Not only is the cerebral lateral *ḷ* found in Rigvedic (though the sound does not occur later in Classical Sanskrit and in some of the modern northern Indo-Aryan languages like Hindi), but an aspirated form *ḷh* is also found, and is unique to Rigvedic. The cerebral sibilant *ṣ* is also found as a sharp and distinct phoneme from the dental sibilant *ś*; and this is particularly significant since, as Zvelebil points out, "proto-Dravidian lacks sibilants completely, even *s*."[11]

3. The cerebral stops in Rigvedic Sanskrit can occur in the initial position in words, and are in this sense as integral a part of the phonological system of the language as the other sets of consonantal stops.

In short, not only are the cerebrals in the Rigvedic language attested at a very much earlier date than in proto-Dravidian, but they are more numerous in number, cover a larger range of consonantal categories, and are more integral a part of the phonological system of the language.

Moreover, not only are the cerebrals found in countless "deśī" words (more about these words in the next chapter) which cannot be demonstrated to be borrowings from Dravidian and Austric languages; they are also found in countless words in Rigvedic and Classical Sanskrit, which are very obviously purely Indo-European words since they are clearly derived from Sanskrit roots and have cognates in Indo-European languages outside India.

It is, therefore, clear that the cerebrals originated in the Indo-Aryan languages; or else they represent a phonological phenomenon which evolved over the entire spectrum of Indian languages at a certain point of time in the remote past—a phenomenon which manifested itself in different ways in different parts of the country, but which had its clearest manifestation in the language of the Rigveda. In any case, the cerebrals are very clearly *not* "the result of Austric and Dravidian influence on the language of the incoming Aryans"[12], as breezily alleged by B.K. Ghosh and other protagonists of the invasion theory.

But if the cerebrals originated, or were most clearly manifested, in the Indo-Aryan languages—that is, in the Indo-European family of languages out of the four families of languages in India in which these sounds are found—why is it that they are not found in the Indo-European languages outside India, and not even in the Iranian languages?

[11] DL, p. 8.
[12] HCIP, p. 202.

Does this prove, as alleged by the invasion theorists, that India cannot be the original Indo-European homeland? Let us examine this question in some detail.

INDO-EUROPEAN LANGUAGES AND THE CEREBRAL SOUNDS

The cerebrals and dentals are two sets of consonants which contain basically the same sounds produced by pressing the tip of the tongue against two different parts of the mouth. The cerebrals are produced by pressing the tip of the tongue against the palate (the roof of the mouth), while the dentals are produced by pressing the tip of the tongue between the teeth.

While Indian languages basically have pure dental sounds and pure cerebral sounds, the Indo-European languages of Europe have only dental sounds. But these "dental" sounds are not pure dentals in the Indian sense of the term; they are only called that since there is only one set of sounds in these languages, and there is no need to be specific about naming them as per the position of the tip of the tongue. When they are specifically compared with the two sets of Indian sounds, it becomes obvious that they are not pure dentals, but "alveolars" which are somewhat in-between the Indian dentals and cerebrals.

On this basis, it has been decided that the proto-Indo-European language also must have had one series of dentals or alveolars. As G.A. Grierson puts it: "The Indo-European languages do not seem to have possessed these letters (cerebrals). They had a series of dentals, which were not, however, pronounced as pure dentals by putting the tongue between the teeth, but probably as alveolars, the tongue being pressed against the root of the upper teeth."[13] Warren Cowgill also describes the tentatively reconstructed proto-Indo-European dentals as being made "with the tip of the tongue against the back of the teeth."[14]

While the single set of dentals found in the European languages consists of consonants which are neither pure dentals nor pure cerebrals in the Indian sense of the terms, the exact pronunciation of these consonants in the different languages of Europe is not exactly uniform. As K.D. Sethna points out: "In expressing *t* and *d*, the Teutons produce a harsh sound by touching with their tongues the gum or fleshy part of the palate just above the teeth. The Southern Europeans make the contact lower down where the teeth issue from the gums, thus producing a softer sound. The Persians and the Indians make it low down on the

[13] LSI, Vol. 4, p. 279.
[14] EB, Vol. 9, p. 434.

teeth almost at their edge and produce the softest sound of all. This sound, being the result of impact on the teeth, is a true dental. The Indian tongue also touches a point very slightly higher than the Teutons do and there comes the harshest note of the scale. This note constitutes the cerebrals."[15]

Compare the situation prevailing in Europe with the situation prevailing in the north Kashmir region (northern Kashmir and eastern Afghanistan), which repeatedly draws our attention as being the region from which the non-Indo-Iranian branches must have spread westwards (Europe) and northwards (Chinese Turkestan). According to the most prominent authority on Burushaski, D.L.R. Lorimer, the Burushaski language has two sets of these consonants, but he does not think that one of the sets can be called "cerebrals according to the Sanskritists' definition of the term".[16] The two sets represent two varieties of alveolar sounds of which one is "produced with tip of the tongue in a *relatively* advanced, and the other with the tip of the tongue in a *relatively* retracted position."[17] In short the two sets are almost identical with the South European set of dentals (alveolars) and the Teutonic set of dentals (alveolars) respectively.

Further, G.A. Grierson, in speaking of the Dardic languages spoken in this region, points out that "a noteworthy feature of the Dardic languages is the confusion between cerebral and dental letters"[18]; and in referring to the Shina language in particular, he interprets this confusion as follows: "The truth probably is that in Shina, the *t* and *d* are pronounced somewhat as in English, neither cerebrals nor dentals, but something between both..."[19]

The facts bear out the following hypothesis: the proto-Indo-European language (postulated by us in the previous chapter) must have had two sets of these consonants—cerebral and dental. However, while the distinct sets developed strongly in the Inner-Indo-European and Central-Indo-European dialects (strongly in the southern, and weakly in the northern, dialects of the latter group), they developed weakly in the Outer-Indo-European dialects. Hence, when these Outer-Indo-European dialects moved out from the Kashmir region and spread out westwards and northwards, they soon lost the distinction between the two sets, which therefore coalesced into one set. Much later, the Iranian dialects,

[15] Karpāsa, p. 126.
[16] TBL, p. 6.
[17] Ibid.
[18] LSI, Vol. 8, pt. 2, p. 243.
[19] LSI, Vol. 8, pt. 2, p. 173.

which moved southwards from the Kashmir region into the Punjab region (from *Airyanam Vaejo* to *Hapta Hindu*, as per the Iranian texts), retained the confusion between the cerebrals and dentals which is even today found in the Dardic languages; hence when they finally moved out of the Punjab region, and by the time they finally settled down in their present habitats, the Iranian dialects had also lost completely the distinction between cerebrals and dentals.

Hence the reconstruction, by philologists, of a single set of dentals (alveolars) in the proto-Indo-European language is correct if we keep in mind the fact that the language reconstructed by them is actually an approximation of the language that we may describe as proto-Outer-Indo-European. However, the language that we have called proto-proto-Indo-European must have had two sets of consonants, and this is confirmed by a consideration of the following two points:

1. G.A. Grierson, after postulating that the proto-Indo-European language must have had dentals (alveolars), goes on to declare: "These sounds have, in India, partly become dentals and partly cerebrals. The cerebrals are in most cases derived from compound letters where the old dentals were preceded by an *l*."[20]

Grierson is not quite correct in his second statement. Most of the dentals and cerebrals in Rigvedic and Classical Sanskrit are, in fact, represented by the equivalent dentals (alveolars) in the cognate words in the non-Indo-Aryan languages, and not necessarily by the equivalent dentals plus something else. Therefore, by and large, a one-equals-two phonological equation can be postulated. Should this be interpreted as one original sound breaking up into two, or as two original sounds coalescing into one?

In a somewhat similar case, when the vowels in the cognate words in the non-Indo-Iranian branches are tabulated, they are found to conform to a pattern which appears to indicate that the proto-Indo-European languages must have had five vowels: *a, e, i, o,* and *u*. When this pattern is compared with the cognate words in the Indo-Iranian branch, it is found that the three vowels, *a, e* and *o*, in this pattern correspond by and large to a single vowel *a* in Indo-Iranian. From these facts, philologists draw the conclusion that proto-Indo-European had three vowels *a, e,* and *o*, which have coalesced in the Indo-Iranian branch into one single vowel *a*.

The reconstruction of proto-Indo-European is a very theoretical process and involves plenty of guesswork and approximation and

[20] LSI, Vol. 4, p. 279.

choosing between alternatives. The reconstruction of the consonants and vowels of proto-Indo-European, as illustrated by Cowgill,[21] demonstrates this fact. If, in spite of this, it can be presumed that the ultimate parent language had three vowels which coalesced into one vowel in Indo-Iranian; then surely, on the same analogy, it cannot be unlikely that the ultimate parent language had two sets of consonants (dentals and cerebrals) which coalesced into one set (dental-alveolars) in the non-Indo-Aryan languages—especially considering the fact that the two sets of consonants are found in the most archaic and oldest attested Indo-European language, the language of the Rigveda.

2. The seeds of cerebralisation were present even in the Outer-Indo-European languages. This is proved by the fact that certain modern European languages have also developed cerebral sounds.

G.A. Grierson, after pointing out that many cerebrals are derived from compound letters where the "old dentals" were preceded by an *l̠*, goes on to state: "Similar changes also occur in other Indo-European languages, and it is therefore quite possible that the Indo-Aryan cerebrals have been developed quite independently."[22]

S.K. Chatterji is more specific: "In modern Swedish, among new Indo-European tongues, however, *ḍ* has developed out of *r+d*, which is paralleled by a similar cerebralisation in Old Magadhi."[23]

From this, it is obvious that certain late formations of cerebral sounds in Indo-Aryan languages are paralleled by identical formations of identical cerebrals, howsoever rare, in certain European languages.

It is therefore clear that the cerebral consonants in the Rigvedic language neither prove an Aryan invasion of India, nor disprove an Indian homeland theory.

[21] EB, Vol. 9, pp. 434-35.
[22] LSI, Vol. 4, p. 279.
[23] ODBL, p. 170.

SIXTEEN

AUSTRIC AND DRAVIDIAN WORDS IN SANSKRIT

S.K. Chatterji provides a list of Sanskrit names, for some basically Indian plants and animals, which he claims are of Austric and Dravidian origin. His point is that the "Aryans" who were outsiders were originally unacquainted with these Indian plants and animals and hence had to borrow the local Austric and Dravidian names for them.

Before examining Chatterji's claims in this respect, it is necessary to examine the broader allegation which forms the background to this claim: viz. that there exists a large number of basic Austric and Dravidian words in Sanskrit and Indo-Aryan.

Therefore, we will be examining two issues:

1. Austric and Dravidian words in Sanskrit and Indo-Aryan.
2. The names of Indian plants and animals in Sanskrit.

AUSTRIC AND DRAVIDIAN WORDS IN SANSKRIT AND INDO-ARYAN

Many European and Indian scholars have expended much effort and scholarship in trying to locate large numbers of Austric and Dravidian words in Sanskrit. What is the reason behind these special efforts?

Now the bare idea of there being a certain number of Austric or Dravidian words in Sanskrit and Indo-Aryan languages would not be an unnatural one. Languages in contact borrow words from each other; and it would be as natural for Indo-Aryan languages to borrow from Austric and Dravidian languages as for those languages to borrow from Indo-Aryan and from each other.

But, given the distribution of languages of the three families (Dravidian languages concentrated in the South, Kol-Munda languages in a small area in East Central India, and Indo-Aryan languages spread out throughout the expanse of North India to the extreme northern and western corners), the natural thing would be for inter-language influence rather than inter-family influence; thus, we find Telugu and Kannada words in Marathi, and Marathi words in Telugu and Kannada; but not Tamil words in Kashmiri or Assamese, or Kashmiri or Assamese words in Tamil.

The only language unrestricted geographically was Sanskrit, which became the great vehicle of literature and the intellectual lingua franca of ancient India; and, therefore, we find every single language in India loaded with Sanskrit words, right down to Tamil and Malayalam in the extreme south, (and, in fact, even Thai, Khmer and Indonesian in Southeast Asia have a considerable number of Sanskrit words). A rebound borrowing by Sanskrit from local languages, including the non-Indo-European ones, and the subsequent filtering down of these non-Indo-European words as "Sanskrit" words into the Indo-Aryan languages of the far north and west, is the only way in which Austric and Dravidian words could reach the Indo-Aryan languages of these far corners; and this process, naturally, would not be likely to transmit a great number of words.

The actual situation in the Indian languages reflects this trend.

However, this does not fit in with the invasion-theorists' concept of what *should have been* the situation. According to them, the whole of India was occupied by speakers of Austric and Dravidian languages before the "Aryan invasion". Therefore, the composers of the Rigveda, as well as the subsequent Classical Sanskrit writers, must have been in close and continuous contact with the Austric and Dravidian languages right in the northwest of India itself. In fact, as per the theory, a majority of the present-day speakers of Indo-Aryan languages (and all of the "lower castes" among them) in North India are the descendants of original Austrics and Dravidians who adopted (or were forced into adopting) the Indo-Aryan languages. Hence, their speech *must* contain very large numbers of Austric and Dravidian words: absence of such large numbers of words goes against the invasion theory.

Hence the zeal expended by these scholars in trying to locate large numbers of Austric and Dravidian words in the Rigvedic and Classical Sanskrit languages or in the Prakrits. Do the actual facts bear out their contentions? Let us examine the facts.

THE QUESTION OF THE DEŚĪ WORDS

The Prakrit grammarians of ancient India had classified Prakrit words into three categories: *tatsama*, *tadbhava* and *deśī*.

The *tatsama* words are those which are found in the same form as in the Vedic and Sanskrit texts. The *tadbhava* words are those Vedic and Sanskrit words which are found in a changed or modified form. Thus the words *sarva* and *satya* are *tatsama* words, and the Hindi words *sab* and *sac* are their *tadbhava* forms. The Hindi word *khet* and the Marathi word *śet* are both *tadbhava* forms of the Sanskrit *kṣetra*.

The grammarians classified all other words as *deśī*. S.K. Chatterji describes them as follows: "When there was no similar Vedic or Sanskrit word to explain them, the grammarians found a label for them in the word deśī, meaning 'of the country', that is 'aboriginal'...."[1]

Thus, Chatterji launches his campaign by translating the word *deśī* as "aboriginal", thereby implying that the Prakrit grammarians themselves were aware of a large number of Prakrit words being "aboriginal" (i.e. "pre-Aryan").

Chatterji's bias thus becomes evident at this very stage:

1. The word *deśī* certainly means "of the country", but how does this mean "aboriginal"? If the grammarians had wanted to imply such a meaning, they would have used a term similar to *ādivāsī* (a term coined by invasionist intellectuals and politicians in modern times). How does Chatterji derive the meaning "aboriginal" from *deśī*?
2. As per Chatterji's description, the grammarians had coined this term for words which had "no similar Vedic or Sanskrit word to explain them". This itself proves that the grammarians classified Prakrit words into literary (*tatsama*), modified-literary (*tadbhava*) and colloquial (*deśī*), taking the Vedic and Sanskrit texts as the standard; and that the classification had nothing whatsoever to do with the language-family affiliations of the words. *Deśī* thus means "spoken" (as opposed to literary), while "aboriginal" means "of the *earlier* original inhabitants".
3. As per the invasionists, even the composers of the Rigveda had retained no "extraterritorial memories". So how could the much later Prakrit grammarians be accused of having such a meaning as "aboriginal" in mind when referring *even* to words in the non-Indo-European languages, let alone in the spoken or semi-spoken (Prakrit) forms of their own Indo-Aryan languages?
4. After having planted the idea that the *tatsama/tadbhava* versus *deśī* classification was a classification of words into "*Aryan*" versus "*non-Aryan*", Chatterji contradicts himself by admitting that many of the *deśī* words (although not found in Sanskrit texts) are Indo-European (in the sense that they have cognates in European languages or can be derived from known Indo-European roots), and by alleging that many of the *tatsama* and *tadbhava* words (i.e. words found in the Vedic and Sanskrit texts) are also "pre-Aryan".

Thus the modern scholars (typified by Chatterji) classify as "non-Aryan" those words, in Sanskrit and Indo-Aryan, which cannot be

[1] ODBL, p. 192.

"satisfactorily" derived from Sanskrit or Indo-European roots, or those "of which counterparts are not found in other Indo-European speeches."[2]

THE IDENTITY OF THE "NON-ARYAN" WORDS

Can Indo-Aryan words which have no counterparts in other Indo-European languages, and cannot be "satisfactorily" derived from Sanskrit or Indo-European roots, be branded as non-Indo-European purely on that basis?

Here is what Warren Cowgill has to say about the sources of English words: "Words in modern Indo-European languages have several sources. They may be *recognizable loan-words* such as English 'skunk', 'chain' and 'inch' (from Algonkian, French and Latin respectively); they may have been formed within the history, or prehistory of the language itself, such as English 'radar' or 'rightness'; they may be of obscure origin, such as English 'drink' which is common Germanic but has no cognates outside Germanic, or 'boy' which is peculiar to English and Frisian; or they may be inherited words that have changed meaning, such as English 'merry' from proto-Indo-European 'mṛǵhu' — 'short'..."[3]

Carl D. Buck points out that many words which cannot be etymologically traced could be words which "were at first colloquial or even slang words (which) gained increasing currency until they superseded the old standard words."[4]

Therefore, the logical thing would be to treat as borrowed words only those which are "*recognizable* loan-words" from Dravidian or Austric languages.

But the zealous invasionist scholars throw all linguistic norms to the winds:

Chatterji, for example, declares: "a great many of the *deśī* words, of which counterparts are not found in other Indo-European speeches, are *probably Dravidian in origin:* (Many are also Kol, and *possibly even* pre-Dravidian and pre-Kol)."[5]

This, he further clarifies as follows: "There is also the *possibility* of non-Aryan speeches (other than Dravidian, Kol and the later Tibeto-Chinese), *speeches now extinct,* being present in India during the first

[2] ODBL, p. 178.
[3] EB, Vol. 9, pp. 437-38.
[4] ADOSS, Preface.
[5] ODBL, p. 178.

half of the millennium AD, and contributing some deśī words and in other ways influencing Indo-Aryan."[6]

In their zeal to brand large numbers of Indo-Aryan words as "aboriginal" and "anything but Indo-European", these scholars are not only determined to speculate about "probabilities" and "possibilities" of their being Austric or Dravidian words even when they are not *recognizable* as such; but they are even willing to invent the "possibility" of *purely hypothetical* "extinct" languages, neither Austric nor Dravidian, which were supplanted by the "Aryan invaders"!

We cannot proceed with these scholars into the twilight zone of non-existent languages. Let us, therefore, examine the case so far as the existing non-Indo-European languages, Austric and Dravidian, are concerned.

THE CASE OF AUSTRIC LOAN WORDS

The Kol-Munda languages of the present-day are heavily loaded with words which are of obvious Indo-Aryan origin: words borrowed either from Sanskrit itself, or from the local Indo-Aryan languages. This is a well-attested fact. Hence the attempt to brand *deśī* words as "Austric", on the basis of the same or similar words being found in the present-day Kol-Munda languages, runs into difficulties at the very outset.

Chatterji, even as he proclaims that "a great many (words) are undoubtedly Kol or Austro-Asiatic", is compelled to admit that "in the absence of any knowledge of the Kol and other Austro-Asiatic speeches of an early period (barring, however, the Khmer of Cambodia) *nothing definite can be said*."[7] This, however, does not prevent him from saying it anyway!

G.A. Grierson is even more unambiguous when he points out: "It is no longer possible to decide to what extent the Munda languages can have influenced the other linguistic families of India. Our knowledge of them only dates back to the middle of the last century... *In the case of Aryan languages, the Munda influence is apparently unimportant*."[8]

Norman H. Zide, the acknowledged authority on the Kol-Munda languages, puts the whole thing very clearly. He points out that "etymological works on Indo-Aryan and Dravidian cannot yet make full use of Munda materials because these are still fragmentary and/or unpublished

[6] ODBL, p. 200.
[7] ODBL, p. 199.
[8] LSI, Vol. 4, Introduction, p. 9.

for the most part. Their use also presupposes a morphological and phonological analysis which has not always been made...The identification of words in Indo-Aryan and Dravidian as Munda loans, even when this has been done by careful scholars, is not often convincing, particularly in the light of newer data."

In fact, Zide gives the specific example of two words *jim/jem*, "to eat", and *marica*, "pepper", which are alleged to be borrowed from Munda. He demonstrates, with linguistic analysis, about the former (in Munda languages) that "it seems much more likely that the occurring form *jim* is a borrowing from, rather than a source for, the Indo-Aryan form"; and that the latter is "a regular borrowing of Oriya *moricho*."[9] Hence, he concludes that "the obvious provenance is Indo-Aryan."[10]

Incidentally, the word *jim* is one of the words to which Chatterji ascribes an Austric origin. He in fact connects the words *cāval* ("rice", Middle Indo-Aryan *cāmal*) with "the Kol or Munda root *jom*, 'to eat'..."[11]

Therefore, it is clear that it is not possible to show borrowings by Sanskrit from Kol-Munda languages, without showing a total disregard for linguistic norms.

S.K. Chatterji,[12] incidentally, even goes so far as to give an example of the alleged borrowings by Indo-Aryan languages from "pre-Dravidian and pre-Kol" languages. He cites the Bengali-Oriya word *bāduḍ/bādaḍi* ("bat") as a negrito word, and derives it from a "root" *bād*, giving the Andamanese words *wót-da, wāt-da, wòt* and *wät* as cognates. Curiously, it does not seem to strike him that the English word "bat" can also then be derived from the same alleged negrito root, with the same cognate forms in Andamanese; and what would this indicate about the original Indo-European homeland?

THE CASE OF DRAVIDIAN LOAN-WORDS

The Dravidian languages being more richly documented than the Austric ones, and for other reasons cited in the introduction to this book, a great number of European and Indian scholars have concentrated more heavily on producing lists of words allegedly borrowed by Sanskrit and other Indo-Aryan languages from Dravidian.

However, the eminent linguist, and a staunch supporter of the inva-

9 CTL, Vol. 5, p. 420.
10 CTL p. 421.
11 HCIP, p. 150.
12 HCIP, p. 147.

sion theory, Thomas Burrow, is compelled to admit grudgingly that "there has been a certain amount of controversy concerning the question of non-Aryan loan-words in Sanskrit, and some scholars (P. Thieme, H.W. Bailey) have adopted a sceptical position in this respect. Alternate Indo-European etymologies have been offered for words for which a Dravidian or Munda etymology had previously been proposed, in some cases successfully... but more dubiously in other cases."[13]

Thus Chatterji, for example, gives a list of words in the Rigveda and the Brāhmaṇas which are allegedly of Dravidian origin. However, he takes great care to refer to them ambiguously as "words of *probable* Dravidian origin..."[14] Among these words are *phala* (fruit), *puṣpa* (flower), *puṣkara* (lotus), *aṭavi* (forest), *kapi* (monkey), *sāyam* (evening), *rātri* (night), *bīja* (seed), *śava* (corpse).

However, Carl D. Buck[15] not only gives the Indo-European derivations of these words, but even gives cognate words in Greek, Persian, Latin, Gothic, etc. Many of the other words cited by Chatterji are either not found in the Dravidian languages at all, or are obviously or demonstrably Indo-Aryan words borrowed by Dravidian languages.

And, quite apart from the fact that words alleged to be of Dravidian origin are often not found in the Dravidian languages at all except as Sanskrit loan-words, the very phonetic structure of the proto-Dravidian language, as reconstructed by linguists and as attested by the Tamil language, debars entire sections of *deśī* words from the likelihood of their being borrowed from Dravidian languages.

1. Even Chatterji admits: "quite a number of *deśī* words begin with a cerebral sound, and many with a palatal. In Dravidian, initial cerebral is rare, if not non-existent...and *deśī* words with an initial cerebral would thus seem to be *not from Dravidian*."[16]

Kamil Zvelebil, one of the foremost authorities on Dravidian linguistics, categorically states: "No consonant of the alveolar or cacuminal-retroflex series...begins a word in Dravidian."[17] He specifies that this includes not only the cerebrals, but also the liquids (*r*, *l*).

Therefore *deśī* words (i.e. words with no cognates in other Indo-European languages, and no "satisfactory" derivation from Sanskrit or Indo-European roots) which begin with *ṭ*, *ṭh*, *ḍ*, *ḍh*, *l* and *r*, would "seem to be not from Dravidian".

[13] CTL, Vol. 5, p. 18.
[14] ODBL, p. 42.
[15] ADOSS, pp. 48, 188, 291, 375, 527, 992, 998, etc.
[16] ODBL, p. 199.
[17] DL, p. 8.

2. Proto-Dravidian had no aspirate sounds at all, not even the basic sound *h*. Therefore all *deśī* words having the sounds *h, kh, gh, ch, jh, ṭh, ḍh, th, dh, ph* and *bh* in them would "seem to be not from Dravidian".

3. Zvelebil also points out that there was a "total absence of sibilants...*wherever sibilants do occur, they are borrowed from Indo-Aryan* which is rich in sibilants. Proto-Dravidian lacks sibilants completely, even (s)..."[18]

Therefore, all *deśī* words having the sibilant sounds *s, ś, ṣ* in them would also "seem to be not from Dravidian".

4. Zvelebil also points out that the voiced and voiceless obstruents had fixed positional pronunciations in proto-Dravidian:

a. "There were no initial voiced stops in Proto-Dravidian—a situation reflected in modern Tamil–Malayalam."

b. "We have no reason to posit voiceless intervocalic obstruents for any stage of Dravidian."[19]

c. "Tense obstruents (pp) are always voiceless."[20]

Therefore, all *deśī* words beginning with *g, j, ḍ, d, b,* or having *k, c, ṭ, t, p* in the middle of a word, or having (doubled) *gg, jj, ḍḍ, dd, bb,* would also "seem to be not from Dravidian".

5. Zvelebil also points out that in proto-Dravidian, "consonant clusters are highly restricted. The first type of clusters consists of homorganic nasal plus obstruent (NP, NPP); another type is the geminates (cc); finally there is the type liquid (L) *l, ḷ* and *y* and (R) *r, ṛ,* with any obstruent or obstruent cluster: *LP, RP, LPP, RPP, RNP*."[21]

Therefore, all *deśī* words having initial consonantal-clusters, or having in them consonantal-clusters not falling in the three above types (having, for example, obstruent + liquid: *pr, tr, kl,* etc. or having obstruent + other obstruent: *tp, pt, dg, db, bd,* etc.) would also "seem to be not from Dravidian".

Therefore, even a staunch protagonist of the Aryan invasion theory, like Bhadriraju Krishnamurti, is compelled to admit: "Indo-Aryan (particularly Middle and Modern) shows large-scale structural borrowing from Dravidian, *but very little lexical borrowing*."[22]

THE GENESIS OF THE "NON-ARYAN" WORDS

What, then, is the exact linguistic position of the *deśī* words?

[18] DL, p. 8.
[19] DL, p. 9.
[20] DL, p. 8,.
[21] DL, p. 12.
[22] CTL, Vol. 5., p. 324.

Warren Cowgill points out: "In prehistoric times, most branches of Indo-European were carried into territories presumably or certainly occupied by speakers of non-Indo-European languages...it is reasonable to suppose that these languages had some effect on the speech of the newcomers. *For the lexicon, this is indeed demonstrable in Hittite and Greek at least.*"[23]

In the case of Vedic and Classical Sanskrit, however, such a situation is *not* demonstrable, as we have already seen, despite the most zealous efforts of the invasionist scholars.

Even S.K. Chatterji after branding the *deśī* words as "aboriginal" and as borrowings from Austric and Dravidian "and possibly even pre-Dravidian and pre-Kol" languages, finally ends his discourse with a discreet admission: "In the present state of our knowledge, the *deśī* words in New Indo-Aryan may be considered *alongwith the tadbhava words as forming part of the inherited element*, citing an attested non-Aryan word for reference only, whenever the latter, from similarity in form and meaning with a *deśī* word in Indo-Aryan, offers itself for comparison."[24]

The *deśī* words are, therefore obviously Indo-European words. But why aren't these or similar words found in the European languages or even in the Vedic language?

As we have already pointed out, the original (proto-proto) Indo-European language had split into at least three groups of dialects: the Outer, the Central and the Inner. Of these, the Outer and Central dialects were confined more or less to the north-west and extreme north of India, while the Inner dialects were spoken in the interior of India. The "proto-Indo-European" language reconstructed by linguists is basically a reconstruction of the proto-languages of the Outer and Central groups, without taking into consideration the Indo-European words and roots peculiar to the Inner groups of dialects. The linguists presume the present-day Indo-Aryan languages to be the latter-day developed forms of the original Vedic language; whereas actually they are the latter-day forms of the ancient dialects of the Inner group of Indo-European dialects, which, in the course of history, were brought closer to the Vedic language through the medium of the artificially constructed Classical Sanskrit language, and by the Sanskrit and Prakrit grammarians.

The *deśī* words are therefore, in short, the words and roots peculiar to the Inner dialects, many of which were incorporated into the literary

[23] EB, Vol. 9, p. 438.
[24] ODBL, pp. 199-200.

Sanskrit and the Prakrits at a later stage, but which do not figure in Vedic or Iranian or in the languages of Europe.

What applies, as discussed above, in the case of Sanskrit and Indo-Aryan words alleged to be of Austric or Dravidian origin, also applies in the case of Sanskrit names of Indian plants and animals. However, let us undertake a short survey, both general and specific, of these names.

GENERAL SURVEY OF NAMES OF PLANTS AND ANIMALS

The names of plants and animals in Sanskrit can be classified into three categories:

1. Those with undisputed Indo-European etymologies.
2. Those with dubious or obscure etymologies.
3. Those obviously or demonstrably borrowed from Austric or Dravidian.

1. *Indo-European etymologies*: The overwhelming majority of the Sanskrit names for Indian plants and animals are obviously or demonstrably derived from Sanskrit or Indo-European roots; and the fact that this should be so is clearest evidence that the ancient Indo-Europeans were native to India.

2. *Dubious or obscure etymologies*: There are some names which are not so easily derivable from known roots, and whose etymology is uncertain. Hence the invasionist linguists hasten to brand them as Austric or Dravidian names—in most cases even when the words cannot be etymologically derived from Austric or Dravidian roots either, and in fact the words are often not even found in the Austric or Dravidian languages, except sometimes as obvious borrowings from Sanskrit or Indo-Aryan.

Can any Sanskrit name for a plant or animal be branded as "non-Indo-European" purely on the ground that the etymological derivation for the name is doubtful, obscure or "unconvincing"?

For the answer to this question, let us see the case of those names of plants and animals of whose Indo-European identity there is the least ground for doubt: viz. those names which are accepted to be inherited Indo-European ones on the ground that they are found occurring in both India and Europe. And we find that here also, etymological derivations are equally doubtful or obscure.

Carl D. Buck makes this fact very clear when referring to the inherited names of animals in the Indo-European languages: "In the inherited names of animals there is little to be said about their semantic nature, for *in most of them, the root connection is wholly obscure.*"[25]

In referring to the few inherited names of plants also, he makes it clear that "*the root connections are mostly obscure*".[26]

Hence, unless one is to presume that the proto-Indo-Europeans were not acquainted with *any* animals or plants *at all*, one has to accept that etymologically obscure names may be "what were at first colloquial or even slang words", and that etymological obscurity need not necessarily indicate a non-Indo-European source unless such a source (for any particular name or word) can be specifically and etymologically demonstrated.

3. *Demonstrably borrowed names*: A small minority of names may be there which could indeed be demonstrated to be loan-words from Austric or Dravidian languages. But these circumstances are perfectly natural.

Thus, for example, it is no-one's claim that the extreme south of India was originally inhabited by speakers of Indo-European languages. It is in fact our claim that the Dravidian languages were always spoken in South India (and not originally in the Mediterranean region as alleged by the invasionist theorists), that the Indo-European languages were always and originally spoken in North India (and not originally in South Russia as alleged by the invasion theorists), and that the Austric languages were always spoken in north-eastern and east-central India (and not originally in Palestine as alleged by some of the scholars).

Now, the plants and animals, which were originally found only in India must have originated in some specific part of India. Cardamom, for example, is known to have originated in Kerala. The Indo-Aryan name for cardamom (Sanskrit *elā*, from which all the modern Indo-Aryan words are derived) is obviously similar to the Dravidian name for it (Tamil *yēla, yelakkāi*). If it is demonstrated that the Sanskrit word is derived from the Dravidian one, what is surprising in the fact that the North Indians should have borrowed the name of the plant, alongwith the plant itself, from the South Indians?

In fact, in such cases, if the common name for any Indian plant is proved to be of Austric or Dravidian origin, it will help in locating the part of India in which the plant had its origin.

In order to have a rational approach to this question, of borrowed names of plants and animals, we must keep in mind the following three

[25] ADOSS, p. 135.
[26] ADOSS, p. 528.

examples:

1. The commonest Sanskrit name for the lizard (with derivatives in most Indo-Aryan languages) is *palli*, and the commonest Dravidian name, as represented by Tamil, is also *palli*. Obviously one of the two languages has borrowed the word from the other. But the lizard is a common animal, and it is extremely unlikely that the speakers of one of the two language-families could have been introduced to the creature itself by the speakers of the other.

Therefore, if one or two of the names (Sanskrit is a rich language having many names for any one object), even the commonest one, for any plant or animal in Sanskrit happens to coincide with the name (or the commonest name, or one of the names) for the same plant or animal in Austric or Dravidian languages, the implied borrowing, in whichever direction, need not *necessarily* indicate previous non-acquaintance with that plant or animal.

2. The commonest Sanskrit name for the peacock is *mayūra* or *mayūraka* (with derivatives in almost all the Indo-Aryan languages). The word has a feminine form *mayūrī*. Sir Monier-Williams[27] derives this word from the root *mā* –, "to bleat."

However, many scholars attempt to brand this as a non-Indo-European word. S.K. Chatterji, for example, goes to the ludicrous extent of deriving it from the Kol-Munda *marak* in one place,[28] and from the Dravidian (e.g. Tamil) *mayil* in another.[29] The fact that the Austric word resembles the form *mayūraka* while the Dravidian word resembles the form *mayūra* would, however, indicate that the Sanskrit word is more likely to be the original.

Mayūra, moreover, is just one of the Sanskrit names for the peacock, others being *barhiṇa, vṛṣin* and *śikhin/śikhaṇḍin*. The Dravidian languages have another word more widely distributed than *mayil*: Tamil *navil*, Kannada *navilu*, Telugu *nemali*.

The most rational explanation is that the common Indian name (common to all the three families) is a colloquial word which gained currency all over the land, superseding in common usage all the other words.

3. The Vedic and Sanskrit words for the dog and the horse are *śvān* and *aśva* respectively. These are attested by most of the other branches of Indo-European languages. Thus, the common words for the dog

[27] SED, p. 789.
[28] HCIP, p. 150
[29] ODBL, p. 42.

(Greek *kuon*, Latin *canis*, Irish *cu*, Lithuanian *suo*, Lettic *suns*, Kashmiri *hun*, German *hund*, etc.) and the horse (Greek *hippos*, Latin *equus*, Irish *ech*, Lithuanian *ešva/ašva*, Illyrian *ikkos*, Old English *eoh*, etc.) have led to the reconstruction of two proto-Indo-European words **kuon* and **ekwo* respectively.

Now in Sanskrit we also find the words *kukkura* and *ghoṭaka*, respectively, for the dog and the horse. Almost all the modern Indo-Aryan words are derived from them (only the Sinhalese language has the word *asuwa* for horse, doubtless a literary word popularized; and the languages in the Kashmir region, and Konkani in the south, which has a tradition of migrating southwards from Kashmir, have words for dog derived from *śvan*). These two words are not found in the Vedic language, but nor can they be derived from Austric or Dravidian (which have words of their own) although persistent efforts have been made by scholars to so derive them. Monier-Williams,[30] however, derives the word *ghoṭaka* from the Sanskrit root *ghuṭ*-, "to protect".

If one is to derive conclusions from these words, what would the conclusions be? Can we brand the words *kukkura* and *ghoṭaka* as "non-Aryan" words simply because they are not found in the Vedic and Iranian and European languages, even when they cannot be proved to be Austric or Dravidian in origin? Can we brand them as "non-Aryan" words simply because their etymological derivations are doubtful, when, according to Carl D. Buck, even the word **kuon* has a "root connection much disputed and dubious",[31] and the word **ekwo* has a "root connection wholly obscure"[32]? Can we, if we accept that the words are borrowed from Austric or Dravidian, presume that the "Aryan invaders" borrowed these words because they were not acquainted with the dog and the horse before the "non-Aryan natives" introduced these animals to them?

The overwhelming majority of Sanskrit names for Indian plants and animals are derived from Sanskrit and Indo-European roots. And any attempt to prove an Aryan invasion on the basis of a few insignificant and flimsy examples of allegedly "borrowed" names proves to be untenable on rational consideration.

SPECIFIC SURVEY OF NAMES OF PLANTS AND ANIMALS

Let us, nevertheless examine the Sanskrit names for some of the

[30] SED, p. 379.
[31] ADOSS, p. 179.
[32] ADOSS, p. 167.

plants and animals native to India.

1. S.K. Chatterji[33] gives seven Sanskrit names which he claims are borrowed from Dravidian languages. Of these, the word *mayūra* has already been dealt with.

Chatterji claims that *markaṭa* and *kapi*, both names for the monkey, are borrowed from Dravidian. But neither of the two words is found in any Dravidian language, the closest being *maṅga* in Kannada. In any case, both the words are clearly derived from Sanskrit roots: *markaṭa* is derived[34] from the root *mark-*, "to move swiftly", (*marka*, "the wind"); and *kapi* is derived[35] from *kapila*, "brownish red" (cognate Greek word *kapnós*, "smoke-coloured").

He also names *taṇḍula* and *vrīhi*, both "rice", as Dravidian loan-words. However, the word *taṇḍula* is clearly derived [36] from the Sanskrit root *taṇḍ-*, "to beat", from *taḍ-*, "to knock, to thud", and refers to the rice grains, dehusked *by threshing*. As for the word *vrīhi*, K.D. Sethna[37] points out at length that it is the Sanskrit word which is the original word from which the Tamil word *arisi* is derived, and not vice versa as alleged by scholars. The Sanskrit word *vrīhi* (with its secondary form *vrīhyam*) is the only one which accounts for the different prevalent forms: Tamil *arisi*, Telugu *varī* (also the name in many Indian languages for another rice-like grain), Sinhalese *wī*, and Telugu *biyyamu*.

Chatterji claims that *tila*, "sesame", is a Dravidian loan-word. But we do not find the word in the Dravidian languages, which have their own two words, cf. Tamil *yeḷ* and *nū*, for sesame.

The seventh word claimed by Chatterji as a Dravidian loan-word is *khaḍgī*, "rhinoceros". But the word, as it occurs in the Dravidian languages (Telugu *khaḍgamrigamu*, Kannada *khaḍgamriga*), is obviously a borrowing from Sanskrit, as indicated by the Sanskrit word *mṛiga*, "animal", used as a suffix. The word, moreover, is very clearly derived[38] from *khaḍga*, "sword", which is itself derived from the Sanskrit root *khaṇḍ-*, "to break".

Thus, not a single one of the seven words, named by Chatterji, proves to be a Dravidian word on examination.

[33] ODBL, p. 42.
[34] SED, p. 791.
[35] ADOSS, p. 188.
[36] SED, p. 432
[37] Karpāsa, pp. 145-51.
[38] SED, p. 335.

2. Chatterji[39] also gives twelve Sanskrit names which he claims are borrowed from Austric languages. His principle seems to be: whenever the etymology of a Sanskrit word seems to be doubtful, brand it as a borrowing from Austric. But, as we have already seen, doubtful etymology is not a valid criterion for branding a word as "non-Aryan", and, as Zide has demonstrated,[40] words glibly branded as Austric words borrowed by Sanskrit prove, on examination, to be Sanskrit words borrowed by the Austric languages.

Let us, nevertheless, examine the more important among the words named by Chatterji.

He claims that the words *gaja* and *mātaṅga*, both names for the elephant, are borrowed from Austric. These words, of course, are not found in the Rigveda; but there we find three other names for the elephant, *hastin*, *ibha* and *vāraṇa*, all three of which are distinctly Sanskrit words. The two words named by Chatterji are also clearly derived from Sanskrit roots; *gaja*[41] from the root *garj-*, "to sound, to roar, to trumpet", and *mātaṅga*[42] from *matam* + *ga*, "roaming at will" (referring to the elephant's progress in the jungle as it crashes through the undergrowth; or as per another derivation, from the root *mad-*, referring to the elephant's drunken, swaying gait).

Moreover, neither of the two words is found in any of the Kol-Munda languages: almost all the languages have words derived from the distinctly Sanskrit word *hastin*, except for the Sora word *ra* and the Gadba word *kom*, neither of which bears the least resemblance to the words *gaja* and *mātaṅga*.

Chatterji brands the Sanskrit words, *kadalī* and *nārikela*, for two of the most important Indian fruits, the banana and the coconut respectively, as Austric words, on the ground that the etymological derivations of the two words are doubtful.

However, a survey of the related words in the Kol-Munda languages clearly shows that the words have been borrowed by these languages from the Indo-Aryan languages. Thus, the words in some of the languages clearly resemble the *tatsama* Sanskrit words, while the words in some others clearly resemble the *tadbhava* forms in the Indo-Aryan languages. Thus, we find the Ho word *kadal* and the Kol word *kodal* resembling the Sanskrit *kadalī*; while the Santali word *kaera*, the

[39] HCIP, p. 150.
[40] CTL, Vol. 5, p. 420.
[41] SED, p. 342.
[42] SED, p. 806.

Mundari word *kela*, the Kharia word *kera*, etc. resemble the *tadbhava* forms. Likewise, the Santali words *narkol/narkor* resemble the Sanskrit words *nārikela/narikera*; while the Kharia word *naryal* distinctly resembles the *tadbhava* forms.

P.O. Bodding, in his monumental Santal–English dictionary unambiguously designates the Santali word *kaera*, "banana", as a borrowing from Hindi, and the words *narkol/narkor*, "coconut", as a borrowing from the more Sanskritized Bengali.

Chatterji also brands the Sanskrit word *kurkuṭa/kṛkavāka* for the domestic fowl as a borrowing from Austric. The word is so obviously an onomatopoeic word, imitative of the crowing and clucking of the fowl, that it is really ridiculous to brand it as a borrowing from one language into another without some solid and substantial evidence; especially in this case, where the Kol-Munda languages have, instead, their own distinctive set of related words for the fowl: cf. Santali *sim sandi*, Korwa *sim*, Juang *sanke*, Sora *kansim*, Gadba *ghusangdang*, etc. Only the Kurku and Nahali *komba* and the Kharia *kokro*, both of which are obviously borrowed from the Indo-Aryan languages, bear any resemblance to Indo-Aryan words.

Another word branded by Chatterji as a borrowing from Austric is *śālmalī*, "silk-cotton". However, the word cannot be found in the Kol-Munda languages, except, if at all, as a borrowing from Indo-Aryan. The Santali word is *murup*, and the Sora word is *kukui*.

Another important Sanskrit word branded as a borrowing from Austric is *karpāsa*, "cotton". Even a scholar like K.D. Sethna (in his book, *Karpāsa*) appears to accept this derivation. It may, of course, turn out that the cultivation of cotton commenced in east-central India in the region of the Austric languages, but the word itself proves no such thing. Sethna[43] accepts the derivation admittedly on the testimony of Chatterji, and the value of Chatterji's testimony in regard to Sanskrit words branded as "Austric" has already been discussed. In this particular case, we may compare the present-day Austric words for cotton: Santali *kaskom*, Kharia *siḍij*, Sora *adi*; of these, only the Santali word *kaskom* can claim similarity with the Sanskrit *karpāsa*; and this word, testified from ancient Sanskrit texts, cannot be arbitrarily declared as a borrowing from a language which is known to be loaded with Sanskrit words, on the basis of similarity with a recently attested word in that language (i.e. Santali), without even explaining the additional sound *rp* in the middle of the Sanskrit word. *Kaskom* is more likely to be a devel-

[43] Karpāsa, p. 5.

opment of *karpāsa*, later *kapāsa*.

Thus, the attempt to prove an Aryan invasion on the basis of names of plants and animals, allegedly borrowed by Sanskrit from Austric and Dravidian languages, fails miserably.

3. In fact, a consideration of the names of three important Indian animals, in the three main language-families of India, only serves to confirm that the present-day geographical distribution of these language-families is more or less the same as that which prevailed in ancient times. These are the camel (found in the northwestern parts of India), the lion (now confined to a part of Gujarat, formerly found all over northwestern and northern India), and the rhinoceros (now confined to Assam, but originally widely spread in the north and northwest, as testified by the Indus seals).

If the north and northwest were originally populated by the Dravidians or Austrics, who were later displaced by the Indo-Aryans, the names for these three animals in Sanskrit should have been borrowed from Dravidian or Austric; or at any rate the Dravidian and Austric languages should have had full-fledged common words of their own for these three animals. On the contrary, while the Indo-Aryan languages have full-fledged common words derivable from Sanskrit roots, the Dravidian and Austric languages have, by and large, borrowed these words from them.

The Sanskrit word for camel is *uṣṭra*, with a cognate form *uštra* in Avestan (Iranian). The words, according to Carl Buck,[44] are derived from the same root as the word *ukṣan*, "ox". All the modern Indo-Aryan words (e.g. Hindi *ū̃t*, etc.); practically all the Dravidian words (Tamil and Malayalam *voṭṭagam*, Kannada and Telugu *voṇṭe*, Toda *voṭṭe*, Brahui *huch*, etc.) with the sole exception of a rare Telugu word (*lōṭipita*) and practically all the Austric words (Santali and Kharia *ū̃t*, etc. and even the Khasi *ut*) with the sole exception of a Sora word *sisalaj*, are derived from the Sanskrit word.

The Sanskrit words for the rhinoceros are *khaḍgī* and *gaṇḍa*, both of which have clear Sanskrit derivations: *khaḍgī*, as already pointed out, is derived[45] through *khaḍga*, "sword", from *khaṇḍ-*" to break', and refers to the rhinoceros' horn; while *gaṇḍa* (also *gaṇḍaka*, *gaṇḍāṅga*) is derived[46] from *gaṇḍa*, "cheek, boil, pimple", and refers to the folds of skin or "armour" on the rhinoceros' body. The Dravidian languages

[44] ADOSS, p. 190.
[45] SED, p. 335.
[46] SED, p. 344.

have words derived from these two names (Tamil *kāṇḍāmirugam*, Telugu *khaḍgamrigamu*, Kannada *khaḍgamriga*). The Austric languages either borrow the Indo-Aryan words, or have no words for the rhinoceros at all. The Santali language also uses a phrase *dak-sadom*, "water-horse", which is like the Greek word coined for the African animal *hippopotamus*, "river-horse". The phrase is clearly a late-coined and artificial word, and in fact, according to Bodding, it is used "only in books"; otherwise the word is just *sadom*, "horse". In short, there is no separate word for the rhinoceros.

The Sanskrit word for the lion is *siṁha*, which is derived[47] from the root *sah-*, and means "the powerful one". (Another word is *keśarī*, derived from *keśa*, "hair", and means "the hairy one"). The Dravidian languages have words derived from the Sanskrit word (Tamil *cingam*, Telugu *simhamu*, Kannada *simha*, etc.), as also the Austric languages (Santali *sinho*, Sora *sinam-kidan*, etc.). In Santali, the word *kul*, originally "tiger", is now used for "lion" as a contraction of the phrase *dhacri-kul*, "maned-tiger" (modelled on the Sanskrit *keśarī*).

The natural interpretation of the above facts is obvious: it is the Indo-Aryan languages, and not the Austric or Dravidian, which were originally spoken in the northern and northwestern parts of India.

4. As already pointed out, most of the "inherited names" (found in both India and Europe) of plants and animals are etymologically "obscure"; and therefore if an Indo-Aryan name or two for an Indian plant or animal is also etymologically obscure (without proving to be of Austric or Dravidian origin) it cannot be branded as "non-Aryan".

But, in fact, a comparison of the names of plants and animals in Sanskrit with those in the European languages will show that the Sanskrit names of plants and animals (which do not have common names in both India and Europe) are derivable from Sanskrit or Indo-European roots, and much more so than the European names. Let us examine the names of three categories of animals: the camel and the elephant (found in India, not found in South Russia or Europe, but known in Europe from North Africa through Greece); the ass and the lion (found in India, not found in South Russia, but found in Southern Europe in ancient times, the European lion now long extinct); and the cat and the fish (generally found everywhere).

Almost all the Sanskrit names for the camel (*uṣṭra*, *maya*, *śarabha*) and the elephant (*hastin*, *ibha*, *vāraṇa*, *gaja*, *mātaṅga*, *kuñjara*, etc.) are

[46] SED, p. 344.
[47] SED, p. 1213.

derived from Sanskrit roots. The European words, according to Carl Buck,[48] are borrowed from a north African source through Greek.

The Sanskrit words for the ass (*gardabha, rāsabha, khara*) and the lion (*siṁha, keśarī, hari, mṛgendra*), are derived from Sanskrit roots. According to Carl Buck, the European words for the ass are derived[49] from Sumerian *ansu* through Greek; and the words for the lion are derived[50] from a north African source through Greek.

The Sanskrit names for the fish are also derived from Sanskrit roots. According to Carl Buck,[51] the Sanskrit word *matsya* (with its Avestan cognate *masya*) is derived from the Indo-European root *mad-*, "to be wet". The European words, however, are all of doubtful origin: the Greek word *ichthys* (with cognates also in the Baltic and Armenian branches, besides the Greek), the Latin word *piscis* (with cognates in the Germanic and Celtic branches, besides the Romance), and the Slavonic word *ryba* are all classified by Carl Buck as words of unknown etymology.

The Sanskrit names for the cat are also derived from Sanskrit roots. According to Buck,[52] the word *mārjāra* is derived from the root *mṛj-*, "to wipe, to clean". The European words, however, are not so smoothly derivable. The ancient Greek *aielouros* and the ancient Latin *feles* are, according to him,[53] words which originally referred to the ferret or marten and were later transferred to the cat. The only proper name for the cat in practically all the European languages, including later Greek and later Latin, are from the Latin words *cattus/gattus/catta*, which is "of dubious origin". (The only other words are the Romanian *pisica* and the Serbocroat *macka*, which are based on "a call word" and "a pet name for Maria" respectively.)

From all this, it is obvious that Sanskrit has etymologically derived names for the overwhelming majority of animals, while the European languages have names which are clearly borrowed or of obscure origin.

5. The Sanskrit texts, right from the Rigveda, have names for practically all the prominent Indian plants and animals, and these names are distinctly Indo-Aryan names and not borrowed ones.

The Rigveda itself mentions, for example, such purely Indian animals as the gaur, blackbuck, muskdeer, chital, buffalo, elephant,

[48] ADOSS, pp. 189-90.
[49] ADOSS, p. 173.
[50] ADOSS, p. 185.
[51] ADOSS, p. 184.
[52] ADOSS, p. 182.
[53] ADOSS, pp. 181-82.

hyaena, monkey, peacock, parrot, and many others. Some, not mentioned by chance in the Rigveda, are mentioned in the immediately post-Rigvedic texts, e.g. the tiger, leopard, mongoose, crocodile, python, and many others. When we consider that the intention of the Vedic poets was not exactly to provide the future generations with documentary evidence about the plants and animals known to them, the evidence is certainly considerable.

So much so that motivated scholars are compelled to clutch at straws, such as the non-mention of the tiger in the Rigveda, to claim that the Rigvedic Aryans were strangers or newcomers in India. That the composers of the Rigveda, who demonstrate such detailed and intimate familiarity with so many animals found only in India, should be supposed to be unacquainted with the tiger merely because they do not mention it in the hymns, does not seem to strike these scholars as ridiculous—inspite of the fact that the name of one of the composers of hymn IX 97, is Vyāghrapāda!

The Sanskrit word *vyāghra* is distinctly derived[54] from the root *ghrā*, "to smell", through *vyā-ghrā*, "to scent out", and is distinct from the common Dravidian word (Tamil *puli*, Kannada *huli*, etc.) and the common Austric words (Santali *kul*, Sora *kinan*, etc.).

In short, all the evidence that can be derived from a study of the Sanskrit names of Indian plants and animals only confirms that the Indo-Europeans were native to India.

[54] SED, p. 1036.

SEVENTEEN

VEDIC SANSKRIT VS. LATER INDO-ARYAN

According to S.K. Chatterji, "the theory of an Aryan invasion of India is borne out by...the character of the Vedic speech, which in its habits differentiates itself from later Indo-Aryan and associates itself with Greek and others in preserving a pure Indo-European structure."[1]

The fact is that there is a significant structural difference between the Vedic language on the one hand, and the later Indo-Aryan languages on the other. While the Vedic language resembles "Greek and others", the later Indo-Aryan languages resemble the Dravidian languages in linguistic structure. The inference drawn from this is that the "earliest" Indo-European speech in India, the Vedic speech, had entered the land from outside, and hence it preserved a "pure Indo-European structure" akin to the other ancient Indo-European languages outside India, and was as yet uninfluenced by the "native" (Dravidian) languages. However, after settling down in India, the speech of the Indo-Aryans was progressively influenced more and more by the "native" languages, and hence took on a similar structure.

This question, of the difference in linguistic structure between the Vedic language and the modern Indo-Aryan languages, and of the implications of this difference, requires to be examined in detail.

We will therefore examine, step by step, the validity of the explanations put forward by the invasion-theorists. There is, as we shall see, an alternate explanation for this linguistic phenomenon, and it is in fact the only one which really fits all the facts of the case. What is more, this explanation, which goes against the invasion theory, has been unwittingly admitted by the invasion-theorists themselves.

We will examine the issue under the following heads:

1. a. The chronology of linguistic change.
   b. The nature of change—"Non-Aryan"?
   c. The nature of change—"Dravidian Influence"?
2. The "other", or Non-Vedic, "Aryans".

THE CHRONOLOGY OF LINGUISTIC CHANGE

Here we will examine a question which does not have to do directly with the alleged linguistic "change" from the Vedic language to the modern Indo-Aryan languages, but which forms the basic logic

[1] ODBL, pp. 26-27.

behind the interpretation of this alleged "change".

If a certain degree of linguistic change has taken place in a language, can this change be chronologically measured (that is, can the time-frame, in which the change must have taken place, be calculated merely by consideration of the change itself)? And is such change always attributable to the inspiration or influence of some other language?

For this purpose, let us take the two languages which B.K. Ghosh[2] takes up in order to illustrate his method of arriving at 1000 BC as the "date" of the Rigveda — viz. English and German.

Both English and German are languages belonging to the Germanic branch of Indo-European languages and in fact to the same southern sub-section of the branch, and at one stage were close to each other in linguistic form and structure. And yet, today, the two have evolved so sharply away from each other that they represent two distinct language types. We shall take the following basic aspects of their vocabulary, syntax and grammar.

Vocabulary

1. While the German language has developed its own vocabulary from its original Germanic root-words, the English language has borrowed heavily from the Italic branch (Latin and the modern Romance languages). Examine, for example, the following list of words picked out at random from a book of comparative vocabulary:

ENGLISH	SPANISH	GERMAN
evidence	la evidencia	der Beweis
evolution	la evolución	die Entwickelung
exact	exacto	genau
exaggeration	la exageración	die Übertreibung
exaltation	la exaltacion	die Erhebung
examination	la examen	die Prüfung
example	el ejemplo	das Beispiel
exasperation	el exasperación	die Erbitterung
excavation	el excavación	die Aushöhlung
exceed	exceder	überschreiten
excellent	excelente	vortrefflich
except	exceptuar	ausnehmen
excess	el exceso	das Übermass
excitable	excitable	erregbar
exclamation	el exclamación	der Ausruf

[2] HCIP, pp. 203-04.

The effect is startling. Going by such evidence alone, English could be branded a Romance language rather than a Germanic one.

2. Not only is the vocabulary distinct, but even the attitude towards words is different. The German style of combining words to an extreme extent is also foreign to English. Douglas Busk, for example (in his book, *The Curse of Tongues and Some Remedies*, parodies this by giving his idea of the headline which a German newspaper would probably give if an assassination attempt were made on the Hottentot emperor's wife on a visit to Germany: "Hottentottenpotentatentantenattentäter... which, despite its thirty-eight letters, would be instantly comprehensible to any German reader."

Syntax

The German vocabulary, as we have seen, is richly distinct from the English. Now see what Frederick Bodmer has to say (in his book, *The Loom of Language*, p. 286) about German syntax: "The most important difference between English and the two German languages is the order of words. It is so great that half the work of translating a passage from a German or Dutch book remains to be done when the meaning of all the individual words is clear, especially if it conveys new information or deals with abstract ideas."

Grammar

In grammar also, the two languages have evolved so differently that German grammar is a nightmare for any English speaker. Just a glance at the articles and the adjective in German will make this point clear.

In English, there are only two articles, "the" (pronounced rather differently before vowels and consonants) and "a/an" (also, for euphonic reasons, having different forms before consonants and vowels).

In German, however, both the definite article as well as the indefinite article change according to gender, number and case. Thus we have masculine, feminine, neuter and plural forms, further differentiated into nominal, accusative, genitive and dative case-forms:

Definite (the)

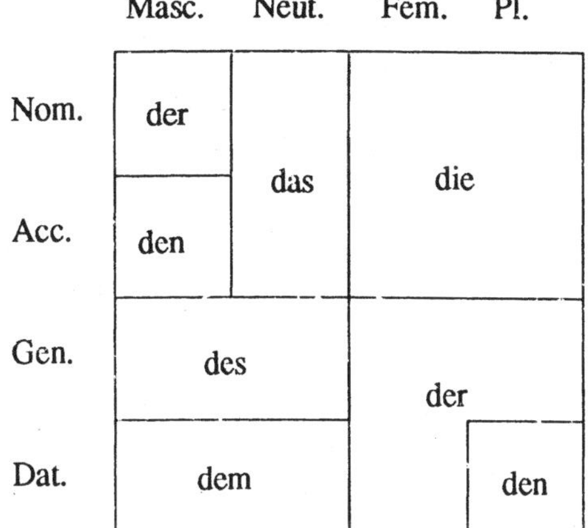

<table>
<tr><th></th><th>Masc.</th><th>Neut.</th><th>Fem.</th><th>Pl.</th></tr>
<tr><td>Nom.</td><td>der</td><td rowspan="2">das</td><td colspan="2" rowspan="2">die</td></tr>
<tr><td>Acc.</td><td>den</td></tr>
<tr><td>Gen.</td><td colspan="2">des</td><td colspan="2">der</td></tr>
<tr><td>Dat.</td><td colspan="2">dem</td><td></td><td>den</td></tr>
</table>

Indefinite (a/an)

<table>
<tr><th></th><th>Masc.</th><th>Neut.</th><th>Fem.</th></tr>
<tr><td>Nom.</td><td colspan="2">ein</td><td rowspan="2">eine</td></tr>
<tr><td>Acc.</td><td>einen</td><td></td></tr>
<tr><td>Gen.</td><td colspan="2">eines</td><td rowspan="2">einer</td></tr>
<tr><td>Dat.</td><td colspan="2">einem</td></tr>
</table>

The behaviour of the German adjective is even more incredible. The English adjective has only one form, but the German adjective changes not only according to gender, number and case, but also according to what precedes it. Take the example of the English adjective "blind", and its German equivalent, also "blind":

a. When used as a predicate, it remains unchanged, e.g. *sie ist blind* = he is blind.
b. When there is a demonstrative or a definite article before it (e.g. that, the, etc.), the adjective has the following forms:

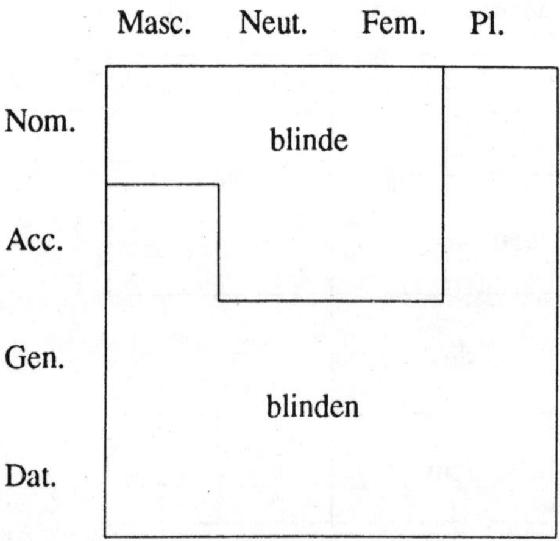

c. When there is a possessive or an indefinite article before it (e.g. my, a, etc.), the adjective has the following forms. But note, also, the forms taken by the possessive (e.g. my) before the adjective:

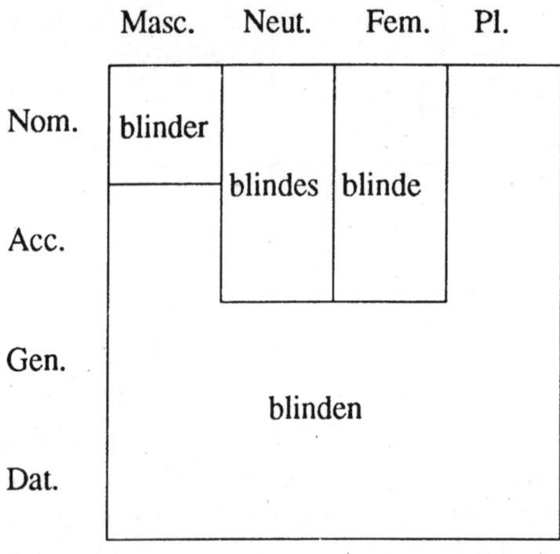

<table>
<tr><td>mein blinder</td><td rowspan="2">mein blindes</td><td rowspan="2">meine blinde</td><td rowspan="2">meine blinden</td></tr>
<tr><td>meinen blinden</td></tr>
<tr><td colspan="2">meines blinden</td><td rowspan="2">meiner blinden</td><td></td></tr>
<tr><td colspan="2">meinem blinden</td><td>meinen blinden</td></tr>
</table>

d. When there is no demonstrative, article or possessive before it, the adjective has the following forms:

<table>
<tr><td></td><td>Masc.</td><td>Neut.</td><td>Fem.</td><td>Pl.</td></tr>
<tr><td>Nom.</td><td>blinder</td><td rowspan="2"></td><td colspan="2" rowspan="2">blinde</td></tr>
<tr><td>Acc.</td><td>blinden</td></tr>
<tr><td>Gen.</td><td colspan="2">blindes</td><td rowspan="2">blinder</td><td></td></tr>
<tr><td>Dat.</td><td colspan="2">blindem</td><td>blinden</td></tr>
</table>

Thus, we find that the English and German languages are, in a structural sense, as different as chalk and cheese. The differences in vocabulary can be attributed to a strong Italic influence on English (although no one will be able to logically explain, much less to linguistically quantify, the exact factors which could have resulted in such a marked difference in degree of Latinization of vocabulary in English and German), but the structural differences cannot be so easily explained. The Italic languages also, like German, have complicated conjugations of the verb, and grammatical gender in nouns; but English does not.

Moreover, structural changes as in English have also taken place in another Indo-European language geographically at a great distance from England: the Persian language. Modern Persian has become so analytic that it stands apart from almost all the other Indo-European languages. As W.B. Lockwood puts it: "Modern Persian has been called the English of the East since it is so highly analytic. Grammatical gender has disappeared, nouns have no case inflexions, adjectives are invariable."[3] These changes cannot be attributed to the influence of other languages, since the neighbouring languages (Semitic, Uralo-Altaic, other Indo-Iranian) are not analytic languages.

Therefore, it is clear that neither can linguistic change be chronologically measured, nor can it be considered as necessarily attributable to the inspiration or influence of some other language or language-group.

THE NATURE OF "CHANGE"—"NON-ARYAN"?

In the case of the Indo-Aryan languages, however, we have not merely the fact that the modern languages show a marked difference in linguistic structure from the Vedic; but that this structure bears similarity with that of the Dravidian languages.

The "changes" alleged to have taken place in Indo-Aryan languages, between Vedic and the modern languages, are alleged to be due to Dravidian influence. In short, they are presumed to be "changes" of a "non-Aryan" kind which have taken place in an originally "Aryan" form of the Indo-Aryan languages.

Let us first examine here whether the features of the Indo-Aryan languages, which are said to constitute these "changes", can be branded as "non-Aryan".

S.K. Chatterji,[4] under the heading, "Points of similarity between Indo-Aryan and Dravidian, showing probable influence of the latter", lists these similarities under four headings: Phonetic, Morphological, Syntactical and Glossic.

So far as Glossic similarities are concerned, Chatterji states: "The Aryan speech has been borrowing words from the Dravidian ever since the former came to India."[5] This amazing contention, sweeping and smug as it is in its presumptuousness, has already been dealt with in the previous chapter, and can be ignored here.

Here we will examine the Phonetic and Morphological similarities

[3] POIEL, p. 250.
[4] ODBL, pp. 170-78.
[5] ODBL, p. 178.

listed by Chatterji:

1. "Paucity of diphthongs..."[6]
2. "Comparative absence of spirants... the change of the Indo-Iranian spirant « Ź (Źh) » to the stop « j (jh) » might have been brought about in India in Dravidian surroundings."[7]
3. "The occurrence of cerebrals... peculiarly Dravidian sounds—not found in any ancient Indo-European speech other than Vedic and Sanskrit."[8]
4. "Insertion of short vowels by anaptyxis..."[9]
5. "The gradual disuse of prepositions..." and the development instead of post-positions, especially "in late Middle Indo-Aryan and New Indo-Aryan—post-positions of nominal and verbal origin..."[10]
6. "Absence of affixes in the comparison of the adjectives in both New Indo-Aryan and Dravidian."[11]
7. "Both New Indo-Aryan and Dravidian had developed the use in a most curious and idiomatic way, of conjunctives and participles with adverbial functions giving rise to what is known as the 'compound verb'..."[12]
8. "An almost wholesale disuse of Old Indo-Aryan moods and tenses, reducing the verb system of Aryan to an indicative present form..."[13] etc.
9. "Onomatopoetic formations on a lavish scale are characteristic of both New Indo-Aryan and Dravidian...Vedic is remarkably poor in onomatopoetics."[14]
10. "Presence of echo-words—this is found in Modern Indo-Aryan and in Dravidian."[15]

The point here is not whether these features are common to both Indo-Aryan and Dravidian. The point is: are these features such as could only have come about, in Indo-Aryan languages, through "Dravidian influence"?

Chatterji's own words give the lie to this. Of the ten points men-

[6] ODBL, p. 170.
[7] Ibid.
[8] Ibid.
[9] ODBL, p. 171.
[10] ODBL, p. 172.
[11] ODBL, p. 173.
[12] ODBL, p. 174.
[13] Ibid.
[14] ODBL, p. 175.
[15] ODBL, p. 176.

tioned by him, his own words prove that at least four of these features are paralleled in Indo-European languages outside the sphere of Dravidian influence:

a. The question of cerebrals has already been dealt with in a previous chapter. Chatterji himself points out that "in modern Swedish, among new Indo-European tongues, however, « ḍ » has developed out of « r+d », which is paralleled by a similar cerebralisation in Old Māgadhī".[16]
b. About anaptyxis, Chatterji himself admits that "it took place also in Italic among other Indo-European languages".[17]
c. About the absence of affixes in the comparison of adjectives, Chatterji admits that many modern Indo-European languages (French fully, and modern Greek and English partly) have also dropped the affixes in the comparison of adjectives and "employed words meaning *more* and *most* before the adjective in question".[18] But this is exactly what has happened in Indo-Aryan languages.
d. About the disuse of old Indo-Aryan moods and tenses, Chatterji himself admits: "a similar decay has taken place in Iranian."[19]
e. About onomatopoetic formations, Chatterji himself admits that; "the onomatopoetic *deśī* formations do not offer any scope for comparison with non-Aryan speeches, except in noticing a general agreement in principle".[20]
f. About the development of post-positions, rather than prepositions in Indo-Aryan languages, Chatterji cannot explain why it should be considered surprising, regardless of other Indo-European languages outside India having developed prepositions, when we consider the fact that the oldest Indo-European languages had inflected forms (which died out, giving rise to prepositions in other Indo-European languages) which must have represented noun + decayed forms of original post-positions.
g. About the "comparative absence of spirants", Chatterji claims that the "change of the Indo-Iranian spirant « ź (źh) » to the stop « j/jh » might have been brought about in India in Dravidian surroundings". But which recorded specimen of "proto-Indo-Iranian" language is Chatterji referring to when he so confidently

[16] ODBL, p. 170.
[17] ODBL, p. 171.
[18] ODBL, p. 174.
[19] Ibid.
[20] ODBL, p. 200.

states that "Indo-Iranian" had spirants rather than stops? If he is deducing it from the presence of spirants, rather than stops, in the other Indo-European languages, then it is a presumption made to explain a fact which is just as easily explained by the theory outlined in this book: viz. that the ancestral forms of the European languages constituted the "Outer Indo-European" dialects spoken in northern Kashmir and Afghanistan, and the ancestral forms of the Iranian languages constituted the northern section of the "Central Indo-European" dialects. These were also spoken in the Kashmir region, while the Rigvedic language, which constituted the southern section of the "Central Indo-European" dialects, was spoken in the Punjab region. Hence it is natural that Iranian should have some similarities with the European branches of Indo-European.

The other features mentioned by Chatterji (paucity of diphthongs, formation of compound verbs, presence of echo-words) also do not constitute, in any sense, features which could be considered as sharp deviations from the natural path of Indo-European linguistic development.

Therefore, we get the following case: The Indo-Aryan and Dravidian languages are remarkably close in linguistic structure, without the points of similarity necessarily being deviations from the natural path of Indo-European linguistic development. What is the explanation for the similarities?

In matters of syntax for example, Chatterji describes it as follows: "It is in syntax that *Indian Aryandom and Indian Dravidiandom are one.*" He further clarifies this as follows: "A sentence in a Dravidian language like Tamil or Kannada becomes ordinarily good Bengali or Hindi by substituting Bengali or Hindi equivalents for the Dravidian words or forms, without modifying the word-order, but the same is not possible in rendering a Persian or English sentence into a New Indo-Aryan language." And it is not only in the case of New Indo-Aryan languages: "this began from early Middle Indo-Aryan as is seen from a comparison of the syntax of Pali and Prakrit with that of the modern vernaculars."[21]

But just before this, Chatterji also admits: "Syntax is regarded as being of greater importance in linguistics, *as an inherited peculiarity*, than phonetics or morphology, which are easily acquired or modified."[22]

[21] ODBL, pp. 176-77.
[22] ODBL, p. 176.

Syntax is, therefore, "an inherited peculiarity" in any normal circumstances. What are the circumstances in which it could be a borrowed phenomenon in the case of the Indo-Aryan languages?

Let us examine whether the reasons for "Indian Aryandom and Indian Dravidiandom" being "one" have to do with "Dravidian influence" on Indo-Aryan.

THE NATURE OF "CHANGE" — "DRAVIDIAN INFLUENCE"?

1. To begin with, the similarities cannot be due to Dravidian influence on Indo-Aryan languages, since such a circumstance would be linguistically unnatural.

Here is how Bhadriraju Krishnamurti, an authority on Dravidian linguistics and a staunch supporter of the Aryan invasion theory, puts it: "While it has been amply demonstrated that Dravidian and Indo-Aryan share many structural features, both in phonology and grammar, the mechanism through which the transmission of such features from one family to another takes place is still not clear. It is true that extensive bilingualism or multilingualism has been invoked as the main factor at work. It is generally accepted that language contact in the initial stages leads to lexical borrowing— with assimilatory (*tadbhava*) phase preceding the appropriation (*tatsama*) phase. Transmission of phonological structural features can thus be a direct consequence of lexical borrowing. Transfer of morphological and syntactic features is expected to follow at a more advanced stage of language contact, *necessarily presupposing extensive lexical borrowing.* The implication of this assumption is that a situation in which a given language or family of languages displays largescale structural borrowing from a neighbouring language or family of languages without extensive lexical borrowing should lead us to question the validity of the above hypothesis. This is relevant in the contact situation between Dravidian and Indo-Aryan. It is the Dravidian languages (particularly South Dravidian) which show evidence of extensive lexical borrowing but only a few traits of structural borrowing from Indo-Aryan. On the contrary, *Indo-Aryan (particularly Middle and Modern) shows largescale structural borrowing from Dravidian, but very little lexical borrowing.* How can we reconcile these conflicting facts in order to work them into the framework of a bilingual situation?"[23]

The facts are crystal clear: Linguistic borrowing always starts out with vocabulary, and it is only at an "advanced stage" of "extensive

[23] CTL, Vol. 5, p. 324.

lexical borrowing" that phonological structural features are borrowed; and only later that morphological and syntactic features are borrowed. This is the case everywhere.

Even the Dravidian languages follow the same pattern. As Krishnamurti points out, they "show evidence of extensive lexical borrowing but only a few traits of structural borrowing from Indo-Aryan".

Therefore, it is very clear that, unless the normal linguistic laws are to be treated as invalid just in order to accommodate the invasion-theorists' insistence that the linguistic structure of Indo-Aryan is borrowed from Dravidian, it will *have* to be accepted that the linguistic structure of Indo-Aryan *cannot possibly be "borrowed" from Dravidian.*

Then what is the explanation for the similarities?

2. Bhadriraju Krishnamurti, being a staunch supporter of the Aryan invasion theory, offers his own theory to explain the similarities: "That Middle Indo-Aryan and New Indo-Aryan have been built on a Dravidian substratum seems to be the only answer. The fact that the invading Aryans could never have outnumbered the natives, even though they politically controlled the latter, is a valid inference. We may formulate the situation as follows: If the speakers of L_1 (mother-tongue) are constrained to accept L_2 (second language) as their 'lingua franca', then an L_3 will develop with the lexicon of L_2 and with a mixture of the dominant structural features of L_1 and L_2. L_2= varieties of Sanskrit. L_3= Middle Indic...The hypothesis that most of present New Indo-Aryan speakers should have been originally Dravidians and also presumably Kolarians (Munda speakers) was suggested long ago..."[24]

Thus, Krishnamurti finds his own method of serving the Aryan invasion theory, and in an even more thorough manner than the normal method of advocating "Dravidian influence". Of course, as he admits, his method is not a new one. Chatterji also, for example, when speaking of the "insertion of short vowels by anaptyxis", suggests that "the adoption of the Aryan speech by Dravidians early in the history of Indo-Aryan had probably something to do with it."[25] However, Krishnamurti lays the entire stress on it due to his sharp awareness of the fact that the linguistic structure of Dravidian *cannot* have been borrowed by the Indo-Aryan languages.

But the theory put forward by Krishnamurti to explain the similarity in structure (by attributing it to an adoption of "Aryan" speech by originally Dravidian speakers) is as incredible as the one rightly re-

[24] CTL, Vol.5, pp. 324-25, footnotes.
[25] ODBL, p. 171.

jected by him (which attributes it to a borrowing of the Dravidian structure by Indo-Aryan speakers).

Krishnamurti hopefully expects us to swallow his idea of millions and millions of people all over North India, constituting the entire population of the land, completely dropping their original Dravidian language and adopting the "Aryan" language, and at the same time retaining the linguistic structure of their original Dravidian tongue by grafting it lock, stock and barrel on to their newly adopted Aryan tongue, but without retaining any significant part of their original vocabulary!

The situation depicted by Krishnamurti is an untenable one. He tries to make it appear plausible by giving what he apparently believes is a parallel situation in modern times: the English language as spoken by Indians.

According to him: "This is also true of modern Indian varieties of English, which have English (L_2) lexicon but a large number of structural features of Indian languages... Indian languages have freely borrowed words from English, but no structural features; transferring of only structural features, excluding the lexicon, is evident when Indians speak English as a second language."[26]

He has the grace to admit that "here of course, the situation is different, since the native languages have not been abandoned."[27] But this is a very great difference indeed, and a fundamental one. If (and it is a very big if) the English spoken by Indians bears any very minor imprint of the structural features of their own languages, it is *because* they have not abandoned their own languages, and *because* they regularly speak their own languages more often and more familiarly than they do English; and therefore when they speak English, a certain "Indian style" of English is inevitable.

But even here, the situation described by Krishnamurti does not prevail. There are many different varieties of Indian English, from that spoken by the consciously westernized and self-alienated sections of "elite" society to the broken English spoken by those with only a working knowledge of the language. But in every single variety, contrary to Krishnamurti's claim, transfer of Indian words is always greater than any alleged transfer of Indian structural features. The use of Indian verbs in English with the addition of the suffix "-fy", for example, is a slang feature of Indian English. The kind of language used in certain

[26] CTL, Vol.5, pp. 324-25, footnotes.
[27] CTL, Vol.5, p. 325, footnotes.

kinds of film magazines, for example, where one finds many Hindi words (in italics, usually) slangily used in English, but where one does not see any transfer of structural features, is a case in point. Even the most westernized sections, who may speak the most idiomatically and grammatically correct English, are likely to use their own native words in many situations.

Therefore, Krishnamurti's idea of a wholesale transfer of Dravidian structural features to the "adopted" Aryan languages, without any transfer of Dravidian vocabulary, by a widely distributed and originally Dravidian-language speaking populace, is a ridiculous one. His explanation, which reduces the Indo-Aryan languages to the level of pidgin English, is totally unsubstantiated by any historical evidence, is incompatible with any linguistic process, and is not a valid explanation for the similarities between Indo-Aryan and Dravidian.

3. The correct explanation for the structural similarity between Indo-Aryan and Dravidian languages is that the similar structure is not "borrowed" by any one of the two from the other. It cannot have been borrowed by the Dravidian languages, since there is no evidence to show that this was the original pan-Indo-European linguistic structure; and it cannot have been borrowed by the Indo-Aryan languages since there is no evidence of the "extensive lexical borrowing" which should precede any structural borrowing.

"Indian Aryandom and Dravidiandom are one" simply because the Indo-Aryan languages and the Dravidian languages developed this common linguistic structure conjointly. It is an "Indian" linguistic structure, and not an "Indo-Aryan" or a "Dravidian" one.

The confusion arises because people insist on presuming that the Vedic language was the earliest form of Indo-Aryan, that Classical Sanskrit developed from Vedic, that the Prakrits (Middle Indo-Aryan) developed from Sanskrit, and that the modern Indo-Aryan languages (New Indo-Aryan) developed from these Prakrits. Hence the features of the Prakrits and modern languages, where they differ from those of Sanskrit or Vedic, are regarded as "changes" that have taken place.

The actual facts, however, are as outlined in this book: The earliest form of Indo-European speech (proto-proto-Indo-European) was spoken in the interior of India, and in late prehistoric times, it spread out as far north and west as Kashmir and Afghanistan. The original language developed into at least three other proto-languages: proto-Outer-Indo-European (in northern Kashmir and Afghanistan), proto-Central-Indo-European (in southern Kashmir and Punjab), and proto-Inner-Indo-European (one or more proto-languages in north India, more or less in the present-day habitat of the Indo-Aryan languages).

The Outer-Indo-European language developed into the dialects which spread out of India into Europe, West Asia and Chinese Turkestan. The Central-Indo-European language developed into the Iranian-Dardic dialects in the north and the Rigvedic dialects in the south. The Inner-Indo-European language developed into the ancestral forms of the modern Indo-Aryan languages.

The modern Indo-Aryan languages, therefore, are not descendants of the Rigvedic dialects, but of other dialects which were contemporaneous with the Rigvedic dialects, but which belonged to a different section of Indo-European speech (the Inner-Indo-European section).

The Vedic dialects died away in the course of time, and their speech-area (the Punjab and its environs) was taken over by the Inner-Indo-European dialects. But long before they died away, the Vedic dialects had set in motion a powerful wave of a cult-movement which covered the entire nation in its sweep. This Vedic cult also finally gave way to the local pan-Indian religion of the Inner-Indo-Europeans and Dravidian-language speakers, but continued to remain in force as the elite layer of this pan-Indian religion.

The Vedic dialects remained the vehicles of the Vedic literature that followed the Rigveda; but soon the "Classical Sanskrit" language was artificially created by the ancient Indian grammarians (Pāṇini was preceded by hundreds of other linguists and grammarians, many of whom are named by him in his *Aṣṭādhyāyī)* in order to achieve a refined via-medium between the Vedic language and the Inner-Indo-European dialects (which had developed conjointly with the Dravidian languages over the course of millenniums, and were therefore structurally different from Vedic, and also had their own roots and words). Later the "Prakrits" (which were also not fully natural forms of speech, but which successively approximated, to a greater and greater degree, the Inner dialects) came into vogue. Finally the Inner dialects came into their own in the form of the "New Indo-Aryan" languages, as heavily Sanskritised as the Dravidian languages.

During the course of the millenniums, upto the present day, the various "Indo-Aryan" (i.e. Central and Inner-Indo-European) dialects and languages influenced each other in innumerable ways, too complicated to be analysed here. The speakers of the Central dialects (in the Punjab region) gradually merged into the Inner-Indo-European speech family, and today we find Inner-Indo-European languages, heavily Sanskritised, spoken all over North India upto the Dardic and Iranian speaking areas.

In short, the linguistic structure of the present Indo-Aryan languages is not a "change" from an originally Vedic-like linguistic structure; but a linguistic structure which developed, in the course of millenniums, in the Inner-Indo-European speech family, in conjunction with the Dravidian languages. This is parallelled by similar situations in pre-Columbian America, where languages belonging to different families (within the Amerindian Super-family of languages) within any single area (e.g. California) developed identical linguistic structures while developing their own vocabularies.

THE "OTHER", OR NON-VEDIC "ARYANS"

The movement of Indo-European languages outwards from within the interior of northern India, as outlined above, is not only the *only* explanation which explains the linguistic facts, but it is also a historical movement which is actually recorded in the historical traditions in the Sanskrit texts, as we shall see when we examine, in subsequent chapters, the evidence of these texts.

Here, however, let us first examine the testimony of various prominent scholars, every one of them a staunch supporter of the Aryan invasion theory, who have unwittingly admitted to certain facts which, in spite of their most strenuous efforts to incorporate them into the invasion theory, cannot be so incorporated, and which instead confirm the theory outlined in this book.

1. S.K. Chatterji has the following to say about the relations between the Vedic language and the modern Indo-Aryan languages: "The Aryan came to India, assuredly not as a single, uniform or standardised speech, but rather as a group or groups of dialects....only one of these dialects or dialect-groups has mainly been represented in the language of the Vedas—other dialects...(might) have been ultimately transformed into one or the other of the various New Indo-Aryan languages and dialects. The mutual relationship of these Old Indo-Aryan dialects, their individual traits and number as well as location, will perhaps never be settled... The true significance of the various Prakrits as preserved in literary and other records, their origin and interrelations, and their true connection with the modern languages, forms one of the most baffling problems of Indo-Aryan linguistics....and there has been admixture among the various dialects to an extent which has completely changed their original appearance, and which makes their affiliation to

forms of Middle Indo-Aryan as in our records at times rather problematical."[28]

Thus S.K. Chatterji unwittingly admits (although he tries to explain it within the framework of the invasion theory) that

a. There were many different dialects, of which the language of the Rigveda was *only one*; and that the New Indo-Aryan languages may well be descended from these other non-Vedic dialects.
b. The relations (within each chronological group: Old, Middle and New, as well as between different chronological groups) between the Old Indo-Aryan (Rigvedic and Classical Sanskrit, as well as the "other" dialects or dialect groups) and Middle-Indo-Aryan (Prakrits) and the present-day New Indo-Aryan languages is "baffling" and "problematical" and "will perhaps never be settled."

2. Even more specifically, these scholars unwittingly admit evidence of the existence of "Aryan"-language speaking people far to the east and south of the Punjab region, deep within India, *prior to the Vedic culture,* who had little to do with the Vedic culture.

a. J.H. Hutton,[29] who sought to draw up a classification of the races of India in 1933, postulated the existence of a race of "Vedic Aryans or Nordics, leptorrhine dolichocephals who brought the Vedic Aryan (Sanskrit) speech"; but he also found it necessary to postulate the existence of *another separate race* of "Alpines, brachycephalic leptorrhine, found in Gujarat and Bengal, *earlier than Vedic Aryans,* but probably speaking Aryan dialects".
b. S.K. Chatterji also points out: "All Aryan speakers, however, were not Vedic in their religion and outlook. There is evidence in the Rigveda that the Vedic Aryans fought not only with the non-Aryans but also with other Aryans, whose ideas and ways of life were probably dissimilar. Some of these non-Vedic Aryans seem to have preceded the Aryans of the Vedic cults in the east, along the Ganges, where the latter followed them from their midland headquarters. Other bodies of Aryans, keeping themselves equally aloof from the Vedic Aryans of the Eastern Punjab, were settled in western and south-western Punjab. These Aryans of the eastern tracts seem to have differed from the Midland or Vedic Aryans in many respects—in religious observances, in many practices, in dialect."[30]

[28] ODBL, pp. 20-21.
[29] HCIP, p. 142.
[30] ODBL, p. 40.

Further, "the Aryans of the Vedic cults called these non-Vedic Aryans 'Vrātyas', outcasts, or riteless people...these Vrātyas were most numerous...(in) Magadha... The rise and progress of the anti-Brāhmaṇa and the anti-sacrificial ideas of the Buddhists and the Jains among the eastern peoples—and these heterodox schools also called their teachings 'Aryan truths'—perhaps shows that other traditions were established before the Brāhmaṇas came, and the Vedic institutions or ideas brought by the Brāhmaṇas from the Midland and the Northwest (Madhyadeśa and Udīcya) sat lightly on the masses—the Vrātya hymns of the Atharvaveda (xv)...suggest the presence of a Śaiva cult among the Vrātyas, and certainly a cult quite different from that presented by the Vedic world."[31]

c. A.R. Hoernle and H.A. Stark (in *History of India*, Calcutta, 1904, pp. 12-13) postulated "a two-fold migration...the advent into India of two separate and antagonistic groups of Aryan speakers, both equally important...a group of Aryans first came into India and settled in the West Gangetic Doab or the midland country. They were followed by another group; and these newcomers dispossessed their kinsmen, who had come earlier, from their original settlements and forced them into tracts west, north, east and south of this Midland region. The newcomers thus became the 'Inner' Aryans, and their predecessors, who had to retreat into the outlying tracts, became the 'Outer' Aryans. It was among these 'Inner' Aryans that Vedic culture and Brahmanical ideas grew up."[32]

d. Ramā Prasad Chanda (in *Indo-Aryan Races*, Part I, Rajshahi, 1916) also reiterated the above views, on the basis of anthropometric evidence based on cephalic index: "According to Chanda, the 'Outer' Aryans were a brachycephalic race derived from a stock totally different from the 'Inner' Aryans, who were dolichocephalic. This difference in race went hand in hand with a difference in dialect. The dolichocephalic 'Inner' Aryans were the ancestors of the people of the Punjab, of the Rājpūts, and of the Brāhmaṇas of the Upper Ganges Valley (Hindostan): among them grew up the Vedic institutions and culture and the system of the four castes. The brachycephalic 'Outer' Aryans, who originally knew nothing of the Vedic cults, and from whose re-

[31] ODBL, p. 46.
[32] ODBL, p. 30.

ligious notions ultimately developed Vaiṣṇavism and Śāktism, were, in later times, profoundly influenced by the religion and ideas of the 'Inner' Aryans..."[33]

From all this, the following points may be noted:

1. All these prominent scholars mentioned above are staunch supporters of the Aryan invasion theory; and, even in representing the above facts, it may be noted that they employ terminology appropriate to the invasion theory: thus, they refer to *two* invasions.
2. But the fact is that they are compelled to postulate the existence of Aryan-language speaking people, who were distinct from the "Vedic Aryans" in race, religion and (within the Indo-European family) language, residing deep within India, and far to the east and south of the Punjab region, earlier than the "Vedic Aryans".
3. All the "evidence" and arguments produced by them, or by anyone else, in support of the Aryan invasion theory, pertains to the Vedic Aryans, whose close connection (religious, linguistic, etc.) with the Iranians has led to the concept of an interim Indo-Iranian homeland. It is *this* presumptuous "evidence" and *these* persistent arguments that we are dealing with, and conclusively disproving, in this book.
4. None of these scholars is able to give the slightest evidence, or the slenderest argument, to show that these non-Vedic Aryans, who are admitted to have been in existence in India far to the east and south of the Punjab region *prior* to the Vedic culture, also "invaded" India or migrated into it from outside. By keeping the question of the "invasion" of India by these Vedic Aryans in high profile, and "proving" this invasion to their own satisfaction, the protagonists of the invasion theory expect the theory of *another and earlier invasion* by racially and linguistically distinct non-Vedic "Aryans", whose very existence is kept in low profile, to be unquestioningly allowed to pass muster. These non-Vedic Aryans, it must be noted again, are admitted by them to be existing in India far to the east and south, *before* the development of the joint Indo-Iranian culture.

All this confirms the theory, outlined in this book, that movement of the Indo-European languages took place from within the interior of northern India, towards the north and west; and that the Rigvedic cul-

[33] ODBL, p. 32.

ture of the Punjab is not the culture of the "Aryans" in their geographically and chronologically first "settlements" in India, but the culture of a section of Indians (Indo-Europeans) who had moved northwestwards from within India.

EIGHTEEN

THE RACIAL EVIDENCE

According to S.K. Chatterji, "the theory of an Aryan invasion is borne out by... the wide difference in racial type between the South Indian Dravidians and the Northwest Indians."[1]

The very fact that the South Indians, who speak Dravidian languages, and the Northwest Indians, who speak Aryan (Indo-European) languages, are different from each other in racial type is, according to Chatterji, proof that there was an Aryan invasion of India. This implies that the Northwest Indian racial type represents—either on the whole, or only in the Indian context—the typical "Aryan race", and the South Indian racial type represents the typical "Dravidian race". We will examine Chatterji's contention in the light of his own exposition of the Indian racial situation.

But before doing that, let us examine the basic concept of an "Aryan race" itself, and see whether it makes any sense in the practical context.

THE "ARYAN RACE"

As we already saw in the chapter on the Aryan invasion theory (background of the theory), most scholars are agreed on the fact that nothing can be said about the racial type of the Original Indo-Europeans (i.e. the original speakers of the Indo-European languages in the Original Homeland, before the speech-family spread out to cover its present habitat from western Europe to Assam and Sri Lanka). It is natural to presume that there may have been an original racial type; but as most of the peoples speaking Indo-European languages, from the earliest recorded times, and at the point of time at which the existence of the language family was recognized, belonged to different racial types, there was no means by which the original racial type could be pinpointed.

The only thing that can be said with certainty is that the various Indo-European languages are related and have a common source, that they must have been spoken originally in a small part of their present area (which part must be their Original Homeland), and that the original speakers may have constituted a single race to begin with. But both the location of the Original Homeland, as well as the original racial

[1] ODBL, p. 27.

type, are subjects of controversy; and at best, it may be presumed that the original racial type may be identifiable with the present racial type in the Original Homeland (once this Homeland is identified; and presuming that there have been no racial changes and intermixtures in that area since that remote period, which is a big presumption indeed).

Hence, most scholars are agreed that the question of racial type is a totally redundant issue in the study of the Aryan problem. Max Müller, for example, was very forthright in this respect. He firmly declared: "Aryan in scientific language is utterly inapplicable to race. It means language and nothing but language."[2]

In his book, *Biographies of Words and the Home of the Aryans*,[3] he is even more categorical. He declares: "Aryas are those who speak Aryan languages, whatever their colour, whatever their blood. In calling them Aryas we predicate nothing of them except that the grammar of their language is Aryan—I have declared again and again that if I say Aryas, I mean neither blood nor bones nor hair nor skull; I mean simply those who speak an Aryan language" (p. 120). And furthermore: "To me, an ethnologist who speaks of an Aryan race, Aryan blood, Aryan eyes and hair is as great a sinner as a linguist who speaks of a dolichocephalic dictionary or a brachycephalic grammar" (p. 245).

But invasionist scholars cannot stomach this logic. They find it necessary to postulate an Aryan race, at least in the Indian context. Thus, P.L. Bhargava takes up the cudgel: "According to Max Müller, 'Aryan in scientific language is utterly inapplicable to race. It means language and nothing but language' (*Collected Works*, Vol. X, p. 90). It should, however, be remembered that the word *Ārya*, of which the word Aryans is an Anglicized form, is used in the Rigveda as the name of a people and not as that of a language. The corresponding word in the Avesta, viz. *Airya*, also means a people and not a language. Whatever meaning may be given to the word Aryan, the fact remains that the original word from which it is derived meant a people or a race and not a language."[4]

Bhargava contends that the original word "meant a people or a race and not a language", thereby lumping together two words, "people" and "race". In respect of the word "people" he is partly right; but on the one hand, he does not fully comprehend the significance of his own words, and on the other, "people", (i.e. community; socially distinct group of

[2] Collected Works, Vol.X, p. 90.
[3] Quoted by A.N. Chandra, RC & IC, pp. 171 and 181.
[4] IVA, p.1, footnote.

people) does not mean the same as "race" (in the sense of a particular type of skull, eyes, hair, skin, etc.).

The Rigveda does appear to use the word *Ārya* in the sense of "themselves" (i.e. the community of people who may be called the Vedic people or the Vedic Aryans) as opposed to others or certain others. But this is a very secondary and subjective use of the word, and no Indian scholar, not even the most ancient one, has understood it to mean a "people" in the primary sense: the *Amarakośa* gives the following synonyms for *Ārya*: of high family, a gentleman, good natured, righteous, noble.

The Vedic composers, therefore, used the word to indicate that they themselves were "noble", while their antagonists were "ignoble". The composers of the Avesta also used the word *Airya* to indicate their own nobility. And the irony of it is that the antagonists, whom the composers of the Rigveda brand as *Anārya*, were none other than these very Iranians, as we shall see in the next chapter.

But, as we said, Bhargava does not comprehend the significance of his own words. It is perfectly true that the modern word "Aryan" means language and not race: the concept of an Aryan (Indo-European) language-family, and therefore of an Original Homeland and dispersion therefrom, came into being because the scholars discovered people *belonging to different races* speaking related languages, and *not* because they found different peoples belonging to a single race. And it is also true that the original word in the Rigveda "meant a people—and not a language". It is just that the scholars have taken this word *Ārya,* Anglicized it into "Aryan", and used it as a name for the Indo-European family of languages.

And yet, we see the amazing spectacle of scholar after scholar, and P.L. Bhargava very much among them, transferring the linguistic sense of the modern word "Aryan" to the Rigvedic word *Ārya;* and presuming that the word *Anārya,* or any other word (*Dāsa, Dasyu,* etc.) contrasted with the word *Ārya* in the Rigveda, refers to enemy peoples who were *linguistically non-Indo-European.*

There were many ancient communities or peoples in Europe (Greeks, Romans, Goths, Celts, etc.) who entered into conflict with each other. If the modern scholars had chosen to adopt the name of any one of these peoples as the name for the Indo-European family of languages, would it have been logical for us to interpret the ancient texts of that particular people in such a way as to presume that their enemies were all speakers of non-Indo-European languages, and that those texts were therefore records of an Aryan invasion of Europe? In the Indian context, furthermore, there is evidence that the enemies were the ancient Iranians.

Therefore, the use of the words *Ārya* and *Anārya* in the ancient texts certainly cannot be interpreted as evidence of conflicts between Indo-European speaking and non-Indo-European speaking peoples.

But Bhargava insists that the *Āryas* were a "people *or a race*". He sees the word as a designation for ethnic features: the very "Aryan race, Aryan blood, Aryan eyes and hair" which Max Müller deprecates in no uncertain terms. This race, according to Bhargava, was "white in complexion": in short, the Nordic race.

THE "NORDIC" ARYANS

S.K. Chatterji, in his exposition of the races of India, approvingly quotes the views of scholars with whom he is in agreement. He describes the Vedic Aryans as "Nordics, leptorrhine dolichocephals who brought the Vedic Aryan (Sanskrit) speech".[5] They were originally "tall, fair-skinned, yellow or golden haired and blue-eyed"[6]: in short, the "Pure Aryans" of Nazi conception.

But what happened to all that yellow or golden hair, and all those blue eyes, in India? "Owing to miscegenation and to climatic conditions, the complexion of the body and the colour of the hair and the eye have been modified or eliminated by natural selection to light brown or brown and to black (for the hair and the eyes), although light-eyed people are not uncommon among the Nordic longheads in India, scattered as they are all over the country."[7]

At any rate, Bhargava (although he refrains from referring to yellow or golden hair and blue eyes: no sane Indian would imagine the Vedic Aryans as having these features) insists that at least in matters of skin colour, "the Aryans were white in complexion and their consciousness of it is shown by the use of the word *śvitnya* (Rigveda I.100.18) (white complexioned) in describing themselves. Many of their families such as the Vasiṣṭhas and the Tṛtsus are similarly called *śvityano* (Rigveda VII.33.1; 83.8). On the other hand, the *Dāsas* or non-Aryans are often called black *(kṛṣṇayoni,* Rigveda II.20.7) or black-skinned *(kṛṣṇatvac,* Rigveda I.130.8)"[8], and "perhaps snubnosed (*anās)* and of

[5] HCIP, p. 142.
[6] HCIP, p. 144.
[7] HCIP, pp. 144-45.
[8] IVA, p. 236.

hostile speech *(mṛdravāc*, Rigveda V.29.10)."[9]

In the entire range of the 1028 hymns of the Rigveda, these are the handful of verses in which the scholars have managed to grab at phrases which can be twisted so as to appear to corroborate their racial theory. It will be worthwhile to examine them.

1. There is no evidence anywhere in the Rigveda to show that the Vedic Aryans called themselves fair-skinned in contrast to their "aboriginal" enemies.

Bhargava cites I.100.18. However, in this verse, the composer does not refer to the Vedic Aryans, but to the Maruts who (like their father Rudra) are often described in the Rigveda as being white or red in colour. The line goes: "The mighty Thunderer with his fair-complexioned friends won the land, the sunlight, and the waters"[10]; and Griffith, in his footnote, remarks: "*His fair complexioned friends:* explained by Sāyaṇa as the glittering Maruts, means probably the Aryan invaders as opposed to the dark-skinned races of the country."[11] It is not the verse which suggests that the Vedic Aryans were fair-complexioned, it is the preconceived notion which leads to the twisted interpretation.

The other verses cited by Bhargava are VII.33.1 and VII.83.8. Bhargava's contention that the verses describe the Vasiṣṭhas and Tṛtsus as white-complexioned is not borne out by the verses which in fact describe the hair-style and the white robes of these warriors. Griffith translates VII.83.8 as follows: "O Indra-Varuṇa, ye gave Sudās your aid when the Ten Kings in battle compressed him about; there where the white-robed Tṛtsus with their braided hair, skilled in song, worshipped you with homage and with hymn."[12] He translates VII.33.1 as follows: "Those who wear hair-knots on the right, the movers of holy thought, white-robed, have won me over..."[13]

Thus, it is clear that the reference is to their white robes and not to their white skin. Moreover, the Rigveda is very clear in showing that Sudās and the Tṛtsus were battling northwards and westwards from the interior side of India; and that their enemies were located to the north in Kashmir, and were driven out further northwestwards as a result of the battle. Moreover, these hymns give the most clinching evidence (as we shall see in the chapter on Positive Evidence in the Purāṇas) of the fact that the enemies of the Vedic Aryans, and of Sudās and the Tṛtsus in

[9] IVA, p. 209.
[10] HOR, Vol. I, p. 130.
[11] Ibid., footnotes.
[12] HOR, Vol. 2, p. 80.
[13] HOR, Vol. 2, p. 34.

the particular context, were the ancestors of the Iranians. Hence the contention that Sudās and the Tṛtsus were white-complexioned in contrast with their enemies is ridiculous in itself.

2. Bhargava cites II.20.7 as evidence that the Rigveda describes the enemies as black. Griffith translates the verse as follows: "Indra the Vṛtra-slayer, Fort-destroyer, scattered the Dāsa hosts *who dwelt in darkness*."[14] And then comes the twist in the footnotes: "*The Dāsa hosts who dwelt in darkness*: the words thus rendered are variously explained. It is uncertain whether the aborigines of the country are meant, or the demons of air who dwell in the dark clouds."[15] However, the hymn clearly refers to the celestial activities of Indra the Thunder-God.

In another verse, IX.41.1, also cited by Bhargava[16], the reference to black skin is a reference to the night. Griffith translates: "Active and bright have they come forth, impetuous in speed like bulls; driving the black skin far away."[17] His footnotes are as double-tongued as in the other case: "The *Black skin*: meaning, apparently, both the black pall or covering of night and the Rākṣasas or dark-skinned Dasyus or hostile aboriginals."[18]

And finally we come to the main verse cited by the invasionist scholars. Griffith translates the verse (I.130.8) as follows: "Indra in battles helps his Aryan worshipper, he who hath hundred helps at hand in every fray, in frays that win the light of heaven. Plaguing the lawless he gave up to Manu's seed the dusky skin; blazing, as it were, he burns each covetous man away, he burns the tyrannous away."[19]

The first part of the above verse very clearly refers to the celestial activities of Indra, as the Thunder-God, who wins "the light of heaven", or, as some scholars have translated it, "in battles sprinkled in heaven". The second part of the verse is either a continuation of the celestial scene, or the transfer of epithet to the more earthly enemies of the composers. The earthly enemies, "the lawless"(i.e. those, Dasyus, who do not worship Indra according to the prescribed rituals), are compared to the celestial enemies of the Thunder-God; and the epithet "black" of the clouds and demons, is transferred to the Dasyus. But the Dasyus were not in fact dark in colour, hence the composer hastens to make the

[14] HOR, Vol. I, p. 285.
[15] Ibid., footnotes.
[16] IVA, p. 209.
[17] HOR, Vol. 2, p. 296.
[18] Ibid., footnotes.
[19] HOR, Vol. I, p. 181.

comparison credible by offering an explanation for the Dasyus acquiring a dark skin: they are burnt black by the blazing fire of Indra's wrath.

Thus, nowhere is there any evidence that the enemies of the Vedic Aryans were dark in colour.

3. Bhargava cites V.29.10 as evidence that the enemies of the Vedic Aryans were "snubnosed", and therefore, must have been racially akin to certain tribal groups, found in some parts of India, who have snubnoses. However, this is a modern, and totally unwarranted, translation of the term. Griffith also translates it as "noseless", but he admits in his footnote that "the word may be, as Sāyaṇa explains it, *an-āsah,* i.e. mouthless, voiceless, unintelligibly speaking."[20] Keith and Macdonell admit that "the Pada text and Sāyaṇa both take it to mean 'without face' *(an-ās).*"[21] The word, thus, does not refer to the nose at all, but to the face as a whole or to the mouth, and is a word of abuse meaning that their speech was unclear or corrupt according to Ārya standards.

As against all these flimsy pieces of "evidence", there is other more solid evidence which demolishes any specific relationship between the Vedic Aryans and a fair skin. The following points may be noted:

1. Malati Shendge, as we shall see in the next chapter, postulates that the Gods in the Rigveda were, in fact, not Gods, but the main contestants in the "Aryan invaders" versus "non-Aryan natives" battle. She decides that all the Gods "with the exception of Indra and Viṣṇu...were the functionaries of the government of the Asura empire" (i.e. the "native non-Aryan" empire). Indra and Viṣṇu, according to her, were the leaders of the invading Aryans. Although her fanciful descriptions are not generally accepted, her classification of Indra as an invader-king is accepted by many scholars. and every other scholar agrees that Indra was the major God invoked by the invaders in their battles against the "non-Aryans". Rudra is the Rigvedic God who is generally accepted as a "non-Aryan" God borrowed by the Aryans from the natives.

Ironically, the Rigveda repeatedly stresses (e.g. throughout hymn X.96) that Indra is greenish-brown in colour. Viṣṇu is also known to be dark or dark-blue in colour. On the other hand, Rudra (II.33.8) is described as white-complexioned.

[20] HOR, Vol. I, p. 489, footnote.
[21] Vedic Index, Vol. I, p. 347.

2. A.D. Pusalker chooses "Rāma and Krișṇa..." as the "true types of Aryan heroes who were pioneers in the spread of Aryan culture and civilization all over India".[22]

Again, we find that the ancient texts, and the entire range of Indian tradition pertaining to Rāma and Krișṇa, are unanimous in describing both of them as being dark in colour.

3. The Aṅgiras rishis are the dominant rishis of the Rigveda. The Aitareya Brāhmaṇa (3.34) describes these rishis as being born of coal. A prominent Aṅgiras rishi, Kaṇva, is specifically described in the Rigveda (X.31.11) as dark-coloured. Another verse (II.3.9) describes the birth of "pious hero", who is described as brown in colour.

4. In fact, descriptions of physical features which could well be identified as Nordic are usually found in respect of demons and the like: Hiraṇyākṣa is the name of a demon (the name means "golden-eyed") and Śūrpaṇakhā is described, in the Rāmāyana (III.17.10) as having red hair. Since, demons, in any culture, are always credited with grotesque and outlandish physical features, this is rather an argument against the prominent presence of any Nordics in India.

Thus, we do not find any reference in the ancient texts to indicate that the "Aryans" were whites and the "non-Aryans" were blacks. In this, the ancient texts are fully in tune with the present situation in India where we do not find any notable Nordic presence in the Indo-Aryan population.

S.K. Chatterji evidently sees the difficulty, and hence he tries to demonstrate the presence, even today, of Nordic elements in India: "Nordic elements are strong in some parts of the North-West Frontier of India, particularly along the upper reaches of the Indus and along its tributaries the Swat, the Panjkora, the Kunar and the Chitral rivers, and in the south of the Hindu Kush range. In the Punjab and Rajputana and in the Upper Ganges Valley, Nordic elements are present (although more and more mixed with other racial elements as we proceed further to the east), particularly among the higher castes or groups; among certain sections in India the Nordic type predominates, e.g. among the Chitpāvan Brāhmaṇas of the Marāthā country."[23]

The region which Chatterji indicates may appear to be the same as occupied by the Rigvedic Aryans, but his claim that Nordic elements are "strong" in these parts has to be taken with a fistful of salt. If a fair skin is to be described as "Nordic", then certainly the people in this

[22] HCIP, p. 315.
[23] HCIP, p. 144.

region are more "Nordic" than people further south; but coloured eyes are a rare feature even in this region, and blonde hair is practically non-existent. Fairness alone does not indicate any connection with "Nordics" outside India and coloured eyes are found as a rare feature among people of every hue of skin colour throughout the length and breadth of India. The northwest, moreover, it must be remembered, was the area where many foreign peoples invaded and settled down in small numbers, getting intermixed with the local population. Most prominent among these were the Greeks under Alexander, whose army included many Nordics of Europe.

Chatterji can locate only one specific community which is noted for a combination of fair skin and coloured eyes: the Chitpāvan Brāhmaṇas of Maharashtra. This, doubtless, is expected to corroborate the theory that the "Aryan invaders" constitute the higher rungs of the caste hierarchy.

Unfortunately for Chatterji, the Chitpāvan Brāhmaṇa community of Maharashtra is in fact a community which, according to its own traditions, consists of people who were not Brāhmaṇas to begin with, and who arrived on the scene long after the establishment of Vedic culture all over India.

The Chitpāvan Brāhmaṇas are the subject of a thesis (ESP/20, University of Bombay, Kalina Campus Library, 1928) by Mrs. Iravati Karve (herself a Chitpāvan). She points out that "as late as AD 1200, they were poor farmers leading a life of seclusion and poverty. The first Peshwa, himself a Konkanastha Chitpavan Brahman, was the first to make conscious attempts to give a lift to his own community... We are told that they were ignorant and despised, and were usually employed as cooks and peons... At first, the Deshasthas would not dine with these intruders" (pp. 1-2 of the thesis).

She also relates (pp. 11-13) "an old and curious myth (which) is inextricably bound up with the Chitpavans and their land. It is widely accepted in Maharashtra as explaining the origin of the Chitpavans as also of their name." According to this myth, Paraśurāma, having donated all his land to Kaśyapa, wanted land of his own. So he reclaimed land from the sea. He had no Brahmans to perform the rituals, since the Brahmans from the mainland refused to perform them. While wandering on the beach, he discovered a wrecked ship and 14 corpses of men washed ashore. He brought the corpses back to life (*citāsthāne pāvanāh,* hence "Chitpāvan"), and made them Brahmans. Later, however, they disobeyed him, and he caused their land, Konkan, to become barren and unproductive. There is another version (p. 22), according to which Paraśurāma initiated into Brahmanhood a group of 60 families of fishermen.

Disregarding the miraculous elements, the purport of this myth is clear: the ancestors of the Chitpāvan Brāhmaṇas were foreigners washed ashore after a shipwreck, and never really accepted as proper Brahmans for a long time by other more orthodox Brahman groups. This, therefore, disproves Chatterji's claim that the Chitpāvan Brāhmaṇas represent the purest racial strain of the "Original Aryan race".

Thus, we find that the invasionist scholars are unable to drum up any credible evidence, either from the ancient texts or from the modern racial situation in India, to support their theory of conflict between originally white "Aryans" and black "non-Aryans".

THE RACIAL SITUATION

But, as we saw, Chatterji insists on seeing "racial evidence" in the fact that the people in the north-west are "different" from the people in the south of India.

The only way in which this could be construed as evidence is by presuming the northwest Indians to be the "original Aryan" racial type and the (unspecified) south Indians to be the "original Dravidian" racial type. (And further, one would have to assume that this automatically proves that the South Indian racial type originally occupied the north-west, from where it was displaced by the present northwestern racial type which came from outside—an assumption which has no base in this "racial evidence" at all.)

But there is one major drawback to this glib assumption: branding any racial sub-type in the country as the "original" Aryan or Dravidian racial type puts an unanswerable question mark on the "original" linguistic identity of every other racial sub-type in the country.

And even S.K. Chatterji (as we shall see), with the help of racial theorists quoted by him, fails to provide even a faintly credible explanation for the racial situation in India if viewed from the point of view of "original" racial-cum-linguistic types.

India provides a true panorama of racial sub-types: it is the only place in the world where one finds all the three racial types (Negroid, Mongoloid and Caucasoid) in its native racial composition. There is no historical evidence of these groups immigrating from outside. In America (whether we take this to mean the USA, or the entire Continent) we find all the three races; but the Caucasoids are historical migrant-invaders from Europe; the Negroids are historical migrant-captives from Africa; and only the native Mongoloid peoples (the "Red Indians") are native to the place. In India, it is only speculation that the Negroids immigrated from Africa (the Andamanese languages are unrelated to the African languages) or that the Mongoloids immigrated from the north and east of Asia.

But we are concerned here only with the Caucasoid races of India. The majority of the speakers of Indo-Aryan, Dravidian and Kol-Munda languages are Caucasoids. Again, among these, we are concerned here only with the alleged racial identity of the "original" speakers of the Indo-Aryan languages. Let us examine the pronouncements of S.K. Chatterji and his school to see if they manage to present even a ghost of a case in support of their theory of originally distinct "Aryan" and "Dravidian" races in ancient India.

There may have been many intra-national migrations of groups of people from one part of the country to another in prehistoric, historical and modern times, resulting in mosaics of racial types in many places. There may, likewise, have been many such migrations of groups of people from outside India into the country. But there is no evidence to show that such immigrations ever resulted in anything more than the absorption of these groups into the mainstream of national culture.

In fact, Chatterji himself admits: "It is strange (and somewhat difficult of explanation) that skeletal remains of Early Man in India, particularly in the prehistoric and early historical times, should be so scanty. This lack of material has not allowed us to postulate with certainty about racial movements in ancient times; and any appraisement or reconstruction of movements of peoples in India, some four or three *or even two thousand years ago,* is bound to remain *largely hypothetical, and based on or inferred from the present situation only."* [24]

In spite of this, Chatterji declares: "No kind of man originated in India, all her human inhabitants having arrived originally from other lands..."[25]; and then he proceeds to enumerate the various peoples immigrating into India in their alleged order of immigration (as detailed by J.H. Hutton in 1933). Other than the Negritos and Mongoloids, he names the following six groups:

1. "Proto-Austroloids: black, dolichocephalic, platyrrhine..."[26]

[24] HCIP, p. 141.
[25] HCIP, p. 142.
[26] Ibid.

("The original Austric speech...would appear to have been brought from the west by the Proto-Australoids."[27])

2. "Early Mediterraneans: leptorrhine dolichocephals, who brought earlier forms of the Austric speech."[28]
3. "Civilized or Advanced Mediterraneans: leptorrhine dolichocephals, who became the 'Dravidians' in India."[29]
4. "Armenoid: a specialized offshoot from the standard Alpine stock—brachycephalic—probably came with the Civilized Mediterraneans (Dravidians) and spoke their language."[30]
5. "Alpines: brachycephalic, leptorrhine; found in Gujarat and Bengal; earlier than the Vedic Aryans, but probably speaking Aryan dialects."[31]
6. "Vedic Aryans, or Nordics: leptorrhine dolichocephals who brought the Vedic Aryan (Sanskrit) speech."[32]

Here, we see the incredible gall of the racial theorists. After being told that there are no clues from the past on the basis of which racial migrations can be definitely characterized, and that all reconstructions of racial movements are "based on or inferred from the present situation only", we are presented with a cut-and-dried story, and a list of various racial-cum-linguistic groups migrating into India, which very obviously could not have been "inferred from the present situation".

At the very outset, we note the following anomalies:

We are told that three different groups of leptorrhine (slender-nosed), dolichocephalic (long-headed) people entered India at three different points of time: the first speaking "earlier forms of the Austric speech", the second being "the Dravidians", and the third bringing "the Vedic Aryan (Sanskrit) speech".

In the same breath, we are also told that two different groups of brachycephalic (round-headed) people entered India at two different points of time: the first speaking the language of the Dravidians, and the second "speaking Aryan dialects". Also, there is an earlier group of platyrrhine (broad-nosed) people who brought "the original Austric speech".

Thus, we are expected to believe in two distinct racial types (one platyrrhine and one leptorrhine), both speaking Austric languages, en-

[27] HCIP, p. 148.
[28] HCIP, p. 142.
[29] Ibid.
[30] Ibid.
[31] Ibid.
[32] Ibid.

tering India at two different points of time; two distinct racial types (one dolichocephalic and one brachycephalic), both speaking Dravidian languages, entering India at two different points of time; and two distinct racial types (one dolichocephalic and one brachycephalic), both speaking Indo-European (Aryan) languages, entering India at two different points of time! And from these hypothetical tales, products of the fertile imagination of scholars determined to drum up some kind of "racial evidence" or the other for the theory of an Aryan invasion of India, we are expected to consider the matter to be logically settled!

Some scholars, perhaps realizing that this plethora of hypothetical race-cum-language types is a bit too thick to swallow, try to provide some relief to our credulity by postulating an original group or two less. R.P. Chanda, for example, postulates two Aryan races: "the 'Outer' Aryans were a brachycephalic race derived from a stock totally different from the 'Inner' Aryans who were dolichocephalic"[33]; but he postulates single Dravidian and Austric races, and mixtures of all these: "the Gujaratis, the Marathas, as well as the Bengalis, Biharis and Oriyas have a preponderance of brachy- and mesaticephals; they are the result of a mixture of the round-headed 'Outer' Aryans with the long-headed Dravidians and Kols, as well as with the long-headed 'Inner' Aryans."[34]

Thus, we see the utter senselessness of the theories cooked up by the racial theorists in their attempts to correlate "race" with language in India. Let us, nevertheless, examine what these scholars have to say specifically about the Dravidian and Aryan "races".

THE "DRAVIDIAN RACE"

S.K. Chatterji admits that it is impossible to search for clues in the past, as regards the racial identities and movements in ancient times, since the skeletal remains are scanty, and claims that the racial theories are "based on or inferred from the present situation only". Let us see if the theories about the "Dravidian race" match these claims:

1. According to Grierson, "The Mundas and the Dravidas belong to the same ethnic stock...the physical type is not uniform throughout... (but) the chief components of the actual race are the Mundas on the one hand and the Dravidas on the other... Anthropology only tells us that the Dravidian race comprises Mundas and Dravidas..."[35]

Now those who are determined to correlate race and language must

[33] Indo-Aryan Races, Part I, Rajshahi, 1916, quoted by Chatterji, ODBL, pp. 31-32.
[34] Ibid.
[35] LSI, Vol. IV, Introduction, p. 5.

find a solution to this. Hence, the cosy theory that there were two groups of "Mediterraneans...leptorrhine dolichocephals" who entered the country at two points of time: the first group, "the early Mediterraneans", being the ones who brought in "earlier forms of the Austric speech"; and the second group, "the civilized or advanced Mediterraneans", being the ones "who became the Dravidians in India". Thus the mystery of one race and two language-families is solved (without upsetting the race-language correlation) by sweeping it outside the borders of India: the same "race" is supposed to have entered India twice, the first time as Austrics, the second time as Dravidians.

S.K. Chatterji, however, offers another solution. He speaks, elsewhere, of "pre-Dravidian stocks like the Kols, who adopted Dravidian speech..."[36] So, a vast majority of the Dravidian-language speaking people in the south are to be presumed to be originally Austrics.

2. The Kadars and Palayans of Cochin and Travancore Hills, and the Rajmahal tribes in eastern Bihar, who all speak Dravidian languages, are supposed to have traces of the Negrito racial stock; and the Chenchu and Kurumba tribes in the south are supposed to be remnants of the proto-Australoid racial stock.

Chatterji informs us that the Dravidians (coming from outside India) "spread along the Indus and Ganges valleys, before pushing into the South, and absorbing there the primitive Negrito and proto-Polynesian people."[37]

3. At this point, let us examine the arbitrary racial generalizations indulged in by Chatterji and his school (noting, at the same time, that these scholars lump together the present-day speakers of each modern language as if they each constituted a racial unit in ancient times).

According to Chatterji, "among the Dravidians, there were tribes in various stages of civilization, from the civilized ancestors of the Kannada, Telugu and Tamil-Malayalam peoples to the wild forefathers of the Brahuis and the Gonds, Khonds and Oraons."[38] Thus, leaving aside for the moment the second part of Chatterji's assertion, we get a racial set consisting of "the Kannada, Telugu and Tamil-Malayalam peoples".

Chatterji quotes R.P. Chanda's racial study, according to which "the Gujaratis, the Marathas, as well as the Bengalis, Biharis and Oriyas...are the result of a mixture of the round-headed 'Outer' Aryans

[36] ODBL, pp. 27-28.
[37] Ibid.
[38] Ibid.

with the long-headed Dravidians and Kols, as well as with the long-headed 'Inner' Aryans."[39] Thus, we get a second racial set consisting of these five peoples presently speaking Indo-Aryan languages.

But Chatterji points out that "the Telugu, Kannada and Kodagu peoples" are also "the result of the same ethnic mixture as the Gujaratis and the Bengalis"[40] (and so, one presumes, are "the Marathas, as well as...Biharis and Oriyas", who have already been placed in the same set as "the Gujaratis and the Bengalis", and are in fact even closer to "the Telugu, Kannada and Kodagu peoples" in geographical distance and in physical features). He also points out that "the Telugu, Kannada and Kodagu peoples...never spoke Aryan."[41] The logical implication of this appears to be that all these groups which are presently speaking Indo-Aryan languages must have originally been speaking Dravidian languages!

4. This is stated explicitly, and rather surprisingly, in respect of a major section of the people of the Punjab and the Upper Gangetic Valley! Chatterji quotes B.S. Guha (Director of the Anthropological Survey of India, 1944) who classifies these peoples as the "true mediterranean/European" type, "taller and fairer", which "represents the civilized pre-Aryan 'Dravidian' people of Northwest India which became Aryanized in language and contributed largely to the evolution of the Hindu people and culture of North India."[42]

5. Finally, we have the Brahui people of Baluchistan who speak a Dravidian language, but "are anthropologically Eranians."[43] Neither Chatterji, nor any other racial theorist, can provide any logical explanation as to why an Iranian-type race should happen to be speaking a Dravidian language. In fact, Chatterji makes a very curious statement about the Brahuis which could be interpreted in an equally curious way.

He classifies the ancient Dravidians into two groups: "the civilized ancestors of the Kannada, Telugu and Tamil-Malayalam peoples", and "the wild forefathers of the Brahuis and the Gonds, Khonds and Oraons". Of the second group, he adds: "These latter may represent earlier pre-Dravidian stocks...who adopted Dravidian speech, and *who might originally have been (as they are now)* quite distinct from the civilized Dravidians."[44] Can we interpret this to mean that Chatterji

[39] ODBL, p. 32.
[40] ODBL, p. 33.
[41] Ibid.
[42] HCIP, pp. 143-44.
[43] LSI, Vol. 4, p. 5.
[44] ODBL, p. 28.

considers the Iranian-like Brahuis to be a "pre-Dravidian" racial stock in India: in short, that the Iranian-like race existed in the Northwest before the hypothetical (and totally concocted) "Dravidian immigration into India"?

In any case, from all these various statements about the "Dravidian race", two things become clear:

1. All these statements are purely products of the fertile imagination of the racial theorists. Chatterji admits that the past provides no racial clues and claims that the racial theories are "based on or inferred from the present situation only", but it is clear that they are not: many of the peoples currently speaking Dravidian languages are branded as having originally been speakers of non-Dravidian languages, and many of the peoples currently speaking non-Dravidian languages are branded as having originally been speakers of Dravidian languages.

2. The racial theorists are at a total loss as to which racial type is to be branded as the "original Dravidian" one. Chatterji on the one hand asks us to consider "the wide difference in racial type between the South Indian Dravidians and the Northwest Indians"[45] as evidence of an Aryan invasion of India, and on the other hand he approvingly quotes a racial theorist who brands a large section of the people of the Punjab as "the civilized pre-Aryan 'Dravidian' people of Northwest India which became Aryanized in language."[46] And he does not care to tell us what we should infer from the wide difference in racial type between the South Indian Dravidians and the Brahuis.

So much for the "Dravidian race" and the "evidence" inferred from it.

THE "ARYAN RACE"

The invasionist scholars postulate the existence of a hypothetical "Aryan race" which invaded India in ancient times. But what exactly is their idea of this Aryan race?

J.H. Hutton,[47] as we saw, postulated invasions or immigrations by two distinct "Aryan" races at two different points of time: the first being an "Alpine" race, "brachycephalic leptorrhine", and the second being a "Nordic" race, "leptorrhine dolichocephal".

It is the second or "Nordic" race "tall, fair-skinned, yellow or golden-haired and blue-eyed"[48] which is the greater favourite of the

[45] ODBL, p. 27.
[46] HCIP, pp. 143-44.
[47] HCIP, p. 142.
[48] HCIP, pp. 144-45.

racial theorists. But as the concept of such a Nordic race in India cannot possibly have been "based on or inferred from the present situation only", it is obvious that the racial theorists require no better material than their fertile imagination in order to concoct these hypothetical "races".

S.K. Chatterji discusses the racial identity of the "Original Aryan race" as follows: "Many scholars, mostly German, assumed the original Indo-European type as being tall, long-headed, straight-nosed, with fair complexion and golden wavy hair, the Nordic type of Europe; others, like Sergi, regarded them as having been a medium, round-headed race, fair, with black hair, the Alpine type; while a third view suggests with greater plausibility that the Indo-European speakers were 'a conglomerate of peoples of different origins who in prehistoric times were welded together into an ethnic unity'..." [49]

So now we are faced with a puzzle: were the "Aryan invaders" Nordics, or were they Alpines, or were they "a conglomerate of peoples of different origins...welded together into an ethnic unity"? Or were there two or three different waves of "Aryan invaders" covering all the different categories?

Chatterji has his own little bit to add to the confusion: "These Indo-European speakers were settled for some time in Eastern Iran before they came into India...in Eastern Iran it is likely that the Aryan speakers absorbed the original speakers who must have differed from them in race, speech and culture."[50]

And after these (one or two or three distinct groups of) "Aryan invaders" finally did enter India, what happened to them? They were exposed to "miscegenation and to climatic conditions."[51] That is: firstly, they got intermixed, in different permutations, combinations and proportions, with the umpteen races (Negritos, Proto-Australoids, various Austric and Dravidian races, etc.) who had preceded them into India from outside (and who had already got intermixed amongst themselves in different permutations, combinations, and proportions); and secondly, due to climatic conditions, "the complexion of the body and the colour of the hair and the eye" became "modified or eliminated."[52]

Thus, to recapitulate the whole story, this "conglomerate of peoples of different origins" entered Iran from South Russia. In Iran,

[49] ODBL, p. 24.
[50] ODBL, p. 25.
[51] HCIP, pp. 144-45.
[52] Ibid.

these people got further mixed up with other peoples who "differed from them in race, speech and culture". Then, this twice-mixed race entered India, in two distinct editions, and here they were subjected to the rigours of the Indian climate, besides getting intermixed with a veritable galaxy of racial types.

After presenting us with this marvellous fairy tale, the racial theorists confidently expect us to believe that this whole story is "based on or inferred from the present situation only"; and at the same time to refrain from asking inconvenient questions about how "the present situation", after all these cataclysmic transformations, could allow of such inferences.

And Chatterji, after presenting us with this story, expects us to swallow his claim that "the theory of an Aryan invasion is borne out by...the wide difference in racial type between the South Indian Dravidians and the North-west Indians."[53]

It is, therefore, time that we got one thing very clear: there is no means, whatsoever, of postulating the exact racial type of the Original Indo-Europeans in their Original Homeland. As we will be seeing presently, the Rigveda and the Purāṇas provide incontrovertible evidence that the Original Homeland lay in the interior of North India; but we will still not postulate the exact nature of this Original "race".

The plain fact is that it was the language-family which spread out from the Original Homeland, and not a racial stock. The question of the Original Homeland is a linguistic one, and not a racial one. In this matter of language and race, Max Müller put the whole thing in a nutshell: "I say that even the blackest Hindus represent an earlier state of Aryan speech and thought than the fairest Scandinavians."[54] And Max Müller certainly cannot be accused of being a Hindu chauvinist.

[53] ODBL, p. 27.

[54] Introduction, p. XXIV, to *Biographies of Words and the Home of the Aryas*, quoted by A.N. Chandra, RC & IC, pp. 171-81.

NINETEEN

NON-EVIDENCE IN THE RIGVEDA

"The Vedic literature is the earliest extant record of the Aryan mind."[1]

Hence, if any evidence of the earliest movements of the Indo-European people is to be found recorded anywhere, it should be found recorded in this literature. And, as we shall see in subsequent chapters, Sanskrit texts actually do provide such evidence.

However, Sanskrit texts provide no evidence whatsoever about any foreign origin of the composers of the texts. Even those invasionist scholars, who have examined these texts in detail in order to dig out such evidence from them, have been compelled to admit their failure. Even while expounding the Aryan invasion theory, these scholars are forced to admit that the theory has no basis in Sanskrit literature. Thus A.L. Basham admits: "Direct testimony to the assumed fact is lacking, and no tradition of an early home beyond the frontier survives in India."[2] T. Burrow, likewise, admits that "the Aryan invasion of India is recorded in no written document and it cannot yet be traced archaeologically."[3]

B.K. Ghosh also admits that "it really cannot be proved that the Vedic Aryans retained any memory of their extra-Indian associations,"[4] and refers to the "total absence of extraterritorial memory in the Rigveda."[5]

John Muir, after his detailed study of Sanskrit texts, comments that, so far as he knows, "none of the Sanskrit books, not even the most ancient, contain any distinct reference or allusion to the foreign origin of the Indians."[6] In fact, his study leads him to declare that the various Indo-European peoples "have sprung from the gradual dispersion of the ancient Aryan race of India, such dispersion being occasioned by political or religious causes."[7]

Therefore, any "evidence" derived from the texts, to show an Aryan invasion of India, can only be something which is in opposition to,

[1] HCIP, p. 216.
[2] *The Oxford History of India*, 1970 edition, p. 53.
[3] *A Cultural History of India*, Clarendon Press, Oxford, 1975, p. 21.
[4] HCIP, p. 204.
[5] HCIP, p. 206.
[6] Original Sanskrit Texts, Vol. 2, p. 323.
[7] Quoted by A.C. Das, RVI, p. 125.

rather than in accordance with, what is expressly stated by these texts.

According to S.K. Chatterji, "the theory of an Aryan invasion is borne out by the general outlook upon life as presented by the Vedic poems, which is that of a warlike and conquering people establishing themselves in a country previously inhabited by another people...and by the totally different form of culture and ideas presented by the Rigveda on the one hand and the oldest Tamil poems on the other..."[8]

What exactly Chatterji intends to suggest, by his statements, is not very clear. On the one hand, it is generally acknowledged that the composers of the Rigveda, in their poems, show a "total absence of extraterritorial memory". On the other hand it is said that the same poems also show "the general outlook upon life of a warlike and conquering people establishing themselves in a country previously inhabited by another people". One wonders how the two statements can be reconciled.

The Rigveda is acknowledged by all the invasionist scholars to be a text of the Punjab. "The oldest Tamil poems" are equally known to be poems from the extreme south of India; these poems give no hint, of any kind, of any association with the Punjab. The Rigveda is datable to at least 4000 BC or 3000 BC; and even the invasionist scholars do not dare to date it later than 1000 BC. "The oldest Tamil poems" are dated *at least* a thousand years after 1000 BC. If two sets of texts, separated from each other in time and space, appear to present "totally different forms of culture and ideas", whatever Chatterji means by that, how does it prove that the composers of the Rigveda were invaders from outside who ousted the Dravidians from the Punjab?

However, the "evidence" of an Aryan invasion, derived by the scholars from the Sanskrit texts, is not confined to these meaningless statements. The scholars derive two distinct categories of "evidence" from them:

1. Negative evidence: The geographical evidence in the Rigveda shows that the hymns were composed in the Punjab region, the Saptasindhu. The subsequent stages of the Vedic literature show an increasingly expanding horizon into the rest of northern India.
2. Positive evidence: The Rigvedic hymns are of a militant and warlike nature, and show that the composers of these hymns were in conflict with various other peoples.

These factors have been interpreted as evidence that the "Aryans" entered India from the northwest, where they established their first set-

[8] ODBL, pp. 26-27.

tlements, and then expanded inwards into the rest of India, being engaged all the while in bitter conflict with the non-Aryan natives.

Let us, therefore, examine these two categories of evidence.

THE GEOGRAPHICAL EVIDENCE IN THE RIGVEDA

An analysis of the geographical references in the Rigveda shows that the composers of the hymns probably occupied a territory from "the south of the Hindu Kush range"[9] to an area "not much further into the interior beyond the frontiers of the Punjab and Rajputana."[10]

The subsequent Vedic texts (the Sāmaveda, the Yajurveda and the Atharvaveda), according to P.L. Bhargava, "make it absolutely clear that the Aryas moved eastward and southward from their original home in the Punjab."[11]

The Sāmaveda is, of course, not a separate text, since an overwhelming majority of its hymns are Rigvedic hymns set to Vedic musical chanting. But, "the Yajurveda introduces us to a new geographical area and a new epoch of religious and social life in India. The centre of Vedic civilization is no longer the region of the Indus and its tributaries, but the land of the Kuru-Pañcālas. In the sphere of religion we find the elaboration of the sacrificial ceremonial as the chief feature of the Yajurveda."[12].

The Atharvaveda shows an even greater shift eastwards: "Its geographical area is much wider, for it mentions the easternmost kingdoms of India such as Aṅga and Magadha. The tiger, native to the marshy forests of Bengal, and therefore still unknown to the Rigveda, appears in the Atharvaveda already as the mightiest and most feared of all beasts of prey. The language of the Atharvaveda is also decidedly later than that of the Rigveda, but earlier than that of the Brāhmaṇas..."[13]

The "evidence" thus furnished by the Vedic texts can be examined from two points of view:

1. Interpretation of the Geographical Data: If the geographical data in the Rigveda shows that the composers were familiar only with the Punjab region, does this prove an Aryan invasion?
2. The Geographical Data itself: Does the Rigveda indeed show ignorance of the rest of northern India?

[9] IVA, p. 49.
[10] HCIP, p. 312.
[11] IVA, p. 4.
[12] IVA, pp. 12-13.
[13] IVA, p. 14.

Interpretation of the Geographical Data

1. We may quote here the words of A.D. Pusalker, a staunch advocate of the invasion theory: "It must be remembered, however, that the Rigveda is not a geographical manual and its various recensions have not come down to us in a complete form. It would, therefore, be unsafe and hazardous to draw any inference from the silence of the Rigveda. *The non-mention of any locality in the hymns cannot be construed as evidence, one way or the other*, unless, of course, it can be proved to be of such importance as to be inexplicable except on the hypothesis of want of knowledge."[14]

2. In spite of his above admission, Pusalker himself treats the non-mention of localities in the hymns as clinching evidence. Thus, he rejects the accounts of the Purāṇas, wherein "the scene of traditional history opens with...the whole of Northern India extending in the east upto Orissa"[15], on the ground that "by the time the Rigveda was composed, the Aryans had not penetrated much further into the interior beyond the frontiers of the Punjab and Rajputana...(therefore) its testimony is decidedly fatal to the geographical views assumed in the Purāṇas."[16]

This, therefore, is the standard and stock argument of the invasion-theorists; even of those among them who, as shown above, admit elsewhere the untenability of the very same argument.

But, then, the Rigveda does not mention any locality to the west of India either. If the Vedic composers can be accused of being ignorant of localities and areas within India, simply because they do not mention them, they should be equally held to be ignorant of localities outside the frontiers of India on identical grounds. But that would be "decidedly fatal" to the invasion theory.

Hence B.K. Ghosh resorts to a last-ditch argument to explain away the non-mention of localities outside India: "The reticence maintained by the Vedic Aryans about immigration from Indo-Irania was, therefore, at least partly intentional..."[16a]

Thus, we have here a typical invasionist argument: the Rigvedic composers did not mention any locality within India because they were ignorant of these areas; but if they did not also mention any localities outside the frontiers of India, it must be because they *deliberately and calculatedly* refrained from doing so!

[14] HCIP, p. 241.
[15] HCIP, p. 311.
[16] HCIP, p. 313.
[16a] HCIP, p. 219.

P.L. Bhargava, himself an invasion-theorist (though an internal invasion-theorist), reacts sharply to the above remark: "The remark of Dr. B.K. Ghosh...that the silence maintained by the earliest Vedic Indians on Iran and the Iranians was at least partly intentional, is really astounding...Surely we cannot think of any organised conspiracy in that primitive age to deliberately omit the name of a people or country from a record containing hymns composed in the course of centuries by hundreds of authors belonging to different families."[17]

3. Bhargava, therefore, carries the principle of non-mentioned localities to its logical conclusion. He treats as evidence the non-mention of localities both within India as well as outside the frontiers of India. He contends that "the Aryans originally lived in the valleys of the rivers Ghorband and Panjshir to the south of the Hindu Kush range...from this region one branch seems to have gone to the West and after wandering in many lands seems to have ultimately settled in the various countries of Europe, while another branch migrated to Saptasindhu... In India also the Aryans spread further and further...inspite of the tough resistance of the aboriginal tribes the Aryans steadily colonized the whole of Northern India and a considerable part of the Deccan."[18]

Bhargava's argument will of course be rejected by the external invasion-theorists. But it is at least more logical in that he treats the principle of non-mentioned localities as evidence in an impartial manner, while they treat it as evidence only in respect of the eastern areas. But is this principle itself right?

The geographical mentions in the Rigveda show that the composers of the hymns lived in the Punjab area and on the banks of the Sarasvati river. But is it logical to conclude from this that the entire body of speakers of Indo-European languages at that point of time, in India or in the world, were confined to the Punjab area? What is the logic which dictates that the composers of the Rigveda constituted *the entire body of speakers of Indo-European languages at that point of time*, whether in India alone or in the whole world?

The Rigveda is not a historical treatise. It is a compilation of hymns. Being, as already pointed out, "the earliest extant record of the Aryan mind", it is certainly more likely, to provide evidence, than any other Indo-European text. But non-mention of localities cannot constitute evidence of the existence or non-existence of Indo-Europeans outside the Punjab region.

[17] IVA, p. 45, footnotes.
[18] IVA, pp. 49 and 56.

The Geographical Data in the Rigveda

In any case, while the Rigveda certainly *does not* mention any locality outside the frontiers of India, it *does* mention or give evidence of localities within India and well outside the range of the Punjab region:

1. The Rigveda repeatedly refers to the eastern and western seas, which can be none other than the seas today referred to as the Bay of Bengal and the Arabian Sea. Bhargava details these references: "In one verse (of Rigveda X.136.5) the sun, addressed as the *keśin* (hairy, i.e. multi-rayed) *muni* (sage) is said to refer to both the seas, the *Pūrva* or the eastern and the *Apara* or the western. The meaning clearly is that it was seen rising in the morning from the eastern sea and retiring for rest in the evening in the western sea. In another verse (Rigveda VII.6.7) Agni Vaiśvānara is praised for removing the investing gloom at the rising of the sun from the heaven and the earth as well as from the avara or the eastern and the para or the western sea. In other verses (Rigveda I.34.7; VIII.12.17; 13.15; 82.1; 97.4; IX. 65.22; X.136.5; 137.2; 187.2) these two seas are called the Arvāvat and the Parāvat seas. The existence of the eastern and western seas is further proved by the fact that in some verses the sun or the morning gods Aśvins are described as rising from the sea (I.163.1; VII.55.7; X.72.7; IV.43.5) while in others as retiring into the sea (I.30.18)."[19]

2. One of the hymns of the Rigveda (IX.96) and one of the three verses in another hymn (X.179.2) are composed by Pratardana, whom the anukramaṇıs clearly describe as *Kāśirāja*, the king of Kashi. Kashi lies in south-eastern Uttar Pradesh, which is certainly not part of the Punjab region. The Purāṇas also confirm that Pratardana was a king of the dynasty ruling in Kashi. Moreover, he is not the first king of Kashi; the Purāṇas name at least six kings preceding him.

3. One entire book (Book III), of the ten books of the Rigveda, is authored by composers belonging to the family of Viśvāmitra. According to the Purāṇas, Viśvāmitra was the ninth descendant of Jahnu, who established the kingdom of Kānyakubja (Kanauj) in Uttar Pradesh, and who gave the Ganga one more new name (Jāhnavī) after his own name. The Rigveda confirms the relation in III.58.6, where the composer of the hymn refers to himself as belonging to the "house of Jahnu". In short, the Pūru kingdom of Kānyakubja was in existence at least nine generations before the composition of any of the hymns in this book.

4. In one hymn (VIII.2.41), the poet Kaṇva Medhātithi praises king

[19] IVA, p. 74.

Vibhindu for his gifts; and in another hymn (VIII.3.21-24) he praises king Pākasthāman for the same reason, and the Bṛhaddevatā (VI.42) clearly identifies these two kings as rulers of Kashi and Bhoja (in eastern Uttar Pradesh, and western Madhya Pradesh) respectively.

5. One hymn (III.53.14) mentions Kīkaṭa and its king Pramaganda. Kīkaṭa is the country later named Magadha under the Pūrus. Thus, we find south Bihar also mentioned in the Rigveda.

Apart from these specific references to eastern Uttar Pradesh, western Madhya Pradesh and south Bihar, and to the Bay of Bengal, in the Rigveda, many of the other people named in the Rigveda are associated by other ancient Indian texts with other parts of India.

In one hymn (VIII.5.37-39), for example, we find a reference to the Cedis and their king Kaśu. Bhargava refers to this and points out that "Cedi was roughly equivalent to modern Bundelkhand."[20] But the Purāṇas, which give the genealogies of the Cedis, point out that the Cedis were Yādavas who migrated northwards to Bundelkhand from Vidarbha in northern Maharashtra. The poetess-composer of one Vedic hymn (I.179), Lopāmudrā, wife of Agastya, is declared by every single ancient Indian text to be the daughter of the king of Vidarbha. All this presupposes that there were "Aryans" in northern Maharashtra well before the composition of these Rigvedic hymns.

Thus, the Rigvedic hymns, in themselves, and in combination with the other texts, show that the Indo-European language-speaking people of the time were not restricted to the Punjab region, but were found as far east as South Bihar and the Bay of Bengal, and as far south as Maharashtra. This is, more or less, the geographical extent of the Indo-Aryan languages, even to this day. This is an inescapable conclusion, and any attempt to deny it can only lead to illogical contradictions. Let us examine the attempts of two scholars, A.D. Pusalker and P.L. Bhargava, in this connection.

Contradictions in Analysis of the Geographical Data

A.D. Pusalker, in his analysis of the data in the Rigveda and the data in the Purāṇas, makes the following comments, which deserve to be noted:

1. He admits that "the Rigveda is not a geographical manual and its various recensions have not come down to us in a complete form. It would, therefore, be unsafe and hazardous to draw any inference from the silence of the Rigveda. The non-mention of any locality in the

[20] IVA, p. 79.

hymns cannot be construed as evidence, one way or the other..."[21]

2. He admits that "the evidence of the Puranas cannot be ruled out altogether...they alone contain something like a continuous historical narrative, and it is absurd to suppose that the elaborate royal genealogies were all merely figments of imagination or a tissue of falsehoods."[22]

3. He admits that "the Vedic literature *confines itself to religious subjects* and notices political and secular occurrences only incidentally so far as they had a bearing on the religious subjects."[23] And immediately after this, he proceeds to quote F.E. Pargiter (in *Ancient Indian Historical Tradition*, London, 1922) as follows: "Ancient Indian history has been fashioned* out of compositions *which are purely religious and priestly*, which notoriously do not deal with history, and which totally lack the historical sense. The extraordinary nature of such history may be perceived if it were suggested that European history should be constructed merely out of theological literature. What would rouse a smile if applied to Europe has been soberly accepted when applied to India."[24]

But after all these admissions, what does Pusalker proceed to do? He gives a logical interpretation of the Puranic genealogies (see the chapter on traditional history in this book) under the heading "Traditional History from the Earliest Times."[25] And then he proceeds to reject the geographical data given in the Purāṇas on the ground that it does not tally with the "geographical evidence" of the Rigveda!

Thus, according to him: "In one respect, however, it seems difficult to accept the traditional account without a great deal of reserve... The Purāṇas say nothing about the original home of the Aryans. The scene of traditional history opens in India with the division of the territory comprising the whole of Northern India extending in the east upto Orissa, among the ten sons of Manu..."[26] In short, the concept of an Aryan invasion does not stand proved by the traditional account, but the traditional account stands disproved because it does not speak of an Aryan invasion!

And further: "This traditional account of the Aryan expansion is, however, in conflict with the evidence of the Vedic texts. ...There are

[21] HCIP, p. 241.
[22] HCIP, pp. 304-05.
[23] HCIP, p. 311.
[24] Quoted in ibid., *fashioned by modern historians.
[25] HCIP, pp. 267-310.
[26] HCIP, p. 311.

good grounds to suppose that by the time the Rigveda was composed, the Aryans had not penetrated much further into the interior beyond the frontiers of the Punjab and Rājputāna...(therefore) its testimony is decidedly fatal to the geographical views assumed in the Purāṇas."[27]

Thus in spite of his own admissions to the contrary, and in spite of the fact that the geographical "evidence" of the Rigveda (as we have already seen) does *not* indeed show that the "Aryans" were confined to the Punjab and Rajputana, Pusalker rejects the "geographical views assumed in the Purāṇas" on the basis of the alleged "testimony" of the Rigveda!

P.L. Bhargava is another scholar who devotes an entire book to describe what he calls "the story of Aryan expansion in India", and who seeks to prove that the Puranic accounts confirm that the "Aryans" of the Rigvedic age were confined to the Punjab region. We will deal with his "story" in the next chapter. Here, let us examine the contradictions or anomalies in his interpretation of the geographical data in the Rigveda.

1. He admits the references, in the Rigveda, to Kashi, Kīkaṭa and the eastern seas, but he tries to deny or downplay the importance of these references:

a. The reference to Kashi is too precise to be avoided. The anukramaṇīs of the Rigveda themselves declare that Pratardana, the composer of IX.96 and X.179.2, is a king of Kashi, and the Purāṇas confirm this. Likewise the Bṛhaddevatā, another supplement of the Rigveda, declares Vibhindu, mentioned in VIII.2.41, to be a king of Kashi.

Bhargava, therefore, allows for the existence of Kashi in the Rigvedic period. However, he shows a map of India[28] entitled "India in the time of King Sudās, c. 2250 BC — Aryan territory" (Bhargava, it must be remembered, is an internal-invasionist, and not an external-invasionist. Hence, while he propagates the concept of an Aryan "invasion" of the rest of north India from an original homeland in the northwest, he is not bound by any idea of a date such as 1500 BC for any earlier "invasion" of Aryans from outside into the northwest), and in this map, he shows the alleged "Aryan territory" of the time on shaded portions of the map. The territory that he shows covers Punjab (east and west), the NWFP, and parts of Kashmir and Afghanistan—and then, far away from this continuous territory, he shows a small shaded portion

[27] HCIP, p. 312.
[28] IVA, opposite p. 220.

around the city of Varanasi, which he tells us is the kingdom of Kashi, surrounded on all sides by "non-Aryan" territory! Bhargava happily informs us that "the only Aryan kingdom outside Saptasindhu, when Sudās came to the throne, was Kashi, and the latter too must have been cut off from Saptasindhu by non-Aryan powers..."[29]

Using this method, of course, geographical references in the Rigveda could be twisted around to any extent to "prove" that the "Aryans" of the time were restricted to Saptasindhu (the Punjab region). Even if Kalinga, Dwarka, Magadha, Vidarbha and Dakṣiṇa Kosala had been specifically mentioned in the Rigveda, all that would be required to be done is to show a map of India with tiny shaded portions in tiny parts of Orissa, Gujarat, Bihar, Maharashtra and Madhya Pradesh respectively, declare these to be tiny colonial outposts of the "Aryans" in India, "cut off from Saptasindhu by non-Aryan powers", and still continue to insist that the "Aryans" were restricted to the Saptasindhu!

This is the kind of evasive and dishonest logic one has to contend with in dealing with invasionist interpretations of Sanskrit texts.

b. He admits the reference to Kīkaṭa and its king Pramaganda, but follows a two-pronged policy to downplay the reference: firstly, he declares the Kīkaṭas to be non-Aryans, thereby denying "Aryan" presence in South Bihar; and secondly, he suggests that "the Kīkaṭas probably dwelt in South Bihar and arrived on their raids in the west,"[30] thereby denying even "Aryan" acquaintance with South Bihar.

Bhargava's suggestion, that the Kīkaṭas were known to the Rigvedic people only because they probably conducted "raids" in the west, right from South Bihar to the Punjab, does not even deserve comment. So far as his contention that the Kīkaṭas were "non-Aryans" is concerned, neither the name Kīkaṭa nor the name Pramaganda can be demonstrated as being "non-Aryan", and many scholars accept them to be "Aryans". Pusalker points out that "Weber...takes them to be Aryans, though at variance with the other Aryan tribes".[31]

c. Bhargava admits the references to the eastern sea, and (as already quoted) mentions them in detail, but he refuses to accept the logical implications of these references: "The identification of the Apara, Para or Parāvat sea does not present much difficulty. There can be no doubt that it was none other than the Arabian sea which could not

[29] IVA, pp. 134-35.
[30] IVA, p. 56, footnotes.
[31] HCIP, p. 248.

have remained unknown to a people who knew the Indus. The Pūrva, Avara or Arvāvat sea is the one which presents some difficulty. It could not have been the Bay of Bengal which is far removed from the home of the Rigvedic Āryas. The problem deserves a detailed investigation."[31a]

Thus, inspite of the fact that the eastern sea could be none other than the Bay of Bengal, Bhargava chooses to simply deny it on no other ground than that it "could not have been" the Bay of Bengal since this clashes with his interpretation of the geographical data in the Rigveda! And, rather than accept the logical identification of the eastern sea with the Bay of Bengal, he is willing (although he does make a last-ditch bid, in his above-referred map, opposite p. 220 in his book, to postulate a sea in western Rajasthan of the Rigvedic period, which he labels the Arvāvat sea), by and large, to leave the identity of the eastern sea as one of those unexplained mysteries of all time!

2. Bhargava also declares that "towards the end of the Rigvedic age...the Aryan settlements had reached upto the banks of the Ganga".[32]

Does this statement tally with his own interpretation of the Puranic data (even when, as we shall see in the next chapter, he converts this data into his "story" of Aryan expansion in India)? Let us examine Bhargava's analysis of the Puranic accounts.

Bhargava, after a logical consideration of the genealogical lists of the different dynasties as given in the Purāṇas, prepares a table of these dynastic lists (see the next chapter for these lists). He classifies the hundred or so generations of the pre-Mahābhārata period into four "ages" according to his insistence that the "Aryans" expanded from the Punjab region into the rest of north India. These four "ages", according to him, are the "Era of Saptasindhu" (Generations 1-27), the "Era of Conquest" (Generations 28-49), the "Era of Expansion" (Generations 50-72) and the "Era of Settlement" (Generations 73-100).

Bhargava summarizes his "story" of "Aryan expansion in India", in these four eras, in the following words:

a. "The Era of Saptasindhu: In the early part of the Rigvedic period, the Aryan people were all settled in the country of the seven rivers—Saptasindhu. The kings of different dynasties ruled in various parts of this compact country, and the easternmost limit of their campaigns was the river Yamunā. No settlement of any Aryan dynasty outside Saptasindhu is recorded till the time of Trasadasyu, the

[31a] IVA, p. 74.
[32] IVA, p. 60.

Aikṣvāku king, and Suhotra, the Paurava king."[33]

b. "The Era of Conquest: Jahnu founded the Kānyakubja kingdom on the bank of the Gangā...Kāśa founded the Kashi kingdom a little further off on the bank of the same river...a new kingdom named Vidarbha was founded south of the Vindhyas and another named Cedi was established south of the Yamunā...."[34]

c. "The Era of Expansion: ...The early part of this period is marked by the expansion of the Āryas in all the different directions of India. ...Some generations later, two more new kingdoms, Vaishali and Aṅga were founded in new regions to the east. This process of expansion was completed in the time of Rāma who went up to the extreme south of India, and whose sons and nephews founded towns and kingdoms in various parts of India."[35]

d. "The Era of Settlement: ...This era was marked by a settled life of cultural development in the territory conquered by the Āryas."[36]

Thus, according to Bhargava's own description of the alleged "expansion" of Aryans inside India, the kingdoms of Kānyakubja and Kashi (in central and south-eastern Uttar Pradesh respectively) were established during the time of Jahnu and Kāśa (both Generation 28); the kingdom of Vidarbha (in northern Maharashtra) was founded during the time of king Vidarbha (Generation 37); the kingdoms of Kosala (in northeastern Uttar Pradesh) and Videha (north-western Bihar) were founded during the time of Bhagīratha and Nimi-Māthava (Generation 50); the kingdom of Aṅga (West Bengal) was founded during the time of Dadhivāhana (Generation 62); the extreme south of India was covered during the time of Rāma (Generation 72) and "towns and kingdoms founded in various parts of India" a generation or two later.

According to all the traditional accounts, the Rigvedic canon was closed by Vyāsa around the time of the Mahābhārata war; and this is confirmed, as admitted by Bhargava, by the fact, that the last king to be named in the Rigveda is Śantanu, who is mentioned in a hymn (x, 98) composed by his brother Devāpī.

In short, as per Bhargava's own description of the alleged "expansion" of Aryans in India, hymns of the Rigveda were being composed 70 generations after the founding of Kashi, 61 generations after the founding of kingdoms in northern Maharashtra, 36 generations after the

[33] IVA, pp. 158-59.
[34] IVA, p. 159.
[35] IVA, p. 160.
[36] Ibid.

founding of kingdoms in Bengal, 26 generations after Rāma's excursions into the extreme south of India, and 25 generations after the founding of towns and kingdoms in various other parts of India.

And yet, Bhargava wants us to believe that "towards the end of the Rigvedic age...the Aryan settlements had reached upto the banks of the Gangā", or, in other words, that the Aryans had penetrated only so far into India, from the Punjab region, as the westernmost regions of the Ganga!

Thus, the scholars, who wish to postulate an original or interim homeland for the Indo-Aryans in the north-west of India, only succeed in tying themselves up into knots, when they try to prove, on the basis of the Rigveda, that the Aryans in India were originally confined to the Punjab region.

All the evidence of the ancient texts, including that of the Rigveda itself, shows that more or less the same areas of India were occupied by speakers of Aryan languages, at the time of the composition of the Rigveda, as they are now. Therefore, just because the Rigveda is the earliest extant text of ancient India, there is no reason to believe that the Aryan-language speakers of the other parts of India originally came from the Punjab region—much less that they came into the Punjab region from outside.

CONFLICTS IN THE RIGVEDA

If the "Aryans" were outsiders who invaded India, established their first settlements in the Punjab region, and then proceeded to conquer their way into the rest of northern India, and if the Rigveda was the earliest record of their religious outpourings during the very first stage of their settlements in the Punjab, then it is essential to identify the "non-Aryan" people with whom they must necessarily have entered into deadly conflict, and of whom evidence must necessarily be found in the Rigveda and other Sanskrit texts.

Identifying conflicts between "Aryans" and "non-Aryans", in the Rigveda and other Sanskrit texts, is therefore an unavoidable aspect of the Aryan invasion theory. Failure to identify such conflicts, and such "non-Aryans", is absolutely fatal to that theory.

Hence, identification of "conflicts", wherever they are found, or can be alleged to be found, in these texts, as conflicts between "Aryans" and "non-Aryans", has become a major industry among invasionist scholars.

These scholars are, of course, handicapped in their efforts by the fact that, just as these texts do not give even the faintest indication of any "homeland" outside India or of any invasion therefrom, they do not give any indication of conflicts between Indo-Europeans and Dravidians or Austrics. And, alas, the oldest Tamil texts also totally refuse to yield even the faintest hint of any such conflicts.

The scholars are, therefore, compelled to give "interpretations" of the textual material to identify these conflicts, even if they have to, in the process of doing so, accuse the ancient Sanskrit authors of a conspiracy of silence to defraud future generations (the ancient Tamil authors, who cannot be accused of similar conspiracy, are perhaps to be supposed to be victims of mass amnesia); or of converting the accounts of such "conflicts" into allegories and mythical stories, or into religious rituals, or into descriptions of natural phenomena; or of deliberately "Aryanising" the collective and individual names of the "non-Aryans" for the purpose of camouflage. Thus, they derive "evidence" not from what the authors say, but from what they claim the authors are deliberately not saying!

The common terms in the Rigveda and later Vedic texts, and in the Purāṇas, which are generally presumed to be references to the "non-Aryan" enemies of the Vedic Aryans, are mainly Dāsa/Dasyu, Asura, Paṇi, Rakṣa/Rākṣasa, Dānava, Daitya, Yakṣa, Gandharva, etc.

Certain scholars have been fully thorough in their branding of these "peoples" as non-Aryans. Thus, Malati Shendge[37] brands them all as non-Aryans, and in fact even assigns particular linguistic identities to them. She locates them all in the north-west of India, and decides that the Dāsas/Dasyus were speakers of Austric languages, the Rakṣas/Rākṣasas were speakers of Dravidian languages (apparently on the analogy of Rāvaṇa of Lanka being a Rākṣasa), and the Asuras were speakers of Semitic languages (identifying the Asuras with the Assyrians!).

P.L. Bhargava[38] rejects the idea of Asuras, Dānavas and Daityas being "non-Aryans"; but he insists that the term Dāsa/Dasyu "undoubtedly meant the aborigines of this country."[39]

As a matter of fact, of all the "peoples" in the Rigveda who are alleged to be in conflict with the Vedic Aryans, the Dāsas/Dasyus alone, as we shall see, are genuinely identifiable as communities of people who were in conflict with the Vedic Aryans. The references to

[37] CDHR, pp. 375-76.
[38] IVA, pp. 57-58.
[39] IVA, p. 47.

these Dāsas/Dasyus are so numerous and so clear that it is evident that they refer to a people more often than to any natural phenomena or mythical beings; and, what is more, many hymns specifically distinguish between Āryas (by which term the composers of the hymns clearly refer to themselves) and Dāsas/Dasyus (by which they refer to their enemies). Many hymns refer to the slaughter of Dāsas/Dasyus in battle.

We will examine, presently, the identity of these various alleged groups of "non-Aryans". But, in the very first stage itself, it must be noted that no one has, as yet, been able to prove from a linguistic point of view (and the question of "Aryans" and "non-Aryans" is basically a linguistic one) that any of the said individuals or groups, mentioned in the texts, are "non-Aryans".

John Muir, after his study of Sanskrit texts, clearly admits: "I have gone over the names of the Dasyus or Asuras, mentioned in the Rigveda, with the view of discovering whether any of them could be regarded as being of non-Aryan or indigenous origin, but I have not observed any that appear to be of this character."[40]

Even V.M. Macdonell, although he (unlike Muir) regards the Dāsas/Dasyus as non-Aryan aboriginals, admits that most of the Dāsa/Dasyu names are derivable from Sanskrit roots. He gives the derivations of the names Pipru, Suṣna, Namuci, Dhuni, Varcin, etc; but he cannot resist the temptation to suggest that at least two Dāsa/Dasyu names (Sṛbinda and Ilībiśa) have "an un-Aryan appearance."[41] What exactly he means by "un-Aryan appearance" is best known only to himself; he cannot prove, and nor does he attempt to prove, that the names are either Dravidian or Austric or Semitic or anything else. There are many names of pure pedigree (names of Gods, rishis and kings) in the Rigveda which can also be accused, in an equally vague manner, of having "an un-Aryan appearance." If Sṛbinda has an un-Aryan appearance, what about Śaśabindu (a prominent Yādava king in the Purāṇas)? If Ilībiśa has an un-Aryan appearance, what about Iḍaviḍa (the name of an Ikṣvāku king, seven generations prior to Rāma)?

Perhaps the best testimony is provided by S.K. Chatterji, that arch-ascriber of a "non-Aryan" origin to Indo-Aryan names, words and customs. He refers to the "Census Report (India) for 1911, p. 327 & 412; Sarat Chandra Roy, *The Mundas and Their Country*, Ranchi 1912, Chap. II, pp. 30-32, 43, 44, 47 ff, 61, 70 ff, and comments: "Mr. Roy's

[40] Original Sanskrit Texts, Vol. II, p. 387, Edition 1819.
[41] VM, p. 162.

attempts to identify names of non-Aryan chiefs in the Rigveda with Mundari names...are rather fanciful."[42]

Chatterji's words show that scholars who try to identify the Dāsa/Dasyu names in the Rigveda as "non-Aryan" names are not even sure whether the names are to be branded as Dravidian or Austric or Semitic; they are only determined that the names must be branded as "non-Aryan". And the efforts of even the most ardent of such scholars, such as Mr. Roy, cannot really succeed in convincing even the other equally ardent scholars of the same brand, such as S.K. Chatterji, about the exact "non-Aryan" identity of the names.

Of the collective names which are branded as names of non-Aryan peoples, the names Asura, Dāsa/Dasyu, and perhaps Paṇi, require special attention. Before examining them, let us examine the other alleged names of "non-Aryan" peoples.

THE "NON-ARYAN" PEOPLES IN THE RIGVEDA

According to Malati Shendge (and innumerable other prominent scholars) the terms Daitya, Dānava, Yakṣa, Gandharva, Rakṣas/Rākṣasa, and Piśāca refer to "non-Aryan" peoples.

1. *Daityas*: The Daityas, according to the Purāṇas, are the progeny of Diti, one of the wives of Kaśyapa. Therefore, it is clear that the Daityas are a class of celestial beings, on par with the Devas. Aditi means "infinity" and Diti means "finity"; the two terms are obviously antonyms, and hence their progeny also depict antonymical concepts: while the Ādityas or Devas are Gods, the Daityas are demons.

2. *Dānavas*: The Dānavas, are likewise, another class of celestial beings, the progeny of Danu, another of the wives of Kaśyapa. Their identity, as a class of celestial beings, is proved by the fact that in Celtic mythology, the Mother-Goddess is named Danu and the Gods are referred to as the "Children of Danu".

3. *Yakṣas*: The word Yakṣa is derived from the root *yakṣ-* "to be quick, to speed on", or, as per Sāyaṇa, from the root *yaj-* "to worship". The word is used in the Rigveda (X.88.13) in the sense of the Supreme God. The Upaniṣads also repeatedly make it clear that the term refers to the innermost spirit. The Bṛhadāraṇyakopaniṣad (S.4.1) speaks of "this mahad Yakṣa, the first-born, the Truth, the Brahma", and the Kenopaniṣad (3-4) identifies Yakṣa with the power of Brahman, surpassing even the strength of the Devas.[43]

[42] ODBL, p. 29, footnote.
[43] CDHR, p. 117.

In fact, Shendge, who insists in the first place that Yakṣas were non-Aryans, admits that the concept of Yakṣa in the ancient texts represents "the supreme force of the universe... Just as the branches cannot exist without the trunk of the tree, the Gods owe their existence to the Yakṣa. It is the creator of the Gods, their *raison d'etre...* Primarily Yakṣa may have been a godhead, a supreme deity which was conceived to be the essence of the universe as well as of the individual."[44]

What was originally a spiritual concept came to be depicted in later texts as a class of celestial spirits, often anthropomorphised as beings living lives of luxury. Kubera, a Yakṣa king, is the guardian of wealth and treasure.

4. *Gandharvas*: The word Gandharva was originally another word for godhead. Throughout the Rigveda (III.38.6, VIII.1.11, IX.83.4, IX.85.12, X.10.4, 80.6, 123.7; etc.) the word clearly and unambiguously refers to the sun. In some hymns (I.22.14, etc.), Gandharva is "the heavenly Gandharva, whose habitation is the sky, and whose special duty is to guard the heavenly Soma, which the Gods obtain through his permission."[45]

Later, the term was converted into the name of a class of celestial beings associated with divine music.

5. *Rakṣas/Rākṣasa*: The word Rakṣas in the Rigveda, is derived from the Sanskrit root *rakṣ-*, "to guard, protect, watch, take care of, save, preserve", or "to guard against, ward off, prevent, injure".

The evidence of the Rigveda shows that the term Rakṣas stood for demoniac spirits and not for any "aboriginal" people. Even Shendge, who wants us to believe that they were "non-Aryan" natives, admits as much: "There are over fifty references to Rakṣas in the Rigveda from the earliest stratum, both in the singular and plural. No Rakṣas is mentioned by name, nor is there any reference to the physiognomy. No fortresses (puras) are associated with any of the Rakṣas. Not much evidence of their being a tribe or clan is available..."[46]

Throughout the Rigveda, the Rakṣas are described in terms which leave no doubt whatsoever that it is supernatural demons which are being referred to (as, for example, in hymn VII.104). Later, the word came to be used even with reference to evil people.

6. *Piśācas*: The word Piśāca is mentioned only once in the Rigveda, in its feminine form Piśācī, in hymn I.133.5. The hymn refers

[44] CDHR, p. 120.
[45] HOR, Vol. I, p. 26, footnote.
[46] CDHR, p. 124.

to demoniac spirits; and the particular word, as it is used therein, unmistakably refers to a kind of banshee or female demoniac spirit, a meaning which it has preserved to this very day.

All these words, therefore, originally referred to celestial beings or spiritual concepts or demoniac spirits. Later these terms came to be used with reference to kings, clans or communities, but in no case is there the slightest evidence that they were "non-Aryans". The term Piśāca, for example, refers today to the speakers of the Piśāca or Dardic languages, which are as "Aryan" as Sanskrit; and as per Shendge's own admission, Pāṇini (in his Aṣṭādhyāyī, V.3.117) refers to certain warrior clans (no less "Aryan") as Rakṣas and Piśācas.

THE ASURAS

The Deva-Asura conflict is a major theme in most of the ancient Sanskrit texts deriving from the Vedic stream. While, in a majority of cases, it is obvious that the stories of this conflict are allegorical tales, there are a large number of stories which leave little doubt in the mind that they refer to mythologized memories of some ancient conflicts.

A.D. Pusalker very happily, and rather simplistically, declares that "the Rākṣasas were aborigines who were hostile to the Brahmanas, while Vānaras, another aboriginal tribe, were allied to the Brahmanas. Asuras, Daityas, Dānavas, and Nāgas, denoted people of different cultures in various stages of civilization, ranging from the rude, aboriginal, uncivilized tribes to the semi-civilized races, offering strong resistance to the spread of Aryan culture."[47]

Further, he claims that there were three stages in the use of words like Asura, Dānava, etc.

a. They were the names of human beings of enemy tribes, and hence evil attributes were associated with the names.
b. Later, even certain Aryan kings were termed Dānavas or Asuras due to their evil character.
c. Finally, the terms came to mean demons.

The twisted logic, and the unscrupulousness, of the invasionist scholars is obvious here. The evidence clearly shows that every single one of these terms originally referred to abstract (divine, celestial or supernatural) concepts, and were later applied to people ("Aryans" in every case), but never to any "non-Aryan" individuals or peoples. We have already dealt with the other prominent names in the Rigveda. We will now deal with the term Asura.

[47] HCIP, p. 303.

As already pointed out in an earlier chapter, the word Asura, in Iranian *Ahura*, refers to the Supreme God. There is no possible explanation which anyone can give as to why the Iranians should have adopted the name of an aboriginal Indian tribe (whether a "rude, aboriginal, uncivilized tribe" or a "semi-civilized race") as the name of their Supreme God, especially when it is alleged that the Iranians and Indo-Aryans had separated outside India.

The truth is that the word Asura originally meant exactly the same thing as the word Deva. As Bhargava points out, "the bulk of the Rigveda...calls everyone of its great Gods both Deva and Asura."[48]

All the Gods in the Rigveda are referred to as Asura: Varuṇa (VIII.19.23; I.24.14; 42.1), Varuṇa and Mitra together (I.151.4; VII.65.2; VIII.25.4), Rudra (V.42.11; II.1.16; V.41.3), Agni (V.12.1; 15.1; VII.6.1; III.29.11), Soma (IX.74.7; 99.1), Savitṛ (VI.53.1; V.49.2), Pūṣan (V.51.11), Ādityas (VIII.27.20), Maruts (I.64.2), Aryaman (V.42.1), Dyaus (I.22.1; 131.1; VII.20.17), Indra (I.174.1; X.105.11; 99.2), Uṣas (X.55.4), etc. The words *asūrya* and *asuratva* are used in the sense of "godliness" when referring to the various Gods.

It is only in certain late hymns that the word seems to acquire an evil meaning. But, as Shendge points out: "Looking at the problem statistically, the term *Asura* is used with good connotation 59/60 times, and 12 times with the connotation of evil, in the Rigveda."[49]

In later texts, the term Asura has been converted into a term for demons. But, even then, they are constantly referred to as a class of beings equal in power and glory to the Devas, and their constant rivals. The explanation for the transformation in meaning of the term lies in a purely Indo-European (i.e. Indo-Iranian) environment. As Bhargava puts it: "It is a well-known fact that whereas in the later Vedic and Sanskrit literature, the words Deva and Asura mean God and demon respectively, in the Avesta the two words convey just the opposite senses... The use of these words in the opposite senses by the Indians and the Iranians was the result of a schism which was perhaps one of the causes of the separation of the two branches of the Aryan race. It is, however, clear that before this schism took place the two words must have been used by the united Āryas *in the same sense*."[50]

Therefore, it is clear that the Deva–Asura antagonism in the later Vedic and Sanskrit literature is a mythologization of the conflict be-

[48] IVA, p. 51.
[49] CDHR, p. 30.
[50] IVA, p. 51.

tween the Vedic "Aryans" and the Iranians.

Realizing this, B.K. Ghosh tries a different tactic to derive evidence of an Aryan invasion from the Deva-Asura conflict. He decides that the term Asura, for God, is "perhaps borrowed from a superior civilization... In innumerable passages in the Brāhmaṇas, the Asuras have been depicted as superior to the Devas in the arts of civilized life..."[51]

He, therefore, places the arena of this Indo-Iranian conflict in the alleged "Indo-Iranian homeland" outside India, where the concept of Asura was, according to him, borrowed from the "superior civilization" of Mesopotamia or Assyria. "The antagonism between the worshippers of the Daiva-Gods and the Asura-Gods...must have been one of the main causes of the estrangement and subsequent secession of those Aryans *who later conquered India*...(who), urged by the spirit of adventure, *advanced further east and at last entered India*", while the Asura-worshippers by and large, "were content to remain in Iran."[52]

His formulation firmly refuses to take into consideration the fact that all the evidence incontrovertibly shows that the Rigveda was composed in the Punjab region and that it shows no evidence whatsoever of any extraterritorial memory, and that the bulk of the Rigveda treats Asura as synonymous with Deva. The conflict, leading to the schism, must therefore have taken place in the Punjab region.

Realizing this, Shendge combines all the different points and presents her own story. According to her, the Aryans were nomadic invaders who invaded India from the northwest, and the Asuras were non-Aryan people, the Harappans, who were settled in the Indus Valley. They were, according to her, affiliated to the Assyrians, and, in fact, part of an Asura empire stretching from West Asia to northwest India. The Aryans invaded the Indus Valley and destroyed the Asura empire. Shendge picturesquely describes the flight of the Asuras: The Aryans "made them vacate the Indus Valley. The pattern of dispersal of the Asuras appears to be like this: A large part went to Iran and the hilly regions in the north-west. Some went via sea to Kaccha and Saurashtra. Others, especially the Dāsas, went to the eastern region. Some Rakṣas probably stayed on in Baluchistan and some went to Southern India, probably to Ceylon. The Gandharvas and the Yakṣas found a place in the Aryan social structure."[53]

[51] HCIP, p. 220.
[52] Ibid.
[53] CDHR, p. 376.

In making up this story, Shendge does not appear to deem it necessary to take the support of any textual reference or any other evidence; her fertile imagination provides all the details. In the process, if she has to convert innumerable things in the Rigveda into "non-Aryan" things, as we shall see presently, that is only part of the game. Incredibly enough, in order to fit into her story the fact that the Deva–Asura conflict could only have been an allegorical account of the conflict between the Vedic people and the Iranians, she concedes that the Asuras were the Iranians, but converts them into "non-Aryans", and even casts doubts on the Indo-European character of the Iranian languages. Referring to the "linguistic affinities of the language of Avesta", she suggests that "(although) at present it is said to belong to the Indo-European family, ...little work has been done on the comparisons of the Avestan language with other, especially Semitic languages. In fact, a comparison of the Ahurian and Daevian vocabularies with some of the more ancient languages may reveal foreign influence."[54]

The only guiding principle behind all these desperate attempts is that the term Asura, in the Deva-Asura conflict, should represent something "non-Aryan", if not an actual "non-Aryan" people in India conquered by the "invading Aryans", then at least a "non-Aryan" cultural influence on the "Aryans" en route to India. The word *Deva*, for God, is purely Indo-European. It is derived from the root *div-*, "to shine", and has cognates in most of the Indo-European languages (Greek *theos*, Latin *deus*, Irish *dia*, Lithuanian *dievas*, etc.). The word *Asura* is therefore branded "non-Aryan". Let us examine whether this is valid.

The word *Asura* is derived from the word *asu*, "life-breath, the life-winds in the body" (on the analogy of *madhura*, "sweet", derived from *madhu*, "honey"), and it means "the essence of life and breath, the innermost spirit, the Paramātmā", which is the sense in which the word is used throughout the bulk of the Rigveda. And what is more, the word is not an isolated word: the Gods in Teutonic mythology are called *Aesir*. According to Carl Buck, the word appears in a Runic inscription as *Ansur* which he derives as "originally 'spirit' from *ans-*, an extension of *an-*, 'breath.' "[55]

Thus, the word *Asura*, which has its exact cognate in the language and mythology of the Teutons at the opposite end of the Indo-European geographical spectrum, is obviously purely Indo-European, and has nothing to do with anything "non-Aryan".

[54] CDHR, p. 29.
[55] ADOSS, p. 1465.

THE DĀSAS/DASYUS

The Dāsas/Dasyus are undoubtedly the enemies of the composers of the Rigveda. The references are too many, and too unambiguous in many cases, to admit of allegorical interpretation. In a very few cases, it is true, the terms seem to refer to demons of darkness who rob the light of the sun and prevent it from reaching the earth; but in a majority of cases, they refer to a people whom the composers of the hymns hold in enmity, and in fact the word *Ārya* is often used in opposition to the words *Dāsa/Dasyu.*

Hence, almost all the invasionist scholars are unanimous in declaring that the Dāsas/Dasyus were the "non-Aryan" people with whom the "invading Aryans" came into conflict in their task of conquering and occupying the Indian territory. Let us examine the case.

The Rigveda, throughout, refers to the Dāsas/Dasyus as *aśraddha,* "faithless", *ayajña,* "offering-less" or "non-sacrificing", and *avrata,* "without rituals". Shendge grabs at this to point out that the Dāsas/Dasyus were indeed human beings and not supernatural or naturalistic phenomena, since "it obviously refers to the religious practices of human beings rather than demons."[56]

But what she misses out is that it *obviously refers to the religious practices, rather than the race or language, of human beings.*

The people referred to as Dāsas/Dasyus were none other than the Iranians, the worshippers of Asura, who were particularly inimical to the cult of Indra and to the sacrifice of animals in the sacred fire. They were, from the very beginning, a community of Indo-Europeans who were different from the Vedic Aryans, and who were in constant conflict with them; but it is only at a very late stage that this enmity resulted in the division of the two words for God, and the conversion by each group of the other group's word for God into a term for demons.

The words *Dāsa* and *Dasyu* are derived from the root *daṁś-*, "to shine" (similar to the word *Deva* from the root *div-*, "to shine") and cannot originally have been words of abuse. The Dāsas and Dasyus are the enemies of the Vedic people throughout the entire range of hymns, therefore, a name akin to the term *Deva* could not have been applied to them by the Vedic Aryans. The people who called themselves by these terms must, therefore, have been Indo-Europeans themselves.

In the Rigveda, the words are used in reference to the enemy people. In later times, therefore, the words became terms of abuse: Dāsa came to mean "servant, slave, demon", and Dasyu came to mean

[56] CDHR, p. 36.

"demon, thief, dacoit, villain." So much so that another cognate word *dasra,* which, throughout the Rigveda, is applied to the Aśvins, and means "shining, glorious, wonderful", also became a term of abuse, meaning exactly the same thing as the word *Dasyu.*

The word is confirmed in Slavonic mythology where the Sun-God is named *Dazh-bog.* The word *Bog* means "God"; and in the Rigveda, also, the cognate word *Bhaga* means both "Sun" as well as "God". The word *Dazh,* is therefore, obviously derived from the root *daṁś-*, and means "Sun". The word *Dazh-bog,* thus, means "Sun-God", or "The Shining God", or "The Shining Sun".

So much for the antecedents of the terms *Dāsa* and *Dasyu.* The evidence for the actual identity of the people so named is even more clear.

The word *Dasyu* is found in the Avesta as *dahyu.* The word *Dāsa* is found in the eastern Iranian dialect of Khotanese as *daha,* meaning "man". In both cases, the words are used by the Iranians in referring to themselves.

Scholars of Indo-European linguistics find themselves at a loss to explain logically the occurrence of these words in Iranian languages. Emile Benveniste, for example, discusses the problem as follows: "The Avestan word for 'country', *dahyu* (anc. *dasyu*) has as its Sanskrit correspondent *dasyu.* In spite of the complete identity of form, some scholars doubt the connection because of the difference in sense. In Avestan and Old Persian, *dahyu* signifies 'country'. In Vedic, *dasyu* is a foreign slave. But the difference can be explained in the light of the older stage of these notions. In Indic, *dasyu* may be taken as an ethnic... An eastern Iranian dialect, Khotanese, possesses the word *daha,* 'man'. We know from other sources that in the Iranian world there was a people, the *Dahae* as they are called by Latin authors. This people, like many others, simply called themselves 'the men'... We can now understand the strange sense of the Sanskrit *dasyu.* If the word at first referred to Iranian society, the name by which this enemy people called themselves collectively took on a hostile connotation and became for the Aryas of India the term for an inferior and barbarous people. Thus, the connexion between the sense of *dahyu/dasyu* reflects conflicts between the Indian and Iranian peoples."[57]

Thus, Benveniste admits that the word "referred to Iranian society" and that it "reflects conflicts between the Indian and Iranian peoples." But he refuses to accept the logical implication of this, since it would

[57] IELS, pp. 260-61.

deal a body-blow to two basic principles of the Aryan invasion theory: (1) that the common Indo-Iranian homeland lay outside India, and (2) that the Rigveda is a saga of Aryan-vs-non-Aryan conflicts. Instead he pleads that while it may have "at first" referred to Iranians, the Indo-Aryans retained the "hostile connotation" of the term, and later applied it to the "ethnic" populace of India. Here we have one more example of the kind of logic which twists every inconvenient fact, and invents new concepts and situation at every step, so as to avoid disturbing the unstable edifice of the invasion theory.

Moreover, the term *dahyu* does not only signify "country", it means both "country" and "people", and in fact, it originally meant only "people". The word is used in the oldest Iranian texts in the sense of "people", and in fact it is used by the Iranians in referring to themselves, and moreover it is used in the specific context of referring to their enmity with the Deva-worshippers.

B.K. Ghosh refers to these oldest Iranian texts, the Yashtas: "It has now been fully established that the civilization of the Gathas is a later reformed civilization of Iran of which a much older phase is reflected in the Yašts, particularly the so-called heathenish Yašts, i.e. the Yašts which have suffered least from Zarathushtrian revision. And the culture reflected in these pre-Zarathushtrian heathenish Yašts is essentially that of Vedic India."[58]

Shapurji K. Hodiwala in his book *Zarathushtra and His Contemporaries in the Rigveda* (published by himself, Bombay, 1913) quotes a passage from the Farvardin Yashta (Sec. 90): "In this passage we are told that Zarathushtra was the first to speak the word against the Devas and in favour of the Ahuramazdaian religion. Then follows this important passage: *yo suro vispo hujyaitish paoiryo-tkaesho dahyunam...* '(Zarathushtra) who was learned, all-happiness-giver and first leader of the Dahyus'..." (p. 9).

The Rigveda also makes it clear (in II.13.9; IV.28.4; V.30.9; X.22.8; etc.) that Dāsas and Dasyus are one and the same; and in one of the few later hymns in which the word Asura has come to acquire an unsavoury connotation (in X.170.2), the Rigveda clearly states that Dasyus and Asuras are one and the same and that the people so referred to are the enemies of the composer of the hymn. Similarly, the Atharvaveda (X.3.11) also stresses the identity between the Dasyus, Asuras and enemies. The most prominent individual *Dāsas* named in the Rigveda (Pipru, Namuci, Varcin, etc.) are also referred to in other

[58] HCIP, p. 223.

hymns as *Asuras*. And Shendge[59] points out that Sāyaṇa and the Mahābhārata treat the word Asura as interchangeable with the words Dāsa/Dasyu.

The Rigveda's contrast of the words Ārya and Dasyu is frequently quoted. But those who see, in this, evidence of the Dasyus being "non-Aryan", in the linguistic sense, may note the following:

1. The Iranians, who call themselves Daha and Dahyu also call themselves Airya.
2. The word *Ārya* was never used by any ancient text in a linguistic sense. The use of the word in that sense is a modern use of the term. Hence the composers of the hymns could never have intended to convey the meaning that they themselves spoke Indo-European languages while the Dasyus spoke non-Indo-European languages. Nor is there the slightest indication that the composers of the hymns used the words in a racial sense. The *Amarakośa* gives the following meanings of the word *Ārya*: 1) of high family; 2) gentlemanly; 3) good-natured; 4) righteous. Thus it is obvious that the composers of the hymns used the words in contrast to indicate that while they themselves were "noble", the Dasyus, in their opinion, were not.
3. This is confirmed by the evidence of the Rigveda itself (X.49.3) where the composer of the hymn expresses his refusal to call the Dasyu enemies by the term Ārya.

Thus, it is obvious that the Ārya-Dasyu conflict in the Rigveda is nothing but the Vedic-vs-Iranian conflict which took place in the Punjab region. After the bulk of the Iranians left the Punjab and migrated westwards, the terms *Dāsa/Dasyu* ceased to be used in reference to a community, and came to be used only in the sense of "slave" and "robber" respectively.

P.L. Bhargava tries to explain the disappearance of the term as the name of a community in post-Vedic times as follows: "The non-Aryan Dāsas, when admitted into Aryan colonies, began to serve the Āryas, and the word Dāsa, therefore, acquired the meaning of servant or slave, just as 'slave' in the Teutonic languages was originally 'Slav'. Probably as a result of this meaning being given to the word, the non-Aryans gave up this name and began to be called Śūdras. Except for this change in the nomenclature of the Dāsas, the condition of the Indian society in the later Vedic period was not much different from that at the

[59] CDHR, p. 31.

end of the Rigveda period. In later Vedic literature, we hear of Āryas and Śūdras as still forming the two sections of Indian society."[60]

In the first place, this favourite leftist ploy of treating the iniquities of the later caste-system as the iniquities of a racial-system (the Aryan race versus the non-Aryan races) is one which does not bear the slightest scrutiny. Dr. Ambedkar, while refuting this ridiculous contention in some detail, categorically declared: "Caste system does not demarcate racial division. Caste system is a social division of people of the same race."[61]

Secondly, the parallel given by Bhargava itself gives the lie to his contention. The word "slave" in the Germanic languages is indeed derived from the name of the Slavonic/Slavic/Slav peoples. As late as this century itself, Hitler declared the Teutons to be the master "Aryan" race and the Slavs to be the "slave" race. But the Teutons and the Slavs are two peoples occupying neighbouring territories as are the Indo-Aryans and the Iranians, and not two strata of a single society in which Teutons from the upper stratum and Slavs the lower stratum. And the Teutons and the Slavs are both Indo-Europeans!

THE PAṆIS

The Paṇis, mentioned in the Rigveda, are regarded as enemies of the Vedic Aryans. A.D. Pusalker sums up the issue: "The Paṇis are often mentioned with the Dāsas and Dasyus as the enemies of the Aryans. Though opulent and rich, the Paṇis never worshipped the Gods or rewarded the priests. They have been described as selfish, non-sacrificing, of hostile speech, greedy like the wolf, niggardly, of cruel speech, Dasyus, Dāsas, of inferior status. They were cattle-owners and notorious cattle-lifters, and *in some passages definitely figure as demons who withheld the cows or waters of the heavens*... The question of the identity of the Paṇis has not yet been settled with any degree of certainty. The words Paṇik or Vaṇik, Paṇya and Vipaṇi, found in Sanskrit, suggest that the Paṇis were merchants par excellence in the Rigvedic age. The Paṇis have been variously identified with an aboriginal non-Aryan people; with Babylonians (on the strength of the word Bekanata); with Parnians, the Dahae and other Iranian tribes; and with non-Aryan caravan traders."[62]

P.L. Bhargava also stresses that the Paṇis were "non-Aryan" na-

[60] IVA, pp. 236-37.
[61] Writings and Speeches, Vol. I, p. 49.
[62] HCIP, pp. 248-49.

tives of India: "As Dr. Altekar has rightly pointed out, it seems fairly probable that the Paṇis of the Vedic literature are identical with the Harappans or with a section of them. The Paṇis are traders, usurers and enormously rich; so were the Harappans..."[63]

Malati Shendge[64] deals at length with the Paṇis and demonstrates that they were the trader-section of the native "non-Aryan" populace, and, being the wealthier section, the prime targets of attacks by the nomadic "Aryan invaders". She quotes hymn X.108, which is in the form of a dialogue between the Paṇis and Saramā, a female messenger sent by Indra and the Gods to the Paṇis. In this hymn, Saramā warns the Paṇis that if they fail to accede to Indra's demand (that they should turn over their cattle and wealth to him), they would be utterly destroyed by the Gods, and their cattle and wealth forcibly acquired by them. Shendge interprets the hymn as a testimony of the mafia-like tactics of the nomadic "Aryan invaders" as they descended on the civilized "non-Aryan" inhabitants of the Indus Valley.

As a matter of fact, the case of the Paṇis in the Rigveda provides us with the most classic expose of the invasionist method of functioning. It shows up the fact that the invasionist scholars examine the Sanskrit texts with invasion-tinted glasses, and blinkers, on their eyes. They do not examine the texts to see what the texts say, but to see how the texts can be twisted around so that they appear to be giving "evidence" of the Aryan invasion, and of conflicts with "non-Aryans". What can be a better example of this than the fact that, although the Rigveda has been deeply studied by the scholars for over two centuries, and many of the most prominent scholars have been Germans, not a single scholar seems to have realized that the Paṇis of the Rigveda are identical with the Vanir of Teutonic mythology?

Some scholars have at least accepted that the Paṇis represent a naturalistic mythological concept. Thus Ralph T.H. Griffith describes the above hymn (X.108) as follows: "The hymn is colloquy between Saramā, the messenger of the Gods or of Indra,...and the Paṇis or envious demons who have carried off the cows or rays of light which Indra wishes to recover."[65] Elsewhere, he points out that "Saramā is the Dawn who recovers the rays of the Sun that have been stolen by the night."[66]

[63] IVA, p. 199.
[64] CDHR, pp. 37-46.
[65] HOR, Vol. II, p. 550, footnote.
[66] HOR, Vol. I, p. 85, footnote.

Later, greater and greater anthropomorphization of the different naturalistic elements in the Rigvedic hymns led to greater and greater resemblance of these elements to human beings. Teutonic mythology shows a later stage of development in which the naturalistic element has not been retained. The Rigveda, however, shows both the original naturalistic element as well as its later transformation into anthropomorphic mythology.

The Paṇis, therefore, have nothing to do with any "non-Aryans".

THE "NON-ARYAN"-MANIA

In their desperate attempts to prove the Rigveda to be a documentation of conflicts between the "Aryans" and "non-Aryans", some scholars seem to have gone berserk in identifying such conflicts and such "non-Aryans". We may take here the example of Malati Shendge.

She decides that "a number of hymns of the Rigveda were not originally understood as myths but were composed to celebrate the victory of the Aryans over the non-Aryans"[67], and that they acquired a religious character by a process of "transformation of historical events into mythopoeic and symbolic."[68] Since most of the hymns depict Indra destroying, or being invoked to destroy, the enemies, Shendge concludes that "the events referred to in the exploits of Indra and Viṣṇu, *the leaders of the Aryans in their conflict*, probably took place historically... When the Aryans created a religion out of these events, they deified their leaders and arrogated to themselves the title of cosmic good. The rituals of this religion have come down to us in the Brāhmaṇas, which are composed of the narratives followed by the ritual prescriptions which are expected to produce magically the desired effect..."[69]

Thus, Shendge makes the alleged Aryan-vs-non-Aryan conflict into the be-all and end-all of the Rigveda and of the Vedic religion or cult derived from it. Therefore, every single reference or indication in the Rigveda, and the later Vedic texts, which shows anything which could be construed as "conflict", is brought by Shendge into her Aryan-non-Aryan scheme. Her book has to be read to be believed. In retrospect, and in the light of other factors and deeper knowledge, especially, as we shall see, of comparative Indo-European mythology, the book is absurd and ridiculous; but at the same time it is rather overpow-

[67] CDHR, p. 3.
[68] CDHR, p. 4.
[69] CDHR, pp. 3-4.

ering, and even frightening, in the intensity and organisation of her arguments.

Shendge decides that Indra was an actual Aryan-invader chieftain who led the marauding bands of barbaric nomads in their conquest of what she claims was the Asura empire of the Indus Valley. Throughout her book, she details the "strategies" devised and "plots" hatched by the Aryans in their campaign of conquest, and the sordid events constituting her incredible story. In the process, she identifies a great many things as "non-Aryan". Some of the prominent items in her list of "non-Aryan" people and things are:

1. *Almost all the Rigvedic Gods:* "The so-called Vedic pantheon, *with the exception of Indra and Viṣṇu,* is composed of the functionaries of the government of the Asura empire having its capital in the Indus Valley...the supreme ruler of this empire was Varuṇa, Rudra was the commander-in-chief of the army, and Sūrya the chief of the intelligence department, and so on..."[70]

2. *Most of the clans and tribes mentioned in the Rigveda:* "Many of the names of the tribes or clans referred to in the Rigveda end in *u* as, for example, Puru, Sigru, Simyu, and appear to be loan-words into Sanskrit. Probably these are the names of the tribes or communities as they were known or as they called themselves. As such, they were borrowed in Sanskrit."[71]

3. *Many of the hymns and most of the rishis of the Rigveda:* "It is evident that at least parts of the Rigveda are probably pre-Aryan. This does not imply that they existed in the same language before. They were composed by the ancient sages in their own language. Amongst such hymns may be counted those addressed to Uṣas, to Agni, to Varuṇa, the cosmogonic hymns, those addressed to Gandharva and so on... Most of the poets were the seven seers and were originally the Asura priests of fire... (these hymns) already existed in the language of the Asuras before the advent of Aryans in India...they were probably, at a later stage, either translated into Sanskrit or on the basis of earlier material new hymns were composed."[72] (Elsewhere, she specifies some of these "pre-Aryan" rishis: Gṛtsamada[73], the Saptarṣi[74], Mātariśvan, Aṅgiras, Atharvan, Atri, Kaṇva, Bhṛgu, Tanu Napāt, Apām Napāt, etc.)

[70] CDHR, p. 290.
[71] CDHR, p. 114.
[72] CDHR, pp. 375 and 379.
[73] CDHR, pp. 38-39.
[74] CDHR, pp. 351-55.

4. *Most of the basic rituals and concepts in the Rigveda:*

a. The concept of Rta.[75]

b. The ritual worship of fire: "Agni was worshipped by the Asuras in an elaborate ritual in which several priests probably participated."[76] The Aryans "thought that the Asuras owed their prosperity to their worship of the fire, (and therefore) they also adopted it and instituted the sacrifices."[77]

c. The ritual use of Soma.[78]

d. "The time-hallowed symbolism of forces of good being represented by light and forces of evil represented by darkness...and...the concept of the God...fighting the evil forces to save his creation."[79]

Thus, almost every single thing in the Rigveda, which would normally be considered as purely "Aryan" by most invasion-theorists, is branded as "non-Aryan" by Shendge: the Vedic Gods, the Vedic tribes and clans, the Vedic rishis and hymns, the Vedic rituals and concepts!

Her conclusions are incredibly ridiculous, but her book is nevertheless a classic: it follows the principle of identification of "Aryan-vs-non-Aryan" conflicts in the Rigveda to its (il)logical conclusion. She unintentionally succeeds in demonstrating that *if the Rigveda is to be treated as a document of Aryan-vs-non-Aryan conflict, then this is what we must unavoidably and inevitably end up with*!

Ultimately the only "Aryans" left in the Rigveda, as per Shendge, are Indra and Viṣṇu ("the leaders of the Aryans in their conflicts", as she fatuously calls them) and presumably, the nameless hordes of "Aryan invaders" led by them. And even these two only narrowly miss being branded as "non-Aryans": "The use of the eponym *Asura* may be indicative of the Asuric origin of the Gods. Only in the case of Indra and Viṣṇu, it is meant as a compliment, as the Aryan origin of Indra and Viṣṇu is beyond doubt."[80]

How she decides that the Aryan origin of Indra and Viṣṇu, alone among the Vedic Gods, is "beyond doubt", is as great a mystery as how she, or any other scholar, decides that anyone or anything in the Rigveda is "non-Aryan".

Shendge tells us that "Indra represents the conquering Aryans, Varuṇa as his powerful equal represents the non-Aryans, the Asuras."[81]

[75] CDHR, pp. 292-94.
[76] CDHR, p. 351.
[77] CDHR, p. 377.
[78] CDHR, pp. 109-13.
[79] CDHR, pp. 376-77.
[80] CDHR, p. 19.
[81] CDHR, p. 295.

In her zeal, she brands the name Varuṇa as "a Sanskritized form of a Semitic name."[82] Ironically, while neither Indra nor Viṣṇu is represented by name in any European mythology, Varuṇa is represented by Uranus in Greek mythology and Woden in Teutonic mythology!

However, there is method in this madness, and the logic of Shendge's non-Aryan mania has to be understood.

But before going into the logic of Shendge's method, it is necessary to understand the motive behind it all, which is indirectly declared by herself.

After elaborating that "a number of hymns of the Rigveda were composed to celebrate the victory of the Aryans over the non-Aryans", and that the entire Vedic religion was instituted as a symbolic celebration of this victory, she tells us that the Śūdras were the non-Aryan natives who were converted into a fourth caste: "the Śūdras were especially debarred from the practice of the Vedic religion. This was not so much for preserving the purity or the monopoly as for the fear which constantly haunted the Aryan mind, and of which it could it never be free, viz. *the revolt of the non-Aryans leading to their (Aryan) expulsion from this land.* Thus, the Śūdra was prohibited even from listening to the Vedic literature simply because if he understood the basis of this religion, he might rebel..."[83]

Shendge's motive, therefore, seems to be to enlighten the "non-Aryans" with the knowledge of the "true nature" of the Vedic religion, so as to initiate the process of "Aryan expulsion from this land", or at any rate, to re-initiate the alleged "Aryan-vs-non-Aryan" conflict once more in modern circumstances.

THE CIVILIZED NON-ARYANS

The main logic of Shendge's book is revealed by herself: "At a time when the Harappan civilization was still undiscovered and when it was assumed that the Aryan invaders of India encountered only a rabble of aboriginal savages...it was safe to regard the whole Vedic corpus as representing in the main an Aryan evolution...(but) the Aryan advent in India was in fact the arrival of barbarians into a region already highly organised into an empire based on a long-established tradition of literate urban culture. The situation is in fact almost reversed, for the conquerors are seen to be less civilized than the conquered."[84]

[82] CDHR, p. 301.
[83] CDHR, p. 378.
[84] CDHR, p. 146.

Thus, Shendge unwittingly reveals the dishonest nature of invasionist scholarship, which, chameleon-like, changes its interpretation of the Vedic hymns to suit its changed perceptions of the exact nature and character of the alleged non-Aryans: Originally, the "non-Aryan" natives were believed to be "a rabble of aboriginal savages", and the hymns were to be interpreted likewise. Now, the discovery of the Harappan civilization, and the need to identify it with the "non-Aryans" conquered by the "Aryan invaders", makes it necessary to reinterpret the hymns so as to show that the "Aryans invaders" were nomadic "barbarians", and the "non-Aryans natives" were "already highly organised into an empire based on a long established tradition of literate urban culture."

Hence, all elements in the Rigveda giving indications of such an empire, and such a tradition, must necessarily be shown to be non-Aryan and pre-Aryan. Shendge, plunges headlong into the task.

To begin with, she identifies the Deva-Asura conflict in the Vedic texts with the "Aryan-non-Aryan" conflict. She quotes innumerable verses and hymns from the Rigveda (IV.42.2, X.124.5, etc.) to show that originally Varuṇa was the king of the Asuras, or of the Asura empire as she calls it, and that Indra usurped his throne, or conquered and took over the Asura empire. Then she proceeds to show that the "Aryans" were nomadic and barbaric, while the Asuras, the "non-Aryans", represented a civilized, urban culture.

1. She quotes Stuart Piggott: "Chariots are described in such detail ...but we hardly know what the Aryan house looked like."[85] She also quotes the Śatapatha Brāhmaṇa (VI.8.1.1-2) as stating that "the *Devas* were moving in carts (*cakramacara*) whereas the Asuras were sitting in houses (*śālās*)."[86] Later, she sums up the matter as follows: "Although much is said about the houses and fortresses of the Asuras and their destruction by the Aryans under the leadership of Indra, nowhere do the Rigvedic hymns mention the houses or even the shelters of the Aryans. On the other hand...the Śatapatha Brāhmaṇa explicitly states that when the Devas were moving in carts, the Asuras were sitting in their houses."[87]

While nothing is mentioned in the Rigveda about the abode of Indra, Varuṇa is repeatedly depicted as sitting in his mansion, observing the deeds and activities of man. His palace is described as made of

[85] CDHR, p. 147.
[86] CDHR, p. 94.
[87] CDHR, p. 271.

gold (V.67.2), having a thousand columns (II.41.5) and a thousand doors (VIII.88.5).

In the Rigveda, Varuṇa is supposed to rule with his powers of magic. The word used, and repeatedly and especially in connection with Varuṇa, is *māyā*. Shendge[88] deals at length with this word. She points out that *māyā* is derived from the root *ma-*, "to measure, mete out, fashion, form, build, make, exhibit", and therefore it properly means building or architecture. In the Mahābhārata, also, the word is used in that sense: *Mayāsura* is the architect of the Asuras who constructs the hall for the *Rājasūya* sacrifice. In the Śāṅkhāyana and Āśvalāyana Śrautasūtras, *Māyāveda* is mentioned as an equivalent of *āsuraveda*. According to Shendge, the nomadic Aryans were so awed by the architectural wonders of the non-Aryan *Asuras* of the Indus Valley, that they considered it to be the result of magic; hence the term *māyā* was construed as a word for magic.

2. Like architecture, agriculture was also unknown to the nomadic Aryans, according to Shendge. She points out that the Śatapatha Brāhmaṇa (I. 61.1.2-4) speaks of how the seasons asked for a share in the sacrifice, and the Gods refused. So the seasons went to the *Asuras:* "Those *Asuras* then throve in such a manner that while the foremost of the *Asuras* were still ploughing and sowing, those behind them were already engaged in reaping and threshing; indeed, even without tilling, the plants ripened for them."[89]

Similarly, according to her,[90] the Śatapatha Brāhmaṇa (VI.6.3.2) relates that the Devas and the Asuras were contesting, and all the herbs went to the Asuras, and only the *udumbara*, ficus glomerata, did not leave the Devas. Having defeated the Asuras, the Devas obtained all the herbs. The Śatapatha Brāhmaṇa (III.6.1.8-9) also relates that all the medicinal herbs deserted the Devas, and only *yava*, barley, was with them.

From all this, Shendge concludes that the Śatapatha Brāhmaṇa "clearly attributes the agriculture to the Asuras. In fact the demand for sacrifice by the seasons and subsequent desertion by them indicates that probably the Aryans were not well-versed in the change of seasons."[90a]

To this, Shendge[91] adds that in Sanskrit, "many terms intimately connected with agriculture are of non-Sanskritic origin", and this "may

[88] CDHR, p. 56.
[89] CDHR, p. 95.
[90] CDHR, p. 96.
[90a] CDHR, p. 241.
[91] CDHR, p. 137.

suggest that the process of agriculture itself was unknown to the Aryans." And she cites 18 Sanskrit words, of which she brands 6 as "Mundari", 2 as "Dravidian", 8 as being "terms of unrecognized origin but of non-Sanskritic appearance", and 2 as being "of doubtful origin."

3. Shendge realizes that many of the characteristics and aspects of the Rigvedic Gods give evidence of association with a materially and spiritually advanced civilization. Hence, on the basis of the word *Asura* being used as an epithet for them, she brands all of them "with the exception of *Indra* and *Viṣṇu*" as "the functionaries of the government of the *Asura* empire"[92], or, in other words, as "the cabinet-members of the non-Aryan government."[93] She "proves", on the basis of innumerable quotations, that Mitra was "the exchequer-general of contracts"[94], Rudra was "the commander of the Asura army"[95] (with the Maruts as his "sons or followers") Sūrya was "the head of the intelligence department"[96], Savitṛ was "the head of the system of redistribution"[97] (with Bhaga and Aṁśa as his assistants), Pūṣan was "the inspector and builder of roads"[98], and so on.

The evidence in respect of Rudra, she claims, is especially strong. Inspite of being heavily equipped with fierce weapons whose power is described in detail, he "is never the partner of Indra in his armed conflicts."[99] His followers, the Maruts or Rudriyas, however, seem to have agreed to join up with Indra. Hence, according to her, they have 33 hymns devoted to them while Rudra has only three. Further, Rudra is maligned throughout the Vājasaneyī Saṁhitā and described in the most insulting terms.

4. Shendge further identifies the main exploit of "the invader king" Indra in the Rigveda: the killing of Vritra by Indra in his conquest of the Asura empire in the Indus Valley. According to her, "Vritra is said to be the serpent who was covering the waters which Indra released by killing the dragon"[100]; but she knows better: Vritra was "an official, who alongwith his men, referred to as Vritrāṇi, was guarding the dam."[101]

[92] CDHR, p. 290.
[93] CDHR, p. 5.
[94] CDHR, p. 303.
[95] CDHR, p. 306.
[96] CDHR, p. 318.
[97] CDHR, p. 321.
[98] CDHR, p. 326.
[99] CDHR, p. 303.
[100] CDHR, p. 50.
[101] CDHR, p. 339.

So, "Indra, by killing Vritra, the guard of the dam across the seven rivers, brought under his control the sluice gates which he opened in order to flood the downstream settlements, thus causing panic and damage to life and property."[102]

The hymns describe the dam, according to Shendge: "One significant feature of the fight is the frequent mention of the mountain which obstructs the waters. In I.32.2, *Ahi* is said to be lying on the mountain. I.57.6 once again refers to a great wide mountain which Indra shatters to pieces by his bolt."[103]

According to Shendge, in IV.30.20, "Indra is said to have submerged with his strokes, for Dabhiti, thirty thousand Dāsas, by magic power, in sleep ...'submergence in sleep' might refer to the inundation of cities at night by the untimely artificial floods."[104]

She identifies Vritra as a non-Aryan Asura, rather than a dragon or serpent: "*Ahhe* and *Ahi* have both formed parts of Assyrian names. The catalogue of tablets in the Kauyunjik collection refers to at least twenty-four names of officials and rulers which begin with *Ahi*... Thus both the words *Vritra* and *Ahi* do not warrant the interpretation 'dragon'."[105]

5. Shendge, as already pointed out, identifies the Paṇis with the "non-Aryan' Harappans (the denizens of her Asura empire), on the basis of the fact that the Paṇis, like the Harappans, are associated with trade and navigation and other features of a settled and flourishing urban culture. On the basis of hymn X.108, she demonstrates that the "Aryans", led or symbolically represented by Indra, were nomads who harassed the settled inhabitants of the area.

6. Shendge realizes, and herself explains in some detail,[106] that the elaborate Vedic system of fire worship could only have been the end-product of a stage-by-stage evolution in a stable, settled society. According to her, therefore, "The cult of fire was associated with God Asura and was probably the religion of the Asuras...Agni was worshipped by the Asuras in an elaborate ritual in which several priests probably participated."[107] The Aryans "thought that the Asuras owed their prosperity to the worship of the fire, (and therefore) they also adopted it and instituted the sacrifices."[108]

[102] CDHR, p. 25.
[103] CDHR, p. 51.
[104] CDHR, p. 35.
[105] CDHR, p. 50.
[106] CDHR, p. 348-55.
[107] CDHR, p. 351.
[108] CDHR, p. 377.

According to her, this is confirmed by the Śatapatha Brāhmaṇa (I.9.2.34-35), where it is stated that the Gods and Asuras contended for the sacrifice, and "thereupon the Gods obtained possession of the whole of the sacrifice and dispossessed the Asuras of it."[109]

She quotes hymn X.124, claiming that "although the hymn is metaphorical it gives some idea of what happened."[110] In this hymn, Indra calls upon Agni to come to their sacrifice. Agni says: "Making myself away from him secretly, I go to the God from the ungod. ...I go from one's regular friendship to the foreign kinship... I say to father Asura a friendly word... Many years I was active in him. As I selected Indra, I give up the father..." All this proves that fire-worship was an Asura institution adopted by the Aryans.

While Shendge's classification of the Rigvedic Gods, as Aryan and non-Aryan combatants in the invasion struggle, is peculiarly her own, the principles underlying her hypothesis are nevertheless the same principles underlying the hypotheses of other invasionist scholars. The identification of Asuras as "non-Aryans", of Indra as an invader king (or at least as representing, in the hymns, the invading Aryans) of the Paṇis as the Harappans, of Rudra as at least a "non-Aryan" God, etc., are all regular invasionist themes.

Even such a noted scholar as F.E. Pargiter, for example, in his zeal to coordinate his interpretation of the Puranic accounts with the theory of an external invasion by "Aryans", ends up reaching some of the same ridiculous conclusions as Shendge. Thus, in his chapter, *The Ancient Brahmans and the Vedas*,[111] he classifies all the Vedic rishis, and all the subsequent Brahmana families, as "non-Aryans", and most of the Vedic hymns as being Sanskrit translations of pre-Aryan hymns. Further, in his interpretation of the Puranic dynasties, he classifies all the dynasties, except the Saudyumnas/Ailas (whom, alone, he classifies as "Aryans"), as "non-Aryan". The Ikṣvākus, in particular, he classifies as "Dravidians". That Aikṣvāku Rāma was a Dravidian, that the Vedic rishis and the Brahmans were "non-Aryans", and that Brahmanism (as Pargiter[112] specifically declares) was a "non-Aryan institution", are certainly conclusions which should provide food for thought to, for example, the ideologues of the Dravida Kaḷagam!

Shendge certainly builds up a seemingly formidable case, but a

[109] CDHR, p. 268.
[110] CDHR, p. 88.
[111] AIHT, pp. 303-21
[112] AIHT, p. 306.

closer look shows that the entire edifice of her arguments is like a house of cards, which collapses at the mere touch of comparative mythology. Not only is the term Asura, and all that goes with it, purely Indo-European; but we find, in European mythology, unmistakable counterparts (as we shall see in the later chapter on Positive Evidence in the Rigveda) for all the "non-Aryans" identified by Shendge: Varuṇa, king of the Asuras, with his magnificent mansion and his magical powers; Rudra, the isolated and reviled outcaste among the Gods; Vritra, the Great Serpent, associated with the mountain and the waters; the Paṇis, with their trade and navigation, and their wealth coveted by the Gods; and institutions like that of fire worship. Here, we will deal only with the question of the allegedly "borrowed" agricultural terms in Sanskrit.

Shendge[113] gives the following list of words, for agricultural terms, which she claims have been borrowed by Sanskrit: *lāṅgala* (plough), *sira* (plough), *khala* (threshing-floor), *ulūkhala* (mortar), *musala* (pestle), *phāla* (ploughshare), as Mundari words; *matya* (harrow, roller), *matikṛ* (to harrow, roll), as Dravidian words; *kīnāśa/kīnāra* (farmer), *pharvara* (field), *karīśa* (manure), *titau*(sieve), *sater* (husk), *sadaka* (unhusked grain), *tsāru* (plough-handle), *tusa* (chaff-husk), as "terms of unrecognized origin but of non-Sanskritic appearance", and *sṛṇī* (sickle) and *stega* (ploughshare) as words "of doubtful meaning."

However, the word *lāṅgala* (plough), according to Monier-Williams,[114] is derived from the root *lag-*, "to penetrate, to attack or to cling" and the derived root *laṅg-*, "to limp, to go". Now, Shendge herself refers to "the heavy type plough preferred by the Punjabi farmers. It *penetrates* deeper into the ground than the lighter one."[115]

The word *sīra* (plough) is cognate to the word *sīta* (furrow); and according to Carl Buck,[116] both are derived from the Indo-European root **se(i)-*, "throw, sow"; the word denotes "a kind of drill-plough", which, he points out, is used in modern India.

The word *khala* (threshing floor) has a straight cognate in the Baltic languages: Lettish *kult* and Lithuanian *kulti* both mean "thresh".[117]

The word *ulūkhala*, "mortar" is obviously derived from the same root.

[113] CDHR, p. 137.
[114] SED, pp. 893, 895, 900.
[115] CDHR, p. 240.
[116] ADOSS, p. 496.
[117] ADOSS, p. 509.

The word *musala*, "pestle", is derived from the root *mus-*, "to break or cut into pieces, to destroy."[118]

The word *phāla*, "ploughshare", is derived from the root *phal-*, "to burst, cleave open or cleave asunder, to bear or produce fruit, to ripen."[119]

The word *matya*, "roller, harrow", has cognates, according to Carl Buck,[120] in other agricultural implements of Europe: Latin *mateola*, "mallet", Old English *mattoc* and Church Slavonic *motyka*, both "hoe", etc.

The word *matikṛ*, "to harrow, to roll", is obviously the verbal derivative of the above word.

Thus, all the 8 words given by Shendge as Mundari or Dravidian words prove to be Indo-European ones. Words vaguely classified as of "unrecognized" or "doubtful" origin can always be taken with a heavy fistful of salt so far as claims of borrowings are concerned, as demonstrated earlier. The words so classified by Shendge can, therefore, be summarily dismissed, especially when we consider that most of them are clearly Indo-European.

Thus, *karīsa* for "manure" is not a difficult derivation when we consider the following Sanskrit words: *kṛṣ*, "plough" (cognate Avestan *karš*[121]), *kṛṣī*, "agriculture", and *kṛṣṭi*, "farmer".

Pharvara, "field", is obviously derived from *phar-*, "to scatter, sow".

Tusa, "chaff, husk", is obviously cognate to Sanskrit *tusta* (English "dust").

Sṛṇī, "sickle", has its direct cognate in Church Slavonic *srūpu*, "sickle", which Carl Buck derives as "an extension of **ser-* in Sanskrit *sṛṇī-*."[122]

Thus, even the few words, from among many Sanskrit agricultural terms, which Shendge tries to brand as "non-Aryan", prove to be as "Aryan" as any other.

THE TRUE NATURE OF "CONFLICTS" IN THE RIGVEDA

From all this, it should be clear that there is no element of "Aryan–vs–non-Aryan" conflict to be found anywhere in the Rigveda. For all

[118] SED, p. 824.
[119] SED, p. 716.
[120] ADOSS, p. 505.
[121] ADOSS, p. 496.
[122] ADOSS, p. 507.

practical purposes, the Rigveda is a purely "Aryan" book of hymns from the Punjab.

The so-called conflicts in the Rigveda are largely the "conflicts" of natural elements. Indra, the Thunder-God of the Rigveda, occupies a central position in the naturalistic aspects of the Rigvedic religion, since it is he who forces the clouds to part with their all-important wealth, the rain. In this task, he is pitted against all sorts of demons and spirits whose main activity is the prevention of rainfall and sunshine. Rain, being the highest wealth, is depicted in terms of more terrestrial forms of wealth, such as cows or *soma*. The clouds are depicted in terms of their physical appearance: as mountains, as the black abodes of the demons who retain the celestial waters of the heavens (i.e. the rain), or even as the black demons themselves. As the poetic imagery, depicting the celestial battles of the natural forces, takes greater and greater recourse to terrestrial terminology and anthropomorphic depictions, the descriptions acquire an increasing tendency to shift from naturalism to mythology. It is these mythological descriptions which are grabbed at by invasion theorists as descriptions of conflicts between Aryans and non-Aryans.

The second category of conflicts in the Rigveda represents the genuine conflicts between the Vedic people and the Iranians. These conflicts are often sought to be poetically blended in with the naturalistic-mythological descriptions, and it requires some care to distinguish between "conflicts" of the first category and genuine conflicts of the second.

That these conflicts of the second category pertain to the Iranians, and not to any "non-Aryans", is proved by the fact (apart from the logical interpretation of the hymns themselves) that nowhere else outside the Vedic literature do the terms, which refer to the enemies of the Vedic people, occur other than in the Iranian texts.

The Iranians not only called their God *Ahura (Asura)* and their demons *Daevas (Devas),* but they also called themselves *Dahas* and *Dahyus* (*Dāsas* and *Dasyus).* The oldest Iranian texts, moreover depict the conflicts between the *Daeva*-worshippers and the *Dahyus* on behalf of the *Dahyus,* as the Vedic texts depict them on behalf of the *Deva*-worshippers. *Indra,* the dominant God of the Rigveda, is represented in the Iranian texts by a demon *Indra.*

The very names of the Supreme God and the Supreme Demon of Iranian theology give evidence of Iranian enmity with the Vedic people.

The name of the Supreme God, *Ahura Mazda*, is composed of the two epithets of the Rigvedic God *Varuṇa: Asura* and *Medhira*. Throughout most of the Rigveda, *Varuṇa* is depicted as the king of the Gods, when the Gods are referred to by the epithet *Asura*. In later, post-Rigvedic literature, the Gods are exclusively referred to by the term *Deva*, and the term *Asura* has been converted into a term for demons; and here *Indra* is undoubtedly the king of the Gods. Hence, when the Iranians broke away from the Vedic people, they adopted the epithets of the king of the Gods, when the Gods were called *Asuras*, as the name of their Supreme God.

The name of the Supreme Demon, *Angra Mainyu*, is composed of the Rigvedic *Aṅgiras* or *Aṅgirā* and *Manyu*.

The Aṅgiras rishis are the predominant rishis of the Rigveda. Of the 7 families of rishis who have composed hymns for the 10 books of the Rigveda, the Aṅgiras rishis alone account for 2 whole books (Books IV and VI); and another third one (Book II) is composed by a rishi who, although nominally a Bhārgava, was born into the Aṅgiras family. Besides these 3 books, Aṅgiras rishis are the composers of 122 (64%) of the 191 hymns in Book I, and 82 (80%) of the 103 hymns in Book VIII, besides a large number of hymns in Books IX and X. The Aṅgiras rishis are so manifestly *the* rishis of the Rigveda that Agni himself is repeatedly addressed as Aṅgiras by rishis belonging to the other families; as, for example, in the very first hymn of the Rigveda, by a composer-rishi belonging to the Viśvamitra family.

The God Manyu in the Rigveda is a particularly destructive form of Indra. He is said to represent "Anger, Passion personified".[123] Two hymns of the Rigveda (X.83 and X.84) are devoted to him. These two hymns are the most blatantly non-naturalistic hymns in the Rigveda. Ralph T.H. Griffith points out that these two hymns "are to be repeated, Sāyaṇa says, at sacrifices to ensure the destruction of enemies."[124] There is no doubt whatsoever that these, and other similar but unrecorded hymns addressed to Manyu represented most clearly the Vedic people's active hostility towards the Dasyus. The second line of X.83.6 fervently calls out: "Come to me, Manyu, Wielder of the Thunder: bethink thee of thy friend and slay the Dasyus."[125] The last verse of the second hymn (X.84.7), in fact, seems to indicate that the two warring sides are worshippers mainly of Varuṇa (=Asura=Ahura) and Manyu

[123] HOR, Vol. 2, p. 499, footnote.
[124] HOR, Vol. 2, p. 500, footnote.
[125] HOR, Vol. 2, p. 500.

(=Indra=Mainyu) respectively, and calls upon both the Gods to ensure the victory of the Vedic side: "For spoil, let Varuṇa and Manyu give us the wealth of both sides gathered and collected; And let our enemies, with stricken spirits, overwhelmed with terror, slink away defeated."[126]

Thus, the Iranian religion calls its Supreme God by the epithets of the superseded Rigvedic king of the Gods; and its Supreme Demon by a combination of the names of the predominant rishis of the Rigveda, and the name of the most militant form of the Rigvedic God Indra.

The fact that the conflicts in the Rigveda were between the Vedic people and the Iranians is half-acknowledged by many scholars. Even Bhargava[127] concedes the fact, although he does not extend his concession to the words Dāsa/Dasyu which, he insists, refer to the "aboriginals" of India. A.C. Das[128] and S.K. Hodiwāla[129] also deal at length with the same subject.

To sum up, there is not the slightest piece of evidence that even the most ardent invasionist scholar can convincingly dig up about any conflicts between the Vedic people and "non-Aryans" of any kind. The circumstances of the Rigveda are purely Indo-European. In fact, as the following chapters will make clear, while the Rigveda represents the viewpoint of only a section of the Indo-European people of the time, it records not merely the oldest Indo-Aryan, or even the oldest Indo-Iranian period known, but in fact the oldest common (or proto-) Indo-European period known to us.

[126] Ibid.
[127] IVA, pp. 50-55.
[128] *Rigvedic India*, pp. 146-47.
[129] *Zarathushtra and His Contemporaries in the Rigveda.*

TWENTY

NON-EVIDENCE IN THE PURĀṆAS

The Rigveda is a book of hymns. It neither is, nor claims to be, either a geographical manual or a historical treatise. The Purāṇas, on the other hand, are, and claim to be, historical treatises giving, incidentally, the geographical particulars concerning the various historical eras or ages with which they profess to deal.

And yet, we find a peculiar and extremely fishy situation prevailing in the study of India's most ancient history: the evidence of the Purāṇas (consisting of what is actually stated in the Purāṇas) is rejected on the basis of the "evidence" of the Rigveda (consisting of evidence inferred from the "non-mentions" in the Rigveda: from the fact that the Rigvedic hymns appear to have been composed mainly in the Saptasindhu region in and around Punjab, and do not appear to mention in detail the places to the far east and south of this region).

This situation is without parallel anywhere else in the world. In the study of the history of the Jews of ancient Israel, for example, no one would even dream of trying to reconstruct the history from those parts of the Old Testament, such as the Book of Psalms, which do not profess to deal with this history, rather than from those parts, such as the Chronicles, which do. And yet, in the case of ancient Indian history, the scholars unblushingly reject the evidence of the Purāṇas on the basis of "evidence" inferred from the Rigvedic hymns!

The basic reason for rejecting the evidence of the Purāṇas is geographical: "The scene of traditional history opens in India with...the whole of Northern India, extending in the east upto Orissa.....(this) is, however, in conflict with the evidence of the Vedic texts...by the time the Rigveda was composed, the Aryans had not penetrated much further into the interior beyond the frontiers of the Punjab and Rājputāna... (therefore) its testimony is fatal to the geographical views assumed in the Purāṇas."[1]

Thus, we have the two allegedly conflicting pieces of evidence: the Puranic evidence which states that the whole of North India was occupied by people, and ruled by dynasties, who very obviously were Indo-European-speaking ones, as far back as almost a 100 generations before the Mahābhārata war, which itself was more than a thousand years, as per the Puranic testimony, before the rule of the Nanda kings in the 4th

[1] HCIP, pp. 311–12.

century BC, and the Vedic "evidence" which shows that the Rigveda (which the scholars insist was composed in 1000 BC, and which, they further insist, represents the earliest Indo-European culture in India) was composed mainly in the Punjab region.

Since the two pieces of evidence are alleged to be "conflicting", one of the two has perforce to be rejected. The compulsions of the Aryan invasion theory naturally dictate that it is the Puranic evidence which is to be rejected. Hence, the scholars reject the Puranic evidence and project the Vedic evidence.

P.L. Bhargava realizes that this rejection of the Puranic evidence, howsoever much it may be the officially accepted position today, is not strictly tenable. Hence, he launches into his powerful thesis which seeks to show that the Puranic evidence does not in fact conflict with the "evidence" of the Rigveda.

To be fair to Bhargava, he tries, or appears to try, to be as logical as possible within the parameters of the "evidence" of the Rigveda. Thus, the Vedic "evidence" has the following three factors:

a. The Rigveda is dated at 1000 BC.
b. The Vedic people are alleged to have come from their original homeland situated as far away as South Russia.
c. The "Aryans" are alleged to have been restricted to the Punjab region within India at the time of the Rigvedic culture.

Bhargava rejects the first contention since he realizes that it is pure hypothesis unsupported by any evidence, and also because he realizes that the number of generations of kings named in the Purāṇas before the rule of the Nandas (who are proved, by Greek records, to have ruled in the 4th century BC) cannot possibly be squeezed into six centuries. Hence he accepts that the Rigveda was composed a few thousand years BC.

He also rejects the second contention on the same grounds as he accepts the third one. In this respect, he shows himself to be at least more honest than the invasion-theorists. Thus, he treats the Vedic Aryans as having been unacquainted as much with the areas outside the boundaries of India as with the areas within India, on the ground that neither of the two areas are specified in detail in the Rigveda.

However, on that same ground, he accepts the third contention. He, therefore, claims, that the original home of all the Indo-European languages lay in the mountains to the north of the Saptasindhu region: "The Aryans originally lived in the valleys of the rivers Ghorband and Panjshir to the south of the Hindu Kush range.... From this region one branch seems to have gone to the West and after wandering in many lands seems to have ultimately settled in the various countries of Europe, while another branch migrated to Saptasindhu from where in course of time it was divided into two sections, one of which left Saptasindhu and settled in Iran."[2]

According to Bhargava, "the Vedic literature makes it absolutely clear that the Aryas moved eastward and southward from their original home in the Punjab."[3] Therefore, realizing that the evidence of the Purāṇas cannot be rejected, he finds it necessary to prove that "the course of Aryan expansion in India as indicated in the (Vedic) literature is fully borne out by Puranic genealogies."[4]

Therefore, Bhargava presents his "evidence" from the Purāṇas to show that "in the early part of the Rigvedic period, the Aryan people were all settled in the country of the seven rivers—Saptasindhu. The kings of different dynasties ruled in various parts of this compact country, and the easternmost limit of their campaigns was the river Yamunā."[5]

In this chapter, we will examine in detail the basic aspects of the "evidence" presented by Bhargava. But before that, let us examine the value of the Puranic accounts as a source of material for the study of India's most ancient history.

THE VALUE OF THE PURANIC ACCOUNTS

The invasionist scholars reject the evidence of the Purāṇas, and project the evidence of the Vedic literature, on the ground that Vedic texts have two strong points in their favour: "Priority of date and comparative freedom from textual corruption"[6], and moreover, as Pusalker points out, they provide "an evidence which is all the more valuable as it is based upon incidental notices not likely to be fabricated in order to serve any preconceived notion."[7]

But what these scholars refuse to note is that these very Vedic texts, in just such "incidental notices", provide valuable evidence about the authenticity of the Puranic evidence: Bhargava points out that "there is actual mention in the Saṁhitā and Brāhmaṇa literature of a work called Purāṇa. Thus the Atharvaveda mentions Purāṇas (Athar-

[2] IVA, p. 49.
[3] IVA, p. 4.
[4] IVA, p. 90.
[5] IVA, pp. 158–59.
[6] HCIP, p. 304.
[7] HCIP, p. 313.

vaveda XI 7.24. The mention of the word in singular number and alongwith Ṛcs, Sāmans and Yajus, each of which forms a single book, shows that there was originally a single Purāṇa). The Śatapatha Brāhmaṇa (X.5.6.8) calls the Itihāsa-Purāṇa and certain other compositions 'honey-offerings to the Gods' and commends their daily study...."[8]

The Chāndogya-Upaniṣad (III.4-1) says: "the (hymns of the) Atharvāṅgiras are the bees, the Itihāsa-Purāṇa is the flower." As Pargiter points out, this "implies that those hymns drew their sustenance from the Itihāsa and Purāṇa, which must therefore have been ancient like those hymns."[9]

The Kauṭilya Arthaśāstra (Book 1, Chapter 3) also puts it as follows: "The 3 Vedas, the Sāman, Ṛc and Yajus are the threefold (scripture). The Atharvaveda and the Itihāsa-Veda are also Vedas."

Thus, it is obvious that the Purāṇa or Itihāsa-Purāṇa (originally there was only one text, which developed 3 recensions, each of which later developed several versions) was a major and basic text in the category of the four Vedas. This is testified by the Vedic literature itself.

The Purāṇas themselves also testify to this fact. They unanimously credit a single person, Vyāsa (who lived at the time of the Mahābhārata war), with the compilation of the ancient hymns into the four present Vedic texts, as well as with the compilation of the original Purāṇa.

The fact that the Vedas must have been compiled around that time is proved by cross-reference with the Purāṇas. Thus the latest datable hymn of the Rigveda is hymn X.98, which is composed by Devāpi. According to the Purāṇas, Devāpi was the brother of Śantanu, the grandfather of Dhṛtarāṣṭra of Mahābhārata fame. And, in fact, the hymn (in X.98.3) does mention Śantanu. Similarly, Dhṛtarāṣṭra himself is mentioned in the Yajurveda (Kāṭhaka Saṁhitā X.6) with his patronymic Vaicitravīrya. The Atharvaveda (XX.129.2) mentions Pratīpa, father of Śantanu and Devāpi. No king, who is mentioned in the Puranic genealogies as living well after the period of the Mahābhārata, is found mentioned in any of the Veda Saṁhitās.

The fact that the original Purāṇa was compiled around that time is proved by the internal evidence of the Purāṇas themselves. Pargiter describes this as follows: "There is much traditional history including fairly copious genealogies down to the time of that battle and the death of Kṛṣṇa and the Pāṇḍavas, and then all the genealogies stop short, ex-

[8] IVA, p. 18.
[9] AIHT, pp. 55–56.

cept those of the three great kingdoms of Hastināpura, Ayodhyā and Magadha, although other old dynasties continued to exist, such as those of Pancala, Kāśī, Mithilā, etc. There is a little historical tradition of the century or so that followed the battle, but only concerning the first five Paurava kings in the first of those three kingdoms. After that century or so, there is no historical tradition, and the genealogies of those three kingdoms are given in prophetic form, but were manifestly compiled long afterwards out of Prakrit chronicles. Yet there were traditions about those 'future' kings, as, for instance, about the kings in Buddha's time and about King Udayana of Vatsa, and none such are noticed in the Purāṇas as far as I am aware. These facts: much traditional history down to the death of the Pāṇḍavas, a very little for a century or so following, and then none whatever in the Purāṇas, prove that there must have been a closing stage in tradition during that century or so—that is, that the original Purāṇa must have been compiled about that time."[10]

Thus the Vedic texts, the Purāṇas, and other independent later sources, are all unanimous in vouching for the antiquity and pedigree of the original Purāṇa, and for the fact that this original Purāṇa was held practically equal in status to the four Vedas. The Rigveda was a book of all the ancient hymns; the Sāmaveda was a book of the hymns arranged differently from the point of view of musical chanting and singing; the Yajurveda was a book of prayers and sacrificial formulas to be recited at the sacrifices, alongwith a presentation of the sacrificial rites and a discussion on them; the Atharvaveda was a book of charms, spells and herbal prescriptions; and last, but definitely not least, the Itihāsaveda or Purāṇa was a book of the general lists of the various dynasties down to the time of the Mahābhārata war, alongwith an account of the historical traditions concerning these dynastics.

Bhargava describes the process as follows: "Every Aryan dynasty had it own Sūtas or bards who maintained its genealogical account. The accounts of these dynasties were compiled at some stage and named Purāṇas or old narrative. It is possible that this compilation was preserved in three recensions out of which the three oldest among the present Purāṇas grew. (According to Viṣṇu Purāṇa, III.6.16–18, the original Purāṇa, was transmitted to Romaharṣaṇa by Vyāsa. Romaharṣaṇa in turn taught it to his disciples, three of whom wrote down three Purāṇa Saṁhitās based on the original Purāṇa learnt by them.)"[11]

Of the 18 major present-day Purāṇas derived from the original "the

[10] AIHT, p. 57.
[11] IVA, p. 19.

oldest Purāṇas, so far as genealogies are concerned, are the Brahma, the Vāyu and the Matsya...next oldest is the Brahmāṇḍa which closely follows the version of the Vāyu....later than these four, but older than the others is the Viṣṇu Purāṇa.... Seven other Purāṇas, viz. the Bhāgavata, the Garuḍa, the Agni, the Padma, the Liṅga, the Kūrma and the Mārkaṇḍeya contain historical matter in varying degree."[12] The other six (Bhaviṣya, Nārada, Brahmavaivarta, Varāha, Vāmana and Skanda) "are purely sectarian works, free from all historical matter."[13]

It is, therefore, evident that it is in the Purāṇas, and not in the Rigveda or the Vedic texts, that we must look for details of India's ancient history.

A very logical viewpoint is expressed, in this context, by A.D. Pusalker:

1. He points out that "there is a difference of opinion among scholars as to the comparative value of the Vedic texts and the Purāṇas in regard to the historical data supplied by them. Keith is excessively sceptical about the historical value of the Purāṇas and is doubtful regarding the historicity of any event which is not explicitly mentioned in the Rigveda. Pargiter goes to the other extreme, and gives more weight to the Puranic tradition than to the Vedic evidence, which he styles as the tradition of the Brāhmaṇas, who possessed no historical sense."[14]
2. He points out the positive points of both the streams of literature: "Priority of date and comparative freedom from textual corruption are doubtless two strong points in favour of Vedic texts. The evidence of the Purāṇas, on the other hand, cannot be ruled out altogether, because despite a good deal of what is untrustworthy in them, they alone contain something like a continuous historical narrative, and it is absurd to suppose that the elaborate royal genealogies were all merely figments of imagination or a tissue of falsehoods."[15]
3. Finally, he recommends the right course to be adopted: "It may be observed that there is no irreconciliable contradiction or conflict between the Vedic texts and the Purāṇas.... *The proper procedure for the writing of traditional history is to take into account the joint testimony of the Vedic and Puranic texts* wher-

[12] IVA, pp. 18–19.
[13] IVA, p. 19.
[14] HCIP, p. 304.
[15] HCIP, pp. 304–05.

ever available, and to try to bring harmony into the apparently conflicting texts. The evidence of the Purāṇas in these matters needs very careful consideration."[16]

P.L. Bhargava tries to bring harmony into the apparently conflicting texts by "proving" that the Puranic testimony confirms the "fact" inferred from the Vedic "evidence" (viz. that the Aryans in India were originally restricted to the Punjab region, and then spread out all over northern India).

BHARGAVA'S STORY OF ARYAN EXPANSION IN INDIA

The original Purāṇa is now found in several recensions or versions, of which the Brahma Purāṇa and the Vāyu Purāṇa are accepted, by all the scholars and students of the Purāṇas, as being the oldest and most authentic. Most of the other Purāṇas follow one or the other of the two versions given by these two Purāṇas. The Matsya Purāṇa seems to follow a third version.

The Purāṇas have been edited and re-edited several times, and hence we find many minor differences in the different versions, but this is the case with all ancient texts (witness the differences in the four Gospels of the New Testament of the Bible) and there is always a standard procedure for studying these ancient texts to iron out the differences and arrive at the original version.

The Purāṇas commence the traditional history of India with the division of the whole of northern India among the ten sons of Manu. Now it is obvious that these ten kings could not have been the sons of a single person, and that this was the mythical way of presenting the relationship between the kings of the ten kingdoms which must have existed in India at the point of time at which the traditional historians commenced their recording. Manu Vaivasvata may have been an emperor who ruled over all the kingdoms. In any case, the ten kings are nominally referred to as the sons of Manu.

However, the Purāṇas do not give any traditional history regarding six of these ten sons. Bhargava, in any case, rejects the very existence of these six sons as founders of royal dynasties in ancient India. The ten sons, according to the Purāṇas, were Sudyumna, Ikṣvāku, Prāṁśu, Śaryāti, Dhṛṣta, Karuṣa, Nariṣyanta, Pṛṣadhra, Nābhāga and Nābhāgodiṣta. According to Bhargava, the first four are "founders of royal dynasties".[17] The next four "are mere names and seem to have

[16] HCIP, pp. 305–06.
[17] IVA, p. 90.

been included in the list to make up the number ten, in order to bring Manu Vaivasvata in line with the other Manus in the cosmological system"[18]; and the remaining two are people who lived long after this period and were not founders of any dynasty, but "have mistakenly been mentioned as sons of Manu Vaivasvata"[19] by the editors of the Purāṇas.

Whether these six names, rejected by Bhargava, were the names of non-Indo-European kings, or of Indo-European kings, or whether they were the names of kings at all, or whether people of these names (in the period in question) ever existed at all, are all irrelevant questions and need not be discussed, since the Purāṇas themselves do not give any material on the basis of which any decisive discussion could be possible. And the history of these persons, or even their identity, is of no importance to our subject here. Like Bhargava, we may concern ourselves only with the four dynasties authenticated by the Purāṇas.

On the basis of synchronisms from within the Puranic accounts themselves, and synchronisms from the epics and the Vedic texts (wherever the names of Puranic kings are mentioned in these texts), Bhargava[20] prepares a genealogical table of the 100 generations in the major dynasties from the time of Manu Vaivasvata to the time of the Mahābhārata war. (The table is presented at the end of this chapter for constant reference.)

It must be added here that the table prepared by Bhargava is a reasonably logical one, except perhaps for a few minor errors in the exact synchronization of the generations of the different dynasties. The Purāṇas give the lists of the different dynasties separately, and with minor differences; hence such minor errors are inevitable, and may be noticed only in the particular contexts. Bhargava's table is a good one: it is only his interpretation of these dynastic lists that calls for an examination.

Thus, Bhargava claims that the kings of all these dynasties, in the earlier part of the Rigvedic age, ruled within the Saptasindhu region, and that they later spread out on a conquering spree and conquered the whole of northern India. He whimsically classifies the dynastic lists, on the basis of this claim, into four "eras" which he calls the Era of Saptasindhu (Generations 1-27), the Era of Conquest (generations 28-49), the Era of Expansion (Generations 50-72), and the Era of Settlement (Generations 73-100), and vividly proceeds to trace out the "course of Aryan

[18] Ibid.
[19] IVA, p. 91.
[20] IVA, pp. 162–65.

expansion", which he claims "is indicated in the Purāṇas by the location of various preceding and succeeding dynasties."[21]

However, the "story of Aryan expansion in India" from the Punjab region to the rest of northern India, which Bhargava claims to be tracing out from the Purāṇas, cannot possibly be "indicated in the Purāṇas by the location of various preceding and succeeding dynasties", since the movement "indicated in the Purāṇas by the location of various preceding and succeeding dynasties" is not from west to east, but from east to west.

Thus, the Purāṇas place the dynasty of Śaryāti in the west (mainly in Gujarat and Western Rajasthan; and as suggested by Bhargava, perhaps also, or mainly, in Haryana), but the other three dynasties are squarely placed in the east: the dynasty Prāṁśu in Western Bihar (around Vaishali), the dynasty of Ikṣvāku in north-eastern Uttar Pradesh (around Ayodhya) and the dynasty of Sudyumna in south-eastern Uttar Pradesh (around Pratiṣṭhāna or Prayāga). The first major movement indicated by the Purāṇas is the establishment of branches of the Sudyumna dynasty on both sides of the ancestral kingdom (around Prayāga): the Kashi branch and the Kānyakubja branch. The next major movement indicated by the Purāṇas is the westward movement of the main Sudyumna dynasty from south-eastern Uttar Pradesh to the region of the Sarasvatī river on the eastern frontiers of the Saptasindhu region!

At this point of time, the Purāṇas shift their major focus on to five dynasties, which they claim to be branches of the Sudyumna/Aila dynasty. These five dynasties are located as follows:

a. The Pūru dynasty: located around the region of the Sarasvatī river (the Punjab, Haryana, and adjoining parts of western Uttar Pradesh).
b. The Anu dynasty: located to the north of the Pūrus, in the region to the north of the Paruṣṇī river (Kashmir).
c. The Druhyu dynasty: located to the west of the Pūrus (the north-west frontiers, Afghanistan).
d. The Yadu dynasty: located to the south-west of the Pūrus (Gujarat, western Madhya Pradesh, northern Maharashtra).
e. The Turvasu dynasty: located to the south-east of the Pūrus (location uncertain, but specifically to the east of the Yadus).

Of these, the Pūrus are most certainly the continuation of the main Sudyumna line. This is proved by both the Vedic evidence (which, as

[21] IVA, pp. 127–28.

we shall see in the next chapter, mentions *Pururavas, Nahuṣa, Yayāti,* and then only Pūru from among the five sons assigned to Yayāti, as authors of Rigvedic hymns) and the Puranic and epic evidence (which clearly states that Pūru inherited the ancestral kingdom, around the Sarasvatī river, from his father Yayāti).

The Anus and Druhyus also appear to be branches of the Sudyumna dynasty. This, also, is indicated by both the Vedic evidence (which, in the only hymn, I.108, which mentions the names of all the five peoples, names the Pūrus, Anus and Druhyus together, and then names the Yadus and Turvasus together), as well as the Puranic and epic evidence (which categorizes Pūru, Anu and Druhyu as the sons of Yayāti by one wife, and Yadu and Turvasu as his sons by another wife).

The Yadus and Turvasus/Turvasas may be branches of the Sudyumna dynasty; but if so they were very distant branches, as indicated by both the Vedic as well as the Puranic and epic evidence (as we shall see in the next chapter).

In any case, we thus get seven dynasties or kingdoms: those of the Prāṁśus, the Ikṣvākus, the Pūrus, the Anus, the Druhyus, the Yadus and the Turvasus. Another and the eighth one indicated above, that of Śaryāti, appears to have ended with him: "The truth seems to be that the kingdom of Śaryāti ended with him....outside this genealogical account, no child of Śaryāti, except Sukanyā, is ever named. In fact, neither in the Purāṇas, nor in the Vedic literature, do we ever find the mention of any Śaryātā prince in connection with any early person or event."[22]

And, except for the dynasty of Śaryāti, which as per Bhargava's own testimony ended with him, and the later dynasty of the Pūrus, whose origin is traced by the Purāṇas to Prayāga in south-eastern Uttar Pradesh, none of the dynasties are located by the Purāṇas in the Punjab region.

So, how does Bhargava claim that the evidence of the Purāṇas, in respect of "the location of various preceding and succeeding dynasties", proves that all the dynasties were originally located in the Punjab and then moved out into the rest of northern India?

Let us have the answer in Bhargava's own words: "The most important thing about which agreement between Vedic and Puranic traditions is supposed to be lacking is the course of Aryan expansion in India. The hymns of the Rigveda, which belong to the earliest period of

[22] IVA, p. 125.

Aryan history, very plainly indicate that the Āryas were settled in that period in the territory later known as the Punjab. The authors of the hymns show their familiarity with the smallest rivers of the Punjab and the north-west frontier.... In the later Vedic literature, the horizon is clearly wider, and kingdoms of the Gangetic valley and the northern part of the Deccan are well-known. The Vedic literature thus clearly indicates that the movement of the Āryas took place from the north-west of India to the east and the south. Unfortunately, the Purāṇas have not been as well studied as the Vedic literature. A thorough study of them reveals that they fully support the Vedic tradition. The present Purāṇas contain two clear layers of matter, viz. the original one consisting of the record of the Sūtas, and the later one consisting of the additions and interpolations introduced by later editors with the object of explaining and amplifying the old records. The original matter of the Purāṇas remarkably agrees with Vedic evidence, and it is only the explanatory matter added by later editors which has given the impression that the Purāṇas go against Vedic evidence."[23]

And why, according to Bhargava, did the later Puranic editors give wrong "explanatory matter" regarding the locations and movements of the dynasties? Bhargava has his answer ready: "Four sons of Manu bacame the first kings of the Indo-Aryan colony. So far as Prāṁśu and his descendants are concerned, the later Puranic editors have refrained from associating them with any well-defined region. As for Śaryāti, the fact that the later Puranic editors have located him in Gujarat is simply due to their mistake of regarding the Śaryāta Haihayas, who settled in Gujarat centuries later, as his descendants. Only in the case of the remaining two kings, whose descendants were actually ruling when the Purāṇas were edited, we find that the Puranic editors have, unmindful of the statements of the original accounts, located them in regions in which their latest descendants ruled. Thus, the Aikṣvākus ruled in the country of Kosala in later times, and so the Puranic editors have located their earliest ancestors in Ayodhya, the most ancient city of Kosala. The Pauravas ruled in the country of Vatsa in later times, and so the Purāṇas have located their earliest ancestors, Sudyumna and Purūravas, in Pratiṣṭhāna, an ancient city of the Vatsa country. The Haihaya Yādavas, another dynasty descended from Sudyumna and Purūravas, ruled in Avanti in later times, and the Puranic editors have therefore located their remotest ancestors in Māhiṣmatī, the most ancient city of that region. That the location of the early kings of these dynasties in

[23] IVA, pp. 127–28.

Ayodhya, Pratiṣṭhāna and Māhiṣmatī is a mistake is fully proved by the older records present in the Purāṇas and the Mahābhārata, which entirely agree with the Vedic evidence, as will be shown presently."[24]

Thus, it is clear that Bhargava's thesis is not based on what the Purāṇas explicitly state, in respect of the locations and movements of the various dynasties, but on what he infers from incidental matter in the Purāṇas, which he claims to be "the original matter of the Purāṇas".

Before we examine the claims of Bhargava about the locations and movements of the various dynasties, one point which must be kept in mind is the misleading way in which Bhargava expresses himself throughout, especially in relating the events and episodes mentioned in the Purāṇas.

Thus, the Purāṇas place the Ikṣvāku dynasty in Ayodhya, far to the east of the Saptasindhu region; but Bhargava locates them not merely within the Saptasindhu region but on the "western confines" of the region, "in a territory situated on the western side of the Indus."[25] And then he proceeds to relate the events in which the Ikṣvākus are involved, using directional phrases appropriate to the location he has assigned to them, almost as if those are the phrases employed in the Purāṇas from which he is relating the events.

Thus, in speaking of the Ikṣvāku king Māndhātṛ, he relates that Māndhātṛ's conquests began "with a conflict with the Druhyu king Aṅgāra whose kingdom probably lay *to the north-east* of the Aikṣvāku kingdom"[26], and in speaking of the Ikṣvāku king Trasadasyu, he hints that "*in the east,* the Pauravas and other ruling families of Saptasindhu seem to have acknowledged his overlordship (Rigveda IV.38.1)."[27] But, in reality, neither do the Purāṇas say that the Druhyu kingdom lay to the northeast of the Ikṣvāku kingdom, nor does the Rigveda (IV.38.1) say that the Pauravas lived to the east of Trasadasyu's kingdom.

A particularly blatant example of this is Bhargava's description of the Battle of the Ten Kings, which is the name given to a battle which is described in four hymns of the Rigveda (VII.18, 19, 33 and 83) and which is acknowledged by all scholars to be the single most important, if not the only major, historical event mentioned in the Rigveda. (This momentous battle will be dealt with in detail in the next chapter.)

In describing the ten tribes which formed a confederacy against Sudās, Bhargava has the following to say: "One of these tribes, the

[24] IVA, p. 128.
[25] IVA, p. 131.
[26] IVA, p. 213.
[27] IVA, p. 215.

Pakthas, were, as the name shows, the ancestors of the Pathans and must have lived beyond the Indus. They thus probably fought under the Ikṣvākus who ruled west of the Indus.... The Ikṣvāku contemporary of Sudās was almost certainly Rohita, son of Hariścandra."[28]

Nowhere in any of the hymns referring to the Battle do we find the faintest hint of any reference to the Ikṣvākus or to any person who could be branded as an Ikṣvāku. And yet, Bhargava determinedly introduces Ikṣvākus into the picture. And the grounds on which he introduces the Ikṣvāku element may be noted: he correctly identifies the Pakthas as the ancestors of the Pathans or Pakhtoons; but, inspite of the fact that the hymns make it very clear that these Pakthas lived in Kashmir in the region to the north of the Paruṣṇī river (the present-day Ravi), Bhargava decides that they "must have lived beyond the Indus". Thereby he commits in actuality the error which he wrongly accuses the later Puranic editors of committing viz. the error of locating the ancestors in the region occupied by their descendants! And then, because he has located the Ikṣvākus also in the same region ("beyond the Indus") in which he now locates the Pakthas, he decides that the Pakthas, "fought under the Ikṣvākus". Then, as the grand finale, he identifies Rohita, son of Hariścandra, as the Ikṣvāku king who led the Pakthas against Sudās!

This is the way in which Bhargava interprets the evidence of the Purāṇas.

Let us now examine Bhargava's arguments about the locations and movements of the various dynasties, taking into account "the joint testimony of the Vedic and Puranic texts".

THE ŚARYĀTI DYNASTY

Bhargava locates the kingdom of Śaryāti as follows: "This king's territory is indicated in a fairly precise manner by the Mahābhārata. It is well known that king Śaryāti met the rishi Cyavana in his own territory and gave his daughter in marriage to him. Now it is said in the Mahābhārata (I.6.8) that Cyavana had his hermitage on the bank of a river called Vadhusara. According to a time-honoured local tradition, the river Vadhusara is identical with the modern Duhan, flowing near Narnaul in Haryana. A village called Dhosi on its bank is still associated with the memory of Cyavana, and has a temple dedicated to him. It is clear that both the names, of the river as well as of the village, are reminiscent of Vadhusara. Cyavana's descendant, Jamadagni son of

[28] IVA, pp. 220-21.

Ṛcika, is similarly described by the Mahābhārata (III.129.7-11) as residing on the bank of the river Raupya near Kurukṣetra. This account is again supported by a very strong local account according to which Jamadagni and his wife Reṇukā lived in the region of the old Sirmur or Nahan State in Himachal Pradesh where a lake is still called Reṇukā in memory of Jamadagni's wife and is regarded as a place of pilgrimage by local Hindus. Thus, according to the Mahābhārata as corroborated by these traditions, Cyavana and his descendants were settled in the region of Haryana and Himachal Pradesh to the west of the Yamunā. The kingdom of Śaryāti thus also lay in this region."[29]

Bhargava's conclusions cannot be argued with. There is no doubt that Śaryāti's kingdom did lie in this region, as per the joint testimony of the epics and the local traditions (ironically, the only place where Bhargava cites local traditions. Elsewhere, he ignores the local traditions which go against his arguments).

And the evidence of the Rigveda confirms this in a significant way. Śaryāti is credited, by the anukramaṇīs, with the composition of hymn X.92. He is also mentioned in the Rigveda thrice (Rigveda I.51.12; 112.17; III.51.7). None of the other three primeval kings (Sudyumna, Ikṣvāku and Prāṁśu) are supposed to be the authors of any Rigvedic hymns, and except for one doubtful reference to Ikṣvāku (X.60.4), none of them is mentioned in any hymn.

This would certainly indicate that while Śaryāti lived in the Saptasindhu region, the other three kings probably did not.

THE IKSVĀKU DYNASTY

The Purāṇas, the epics, and the local traditions, all locate the Ikṣvāku dynasty in Ayodhya in north-eastern Uttar Pradesh. But Bhargava on the basis of inferences drawn by him, from what he claims is "the original matter of the Purāṇas" lying within the present Purāṇas, locates the Ikṣvākus not only in the Punjab, but in the "western confines" of the Punjab.

"The wars and conquests of these (early Aikṣvāku) kings clearly indicate the region where they ruled. The greatest conqueror among the early Aikṣvāku kings was Māndhātṛ. He is said to have made wide conquests. Yet he is never associated with any river or region to the east of the Yamunā while in the northwest his conquests extended as far as Gandhāra (Mahābhārata III.125.25-26: *Eṣā Sā Yamunā rājanmaharṣi-gaṇa-sevitā. Atra rājā maheṣvaso Māndhātā yajat svayam*). In-

[29] IVA, pp. 132-33.

deed the fact that he sacrificed on the bank of the Yamunā shows that it was the limit of his conquests. It could not have been the western limit, for in the west his conquest extended beyond the Yamunā. It must, therefore, have been the eastern limit. This proves that the Aikṣvākus ruled somewhere in the country west of the Yamunā. The Rigveda clearly associates the Aikṣvāku king Trasadasyu with the region to the west of the Indus for he is said to have conferred gifts on the rishi Sobhari on the bank of the river Suvāstu. The conquest of Gandhāra by Māndhātṛ and the granting of gifts by Trasadasyu on the banks of the Suvāstu makes it certain that the early Aikṣvākus ruled in a territory situated on the western side of the Indus. There is one strong point which helps us in determining the exact location of this territory. It is well-known that the Aikṣvākus later settled in the country of Kosala. Now two of the most important rivers of Kosala, Gomatī and Sarayū, bear the same names as two of the western tributaries of the Indus, now known as the Gomal and the Siritoi. It has been pointed out that new places are given the old names of those very places with which the newcomers had been associated. This makes it highly probable that the exact territory where the early Aikṣvākus ruled lay on the banks of the Gomal and the Siritoi."[30]

Bhargava also names the precise point in history when the Ikṣvākus moved eastwards: "The first Aikṣvāku king who is definitely associated in the Purāṇas with the river Gangā is Bhagīratha.... The ancient Vāyu and Brahmāṇḍa Purāṇas make a very simple but clear statement about it in a remarkable verse occurring in both of them....the whole verse means that Bhagīratha, who came from a long distance, adorned the banks of the Gangā with a large number of chariots and made her his daughter, i.e. gave her his name. This is one of the most remarkable statements found in the Purāṇas, and makes it absolutely certain that the early Aikṣvākus ruled in a region so distant from the Gangā that none of them previous to Bhagīratha had set his foot on its banks. Moreover, in saying that Bhagīratha adorned the Gangā with multitudes of chariots, the statement makes it absolutely clear that Bhagīratha had come with a large number of followers with the intention of conquering and establishing a new kingdom. The ancient Ṣoḍaśarājikā of the Mahābhārata supports these older Purāṇas when it says that Bhagīratha covered the Gangā with heaps of gold (given as sacrificial gifts to brahmans) and the river chose him as her father, i.e. took his name. It need hardly be added that the epic statement also

[30] IVA, pp. 131-32.

implies that Bhagīratha came to the river Gangā with a large number of followers. Bhagīratha, therefore, must have been the founder of the Kosala kingdom of Ayodhyā, whose name unassailable was thus appropriately given to commemorate his victorious career."[31]

Thus, Bhargava "proves", on the indirect "evidence" of incidental statements in the Purāṇas and epics, that the Ikṣvākus originally lived to the west of the Indus and migrated eastwards only at the time of Bhagīratha. However, his story is not only directly contradictory to the explicit accounts of the Purāṇas, it also contradicts the joint testimony of the Vedic and Puranic texts:

1. Māndhātṛ is the 20th king of the Ikṣvāku dynasty, and the Purāṇas name 18 other Ikṣvāku kings between Māndhātṛ and the original Ikṣvāku. All these 18 kings are located by the Purāṇas in Ayodhya, and not one of them is reported by the Purāṇas as having had anything to do with the Punjab. In the case of Māndhātṛ, however, the Purāṇas have a different story to relate.

Pargiter describes the following major historical event: "The Druhyus occupied the Punjab and Māndhātṛ of Ayodhya had a long war with the Druhyu king Aruddha or Aṅgāra. The latter's successor was Gandhāra."[32]

Moreover, the Purāṇas make it clear that the direction from which Māndhātṛ attacked the Druhyu king was from the east. Pargiter points out: "The next Druhyu king Gandhāra retired to the northwest and gave his name to the Gandhāra country."[33] (Bhargava, as already pointed out, firmly ignores the directions explicitly stated and implicitly indicated in the Purāṇas, and tries to suggest that the Druhyu kingdom "probably lay to the north-east of the Aikṣvāku kingdom".)

The evidence of the Rigveda confirms the Purāṇic evidence. None of the 18 Ikṣvāku kings, before Māndhātṛ, is mentioned in the Rigveda. However, Māndhātṛ is mentioned thrice in the Rigveda (I.112.13; VIII.39.8; 40.12) and is even credited with the composition of a Rigvedic hymn (X.134). This would appear to indicate that the Ikṣvāku kings before Māndhātṛ were unknown to the Vedic composers of the Saptasindhu region, being located well to the east of that region.

Here, indeed, is joint testimony of the Rigveda and the Purāṇas. The Rigvedic evidence by itself would not amount to much, since it is quite possible that kings could not be mentioned in the Rigveda and yet

[31] IVA, p. 137.
[32] AIHT, p. 167.
[33] AIHT, p. 262.

have been kings of the Punjab. The Puranic evidence by itself would be unacceptable to the invasion-theorists. But the combined evidence of the Rigveda and the Purāṇas cannot be wrong, and cannot be logically rejected, unless the composers of the Rigvedic hymns and the editors of the Purāṇas are to be accused of having been partners in a grand, and extremely subtle, conspiracy to befool future historians.

2. Śrāvasta was the 9th king of the Ikṣvāku dynasty (10th in the generation table, which includes Manu Vaivasvata), and he founded the historical city of Śrāvastī in north-eastern Uttar Pradesh (to the north-west of Ayodhya). This confirms that the early Ikṣvāku kings ruled in Ayodhya.

Bhargava foresees this point, and argues as follows: "The tenth king Śrāvasta is credited by some Purāṇas with the foundation of the city of Śrāvastī. This is no doubt a mistake.... for this statement is contradicted by another statement of the Purāṇas which makes all the sons of Rāma and his brother the founders of cities, and the city of which Lava, the second son of Rāma, was the founder is called Śrāvastī... This second statement is in perfect keeping with the history of the Aikṣvākus according to Puranic as well as Vedic evidence.... The first statement is therefore wrong."[34]

It is difficult to understand why Bhargava should expect us to believe that the two statements contradict each other, though it is easy to understand why he himself should grab at the second statement in order to discredit the first one which goes against his thesis.

Bhargava himself, in locating the Ikṣvākus in the Punjab, remarks that "new places are given the old names of those very places with which the newcomers had been associated". What is more natural, then, but that Lava, when founding another city in some other part of India (Bhargava himself states that Rāma's sons and nephews "founded towns and kingdoms in various parts of India"), should have given it the name of one of the most prominent cities in his native kingdom of Kosala, which had been named by his remote ancestor Śrāvasta after himself?

Instead of accepting the logical implications of the two Puranic statements, Bhargava wants us to regard the first statement as wrong; and to believe, instead, that the Ikṣvākus lived in the Punjab for 49 generations, that Bhagīratha (the 49th Ikṣvāku king) first crossed the Yamuna and established the kingdom of Kosala in the far east, that none of the records in the Punjab (the Vedic texts) recorded the exis-

[34] IVA, pp. 117-18.

tence of Śrāvasta (the 9th Ikṣvāku king, whose only major claim to fame seems to be the city founded by him, according to the Purāṇas) but that his far descendant (Generation 73), for some mysterious reason and in some mysterious way, chose to name a city after his obscure (and nowhere-else-recorded) ancestor!

3. Bhargava argumentatively insists that the Ikṣvākus lived to the west of the Yamuna, and in fact to the west of the Indus, before the time of Bhagīratha (the 49th Ikṣvāku king), who crossed all the rivers and established the kingdom of Kosala in north-eastern Uttar Pradesh.[35]

However, the evidence of hymn X.179 of the Rigveda indirectly confirms that Vasumanas (the 33rd Ikṣvāku king) must have been a king of Ayodhya. This hymn consists of three verses, the composition of which is attributed to Śivi Auśināra, Pratardana and Vasumanas respectively.

According to the Puranic genealogies, Śivi was an Ānava king of the north-eastern Punjab, Pratardana was a king of Kashi and Vasumanas was a king of Ayodhya.

While the Rigveda gives no evidence to show that any of these three kings was not what the Purāṇas claim him to be, in the case of Pratardana at least the anukramaṇīs of the Rigveda clearly state that he was the king of Kashi.

It would, therefore be natural to presume that the Purāṇas are right in the matter of Vasumanas as well, and that Vasumanas was indeed ruling in Ayodhya. If one of the three kings was definitely the king of Kashi (in south-eastern Uttar Pradesh) there is no ground to presume that the Purāṇas are wrong in declaring another of them to be the king of Ayodhya (in north-eastern Uttar Pradesh). In fact, the hymn seems to be a joint composition of three untypical Rigvedic composer-kings: two being kings from well outside the Punjab region, and the third being an Ānava (Anu) king of the Punjab who, as per the testimony of the Purāṇas, had migrated southwards from Kashmir to the fringe area of north-eastern Punjab.

Since the whole thing seems to be a question of choosing between the testimony of the Purāṇas (half-confirmed, and nowhere contradicted, by the Rigveda) and the testimony of P.L. Bhargava (unsupported by any source), it is obvious that Vasumanas has to be accepted as a king of Ayodhya, 16 generations before Bhagīratha.

4. Now, we come to the story of Bhagīratha, which Bhargava inter-

[35] IVA, p. 160.

prets, as a story of the Ikṣvāku migration from the Punjab to Ayodhya. The whole of Bhargava's "evidence" hinges on Bhagīratha since there is no particular way in which the early Ikṣvāku kings can be shown not to have been ruling in Ayodhya without showing a certain point at which they can be alleged to have arrived in Ayodhya from outside. Hence he treats what he terms the "discovery" of the Ganga by Bhagīratha as the point of arrival of the Ikṣvākus at the Ganga on their way towards Ayodhya.

Therefore, he makes a big thing out of what he describes as "a very simple but clear statement...in a remarkable verse occurring in the Vāyu and Brahmāṇḍa Purāṇas". According to him "the whole verse means that Bhagīratha, who came from a long distance, adorned the banks of the Gangā with a large number of chariots, and made her his daughter, i.e. gave her his name". He interprets "from a long distance" as meaning from the Punjab region, and the reference to the large number of chariots as meaning that "Bhagīratha had come with a large number of followers with the intention of conquering and establishing a new kingdom". He also quotes a verse from the Mahābhārata which says that "Bhagīratha covered the Ganga with heaps of gold (given as sacrificial gifts to brahmans) and the river chose him as her father, i.e. took his name".

It is obvious that the "remarkable verse" is only a description of a huge ceremony conducted by Bhagīratha on the banks of the Ganga on the occasion of naming it after himself, but Bhargava chooses to treat it as a story of migration and conquest. His thesis is totally unsupported by the evidence of the Rigveda: if Bhagīratha was king from the western confines of the Punjab who crossed a number of rivers (the Indus, the Sarasvatī, the Yamuna, etc.) with a huge army of chariots, soldiers and rishis/brahmans, and broke new ground in "Aryan" conquest and expansion, he should have been a prominent figure in the Rigveda. However, the Rigveda seems totally unaware of his very existence.

Now, Bhargava's entire interpretation of the verse hinges on the phrase "from a long distance" which he rather presumptuously interprets as making it "absolutely certain that the early Aikṣvākus ruled in a region so distant from the Gangā that none of them previous to Bhagīratha had set his foot on its banks". But what is even more "remarkable", than Bhargava's packing of so much meaning into so simple a phrase as "from a long distance", is the fact that the verse does not even contain the phrase in the first place!

The verse is found in the Vāyu Purāṇa (88.168) and it says: *yena gaṅgā saricchreṣṭhā vimānairupaśobhitā; ījānena samudrādvai duhitṛtvena kalpitā*. Bhargava quotes this whole verse and then adds: "The words *ījānena samudrādvai* do not yield any sense. The Brahmāṇḍa (III.63.167) has the reading *sureśādvai* in place of Vayu's *samudrādvai*, but this reading does not make any sense either. The true reading seems to have been *āyātenā sadūrādvai*."[36] In this manner, Bhargava himself introduces the phrase "from a long distance" into his "remarkable verse".

And Bhargava himself indirectly proves that the actual phrase must indeed have something to do with *samudra* (sea) rather than with *sadūra* (distance). The parallel quotation from the Mahābhārata (VII.60.8) which he quotes immediately, as saying "the river chose him as her father, i.e. took his name", is as follows: *gaṅgā samudragā devī vavre pitaramīśvaram*.[37]

Thus, Bhargava's "original matter of the Purāṇas", which, he claims, shows that the Ikṣvākus moved from the Punjab to Ayodhya, seems to consist only of statements that Māndhātṛ sacrificed on the Yamuna and Bhagīratha sacrificed on the Ganga; which he interprets, without rhyme or reason, to mean that Māndhātr and Bhagīratha, coming from the west, had managed to conquer all that way eastwards for the first time in Ikṣvāku history!

Therefore, it is clear that Bhargava cannot produce the slightest bit of evidence to contradict the Puranic accounts which locate the Ikṣvāku dynasty in Ayodhya from the very beginning and in fact a consideration of the evidence of the Rigveda only confirms this location.

In these circumstances, it is obvious that the ancient names of two of the western tributaries of the Indus, now known as the Gomal and the Siritoi, must have been based on the names of the two important rivers of Kosala, the Gomati and the Sarayu, and not vice versa as alleged by Bhargava.

The Gomati and the Sarayu in north-eastern Uttar Pradesh have borne these names from time immemorial, and bear those names to this very day. In the case of the Gomati and the Sarayu of the western Indus, it is obvious that they bore those names only at the time of the composition of the Rigvedic hymns; their identification today with the Gomal and the Siritoi is a matter of speculation (even if, doubtless, a correct speculation). It is more logical to presume that the north-western rivers were named after the two prominent rivers of the Kosala

[36] IVA, p. 137, footnote.
[37] Ibid.

region by a group of Ikṣvāku emigrants who settled on the banks of the Indus, than to presume that the Kosala rivers were named after two obscure tributaries (rather than after the more important rivers) of the Saptasindhu region by a group of emigrants from the Punjab who settled in Kosala.

Especially in view of the fact that while the Purāṇas give no evidence whatsoever of any Ikṣvāku migration from the Punjab to Kosala, despite the most desperate arguments of Bhargava, they do give repeated testimony to the migration of Ikṣvāku groups from Kosala to the Punjab. Thus, Māndhātṛ is depicted in the Purāṇas as moving all the way from Ayodhya to the Punjab to drive out the Druhyus. Likewise, Trasadasyu, four generations later, is depicted as venturing into the Punjab for similar reasons, his name Trasadasyu being a testimony to his activities, and Bhargava himself points out that the Rigveda depicts him conferring gifts on the rishi Sobhari on the bank of the river Suvāstu. A Rigvedic hymn, X.33, in fact refers to three descendants of Trasadasyu (Kuruśravaṇa, Upamaśravas and Mitrātithi), who are not found in the Puranic genealogies of Ayodhya and must therefore have been descendants who settled in the Punjab. Bhargava himself testifies[38] to the fact that the sons and nephews of Rāma (by whose time even Bhargava is compelled to admit that the Ikṣvākus were ruling in Ayodhya) established towns and kingdoms in different parts of India, *including in the Punjab*; and the Rigveda, which has nothing to say about Rāma himself, refers to a king Māyava (not mentioned in the Puranic genealogies as a king of Ayodhya, and therefore, obviously, a settler in the Punjab) as a descendant of Rāma (in hymn X.93).

Therefore, it is clear that the Purāṇas are perfectly correct in locating the Ikṣvāku dynasty in north-eastern Uttar Pradesh.

THE PRĀṀŚAVA DYNASTY

All the Purāṇas locate the dynasty of Prāṁśu in north-western Bihar around Vaishali. The dynasty was founded by Prāṁśu, and came into particular prominence under his descendant Marutta Āvīkṣita who is recorded as one of the earliest great conquerors in all the Purāṇas and the Mahābhārata. After some generations, it passed into historical obscurity before coming into prominence under Viśāla, who either founded, or renamed after himself, the capital city of Vaishali.

Bhargava, however, treats this Puranic account as being wrong on two counts: firstly, he rejects the connection between the early Prāṁśu

[38] IVA, p. 118.

dynasty and the later one (which he brands as a separate Vaishali branch of the Ikṣvāku dynasty), and secondly, he denies that the early Prāṁśu dynasty was located in Vaishali.

His arguments for rejecting the connection between the dynasty of Prāṁśu and the later dynasty of Vaishali are as follows: "In the first place, the kings of the Prāṁśava dynasty ruled in the very earliest ages, and there must have been a difference of several generations between the last king of their line and the first king of the Vaiśāla dynasty. In the second place, the Prāṁśavas certainly ruled in the northwest of India, as will be shown in the next chapter, and there is no reference anywhere of their migration to the east. Lastly, the position of Vaishali so near to the Aikṣvāku kingdoms of Kosala and Videha gives strong support to the Rāmāyaṇa that the founder of this kingdom must have been a scion of the ruling dynasty of either of these kingdoms."[39]

Let us examine his second argument first, as it is the one with which we are basically concerned, before examining the other two subsidiary arguments. Bhargava claims that "the Prāṁśavas certainly ruled in the north-west of India, as will be shown in the next chapter". This is how he "shows" it in his next chapter: "Nothing definite is said in the Purāṇas about the location of this dynasty, but whatever is said about it proves that it also ruled in the country watered by the Indus and its tributaries. Thus the most famous conqueror of this dynasty, Marutta, is, like Māndhātṛ, said to have sacrificed on the Yamunā (Mbh. III.129.13–16). That it must have been the eastern limit, as in Māndhātṛ's case, is proved by another thing. The fact that the rishi Ucathya is connected with Māndhātṛ in the Mahābhārata (XII.90) and Ucathya's brother Saṁvarta is connected with Marutta in the same epic, as well as in the Purāṇas (Vāyu 86.9-11; Bhāgavata IX.2.26, etc.) and in the Aitareya Brāhmaṇa (39) means that the Prāṁśava and the Aikṣvāku dynasties could not have ruled in two widely different regions. This dynasty has thus also to be placed in the country later called Punjab. As for the part of the Punjab occupied by it, we can only say that it must have ruled on its western confines like the Ikṣvākus, because it survived the conquests of Yayāti."[40]

Since the Purāṇas locate the dynasty in north-western Bihar, which is what Bhargava is trying to refute, his statement that "nothing definite is said in the Purāṇas about the location of this dynasty" is rather strange. And the only evidence he can give to show that they lived in

[39] IVA, p. 123.
[40] IVA, p. 132.

the Punjab is to show that the Ikṣvāku and Prāṁśu dynasties must have been neighbours! But of course they were neighbours—the Ikṣvākus in north-eastern Uttar Pradesh and the Prāṁśus in north-western Bihar were certainly neighbours! But Bhargava, after "proving", against the joint testimony of the Rigveda and the Purāṇas, that the Ikṣvākus lived in the western Punjab, expects us to have swallowed his "proof" so completely that we will accept unquestioningly the location of the Prāṁśus also in the western Punjab, merely on the ground that they were neighbours of the Ikṣvākus! And this is his only "proof" of the location of the Prāṁśus in the Punjab.

The fact that any king performed a sacrifice on the banks of any particular sacred river certainly has nothing whatsoever to do with the "limits" of his "conquests". And there is a basic difference between the conquests of Māndhātṛ and the conquests of Marutta. The Purāṇas specifically describe Māndhātṛ as having moved into the Punjab to drive out the Druhyus who had occupied it. However, Marutta is not shown by the Purāṇas to have ventured into the Punjab.

And this situation (the Prāṁśavas ruling in far off north-western Bihar, and not being associated in any way with the Punjab) is confirmed by the evidence of the Rigveda: not a single king of the Prāṁśu dynasty is mentioned in the Rigveda: neither Prāṁśu, nor "the famous conqueror of this dynasty, Marutta", nor any other. The Rigveda is totally oblivious of, and indifferent to, the very existence of the Prāṁśu dynasty.

Bhargava's argument that "there is no reference anywhere of their migration to the east" is, therefore, pathetic. The Purāṇas do not claim that the dynasty ruled in the Punjab; they locate it in north-western Bihar from the very beginning. Hence the question of referring to their "migration to the east" just does not arise. It is only Bhargava who locates them in the Punjab, against the joint testimony of the Rigveda and the Puranic texts.

Moving from the early Prāṁśu dynasty to the later one (which he totally separates from each other by declaring the first to be a Prāṁśu dynasty of the Punjab, and the latter one an Ikṣvāku dynasty of Vaishali) Bhargava argues that "the position of Vaishali so near to the Aikṣvāku kingdoms of Kosala and Videha gives strong support to the Rāmāyaṇa that the founder of this kingdom must have been (an Ikṣvāku)".

This is a really senseless argument to make: that the Vaishali dynasty must have been founded by an Ikṣvāku, since there were Ikṣvāku kingdoms in the neighbourhood! Especially since, as we have already seen, the Prāṁśu identity of the Vaishali dynasty stands proved by the fact that Bhargava himself gives testimony to the Ikṣvākus and Prāṁśus being neighbours!

The Rāmāyaṇa apparently makes a statement which indicates that it "regards his (Viśāla's) father as an Ikṣvāku prince."[41] Bhargava grabs at this statement as evidence. The Vaishali dynasty is identified as a Prāṁśava dynasty by the Vāyu, Brahmāṇḍa, Viṣṇu, Garuḍa and Bhāgavata Purāṇas. Against this, Bhargava can only produce negative evidence: "the Brahma and Markaṇḍeya Purāṇas and the Mahābhārata and Harivaṁśa do not connect the Vaiśāla dynasty to it."[42] However, these Purāṇas; do not deny or contradict the statement of the other Purāṇas, they are merely silent on the point; and Bhargava cannot produce a single quotation from the Purāṇas to connect the Vaishali dynasty with the Ikṣvākus. His sole "evidence" of a statement in the Rāmāyaṇa is negated by himself when he demonstrates, elsewhere,[43] that the Rāmāyaṇa is in the error, whenever it contradicts the Purāṇas, even in respect of the Ayodhya dynasty itself!

Bhargava's argument that the later Vaishali dynasty cannot be a continuation of the earlier Prāṁśu one since "there must have been a difference of several generations between the last king of their line and the first king of the Vaiśāla dynasty", is irrelevant. The editors of the Purāṇas were undoubtedly living in the Kuru-Pañcāla area of northern India, as admitted by all the scholars, and yet Bhargava himself admits that there are big gaps, in the present Purāṇas, in the genealogical lists of even the Pūru kings of the region. But Bhargava does not deny the connection between the latter Kuru dynasty and its earlier ancestral Pūru dynasty. The Prāṁśu dynasty ruled in the far east (north-western Bihar), and therefore any big gaps in the genealogies are understandable. In speaking of a similar big gap in the Haihaya genealogy after their defeat by Sagara, Bhargava himself explains it on the ground that "the account of their successors in central and western India was not available to the Puranic editors of northern India."[44]

Therefore, it is clear that the location of the Prāṁśu dynasty in north-western Bihar, by the Purāṇas, is correct.

[41] IVA, p. 123.
[42] IVA, p. 123.
[43] IVA, p. 117.
[44] IVA, p. 136.

THE SUDYUMNA DYNASTY

Now we come to the Sudyumna dynasty, which plays the predominant role, not only in Vedic and Puranic history, but, as we shall see in the next chapter, in what scholars would describe as proto-Indo-Iranian and proto-Indo-European history as well.

According to the Purāṇas, Sudyumna ruled in south-eastern Uttar Pradesh, around Pratiṣṭhāna (Prayāga) which was his capital. His son Purūravas had two sons: Āyu and Amāvasu. Amāvasu established the kingdom of Kānyakubja (around Kanauj). Āyu had many sons of whom Nahuṣa and Kṣatravṛddha/Vṛddhaśarman were the two most prominent ones. Kṣatravṛddha established the kingdom of Kashi, to the east of Prayag. Nahuṣa had two sons, Yati and Yayāti. Yati became a rishi, but Yayāti inherited his paternal kingdom. Yayāti had 5 sons: Yadu, Turvasu, Druhyu, Anu and Pūru. Pūru inherited the paternal kingdom, while the remaining sons established kingdoms in four directions relative to the location of Pūru's kingdom: Turvasu to the south-east, Yadu to the south-west, Anu to the north, and Druhyu to the west.

The combined evidence of the Purāṇas and the epics shows that although Sudyumna ruled in Prayāg in south-eastern Uttar Pradesh, his most prominent descendants had shifted to the west and were ruling in the region of the Sarasvatī river at the eastern end of the Saptasindhu. Thus, Yayāti undoubtedly had his capital on the banks of the Sarasvatī, and the kingdom ruled over by the Pūru dynasty (on the evidence of both the Rigveda as well as the Purāṇas) lay on the banks of the Sarasvatī. Therefore, it seems likely that the westward migration took place in the time of Nahuṣa, one of whose less important brothers took over the reins of the ancestral kingdom in Prayag, which remained historically irrelevant in later times.

F.E. Pargiter[45] ignores the evidence of the Rigveda and the Purāṇas, in respect of the location of Yayāti and Pūru, and continues to treat them as ruling in Prayag. Hence, also, he locates the other 4 sons to the south-east, south-west, north and west of Prayag. He thus fails to keep up with the geographical movements in the Purāṇas.

Bhargava, on the other hand, stresses the evidence of the Purāṇas and epics in respect of Yayāti and Pūru, and, reasoning backwards in time, decides that their ancestors were also located in the same region i.e. in the eastern Punjab. Further, he locates all the five kingdoms, which the Purāṇas claim were established by the five sons of Yayāti,

[45] AIHT, p. 259.

within the Punjab: "Anu is said to have got the north, Druhyu the west and Yadu the south-west. Various facts preserved in the Rigveda, the Purāṇas and the Mahābhārata confirm the location of the Anus in the northern and of the Druhyus and the Yadus in the north-western and south-western parts respectively of what later came to be called Punjab."[46]

By and large, Bhargava does not deny the location of the Pūrus (in the Punjab), the Anus (in Kashmir) and the Druhyus (in the northwest frontiers and in Afghanistan); and the location of the Turvasus is neither clear nor important. What Bhargava basically denies is:

a. The location of Sudyumna in south-eastern Uttar Pradesh.
b. The location of the early Yadus (Yādavas) in Central and Western India (Gujarat, western Madhya Pradesh, and northern Maharashtra).
c. The very existence of the early Kashi and Kānyakubja dynasties.

He insists, instead, that:

a. Sudyumna was located in the Punjab.
b. The Yadus were located in south-west Punjab (to the west of the Indus).
c. The Kashi and Kānyakubja kingdoms came into being at a later date when they were founded by sons of Suhotra, the Pūru king.

However, the location of Sudyumna in south-eastern Uttar Pradesh cannot be incorrect. All the Purāṇas are unanimous in declaring that Sudyumna was located in Prayag, and there is no reason whatsoever why they should make such a claim if it were not true. Bhargava claims that "the Pauravas ruled in the country of Vatsa in later times, and so the Purāṇas have located their earliest ancestors, Sudyumna and Purūravas, in Pratiṣṭhāna, an ancient city of the Vatsa country."[47] But this is ridiculous: the Puranic editors are generally located, by all scholars, in the Kuru-Pañcāla region, and the Kuru and Pañcāla dynasties were Pūru dynasties. The main event after which the original Purāṇa closed its traditional account was the Mahābhārata war—and this war, in which the main combatants were also Pauravas, took place in Haryana. And, as Pargiter points out,[48] the post-Mahābhārata traditions, interpolated by the later Puranic editors into the Purāṇas, give only the genealogies of the three great kingdoms of Hastināpura, Ayodhya and Magadha, in the future tense; and so far as traditional accounts are

[46] IVA, p. 130.
[47] IVA, p. 128.
[48] AIHT, p. 57.

concerned, they give only the traditions concerning the first five Paurava kings of Hastināpura. The major thrust of the Purāṇas, from beginning to end, is on the western Paurava dynasties. If, therefore, the Puranic editors should have been led to suggest a wrong location to Sudyumna and Purūravas, they would have suggested Hastināpura as the location of Sudyumna's kingdom. The fact that the Purāṇas insist on Pratiṣṭhāna (Prayāga) being the location of Sudyumna's kingdom is, therefore, strong evidence that the Puranic editors were unbiasedly reporting the original historical tradition.

This tradition is all the more important since it provides the traditional recorded testimony of a circumstance which explains a major linguistic fact already recorded in a previous chapter—viz. the Indo-European linguistic connection with the Austronesian-Austric languages. As pointed out, the original Indo-European languages, in their formative stages, must have been closely associated with the Austric languages in their formative stages; and the place where such an association could have come about is precisely the place indicated by the Purāṇas. The original Indo-European languages must have been spoken in eastern Uttar Pradesh and western Bihar while the original Austric languages must have been spoken in southern Bihar and Orissa. The Sudyumnas/Ailas, as we shall see in the next chapter, included the speakers of the ancestral forms of the European, Iranian and Vedic languages; and the Purāṇas show them moving from eastern Uttar Pradesh to the Punjab-Kashmir area.

In the matter of the Sudyumna dynasty, the Purāṇas introduce a peculiar mythical element: it reports that Sudyumna was converted into a woman named Ilā, and gave birth to Pururavas after marrying Budha, son of Soma (a Vedic rishi). Bhargava[49] provides the most rational explanation of this: according to him, Sudyumna must have been childless, since "the sons assigned to him by late Puranic editors are absolutely mythical, being mere eponyms of Gaya, Utkala, etc. and nothing is said about them ever after", therefore Sudyumna must have adopted Purūravas, son of his sister Ilā. Therefore, "the later Puranic editors have given a fabulous turn to the relations between Sudyumna and Purūravas. It is said that Sudyumna was transformed into a woman named Ilā, and gave birth to Purūravas by a union with Budha, son of Soma."[50] As a result of this, the descendants of Purūravas (and especially the Pūrus) were regarded as both Saudyumnis (descendants of

[49] IVA, pp. 94-95.
[50] IVA, pp. 94-95.

Sudyumna) or Ailas (descendants of Ilā) and Ātreyas (descendants of Atri family). Therefore, the Rigveda (X.95.18) and the Śatapatha Brāhmaṇa (XI.5.1) call Purūravas "Aila" or "son of Ilā"; the anukramaṇīs of the Rigveda call Pūru (as author of V.16;17) "Ātreya", and likewise the Matsya Purāṇa (198.1) calls the Viśvāmitra family of rishis a branch of the Atri family; and Bharata, the greatest Pūru king (after whom all the later Pūru dynasties—the Tṛtsus, the Kurus and Pāñcālas, the later Kashi and Kānyakubja dynasties, etc.—are called Bharatas) is called "Saudyumni" by the Śatapatha Brāhamaṇa (XIII.5.4.11-14).

It is clear that it is the Ātreya element in their ancestry which must have led the Sudyumnas (in the time of Nahuṣa) to migrate towards the Saptasindhu region.

THE YĀDAVA DYNASTY

The Purāṇas locate the five dynasties, which are classified as Sudyumna dynasties, as follows:

1. The Pūru dynasty: the central region (Punjab, eastern Uttar Pradesh, Haryana, Delhi and Himachal Pradesh).
2. The Anu dynasty: the northern region (Kashmir).
3. The Druhyu dynasty: the western region (northernmost Kashmir, the northwest frontiers, Afghanistan).
4. The Turvasu dynasty: the south-eastern region (not stated clearly, and not identifiable; but supposed to be to the east of the Yadus. In any case, the dynasty fades away into obscurity in the Purāṇas itself).
5. The Yadu dynasty: the south-western region (Gujarat, western Madhya Pradesh, northern Maharashtra).

Bhargava, however, insists that all these five dynasties ruled in different parts of the Punjab itself. He, in fact, locates them in the same directions as indicated above, but within the Punjab: the Pūrus in the centre, the Anus to the north, the Druhyus to the west, the Turvasus to the south-east and the Yadus to the south-west.

But the Pūrus, by all accounts, have to be placed on the banks of the Sarasvatī, and cannot be restricted only to the central part of the Punjab. Hence, it is rather difficult for Bhargava to place the Turvasus and Yadus to the south-east and south-west respectively of the Pūrus, and yet show them located within the Punjab. Hence, when showing the locations of the five dynasties, in the map[51] shown by him, Bhargava

[51] IVA, map opposite p. 220.

places his trust in the indulgence, or carelessness, of his readers, and depicts them as follows:

He shows the Pūrus on the northern side of the Sarasvatī, and the Anus to their north, and the Druhyus to the west and north-west; but he shows the Turvasus not to the south-east of the Pūrus, but very much to the northwest of them! And he shows the Yadus, not to the south-west of the Pūrus, but even further to the north-west, even beyond the Turvasus! In this clever way, he shows all the five dynasties located within the Punjab, in contradiction to the description given by himself.

We are concerned here only with the location of the Yadus or Yādavas. The Purāṇas show two different dynasties from the very beginning, which are classified as Yādava. They are attributed to the two sons of Yadu. Of these, the Haihayas are located mainly in western Madhya Pradesh, and the Yādavas proper in Gujarat and northern Maharashtra (Vidarbha). Bhargava, however, insists that they lived originally in the south-east of the Punjab, and later migrated to these parts. Let us examine his evidence in respect of the Haihayas and the Yādavas.

The Haihayas: Bhargava argues as follows: "The association of the earliest Haihaya kings with Māhiṣmatī and Avanti by later Puranic editors is on a par with the association of the earliest Aikṣvāku kings with Ayodhyā and the earliest Saudyumna kings with Vatsa. That the early Haihaya kings, Arjuna and Jayadhvaja, could not have been kings of Avanti is proved by many important facts. In the first place, the country of Avanti was named after the Avantis, one of the five branches descended from Arjuna's grandson Tālajangha. The Avantis, therefore, must have been the founders of the Avanti kingdom. It is thus clear that Avanti could not have been under the rule of Arjuna and Jayadhvaja, if founded by their descendants. Secondly, the rishi Jamadagni, with whom Arjuna came into conflict, is said by the Mahābhārata (III.129.7-11) to have practised austerities near Kurukṣetra, far from Avanti. Thirdly, it is clearly said in the ancient Brahmāṇḍa Purāṇa (III.47.67-73) that when there was a war between Paraśurāma and the Haihayas, the Haihaya princes took refuge a long time at the Himalayas. Now if the Haihayas had been ruling in Avanti, the natural place of refuge would have been the Vindhyas and not the distant Himalayas. This again proves that Arjuna and his near descendants did not rule in Avanti. The point, at which the Haihayas left their original home (in the Punjab) and settled in Central and Western India, is fairly well indicated by the Purāṇas. The Aikṣvāku king Sagara is said to have completely routed the Haihayas and it is remarkable that the account of the Haihaya kings closed about the time of Sagara. What could have been the cause of the closing of this account? It is certain that the Haihayas did not become extinct, for they ruled in Central India for centuries after, till overthrown by Puṇika, the father of Pradyota. The reason plainly was that after their defeat by Sagara, they left their original home, and the account of their successors in central and western India was not available to the Puranic editors of northern India."[52]

Thus Bhargava denies the early presence of the Haihayas in Avanti and Māhiṣmatī, and places them in the Pūnjab, *not* on the basis of any statement in the Purāṇas, but on the basis of certain inferences drawn by him. And these inferences are totally baseless.

Firstly, The Purāṇas clearly state that the Haihayas lived in Avanti and Māhiṣmatī (in western Madhya Pradesh) and that the Yādavas lived further south in Gujarat and Vidarbha. This is confirmed by the evidence of the Rigveda: not a single early Yādava king is mentioned in the Rigveda, and the only Haihaya kings mentioned are Arjuna and Vītahavya; and Vītahavya is the very king, referred to by Bhargava above, whom the Purāṇas describe as having gone on a major raid into the north (and as having taken "refuge a long time in the Himalayas") with his father Talajangha. Arjuna is stated by the Purāṇas to have made deep conquests into the north, and subsequently entered into conflict with Jamadagni. Thus the only two kings cited by Bhargava, to "prove" his point that the early Haihaya kings were associated with the Punjab, are in fact the only two Haihaya kings asserted by the Purāṇas to have come into active conflict with the kings of the Punjab, but not with the rishis (since, except for the later conflict with Jamadagni, Arjuna is in fact depicted as being a liberal donor of gifts to the rishis; and a branch of the descendants of Vītahavya became Vedic rishis, known as "Vaitahāvya brahmans", and settled in the Punjab, and Vītahavya himself is credited with the composition of a Vedic hymn, VI.15, and hence the references to them are not necessarily hostile. The Rigvedic evidence proves that the Haihayas did indeed live in western Madhya Pradesh, since none of the kings were known to the Rigveda except those who are described by the Purāṇas as having entered into Rigvedic territory (i.e. the Punjab).

Bhargava cannot insist that Arjuna or his descendant Vītahavya must have lived in the Punjab itself, on the ground that people from the south, far from the Rigvedic territory, could not have made raids into

[52] IVA, pp. 135-36.

the Rigvedic territory in the remote past. The Purāṇas very distinctly, repeatedly, and in detail, describe the Haihayas as having done just that. And Bhargava himself reports, in respect of the Haihaya king Bhadraśreṇya, 4 generations prior to Arjuna, that "Bhadraśreṇya, the Haihaya, seized the kingdom of Divodāsa of Kashi...until Divodāsa and his son Pratardana recovered it."[53] He, of course, would like us to believe that Bhadraśreṇya ruled in the Punjab. Even a cursory look at a map of India will show that Kashi is even further away from the southwest Punjab, west of the Indus (or even east of the Indus), where Bhargava locates the Haihayas, than is Avanti. He expects us to believe that Bhradaśreṇya conducted a raid all the way from the western Punjab to Kashi; but that Arjuna, four generations later, could not have conducted a raid from Avanti to Kurukṣetra (about two-thirds the distance from western Punjab to Kashi), and that Vītahavya, three generations later, could not have conducted a raid from Avanti to eastern Punjab near the Himalayas (still much less a distance than that from western Punjab to Kashi). The very fact that the Purāṇas describe the activities of Arjuna and Vītahavya in the Punjab, even when they also specifically describe these Haihaya kings as rulers of Avanti on raids in the north, should, according to Bhargava, be accepted as "evidence" that these Haihaya kings ruled in the Punjab itself. That the activities of their ancestor, Bhadraśreṇya, in Kashi, should also, on the same logic, be taken as "evidence" that he ruled somewhere in the region of Kashi, does not seem to strike Bhargava as an equally valid proposition.

In fact, Bhadraśreṇya's conquest of Kashi proves that he must have ruled in Avanti and not in the Punjab. The Purāṇas report that he ruled in Avanti; the Rigveda, by its total silence on Bhadraśreṇya, indicates that he not only did not rule in the Punjab, but that he did not even cross through the Punjab in the course of his conquests; and the fact that the distance from Avanti to Kashi is almost half the distance from the western Punjab to Kashi makes the former event more likely.

According to Bhargava, the Puranic account of the Haihaya kings closes about the time of Sagara, who, according to the Purāṇas, completely routed the Haihayas. Bhargava declares that this was "the point at which the Haihayas left their original home in the Punjab and settled in central and western India." According to him, the fact that the Haihaya kings till that point of time are described in the Purāṇas proves that they ruled in the Punjab till then; and later, when they moved southwards, they ceased to be described by the Puranic editors, since

[53] IVA, p. 154.

"the account of their successors in central and western India was not available to the Puranic editors of northern India".

Incidentally, a very significant point may be noted here. If the Puranic editors, at a far later date and with far greater geographical knowledge, and with their avowed aim of recording dynastic genealogies, could have been unable to record the less prominent kings of western Madhya Pradesh who were descended from kings already listed by them; how can the non-mention of kings and dynasties of interior India by the Rigvedic poets, who were composing hymns and *not* dynastic lists, and who were demonstrably indifferent to distant peoples not following their cult, be interpreted as the non-existence of "Aryan" kings and dynasties in interior India?

So far as Bhargava's argument is concerned, note what he says in respect of the Pūru dynasty: "The Paurava dynasty's list ends with the foundation of its branch, the Tṛtsus, who ruled very near the (main-line) Paurava territory and put the Pauravas entirely into shade. The list of the Paurava dynasty is, therefore complete up to the foundation of the Tṛtsu dynasty, but the Paurava kings who ruled simultaneously with the Tṛtsus are practically unknown. The Paurava dynasty was revived by Parīkṣit-I ages after, and was known as the Kuru dynasty. The list of the Kuru kings is no doubt exhaustive."[54]

Can this be interpreted to mean that the main-line of Pauravas left northern India, after the Tṛtsu branch-dynasty was established, and settled elsewhere far away, and returned back at the time of Parīkṣit-I? Obviously, the reason why the Purāṇas ignored the main Paurava line in the intervening period, and concentrated on the branch-line (Tṛtsus), is because the Paurava kings were minor and obscure ones, although they lived plumb in the heart of northern India. Therefore the non-mention of the Haihaya kings after the time of Sagara is not because the Haihayas ruled in the Punjab till that moment and then left for Central India; but because the Haihaya dynasty became a minor and obscure one, in the eyes of the Puranic editors, after Sagara had broken the back of their raids, conquests and rule in the north. The Haihayas, first and last, were located in central and western India.

Bhargava's glib conclusion that "Avanti was named after the Avantis ...(who were) descended from Arjuna's grandson Tālajangha ...the Avantis therefore must have been the founders of the Avanti kingdom...Avanti could not have been under the rule of Arjuna and Tālajangha if founded by their descendants...." is astounding. Even if

[54] IVA, pp. 149-50.

one presumes that Avanti was named after the Avantis (and not vice versa), the capital Māhiṣmatī, even further to the south, was named after Mahiṣmant, who was six generations before Arjuna. Thus, both Arjuna and Vītahavya, the two kings mentioned in the Rigveda (which fact Bhargava cites as "evidence" of their being residents of the Punjab) must have lived in Central India as per Bhargava's own logic of place-names.

The Purāṇas, in fact, state very clearly that the very earliest Haihayas, generations before Mahiṣmant, lived in the same region. If Avanti was named after the descendants of the 39th generation king, and if Māhiṣmatī, even further south, was named after the 31st generation king, can place-names be cited as evidence of the first arrival of the dynasty in the region, even when historical traditions insist that they were present in the same region long before? And in this case, it is not only the Haihaya dynasty, but the Indo-European language-family itself, whose first "arrival" into the region is determined by Bhargava on the basis of place-names!

Despite Bhargava's strongest efforts, the Haihayas have to be located in western Madhya Pradesh and not in the Punjab.

The Yādavas: About the non-Haihaya Yādavas, Bhargava argues as follows: "We find that the Rigveda (IV.30.17–18) mentions their raid on the river Sarayū, which was an affluent of the Gomatī, a western tributary of the Indus. The Mahābhārata (III.130) says that Lopāmudrā, the Yādava princess, married Agastya at a great *tirtha* on the Indus. ....These statements imply that the Yādavas lived somewhere on the western confines of the land of the five rivers."[55]

Here we have a repeat performance of Bhargava's logic: The Rigveda mentions the Yādava raid on a western tributary of the Indus, therefore the Yādavas also must have been residents of the "western confines" of the Punjab!

As a matter of fact, the incident referred to in the above hymn (IV.30.17–18) seems to be an important one concerning both Yadus and Turvasus, since there are 15 references in the Rigveda which mention the Yadus and Turvasus together, and most of these seem to refer to the above incident. Four of them (I.174.9; IV.30.17; V.31.8; VI.20.12), in fact, consist of laudatory references to Indra for bringing the Yadus and Turvasus safely across the stormy river. The incident, therefore, is not so much a "raid" by the Yadus, as it is an incident in which the Yadus and Turvasus responded to a call by the Vedic rishis

[55] IVA, p. 130.

to come to their aid in fighting their foes.

And the references make it very clear that the Yadus and Turvasus were a very distant people, who were certainly not residents of the "western confines" of the Punjab to the west of the Indus. They were in fact, peoples who lived *far to the east* of the Sindhu river, and they had to cross the raging waters of that stormy river, in a particularly stormy mood, in order to reach the region to the west of the Indus where the important historical incident (the exact nature of which is not very clear from the hymns) took place.

Thus, hymn I.36.18. is as follows: "We call on Ugradeva, Yadu, Turvasa, by means of Agni, *from afar:* Agni, bring Navavāstva and Bṛhadratha, Turviti to subdue the foe."[56] And hymn VI.45.1: "That Indra is our youthful friend, who, with his trusty guidance, led *Turvasa and Yadu from afar.*"[57]

In like manner, Bhargava decides, on the basis of the Yādava princes Lopāmudrā having married Agastya at a great *tirtha* on the Indus, that the Yādavas were located on the "western confines" of the Punjab on the banks of the Sindhu, and that this Yādava princess could not have been a princess of Vidarbha in the south although the Purāṇas say so in no uncertain terms.

But note what Bhargava says in another context; while drawing out a synchronism, he proves it by citing the following: "Alarka of Kashi...was a contemporary of Agastya, whose wife Lopāmudrā blessed him (Vāyu 92.67; Brahmāṇḍa III.67.71; Brahma 11.53; 13.74; Harivaṁśa 29.75-76; 32.34)."[58] Thus, he admits that Lopāmudrā and Agastya went to Kashi (or perhaps the king of Kashi came to them?).

In short, Bhargava accepts that Lopāmudrā, living on the "western confines" of the Punjab to the west of the Indus could have gone all the way to Kashi merely to bless the king. He does not deduce from this that Lopāmudrā lived in Kashi. But he finds it so difficult to believe that Lopāmudrā, if living in Vidarbha, could have gone all the way to "a great *tirtha* on the Indus", even for the special occasion of her marriage, that he considers it as evidence that she and her entire race (the Yādavas) lived beside the Indus!

In fact, the explanation for Lopāmudrā's marriage taking place "at a great *tirtha* on the Indus" is obvious and natural. Agastya is credited by the Purāṇas with having brought the Vedic cult (*not* the "Aryan

[56] HOR, Vol. 1, p. 52.
[57] HOR, p. 604.
[58] IVA, p. 151.

race", or "Aryan" rule, or the Aryan language family; but only the Vedic cult, which was not originally a pan-"Aryan" cult, but, as we shall see in the next chapter, basically a Pūru cult of the Punjab) to the south of the Vindhyas. He became the priest of Vidarbha, king of northern Maharashtra (who named his kingdom after himself; although it was not founded by him, but was his ancestral kingdom), and married Lopāmudrā, Vidarbha's daughter. There is, therefore, nothing very surprising about it if Agastya should have chosen to solemnize his marriage at a "great *tirtha*" in his native province, the Punjab.

The evidence of the Rigveda confirms the location of the Yādavas in central and western India. Not a single one of the Yādava kings is credited with the composition of a Vedic hymn; the only Yādava composer is Lopāmudrā (I.179). And the only Yādavas specifically referred to in the Rigveda are the Cedis (of Bundelkhand in southern Uttar Pradesh and northern Madhya Pradesh) and their king Kaśu. And these Yādava kings of Cedi (referred to in hymn VIII.5.37-39), who were later conquered by the Pūru king Vasu (who established his own Pūru dynasty in Cedi), are admitted even by Bhargava to have been the descendants of Vidarbha (whom he credits with the founding of the Vidarbha kingdom in northern Maharashtra): "Another son of Vidarbha was Kaiśika, whose son Cidi founded the Cedi kingdom in the country lying along the south of the Yamunā."[59]

Thus, even Bhargava admits that the only Yādava kings, specifically mentioned in the Rigveda, are descendants of kings who had migrated from Vidarbha in the south to Cedi (Bundelkhand) in the north. If Bhargava also claims that these Yādavas had earlier migrated from the Punjab to Vidarbha in the south, he cannot produce any statement from the Purāṇas or reference from the Rigveda to support his claim.

The Kashi and Kanyakubja Kingdoms: According to the Purāṇas, the kingdom of Kānyakubja (Kanauj) was founded by Amāvasu, one of the two sons of Purūravas, and brother of Āyu; and the kingdom of Kashi was founded by Kṣatravṛddha, one of the many sons of Āyu, and brother of Nahuṣa. These kingdoms, in their early stages, seem to have been obscure and insignificant, and do not form an important part of the Puranic accounts. However, they form a very basic and significant factor in the history of locations and movements of the dynasties: they were established, according to the Purāṇas, even earlier than the kingdom of Yayāti and Pūru and they thus confirm that the movement of

[59] IVA, pp. 222-23.

the Sudyumna dynasty was from east to west.

For this reason, Bhargava finds it imperative to disprove the early existence of these two kingdoms. In this, he finds what he believes to be "evidence" in some of the Purāṇas. Thus, the Brahma (which, as per most scholars, including Bhargava, is the oldest version among the existing Purāṇas) and Agni Purāṇas, and the Harivaṁśa (which always follows the Brahma version) mention all the kings of the later Kashi and Kānyakubja kingdoms, by which time both these kingdoms had become extremely important ones, as descendants of Suhotra of the Pūru dynasty.

According to Bhargava, therefore, the founders of the Kashi and Kānyakubja kingdoms were two sons of Suhotra, Kāśa and Jahnu respectively.

However, there is another contradictory account which is given by a great number of Purāṇas. This account is found in "the Vāyu, Brahmāṇḍa, Viṣṇu, Garuḍa and Bhāgavata Purāṇas, *as well as in the Brahma Purāṇa and the Harivaṁśa.*"[60] According to this account, the Kānyakubja line consists of Sudyumna/Ilā-Purūravas-Amāvasu-Bhīma-Kañcanaprabha-Suhotra-Jahnu; and the Kashi line consists of Sudyumna/Ilā-Purūravas-Āyu-Kṣatravṛddha-Sunahotra/Suhotra-Kāśa. Thus, even according to this account, both Jahnu and Kāśa have fathers named Suhotra.

Bhargava proves that the first version (which makes both Jahnu and Kāśa sons of the Pūru king Suhotra), is correct, by moving backwards from a synchronism which shows that Vadhryaśva (a king of the Tṛtsu branch of the Pūru dynasty), Gāthin (a king of Kānyakubja, and father of Viśvāmitra) and Alarka (a king of Kashi) were contemporaries. Moving back 9 generations from each of these three kings, one comes upon their ancestor King Suhotra. It is therefore obvious, according to Bhargava, that this King Suhotra must be one and the same person; and therefore the two Purāṇas and Harivaṁśa, which declare Jahnu and Kāśa to be sons of the Pūru king Suhotra, must be correct. Therefore, the Purāṇas which make Jahnu a descendant of Amāvasu and Kāśa a descendant of Kṣatravṛddha/Vṛddhaśarman must be mistaken in their account. Therefore, the Kānyakubja and Kashi kingdoms must have been founded by Jahnu and Kāśa respectively; and the accounts which claim that they were founded 24 generations before Jahnu and 23 generations before Kāśa respectively must be wrong.

Bhargava's reasoning is logical, but there is one factor which acts

[60] IVA, pp. 108 and 111.

as a stumbling block in his theory: the fact that a great number of Purāṇas firmly state that Amāvasu founded Kānyakubja, and that Kṣatravṛddha founded Kashi. There is no way in which it can be explained why the Purāṇas should have made up such a pointless story if it were not true. Even more significant is the fact that the Brahma Purāṇa and the Harivaṁśa, which declare Jahnu and Kāśa to be sons of the Pūru king Suhotra also give this version concerning Amāvasu and Kṣatravṛddha! This version cannot, therefore, be rejected, and Bhargava is compelled to furnish an explanation. His explanation is as follows.

According to him, due to the passage of time, "In some cases, it was not easy for the priestly editors of the Purāṇas to definitely identify these ancestors. In such cases, often double origins were given; and when one of them was later on rejected, it was often the correct one."[61] The Brahma Purāṇa, being the oldest, gives both the versions, but in the case of the second oldest Purāṇa: "the Vāyu has manifestly been 'improved' by rejecting one version in such cases."[62] This is one such case, according to Bhargava, where the version rejected by the Vāyu Purāṇa happens to be the correct one.

Bhargava's explanation is woefully inadequate in that it fails to explain why, in the first place, the "wrong" version was concocted at all. In this particular case, for example, there is no explanation for the Puranic editors allegedly concocting an Amāvasu and Kṣatravṛddha and crediting them with the founding of the Kānyakubja and Kashi kingdoms.

A closer examination of the problem, however, furnishes the logical explanation. The explanation is that *both the versions given by the Brahma Purāṇa are correct.*

The Kānyakubja and Kashi kingdoms were indeed founded by Amāvasu and Kṣatravṛddha respectively. The subsequent kings were insignificant ones, and hence most of them remained unrecorded by the editors of the Purāṇas, and, before them, by the compilers of royal genealogies. Only two other kings of the Kānyakubja kingdom (Bhīma and Kañcanaprabha), and none of the kings of Kashi, are recorded in the Purāṇas.

However, Suhotra, the fourth-generation descendant of the famous Pūru king Bharata, is recorded in the Ṣodaśarājikā of the Mahābhārata as one of the 16 cakravartins (great conquerors) of all time. The king-

[61] IVA, p. 21.
[62] IVA, p. 19.

doms of Kānyakubja and Kashi were obviously among his conquests, and the original dynasties of these two kingdoms were thereafter supplanted by dynasties descended from his two sons, Jahnu and Kāśa. The Kashi kingdom may have received its name from that of Kāśa, and the original name of the kingdom remains unknown (the Puranic editors referred to it as Kashi even in its pre-Kāśa days, in the same manner as the names eastern Uttar Pradesh and northern Maharashtra have been used in this book to describe the location of the ancient kingdoms).

A third son of Suhotra, Bṛhat/Hastin, retained the ancestral Pūru kingdom, but shifted his capital slightly eastwards and founded the Pūru capital of Hastināpura, named after himself.

The list given by the Brahma Purāṇa and Harivaṁśa, in which Jahnu and Kāśa are shown as the sons of the Pūru king Suhotra, therefore, represents the actual genealogical list; while the other list, given by all the Purāṇas, including also these two, represents the list of kings of Kānyakubja and Kashi, without reference to the actual blood-relationship between successive kings.

THE JOINT TESTIMONY OF THE RIGVEDA AND THE PURĀṆAS

The Rigveda and the Purāṇas, as we already saw, are accused of giving "conflicting" testimony of India's earliest historical period, especially in regard to the geographical factor. This is rather like claiming that the Book of Psalms and the Chronicles, in the Old Testament, give "conflicting" testimony about the earliest historical period of the Jews.

However, as we also saw, there is no real contradiction between the two. The Rigveda is a book of the ancient hymns of the rishis of the Saptasindhu, and of other rishis and kings who came into intimate contact with the Saptasindhu region. The Purāṇas are a reasonably well-maintained record of the ancient historical traditions of the prominent rishis and kings, and the major dynasties, of the major part of northern India. By the time the Purāṇas were finally edited, the Vedic cult had spread all over India; and hence the Purāṇas (like the different systems of *darśanas*, or philosophies, which were often as different from each other as chalk from cheese) also gave prime importance to the Vedic traditions, and often imparted a Vedic hue to the historical accounts, besides giving plenty of mythological material alongside, or even within, the historical narratives. But, by and large, as Pargiter puts it, "the Puranic stream of tradition flowed independently of the Vedic stream."[63]

[63] AIHT, p. 43.

There is no real contradiction between the two, but there is the natural difference which flows from the different aims (hymnology and traditional historiography, respectively) and the different geographical vistas (incidentally the Punjab region and intentionally the major part of northern India, respectively) of the Vedic and Puranic streams of literature. Thus the Rigveda refers to kings and rishis of the Punjab region who may not have been really important enough to be noted by the Purāṇas (Pargiter, rather spitefully but not wholly without justification, puts it as follows: "the hymns celebrate not the really great kings, but those who specially favoured and enriched poetical rishis. The praise is no measure of the king's greatness or fame, but rather the rishi's grateful laudation of the king's dignity and generosity...."[64]); while the Purāṇas contain the names of kings and rishis who may never have ventured near the Saptasindhu region at all, or were not significant enough, in the eyes of the composer-rishis of the hymns, to be mentioned anywhere in any manner.

In the face of all these facts, it is all the more remarkable that the genealogical lists and traditional accounts given by the Purāṇas can be confirmed, in their geographical aspects, by comparing them with the relevant names attested by the Rigveda. The fact that the Rigveda seems to confirm the Puranic accounts in every case is positive proof of the geographical validity of the Puranic accounts.

Thus, of the 4 relevant dynasties, the Prāṁśu dynasty is located by the Purāṇas farthest away from the Punjab (in western Bihar), and no king is described as coming into contact with the Punjab region. Appropriately, the Rigveda does not mention the name of any Prāṁśu king, and nor does it mention the name of Prāṁśu himself.

The Ikṣvāku dynasty is located by the Purāṇas slightly closer to the Punjab (i.e. in Ayodhya in north-eastern Uttar Pradesh), and some of the kings are described as coming into close contact with the Punjab, the first such king being Māndhātṛ (Generation 21). Appropriately, he is the first Ikṣvāku king whose name appears in the Rigveda, the kings before him being unknown to the hymns.

The Sudyumna dynasty is originally located by the Purāṇas in south-eastern Uttar Pradesh, but then the Purāṇas describe this dynasty as moving right into the Punjab region and (a major branch of it) settling down there. Appropriately, the Rigveda mentions most of the early kings: Purūravas, Āyu, Nahuṣa, Yayāti, Pūru, etc. (Generations 3, 4, 5, 6, and 7 respectively).

[64] AIHT, p. 8.

The Śaryāti dynasty, which either ended with him (as suggested by Bhargava), or migrated southwards to Gujarat (if the Puranic accounts are so interpreted), is located by the Purāṇas in the west of India, the exact location suggested being Haryana–East Punjab. Appropriately, Śaryāti (Generation 2) is mentioned in the Rigveda; the earliest generation, from among the different dynasties, to be mentioned in the hymns.

In respect of the five dynasties which are classified as Saudyumna also, the same case prevails. The Rigveda mentions the names of all the five dynasties (Pūru, Anu, Druhyu, Yadu and Turvasu/Turvasa), but so far as actual kings of the dynasties are concerned, the case is as follows.

The Pūrus are located by the Purāṇas in the Punjab region. Appropriately, Pūru is the only one, of the five, to whom Rigvedic hymns (V.16;17) are attributed. A large number of Pūru kings are either mentioned in the Rigveda, or have Rigvedic hymns attributed to them, as we shall see in the next chapter.

The Anus and Druhyus are located to the north and west, respectively, of the Pūrus. They are located closest to the Punjab; and their culture was, therefore, more akin to that of the Punjab than was the culture of the Yadus or Turvasus, who are located far to the south of the Punjab region (to the south-west and south-east respectively) by the Purāṇas (confirmed, as already pointed out, by the Rigveda which locates them far away); but, as we shall see in the next chapter, they were on more or less inimical terms with the people of the Punjab.

Therefore, the only hymn which is attributed to the Anus is X.179.1. But this hymn is attributed to Śivi Auśināra, who belongs to a branch of Anus which is specifically mentioned as moving southwards, in the time of Śivi's father Uśīnara, from Kashmir to the Punjab. The only other Anu, of the genealogies, who finds doubtful mention in the Rigveda may be Uśīnara; hymn X.59.10 refers to Uśīnarāṇī, who is interpreted by many to be the wife of Uśīnara.

No Druhyu king has any hymn attributed to him; and nor is any Druhyu king, of the genealogies, mentioned in the Rigveda.

Likewise, no Turvasu king has any hymn attributed to him; and nor is any Turvasu king, of the genealogies, mentioned in the Rigveda.

Of the two Yadu dynasties, the Haihayas are located by the Purāṇas in western Madhya Pradesh, while the Yādavas proper are located further to the south, in northern Maharashtra. The only Yadu king to have a hymn attributed to him is the Haihaya king Vītahavya, who, as we have already seen, is described by the Purāṇas in association with the Punjab region, and from whom were descended the Vaitahāvya rishis. The only other king to be mentioned is Arjuna, who is also described in the Purāṇas as moving towards the Punjab region in his conquests and conflicts. Arjuna is often mentioned in connection with his son Kutsa (not known to the Puranic genealogies, but known as the progenitor of the Kutsa rishis).

Thus, in every case, those kings of the Puranic genealogies, who are found mentioned in the Rigveda, are precisely those kings who are described, in the traditional accounts of the Purāṇas, as being closely associated with the Punjab. All these cannot be coincidences.

Can it be argued that perhaps those other kings of the genealogies, who are *not* mentioned in the Rigveda, may have been unimportant ones with no particular deeds or events to their credit; and hence, on the one hand, they found no mention in the Rigveda, in spite of being kings of the Saptasindhu; and, on the other hand, the Puranic editors were not equipped with precise details of their activities in the Punjab and hence did not mention anything about them in connection with the Punjab?

The above argument would be wrong: there *were* kings, of the genealogical lists, who are described in the Purāṇas as having great achievements to their credit; but neither do the Purāṇas associate them with the Punjab, and nor does the Rigveda refer to these kings. Bhargava (who, of course, insists on locating all the early kings within the Punjab, despite explicit statements to the contrary in the Purāṇas) describes the earliest history of the dynasties as follows:

"At this time, the Aryan colony of the Saptasindhu had developed into seven principal kingdoms, those of Yayāti's five sons and the two earlier of the Aikṣvākus and the Prāṁśavas. The first noted Aikṣvāku king was Kuvalayāśva, who lived some five generations after Yayāti. He is said to have rescued the sage Uttaṅka and earned the title Dhundhumāra by killing a powerful rākṣasa named Dhundhu who lived near a sand-filled sea called Ujjalaka. As has already been pointed out, this sea lay in a part of what is now called Rajasthan, and Kuvalayāśva must have gone thither in the course of his conquests...for about six generations after Kuvalayāśva, no eminent king was born in any of the dynasties and there was no event worthy of mention. This period of lull was, however, followed by one which produced a series of great conquerors and sacrificers. The first great king after this period of lull was the Prāṁśava monarch Marutta Āvikṣita.... He was a great conqueror and carried his arms upto the river Yamunā.... The Yādavas... rose to power under king Śaśabindu, who was a famous cakravartin, and extended his sway over neighbouring states...the Aikṣvākus then rose to great prominence under their king Māndhātṛ..."[65]

This is the Puranic account as related by Bhargava himself. Significantly, of the first four great kings described by him, the first three are not mentioned even once throughout the Rigveda, while the fourth is not only mentioned prominently many times, but is credited with the composition of a Rigvedic hymn (X.134).

Bhargava, who places all these kings within the Saptasindhu region, and describes them as conquering kingdoms right and left within the region itself, has no explanation to offer for the Rigveda's blissful ignorance of the very existence of these first three great monarchs and conquerors, or for Māndhātṛ's being the first to receive mention and prominence in the Rigveda.

The Purāṇas, however, have the natural explanation within their historical accounts: the first 3 great monarchs and conquerors ruled and conquered outside the Saptasindhu; the fourth one also ruled outside the Saptasindhu, but he conquered his way into the Punjab and drove out the Druhyu invaders.

Can it be argued that these kings, not mentioned in the Rigveda, may have been fictitious ones invented by the Puranic editors?

Such an argument, besides being insolent, would be wrong: the Rigveda, whose composers restricted their sights to the Saptasindhu region, does not mention these kings. But the later Vedic literature, which, in the wake of the spread of the Vedic cult all over India, takes cognizance of the ancient traditions of those regions, mentions the names of these kings: the Maitrāyaṇīya Upaniṣad (I.4-5) mentions Kuvalayāśva and Śaśabindu, and the Śatapatha Brāhmaṇa (XII.4.5.6.) and the Aitareya Brāhmaṇa (39.7) mention Marutta Āvīkṣita.

Can it, as a last-ditch argument, be argued that these kings, *not* mentioned in the Rigveda but mentioned in the later Vedic literature, are kings who were actually descendants of the kings (mentioned in the Rigveda) who ruled in the Saptasindhu region; but that the Puranic editors, either out of utter villainy or utter stupidity, wrongly designated them, in the genealogical lists, as their ancestors?

Let us take the example of Sudyumna. He is not mentioned in the Rigveda, nor in any of the other Veda Samhitas. But he is not a fictitious king invented by the Puranic editors, since he is mentioned in the Maitrāyaṇīya Upaniṣad (I.4). Is he therefore a descendant of the kings mentioned in the Rigveda, or is he an ancestor? The Śatapatha Brāhmaṇa (XIII.5.4.11-14) describes Bharata Dauṣyanti as Saudyumni,

[65] IVA, pp. 212-13.

"descendant of Sudyumna". And Bharata, who is a very prominent king mentioned many times in the Rigveda, is repeatedly described in the Rigveda (III.33.12; 53.12; etc.) as the ancestor of the Viśvāmitras, who are the composers of the entire third book of the Rigveda and of many hymns in other books.

Therefore, unless it is to be alleged that the ancient composers of the Rigvedic hymns and the editors of the Purāṇas hatched a deep, and extremely subtle, conspiracy to doctor their texts in such a way as to give a false picture of the locations and movements of the ancient dynasties, it will have to be accepted that the joint testimony of the Rigveda and the Purāṇas provides incontrovertible evidence that there were these different dynasties ruling in different parts of northern India (upto at least Bihar in the east and northern Maharashtra in the south) during, and even before, the composition of the majority of the hymns of the Rigveda; and that the movement of these dynasties took place from east to west, and not vice versa.

Thus, we have seen that the joint testimony of he Rigveda and the Purāṇas confirms the basic validity of the geographical details given in the Purāṇas regarding the locations and movements of the various dynasties. Since many of these movements antedate the composition of the Rigveda, it seems logical to presume that the Purāṇas should also contain clues as to the location of the original homeland of the Indo-European language-family, and of the initial stages of the dispersion of these languages from their original homeland.

We will examine, in the next chapter, the positive evidence found in the Purāṇas in this regard.

Note: The kings mentioned in this chapter are marked by an asterisk in the dynastic lists (as prepared by P.L. Bhargava) appended to the chapter. (Bhargava has given only the main lists: thus, he has given the dynastic list of the Tṛtsu branch descended from Nīla, son of Ajamīdha; but not the main Pūru line descended from Ajamīdha's other son, Ṛkṣa.)

THE DYNASTIC LISTS IN THE PURĀṆAS
TABLE PREPARED BY P.L. BHARGAVA
(India in the Vedic Age, pp. 162–65)

The "Era of Saptasindhu", according to Bhargava

	Prāṁśavas	*Aikṣvākus*	*Yādavas*	*Haihayas*	*Druhyus*	*Ānavas*	*Pauravas*	*Turvaśas*
1.	Manu	Manu					Manu	
2.	Prāṁśu*	Ikṣvāku*					Sudyumna*	
3.	—	Vikukṣi					Purūravas*	
4.	Prajāpati	Kakutstha					Āyu*	
5.	—	Anenas					Nahuṣa*	
6.	Khanitra	Pṛthu					Yayāti*	
7.	—	Viṣṭarāśva	Yadu*		Druhyu*	Anu*	Pūru*	Turvaśa*
8.	Kṣupa	Ārdra	Kroṣṭu	Sahasrajit	—	—	Janamejaya	—
9.	—	Yuvanāśva-I	—	—	—	—	Pracinvant	—
10.	Viṁśa	Śrāvasta*	—	—	—	—	Pravīra	Vahni
11.	—	Bṛhadaśva	Vṛjinīvant	—	—	Sabhānara	Manasyu	—
12.	Viviṁśa	Kuvalāśva*	—	Śatajit	Babhru	—	Abhayada	—
13.	—	Dṛḍhāśva	—	—	—	—	Sudhanvan	Garbha
14.	Khaninetra	Pramoda	Svāhi	—	—	—	Bahugava	—
15.	—	Haryaśva-I	—	—	—	Kalānala	Śaṁyāti	Gobhānu
16.	Ativibhūti	Nikumbha	—	Haihaya	—	—	Ahaṁyāti	—
17.	Karandhama	Saṁhatāśva	Ruśadgu	—	Setu	Sṛñjaya	Raudrāśva	Trisānu
18.	Avikṣit	Akṛśāśva	—	—	—	—	Ṛceyu	—
19.	Marutta*	Prasenajit	Citraratha	Dharma	—	Purañjaya	Matināra	Karandhama
20.	Nariṣyanta	Yuvanāśva-II	Śaśabindu*	—	—	—	Taṁsu	—

	Prāṁśavas	*Aikṣvākus*	*Yādavas*	*Haihayas*	*Druhyus*	*Ānavas*	*Pauravas*	*Turvaśas*
21.	Dama	Māndhātṛ*	Pṛthuśravas	—	Aṅgāra*	Janamejaya	Dharmanetra	Marutta
22.	Rāṣṭravardhana	Durgaha	Antara	Dharmanetra	Gandhāra*	—	Duṣyanta	—
23.	Sudhṛti	Girikṣit	—	—	—	—	Bharata*	Varutha
24.	Nara	Purukutsa	Suyajña	—	—	—	Vidatha	—
25.	Kevala	Trasadasyu*	—	Kunti	—	Mahāśāla	Bhuvamanyu	Aṇḍīra
26.	Bandhumant	—	Uśanas	—	—	—	Bṛhatkṣatra	—
27.	Vegavant	Sambhūta	—	—	Dharma	—	Suhotra*	—

The "Era of Conquest", according to Bhargava

						Pauravas		
	Aikṣvākus	*Yādavas*	*Haihayas*	*Druhyus*	*Ānavas*	(*Bhāratas*) *Tṛtsus*	(*Bhāratas*) *Jahnus*	(*Bhāratas*) *Kāśis*
28.	Viṣṇuvṛddha	Śineyu	Sāhañja	—	—	Bṛhat*	Jahnu*	Kāśa*
29.	Anaraṇya	—	—	—	Mahāmanas	Ajamīḍha	Sunaha	Dīrghatapas
30.	Trasadaśva	Marutta	—	—	—	Nīla	Ajaka	Dhanvantari
31.	Haryaśva-II	—	Mahiṣmant*	Dhṛta	—	Suśanti	Balakāśva	Ketumant-I
32.	Hasta	Kambalabarhis	—	—	—	Purujānu	Kuśa	Bhīmasena
33.	Rohidaśva	—	Bhadraśreṇya*	—	Uśīnara	Tṛtsu	Kuśāmba	Divodāsa*
34.	Vasumanas*	Rukmakavaca	Durdama	—	Śivi*	Bhṛmyaśva	Iṣīratha	Pratardana*
35.	Trivṛṣan	Parāvṛt	Kanaka	Durdama	—	Mudgala	Kuśika	Vatsa
36.	Tryaruṇa	Jyāmagha	Kṛtavīrya	—	Vṛṣadarbha	Vadhryaśva	Gāthin	Alarka*
37.	Triśanku	Vidarbha*	Arjuna*	—	—	Divodāsa	—	—
38.	Hariśchandra*	—	Jayadhvaja*	—	—	Pijavana	Visvamitra*	Sannatī

						Pauravas		
	Aikṣvākus	*Yādavas*	*Haihayas*	*Druhyus*	*Ānavas*	(*Bhāratas*) *Tṛtsus*	(*Bhāratas*) *Jahnus*	(*Bhāratas*) *Kāśis*
39.	Rohita*	—	Tālajangha*	Pracetas	—	Sudās*	—	—
40.	Harita	Bhīma-I	Vītahavya*	Sucetas	—	Sahadeva*	—	Sunītha
41.	Cancu	—	—	—	—	Somaka*	—	—
42.	Vijaya	Kunti	Amanta	—	—	—	—	Kṣema
43.	Ruruka	—	—	—	—	—	—	—
44.	Vṛka	Dhṛṣṭa	Durjaya	—	—	—	—	Ketumant-I
45.	Bāhu	—	—	—	—	—	—	—
46.	Sagara*	Nirvṛti	Supratīka	—	—	—	—	Suketu
47.	Asamañjas	—	—	—	—	—	—	—
48.	Aṁśumant	Vidūratha	—	—	—	—	—	Dharmaketu
49.	Dilīpa	—	—	—	—	—	—	—

The "Era of Expansion", according to Bhargava

		Pauravas				
	(*Yādavas*) *Vidarbha*	(*Bhāratas*) *Kāśi*	(*Bhāratas*) *Aṅga*	(*Aikṣvākus*) *Kosala*	(*Aikṣvākus*) *Videha*	(*Aikṣvākus*) *Vaiśālī*
50.	Daśārha	Satyaketu	—	Bhagīratha*	Nimi Māthava	—
51.	—	—	—	Suhotra	Mithi Janaka	—
52.	Vyoman	Vibhu	—	Śruta	Udāvasu	—
53.	—	—	—	Nābhāga	Nandivardhana	—
54.	Jimūta	Suvibhu	—	Ambarīśa	Suketu	—
55.	—	—	—	Sindhudvīpa	Devarāta	—

	Pauravas					
	(Yādavas) Vidarbha	*(Bhāratas) Kāśī*	*(Bhāratas) Aṅga*	*(Aikṣvākus) Kosala*	*(Aikṣvākus) Videha*	*(Aikṣvākus) Vaiśālī*
56.	Vikṛti	Sukumāra	—	Ayutāyus	Bṛhaduktha	—
57.	Bhīma-II	—	—	Ṛtuparṇa	Mahāvīrya	—
58.	Rathavara	Dhṛṣṭaketu	—	Sarvakāma	Sudhṛti	—
59.	Navaratha	—	—	Sudās	Dhṛṣṭaketu	—
60.	Daśaratha	Veṇuhotra	—	Mitrasaha	Haryaśva	—
61.	Ekādaśaratha	—	—	Aśmaka	Maru	Tṛṇabindu
62.	Śakuni	Bharga	Dadhīvāhana	Mūlaka	Pratīndhaka	Viśāla*
63.	Karambha	—	—	Śataratha	Kīrtiratha	Hemacandra
64.	Devarāta	Bhargabhūmi	Diviratha	Iḍaviḍa	Devamīḍha	Sucandra
65.	Devakṣatra	—	—	Vṛddhaśarman	Vibudha	Dhūmrāśva
66.	Devana	—	Dharmaratha	Viśvasaha-I	Mahādhṛti	Sṛñjaya
67.	Madhu	—	—	Dilīpa Khaṭvāṅga	Kīrtirāta	Sahadeva
68.	Puruvaśa	—	Citraratha	Dīrghabāhu	Mahāroman	Kṛśāśva
69.	Purudvant	—	—	Raghu	Suvarṇaroman	Somadatta
70.	Purūdvaha	—	Satyaratha	Aja	Hṛasvaroman	Janamejaya
71.	Satva	—	Lomapāda	Daśaratha	Sīradhvaja	Sumati
72.	—	—	—	Rāma*	Bhānumant	—

The "Era of Settlement", according to Bhargava

		Pauravas				
	(Nīpas) *Pañchāla*	*(Bhāratas)* *Kurus*	*(Bhāratas)* *Magadha*	*(Bhāratas)* *Aṅga*	*(Aikṣvākus)* *Kosala*	*(Aikṣvākus)* *Videha*
73.	—	—	—	Caturaṅga	Kuśa	Pradyumna
74.	—	—	—	—	Atithi	Muni
75.	—	—	—	Pṛthulākṣa	Niṣadha	Ūrjavaha
76.	—	—	—	—	Nala	Sanadvāja
77.	—	—	—	Campa	Nabhas	Śakuni
78.	—	—	—	—	Puṇḍarīka	Añjana
79.	—	—	—	Haryaṅga	Kṣemadhanvan	Ṛtujit
80.	—	—	—	—	Devānīka	Ariṣṭanemi
81.	—	—	—	Bhadraratha	Ahīnagu	Śrutāyus
82.	—	Saṁvarana	—	—	Pāriyātra	Supārśva
83.	Samara	Parīkṣit-I	—	—	Śala	Sañjaya
84.	—	Jahnu	Sudhanvan	Bṛhatkarman	Uktha	Kśemāṅg
85.	Pāra	Suratha	Suhotra	—	Vajranābha	Anenas
86.	—	Vidūratha	Cyavana	—	Śankhana	Mīnaratha
87.	Pṛthu	Sārvabhauma	Kṛta	Bṛhadratha	Vyuṣitāśva	Satyaratha
88.	—	Jayatsena	Vasu	—	Viśvasaha-II	Upaguru
89.	Sukṛti	Arādhin	Bṛhadratha	Bṛhadbhanu	Hiraṇyanābha	Upagupta
90.	—	Mahāsatva	Kuśāgra	—	Puṣya	Svāgata
91.	Vibhrāja	Ayutāyus	Ṛṣabha	Bṛhanmanas	Dhruvasandhi	Suvarcas
92.	Aṇuha	Akrodhana	Puṣpavant	—	Sudarśana	Suśruta
93.	Brahmadatta	Devātithi	Puṣya	Jayadratha	Agnivarṇa	Jaya

		Pauravas				
	(Nīpas) *Pañchāla*	*(Bhāratas)* *Kurus*	*(Bhāratas)* *Magadha*	*(Bhāratas)* *Aṅga*	*(Aikṣvākus)* *Kosala*	*(Aikṣvākus)* *Videha*
94.	Viśvakṣeṇa	Ṛkṣa	Satyahita	—	Śīghra	Vijaya
95.	Udaksena	Bhīmasena	Sudhanvan	Dṛḍharatha	Maru	Ṛta
96.	Bhallāta	Pratiśravas	Ūrja	—	Prasuśruta	Sunaya
97.	Janamejaya	Pratīpa*	Sambhava	Viśvajit	Susandhi	Vītahavya
98.	Nila	Śantanu*	—	—	Sahasvant	Dhṛti
99.	Pṛṣata	Vicitravīrya*	Jarāsandha	—	Viśrutvant	Bahulāśva
100.	Drupada	Dhṛtarāṣṭra*	Sahadeva	Karṇa	Bṛhadbala	Kṛtakṣaṇa

TWENTY ONE

POSITIVE EVIDENCE IN THE PURĀṆAS

The concept of an Indo-European language family, and of an original homeland for this family, is only a few centuries old. But since it is a logical concept, there obviously *must* have been an original homeland from which the dispersion of the languages took place. If recorded evidence of this is to be searched for, it must be searched for in the most ancient historical texts of the various Indo-European peoples.

The oldest Indo-European text is the Rigveda; but it is a book of hymns. Its companion text, which dealt with history, was the Original Purāṇa, which is today extant in the form of different recensions each of which is known by a separate name (Brahma Purāṇa, Vāyu Purāṇa, etc.). These recensions, the present-day Purāṇas, must therefore be looked to for any possible details of the historical movements of the original speakers of Indo-European languages.

And, incredible though it may seem, especially to those who are accustomed to viewing the subject through the blinkered vision of the generally accepted theory on the subject of the original homeland, *the Purāṇas do provide the basic details of these historical movements.*

Thus, unlike the generally accepted theory on the subject of the proto-Indo-European homeland which requires almost everything to be accepted on trust, and which fails to account for the majority of linguistic and other factors, the theory outlined in this book is borne out by the evidence of the most ancient Indo-European historical texts, and it accounts for practically all the factors.

As we have outlined earlier in this book, the earliest Indo-Europeans must have formed into three distinct linguistic groups in very ancient times: the Inner Indo-Europeans (within the interior of India), the Central Indo-Europeans (in the Punjab region, and in southern Kashmir), and the Outer Indo-Europeans (in the areas to the north and west of the Central Indo-Europeans).

Now, as per the Puranic accounts, we find three peoples who are depicted as occupying the north-western regions: the Pūrus in the Punjab region, the Anus in southern Kashmir, and the Druhyus in the areas to the north and west of the Punjab region and Kashmir. The other peoples (the Prāṁśus in western Bihar, the Ikṣvākus in north-eastern Uttar Pradesh, the Yadus in Western and Central India, and the Turvasus to the east of the Yadus) occupied the interior parts of India.

If our analysis, in the previous chapter, of the joint testimony of the Rigveda and the Purāṇas, is correct, the Pūrus should be the Rigvedic people, the Anus should be the Iranians, and the Druhyus should be the western Indo-Europeans. Do the Purāṇas and the Rigveda give any evidence in this regard?

Let us examine the positive evidence given in the Purāṇas, supported by the Rigveda, pertaining to the Pūrus, the Anus and the Druhyus.

THE PŪRUS: THE RIGVEDIC ARYANS

As per the Aryan invasion theory, the "Aryans" in India originally settled in the Punjab region, and their culture of that period is represented by the hymns of the Rigveda. Applying that logic to the genealogical lists given in the Purāṇas, P.L. Bhargava tries to "prove" that all the different dynasties listed in the Purāṇas were originally settled in the Punjab, and later on spread all over northern India from their base in the Punjab.

However, the Purāṇas have a totally different story to relate. They locate the different dynasties in different parts of northern India, and the only dynasty which is located in the Punjab is that of the Pūrus. According to a logical interpretation of the evidence, the Pūrus, and the Pūrus alone of all the different peoples described in the Purāṇas, must be the Rigvedic Aryans. The evidence of the Rigveda, and of the subsequent Veda Saṁhitās, confirms this:

1. Firstly, let us examine the matter statistically. Ten dynasties or peoples are mentioned in the Purāṇas, of which four are described in some detail: These four are the Śaryātis, the Prāṁśus, the Ikṣvākus and the Sudyumnas. The Sudyumnas, are again divided, later, into the Druhyus, Anus, Turvasus, Yadus and Pūrus. Therefore, if all the dynasties or peoples mentioned or described in the Purāṇas are to be presumed to have constituted sections of the Rigvedic Aryans, the Pūrus alone should constitute (in bare proportions) either a one-fiftieth, or one-twentieth, or one-seventh section of the Rigvedic Aryans. But in fact, we find that the Pūrus dominate the Rigveda as well as the subsequent Saṁhitās. Let us examine the names of the kings (with their generation-numbers as per Bhargava's collated list) who are either mentioned in the Saṁhitās or credited with the composition of Rigvedic hymns.

Among the kings of the Śaryāti dynasty, only Śaryāti (2) is mentioned in Rigveda I.51.12; 112.17; III.51.7, etc. (As pointed out earlier, his dynasty probably ended with him, or his descendants moved southwards.)

Among the kings of the Prāṁśu dynasty, none is mentioned in the Rigveda or in the subsequent Veda Samhitās.

Among the kings of the Ikṣvāku dynasty, we find the following:

i. *Ikṣvāku* (2) mentioned vaguely in X.60.4, and also in the Atharvaveda (XIX.39.9).
ii. *Māndhātṛ* (21) mentioned in I.112.13; VIII.39.8; 40.12; etc., and as composer of X.134.
iii. *Purukutsa* (24) mentioned in I.64.7; 112.7; 174.2; IV.33.8; V.33.8; VI.20.10; VIII.19.36; etc.
iv. *Trasadasyu* (25) mentioned in I.112.13; IV.38.1; 42.8-9; V.33.8; VII.19.3; VIII.8.21; 19.32; 36.7; X.150.5; etc.
v. *Vasumanas* (34) mentioned as composer of X.179.3.
vi. *Trivṛṣan* (35) mentioned in V.27.1.
vii. *Tryaruṇa* (36) mentioned in V.27.1, and as composer of V.27 and IX.110.
viii. *Sindhudvīpa* (55) mentioned as composer of X.9.

The five dynasties or peoples, referred to as Sudyumnas, are all referred to eponymously; but so far as kings of the dynasties are concerned, we find the following:

Among the kings of the Druhyu dynasty, none is mentioned in the Rigveda or in the subsequent Veda Saṁhitās.

Among the kings of the Anu dynasty, Śivi Auśināra (34) is credited with the composition of X.179.1; and it is speculated that Uśīnarāṇī, in X.59.10, refers to his mother.

Among the kings of the Turvasu dynasty, none is mentioned in the Rigveda or in the subsequent Veda-Saṁhitās.

Among the kings of the Yadu dynasty, Arjuna (37) is mentioned in I.122.5; VII.19.2, etc. and Vītahavya (40) is mentioned in VII.19.3, and in the Atharvaveda (VI.137.1) and as composer of VI.15.

But when we come to the Pūru dynasty, we find a whole range of Pūru kings:

i. *Pūru* (7) mentioned as composer of V.16-17.
ii. *Bharata* (23) mentioned in II.36.2; III.53.12; V.54.14; VI.16.4; etc.
iii. *Vidatha* (24) mentioned in V.33.9.
iv. *Suhotra* (27) mentioned as composer of VI.31-32.
v. *Jahnu* (28) of Kānyakubja, mentioned in I.116.19; III.58.6; etc.
vi. *Ajamīdha* (29) mentioned in IV.44.6, and as composer of IV.43-44.

vii. *Ṛkṣa* (30) mentioned in VIII.68.15 (or 57.15 in HOR).
viii. *Bhīmasena* (32) of Kāśī, mentioned in the Yajurveda (Kāṭhaka Saṁhitā, VII.1.8).
ix. *Divodāsa* (33) of Kāśī, also mentioned in the Yajurveda (Kāṭhaka Saṁhitā, VII.1.8), and in the anukramaṇīs as father of Pratardana.
x. *Tṛtsu* (33) mentioned in VII.18.13; 33.6; 83.6; etc.
xi. *Pratardana* (34) of Kāśī, mentioned in the Yajurveda (Kāṭhaka Samhitā, XXI.10), and as composer of IX.96 and X.179.2.
xii. *Mudgala*(35) the Tṛtsu, mentioned in X.102, and as composer of III.3.
xiii. *Kuśika* (35) of Kānyakubja, mentioned in III.26.1, and as composer of III.3.
xiv. *Gāthin* (36) of Kānyakubja, mentioned as composer of III.19-22.
xv. *Śrutarvan* (36) of the main line, mentioned in VIII.74.13 (or 63.13 in HOR).
xvi. *Vadhryaśva* (36) the Tṛtsu, mentioned in X.69.1.
xvii. *Divodāsa* (37) the Tṛtsu, mentioned in I.112.14; VI.61.1; etc.
xviii. *Viśvāmitra* (38) of Kānyakubja, mentioned as composer of most of Maṇḍala III of the Rigveda.
xix. *Pijavana* (38) the Tṛtsu, mentioned in VII.18.22-25, and in the anukramaṇis as father of Sudās.
xx. *Sudās* (39) the Tṛtsu, mentioned in I.112.14; VII.18; 19; 33; 83; etc., and as composer of X.133.
xxi. *Sahadeva* (40) the Tṛtsu, mentioned in IV.15.7-10.
xxii. *Somaka* (41) the Tṛtsu, mentioned in IV.15.8-10.
xxiii. *Parīkṣit-I* (83), mentioned in the Atharvaveda (XX.127.7-10).
xxiv. *Pratīpa* (97), mentioned in the Atharvaveda (XX.129.2).
xxv. *Śantanu* (98), mentioned in X.98, composed by his brother Devāpi.
xxvi. *Vicitravīrya* (99), mentioned in the Yajurveda (Kāṭhaka Saṁhitā, X.6)
xxvii. *Dhṛtarāṣṭra* (100), also mentioned in the Yajurveda (Kāṭhaka Saṁhitā, X.6)

In addition to these, we also have the following immediate ancestors of Pūru:

i. *Purūravas* (3), mentioned in I.31.4; X.95; etc.
ii. *Āyu* (4) mentioned in I.53.10; 31.11; II.14.7; etc.
iii. *Nahuṣa* (5) mentioned in I.31.11; V.12.6; etc., and as composer of IX.101, alongwith his father.

Thus, the Pūru kings mentioned in the Rigveda range from Pūru (Generation 7) to Śantanu (Generation 98), and, in the other subsequent Veda-Saṁhitās, the range extends to Dhṛtarāṣṭra (Generation 100) besides going back four generations beyond Pūru to Purūravas (Generation 3). The entire range of generations, and a great number of kings, are covered.

2. Even the few kings of the other dynasties, who are found mentioned in the Rigveda, are kings (ruling in other parts of India) who became associated with the Punjab in some way, as per the Puranic accounts (already discussed in the previous chapter). But even more significant is the fact that the Rigveda and the Purāṇas show that even here, the *Pūru* factor played an important part in the importance given to these non-Pūru kings in the Rigveda.

Thus, among the non-Pūru kings, the Rigveda does not mention any king of the Prāṁśu, Druhyu and Turvasu dynasties, and mentions only two occasional kings or so, each, of the Anu and Yadu dynasties. However, we find that the Ikṣvāku dynasty has a slightly more important position in the Rigveda: at least eight kings, as we saw, are associated with the hymns.

Of these, the name Ikṣvāku, which occurs only once in the Rigveda, does not refer to the king of this name. It is either an eponymous use of the term (symbolically referring to the help rendered to the Pūrus by the Ikṣvāku kings), or, more likely, an appellation for the sun: "Him in whose service flourishes Ikṣvāku, rich and dazzling bright as the five tribes that are in heaven."[1] (The Ikṣvākus represent the solar race while the Pūrus represent the lunar race.)

The three Ikṣvāku kings who are most frequently mentioned in the Rigveda are Māndhātṛ (21), Purukutsa (24) and Trasadasyu(25). The association of the Ikṣvākus with the Rigvedic culture thus commences with Māndhātṛ; and what is significant about this is that Māndhātṛ, although an Ikṣvāku king, was the son of a Pūru princess, and hence half a Pūru himself. Bhargava points out the specific evidence in the Purāṇas: "The Aikṣvāku genealogy says that Yuvanāśva-II married Gaurī, the daughter of Atīmāna (= Atināra, Ratināra or Matināra), and their son was Māndhātṛ. The Paurava genealogy says Matināra's daughter Gaurī was mother of Māndhātṛ."[2]

And about the *Purukutsa* and *Trasadasyu* mentioned so frequently in the Rigveda, this, according to Bhargava, is the opinion of many

[1] HOR, Vol. 2, p. 464.
[2] IVA, p. 150.

prominent scholars: "According to Macdonell, Keith (*Vedic Index*, Vol. I, pp. 541-42, *Cambridge History of India*, Vol. I, Ch. IV), Rapson (*Cambridge History of India*, Vol. I, p. 305), and other scholars, the Rigvedic kings of these names belonged to the Paurava family."[3]

The Pūru identity of the Rigvedic Aryans is so clear that these scholars subconsciously decided that kings of such prominence in the Rigveda could only be Pūrus; hence they decided that the Purukutsa and Trasadasyu mentioned in the Rigveda must be Pūru kings, distinct from the Ikṣvāku kings of the same name in the Purāṇas.

While the subconscious reason at the back their contention is worthy of note, their actual contention is not correct. The Purukutsa and Trasadasyu mentioned in the Rigveda are the same Ikṣvāku kings of the Purāṇas. However, it is still a fact that it is the Pūru factor which is responsible for the prominence given to these Ikṣvāku kings in the Rigveda, quite apart from the fact that their close ancestor, Māndhātṛ, was half a Pūru.

Thus, the Rigveda (IV.38.1) clearly states: "From you two (Mitra-Varuṇa) came the gifts in days aforetime which Trasadasyu granted to the Pūrus. Ye gave the winner of our fields and plough-lands, and the strong smiter who subdued the Dasyus."[4] The phrase "which Trasadasyu granted to the Pūrus" is also translated by some as: "Ye who gave Trasadasyu to the Pūrus."[5]

Thus, the Rigveda clearly declares that Trasadasyu was a non-Pūru who came to the aid of the Pūrus in their battle against their enemies, the Dasyus, and who recovered their fields and plough-lands which had been captured by the Dasyus. It was this spectacular assistance rendered to the Pūrus which gave Trasadasyu, and his father Purukutsa, so much prominence in the Rigveda; and in fact it is this which gave him his title Trasadasyu. The next great Ikṣvāku king, Tryaruṇa (36), who is mentioned in the Rigveda, is also given the title Trasadasyu; and it is logical to suppose that Tryaruṇa rendered similar aid to the Pūrus, resulting in his receiving the same title as his illustrious ancestor (who is known to us only by his title, his original name being lost to both the Rigveda and the Purāṇas). Tryaruṇa's father Trivṛṣan (35) is also mentioned in the Rigveda only because of, and in the company of, his Pūru-aiding son.

Significantly, Māndhātṛ (21) had also rendered similar aid to the

[3] IVA, p. 118.
[4] HOR, Vol. 1, p. 443.
[5] HOR, Vol. 1, p. 444, footnote.

Pūrus, who were his maternal relations: "The Druhyus occupied the Punjab, and Māndhātṛ of Ayodhya had a long war with the Druhyu king Aruddha or Aṅgāra,"[6] so that "the next Druhyu king Gandhāra retired to the north-west and gave his name to the Gāndhāra country."[7]

Vasumanas (34) is mentioned in the anukramaṇīs as the composer of X.179.3. It is obvious that this is due to his association with the Pūru king Pratardana (34) of Kāśī. X.179 is a hymn which contains only three verses, of which Pratardana is the composer of X.179.2. (The composer of the third verse, X.179.1, is Śivi (34). He is the only Anu king properly associated with the Rigvedic hymns; and it is obvious that both Vasumanas and Śivi figure as composers only due to their association with the Pūru king Pratardana, who is also the composer of another entire hymn, IX.96.)

Thus, it is obvious that the few non-Pūru kings, associated with the hymns of the Rigveda, have strong Pūru associations.

3. Let us examine the matter even more specifically by analysing the exact nature of the Rigvedic references to the eponyms of these various peoples.

In the Rigveda, there is no mention of the Prāṁśus at all; and the single, and rather ambiguous, reference to the Ikṣvākus has already been dealt with. There were, perhaps, no Śaryātis as such if the line ended after Śaryāti, hence the name is nowhere found as an eponym for a people.

But there are plentiful references to the five Sudyumna/Aila peoples. I.108.8 mentions all five of them together, and, significantly, it mentions the two southern peoples (Yadus and Turvasus) together in one line, and the three northern peoples (Druhyus, Anus, Pūrus) together in the next line. What is particularly significant about this verse is that it proves that there were indeed five distinct peoples of whom the Pūrus were only one. This precludes the possibility of any attempt to discount the evidence being presented here, which shows that the Rigvedic Aryans were the Pūrus, on the argumentative ground that perhaps all the "Aryans" in India at that time were known as Pūrus, and that the other peoples described in the Purāṇas may be figments of the Puranic imagination.

In another verse (VIII.10.5), four of the five peoples are mentioned together: "Whether ye, lords of ample wealth, now linger in the east or

[6] AIHT, p. 167.
[7] AIHT, p. 262.
[8] HOR, Vol. 2, p. 131.

west, with Druhyu, or with Anu, Yadu, Turvaśa, I call you hither; come to me."[8] It is clear that the four non-Pūru peoples are being depicted as residing in different directions far away from the composer of the hymn, who is very obviously a Pūru; and the Gods are being entreated to desert these peoples and come to the Pūrus.

There are about 17 verses which refer to any two of the five peoples together, and of these 15 refer to the Yadus and Turvasus together. The fact that these two distinct peoples were almost invariably clubbed together shows that they resided at so great a distance away from the Vedic Aryans that they did not have distinct identities of their own, and were always thought of as a pair.

The actual references confirm this: at least 10 of the verses seem to refer to an incident in which the Yadus and Turvasus are described as coming "from afar", crossing tumultuous rivers or seas, apparently in response to an appeal (contained in I.36.18) by the Vedic Aryans for help in their battle against their foes. These verses (I.36.18; I.54.6; I.174.9; IV.30.17; V.31.8; VI.20.12; VI.45.1; VIII.4.7; VIII.7.18; VIII.9.14) make it clear that the Yadus and Turvasus, though in a sense the heroes of the verses, are distinct from the Vedic Aryans. Of the other 5 verses, two (VII.19.8; IX.61.2) are positively hostile towards the Yadus and Turvasus, one (X.62.10) depicts them as givers of gifts, and two others (VIII.45.27; IX.61.2) are rather ambiguous in content.

Outside of these joint references, there are few other references to the Yadus and Turvasus. One verse refers to the Turvasus along with the Anus (VIII.4.1): "Though, Indra, thou art called by men eastward and westward, north and south; thou chiefly art with Ānava and Turvaśa, brave champion! (Thou art) urged by men to come."[9] This is obviously another of those verses which refer to the glory of the Gods (Indra, in this case) pervading the different directions, from the regions of the Anus in the north to that of the Turvasus in the south.

There are five other verses which refer to the Yadus or the Turvasus alone. One verse (I.47.7), as in the above one, uses the Turvasus as a criterion of distance and direction, another one (VIII.4.19) refers to them as givers of gifts, and the third (VI.27.7) refers to them in a hostile sense, exulting in their defeat at the hands of Sṛnjaya. One verse (VIII.1.31) refers to the cattle-wealth of the Yadus, and the other (VIII.7.46) refers to them as givers of gifts.

Thus, it is clear that the Yadus and Turvasus were peoples, different from the Rigvedic Aryans, who resided at a very great distance

[9] HOR, Vol. 2, p.113.

from the Saptasindhu centre of Rigvedic culture; and who at least on one occasion came to the aid of the Rigvedic Aryans in their battle against their Dasyu foes, but who were on occasion themselves pitted against the Rigvedic Aryans.

So far as the Anus and Druhyus are concerned, there are very few references to them by these names (outside of the Dāśarājña hymns, with which we will deal later). Thus, there is one vague reference (V.31.4) to the Anus: "Anus have wrought a chariot for thy courser, and Tvaṣṭar, much invoked, thy bolt that glitters..."[10] Likewise, there is one reference to the Druhyus in juxtaposition with the *Pūrus* (VI.46.8): "Or, Maghavan, what vigorous strength in Trikṣī lay, in Druhyus or in Puru's folk; fully bestow on us, that in the conquering fray, we may subdue our foes in fight."[11]

But we find 13 references to the Pūrus alone (and this is without counting the references to the Bhāratas or Tṛtsus who were branches of the Pūrus). Even more significant than the large number of references is the fact that these references make it clear that the word Pūrus is being used in a first-person sense by the composers, to refer to themselves or to mankind in general.

Thus, we already saw, in the reference to Trasadasyu, that the composer speaks of the Gods giving Trasadasyu to the Pūrus, and then immediately shifts to the first person: "Ye gave the winner of our fields and plough lands..."[12]

The following verses may also be noted, with the comments, in footnotes, by R.T.H. Griffith:

One verse (I.59.6), in praise of Agni, is as follows: "Now will I tell the greatness of the Hero whom Pūru's sons follow as Vṛtra's slayer..."[13] A line of a previous verse (I.59.2) of the hymn declares: "Vaiśvānara, the Deities produced thee, a God, to be a light unto the Ārya."[14] It is obvious that the composers, who consider themselves to be "Ārya" (noble), are Pūrus. In his footnote, Griffith gives the following definition: "Pūru's sons: men in general, Pūru being regarded as their progenitor."[15]

Another verse (VI.20.10) is even more explicit: "May we, O Indra, gain by thy new favour: so Pūrus laud thee with their sacrifices..."[16]

[10] HOR, Vol. 2, p. 492.
[11] HOR, Vol. 1, p. 608.
[12] HOR, Vol. 1, p. 443.
[13] HOR, Vol. 1, p. 81.
[14] Ibid.
[15] HOR, Vol. 1, p. 81, footnotes.
[16] HOR, Vol. 1, p. 580.

Here, again, it is clear that "we" are the Pūrus.

Another verse (VIII.53.10) goes: "For thee, among mankind, among Pūrus, is this Soma shed. Hasten thou hither, drink thereof."[17] The Pūrus obviously represent "mankind" to the composers of the hymn.

In another verse (X.48.5) Indra is depicted as addressing the Pūrus: "Indra am I, none ever wins my wealth from me: never at any time am I a thrall to death. Pressing the Soma, ask riches from me alone: Ye Pūrus, in my friendship, shall not suffer harm."[18] In his footnote, Griffith notes: "Ye Pūrus: 'O men'— Wilson"[19]

In two other verses (VII.5.3 and X.4.1) also, Griffith points out that the word Pūru is treated as synonymous with mankind in general.

There are only two verses in which Pūrus are referred to disapprovingly, but both these verses (VII.8.4; 18.13) represent the rivalry between the main line of Pūrus and the Tṛtsu branch of Pūrus; and in both the verses, the Tṛtsus are the heroes and composers.

The analysis of the references to the various peoples, thus, proves that the Pūrus were the Vedic Aryans.

4. Finally, we have the most clinching piece of evidence: the evidence inherent in the very interpretations and arguments of the invasion-theorists themselves.

The invasionist analysis, of the geographical references in the Vedas, has shown that the Vedic Aryans moved eastwards from an original base in the Saptasindhu.

Thus, all the scholars are agreed on the fact that the centre of activity in the Rigveda is in the Saptasindhu region. As P.L. Bhargava puts it: "the bulk of the hymns, of which this work consists,... show that the centre of Aryan activity was still the region around the Sarasvatī."[20]

But, "the Yajurveda introduces us to a new geographical area and a new epoch of religious and social life in India. The centre of Vedic civilization is no longer the region of the Indus and its tributaries, but the land of the Kuru-Pañcālas..."[21]

The Atharvaveda takes us even further afield: "Its geographical area is much wider, for it mentions the easternmost kingdoms of India such as Aṅga and Magadha."[22]

[17] HOR, Vol. 2, p. 207.
[18] HOR, Vol. 2, p. 449.
[19] HOR, Vol. 2, p. 449, footnote.
[20] IVA, p. 159.
[21] IVA, pp. 12-13.
[22] IVA, p. 14.

Thus, the scholars are unanimous in deducing that the Veda Saṁhitās give evidence of the movement of the Vedic Aryans from the Punjab towards the east. This is, in fact, the most fundamental invasionist dogma that is derived from the interpretation of the Vedas. On this ground alone, we find that

a. Most scholars, as exemplified by A.D. Pusalker, reject the geographical details given in the Purāṇas on the ground that "by the time the Rigveda was composed, the Aryans had not penetrated much further into the interior beyond the frontiers of the Punjab and Rājputāna... (therefore) its testimony is decidedly fatal to the geographical views assumed in the Purāṇas."[23]
b. Others, like P.L. Bhargava, try to show that the Purāṇas do, in fact, conform to the "testimony" of the Rigveda. Thus Bhargava insists that "the present Purāṇas contain two clear layers of matter, viz. the original one consisting of the records of the Sūtas, and the later one consisting of the additions and interpolations introduced by later editors...the original matter of the Purāṇas remarkably agrees with the Vedic evidence."[24] We have already examined, in the last chapter, Bhargava's attempts to show that the mysterious "original matter" of the Purāṇas gives evidence of all the Purāṇic dynasties being originally located in the Punjab.

Both these sets of scholarly conclusions are, in fact, acts of intellectual surrender on being unable to coordinate the available material. The Vedic evidence shows that the Vedic Aryans appear to have moved eastwards from an original base in the Punjab. The Purāṇas, on the other hand, commencing their narrative nearly a hundred generations before the Mahābhārata war, open "the scene of traditional history in India with...the territory comprising the whole of Northern India extending in the east upto Orissa."[25] Thus, they fail to describe this movement from the Punjab towards the east, and thereby stand rejected in the eyes of the invasion theorists.

But, as we have seen here, the Pūrus alone, among the different dynasties and peoples described in the Purāṇas, constituted the Vedic Aryans. When we examine the Purāṇas in the light of this fact, we find that they do indeed describe exactly this same movement in respect of the Pūrus.

[23] HCIP, p. 312.
[24] IVA, p. 127.
[25] HCIP, p. 311.

Thus, the Purāṇas describe the Pūrus as dwelling in the Punjab and on the banks of the Sarasvatī. The Mahābhārata confirms this. The Rigvedic hymn in praise of the Sarasvatī refers to the Pūrus (VII.96.2): "...the Pūrus dwell, Beauteous one, on thy two grassy banks..."[26]

The Purāṇas describe the Pūrus as they move eastwards: conquering the Kānyakubja and Kāśī kingdoms, establishing the Kuru and Pañcāla kingdoms, and finally establishing the Aṅga and Magadha kingdoms (Bhargava proves that the Aṅga kingdom was also a Pūru kingdom). The failure of the scholars to comprehend the significance of this description in the Purāṇas is based on the fact that their theory suffers from two fundamental flaws.

Firstly, they presume that the Vedic Aryans represented the entire body of the speakers of Indo-European languages within India. But, as we have seen, the Vedic Aryans consisted only of the Pūrus. Thus, their failure is a failure to identify the Vedic Aryans from among the different peoples described in the Purāṇas.

Secondly, they presume that the Vedic culture represented the culture of a people who had moved into the Punjab from outside (i.e. from the west). Hence they presume that the Indo-European presence in India commenced with the Vedic Aryans in the Punjab. However, as we have seen, the Purāṇas not only describe the movement of the Vedic Aryans (i.e. the Pūrus) from the Punjab to the east, but they also describe the earlier, pre-Rigvedic, movement of the ancestors of the Vedic Aryans (as well as of the Iranians and Western Indo-Europeans) from the interior of India to the Punjab.

Most scholars tend to view the question of the identity of the Vedic Aryans through the blinkers of the invasion theory. This goes even for those scholars who do not accept the invasion theory (such as K.D. Sethna or P.L. Bhargava, in different ways), and even for those among them who are ideologically disinclined to accept the invasion theory (such as V.D. Savarkar, and other Hindu-minded scholars of various degrees). Hence all these scholars focus on the culture of the Rigveda as the chronological starting-point of Indian, or at least Indo-Aryan, culture and history. Starting with this shaky premise, it is hardly surprising that they are left with nothing positive to say against the invasion theory.

However, as we have seen, the evidence of the Purāṇas and the Rigveda is capable of only one interpretation: that the Pūrus, one of the branches of a people who migrated to the north-west from eastern U.P.

[26] HOR, Vol. 2, p. 91.

in earlier times, were the Vedic Aryans.

THE ANUS: THE IRANIANS, ETC.

The Pūrus were the Vedic Aryans. This makes it clear that the other Indo-European peoples of the present-day, or rather their genetic or linguistic ancestors, must be present among the other peoples named in the Purāṇas. The evidence of the Rigveda shows that the Iranians were very closely associated with the Vedic Aryans, and were on inimical terms with them almost throughout (since nowhere in the Rigveda are the Dāsas/Dasyus spoken of other than in a hostile sense). Of the other peoples, the Yadus and the Turvasus, the Ikṣvākus, the Prāmśus, and even the Druhyus, were geographically located, according to the Purāṇas, at a greater distance from the Pūrus, and the Anus were the most closely located people. Moreover, the Ikṣvākus, the Yadus and the Turvasus are often depicted in the Rigveda as coming to the aid of the Pūrus in their conflicts with the Dāsas/Dasyus. Hence, the Anus are obviously the ones, among the Puranic dynasties or peoples, who represent the Iranians.

This fact is confirmed by the combined testimony of a great number of different sources:

1. The Purāṇas depict the Anus as living in Kashmir, to the north of the river Paruṣṇī (the modern Ravi), and therefore to the north of the Pūrus in the Punjab. This is confirmed by the Rigveda. According to Bhargava, "the Anus...dwelt on the banks of the Paruṣṇī according to the Rigveda *(footnote:* Rigveda VII.18.13. The fact that Indra is said to have given away the possession of the Anu king to the Tṛtsus in the battle of Paruṣṇī shows that the Anus dwelt on the banks of the Paruṣṇī. Similarly, in VIII.74, king Śrutarvan is said to have sacrificed in the fire of the Ānavas and given gifts on the banks of the Paruṣṇī)."[27]

But a major branch of the Anus later moved southwards and conquered, and established kingdoms in, the major part of the Punjab. Bhargava relates: "About the time of Tṛtsu lived the Ānava king Uśīnara. His son was the famous Śivi. Śivi made conquests on both sides of the Paruṣṇī and enlarged his kingdom. His eldest son was Vṛṣadarbha, whose descendants were in later times known as the Śivis. From his other sons were descended the Sauviras, Kekayas and Madrakas, who all established separate kingdoms in the Punjab in the later Vedic age."[28]

[27] IVA, p. 130.
[28] IVA, p. 216.

Pargiter also relates this history: "One branch, headed by Uśīnara established separate kingdoms on the eastern border of the Punjab, namely those of the Yaudheyas, Ambaṣṭhas, Navarāṣṭra and the city Kṛmilā; and his famous son Śivi originated the Śivis (footnote: called *Śivas* in Rigveda VII.18.7) in Śivapura, and extending his conquests westwards, founded through his four sons the kingdoms of the Vṛṣadarbhas, Madras (or Madrakas), Kekayas (or Kaikeyas), and Suviras (or Sauviras), thus occupying the whole of the Punjab except the north-west corner."[29]

Thus, the Purāṇas locate the Anus originally in Kashmir, and later depict them as moving southwards and conquering the Punjab.

This same history is related by the most ancient Iranian texts in respect of the Iranians. Bhargava points out: "The first chapter of the Vendidad or the handbook of the Parsees enumerates sixteen holy lands created by Ahura Mazda which were later rendered unfit for the residence of man (i.e. the ancestors of the Iranians) on account of different things created therein by Angra Mainyu, the evil spirit of the Avesta. This clearly means that the Iranians had lived turn by turn in all these lands before they finally settled in Iran, and that is why they regarded them as holy. The first of these lands was, of course, Airyana Vaejo which was abandoned by the ancestors of the Iranians because of severe winter and snow. Of the other lands, one was Hapta Hindu, i.e. Saptasindhu. This is the clearest proof of the fact that the Aryan ancestors of the Iranians were once a part and parcel of the Aryans of Saptasindhu before they finally settled in Iran. Excessive heat created in this region by Angra Mainyu was, according to the testimony of the Vendidad, the reason why the ancestors of the Iranians left this country."[30]

Hapta Hindu, naturally, is the Sapta Sindhu. And Airyana Vaejo, which the ancestors abandoned "because of severe winter and snow," can obviously be none other than Kashmir.

The evidence of the Purāṇas and the Iranian Vendidad is curiously confirmed by a third, and totally unconnected non-Indo-European source: the cuneiform records of the Assyrians. The earliest recorded evidence of the existence of the Iranians is in these cuneiform texts, and this is what they record: "By the mid-ninth century BC, two major groups of Iranians appear in cuneiform sources: the Medes and the Persians. Of the two, the Medes were the more widespread, and, from an Assyrian point of view, the more important. What is reasonably clear

[29] AIHT, p. 264.
[30] IVA, pp. 50-51.

from the cuneiform sources is that the Medes and Persians (and no doubt other Iranian peoples not identified by name) were moving into western Iran *from the east*."[31]

The *Larousse Encyclopaedia of Mythology* also confirms: "We find no mention of the future 'Iranians' previous to the ninth century BC. The first allusion to the Parsua or Persians, then localized in the mountains of Kurdistan, and to the Madai or Medes, already established on the plain, occurs in 837 BC, in connection with the expedition of the Assyrian king Shalmaneser III. About a hundred years afterwards, the Medes invaded the plateau which we call Persia (or Iran), driving back or assimilating populations of whom there is no written record..."[32]

Thus, we see that the Medes and Persians are first recorded, by the Assyrian cuneiform sources, as invading Iran *from the east* in the ninth century B.C. The ancient Iranian texts record the earlier movement of their ancestors from Airyana Vaejo (Kashmir, as we saw) to regions to the west and south-west, including Hapta Hindu (Saptasindhu) and 14 other areas which have been identified with the names of present-day areas situated between the Punjab-Kashmir region and Western Iran. The Purāṇas record this history of the migration of the Iranians (whom they refer to as the Anus) from Kashmir to the whole of the Saptasindhu region; and even record the name of one section of these Anus, the Madras, who can be none other than the Madai (the Medes) recorded by the later Assyrian texts.

Even more significantly, the earliest Assyrian reference to the Madai and the Parsua, showing them both moving westwards from the east in the ninth century BC, locates the Madai on the plain and the Parsua in the mountains. The Rigveda and the Purāṇas in relating the history of an earlier period, locate the Madras on the plains of the Punjab and the Parśus in the mountain regions of Kashmir to the north of the Paruṣṇī. Thus, the two earliest groups of Iranians, recorded in the cuneiform texts, prove to be groups of Anus, whose migration to Iran from Kashmir stands confirmed by the combined testimony of so many diverse sources.

2. Another factor which would appear to confirm that the Iranians lived originally in Kashmir is the fact that the Soma plant, which plays such an important ritualistic role in both Vedic as well as the earliest Iranian religious rituals, is located by the Rigveda in and around Ka-

[31] EB, Vol. 9, p. 832.
[32] LEM, p. 321.

shmir. One verse (VIII.53.11 in Griffith's translation) describes Soma as "growing by Suṣomā and by Śaryaṇāvan (and)...in Ārjīkīya..."[33]; and another verse (X.34.1) refers to "Mūjavān's own Soma", and Griffith, in his footnote, clarifies that Mūjavān is "said to be a mountain on which the finest Soma plants grew."[34]

Bhargava[35] proves that the three mountains referred to in VIII.53.11 (VIII.64.11 in Max Müller's translation) are located in Kashmir. The Mūjavān mountain, referred to in X.34.1, is located in the extreme north of western Punjab, to the west of the Kashmir area referred to in VIII.53.11.

However, the most substantial evidence of the fact that the Anus were the Iranians, who originally lived in Kashmir, is provided by the Rigveda in its description of the "Battle of the Ten Kings", or the "Dāśarājña", which is the most important political event depicted in the Rigveda. We will now examine the details of this great battle, which has been consistently, and amazingly, misinterpreted by all the modern scholars who have chosen to study it.

THE BATTLE OF THE TEN KINGS

The Dāśarājña is the name given to a great battle, described in two hymns (VII.18;83) and prominently referred to in two others (VII.19; 33), which took place between Sudās, the Tṛtsu king, on the one hand, and a confederacy of ten peoples, on the other.

Five of these peoples are clearly named, in VII.18.7, which is as follows: "Together came the Pakthas, the Bhalānas, the Alinas, the Śivas, the Viṣānins. Yet to the Tṛtsus came the Ārya's comrade (Indra), through love of spoil and heroes' war, to lead them."[36]

So far as the other five peoples (who formed the confederacy against Sudās) are concerned, most scholars have chosen to decide, for some unfathomable reason, and without the least confirmation from the hymns, that they were, in the words of Bhargava, "the well-known families descended from Yayāti, viz. Yadu, Turvasa, Druhyu, Anu and Pūru."[37] But this, as we shall see presently, is absurd.

The hymns clearly name the other five peoples who took part in the battle against Sudās. Thus, the two verses (VII.18.5-6) prior tc the one which names the five peoples (Pakthas, Bhalānas, Alinas, Ś:vas,

[33] HOR, Vol. 2, p. 207.
[34] HOR, Vol. 2, p. 429.
[35] IVA, pp. 76-77.
[36] HOR, Vol. 2, p. 18.
[37] IVA, p. 220.

Viṣānins) name three more of them. The verses are as follows: "What though the floods spread widely, Indra made them shallow and easy for Sudās to traverse. He, worthy of our praises, caused the Śimyu, foe of our hymn, to curse the river's fury. Eager for spoil was Turvaśa Puroḍās, fain to win wealth, like fishes urged by hunger, the Bhṛgus and the Druhyus quickly listened: friend rescued friend mid the two distant peoples."[38]

And, the very first verse of VII.83 names the last two peoples who took part in the confederacy against Sudās: "Looking to your wealth, the Pṛthus and Parśus marched forward. O Indra-Varuṇa, these Dāsa and Ārya enemies were killed by you."[39]

Thus, we have the names of the ten peoples who fought against the Tṛtsus: they were the Pakthas, Bhalānas, Alinas, Śivas, Viṣānins, Śimyus, Bhṛgus, Druhyus, Pṛthus and Parśus. They were the ten peoples, but together they constituted groups among the Anus and the Druhyus, as the main verses describing the battle (VII.18.12-14) make clear: "Thou, thunder-armed, overwhelmedst in the waters famed ancient Kavaṣa and then the Druhyu. Others here claiming friendship to their friendship, devoted unto thee, in thee were joyful. Indra at once with conquering might demolished all their strong places and their seven castles. The goods of Anu's sons he gave to the Tṛtsus. May we in sacrifice conquer scornful Pūru. The Ānavas and Druhyus, seeking booty, have slept, the sixty hundred, yea, six thousand, and six and sixty heroes. For the pious were all these mighty exploits done by Indra."

Thus, while describing the different groups or peoples moving in for the battle, the hymns describe them by their specific names. But in describing the actual battle itself, the collective names of all these ten peoples, viz. Anus and Druhyus, are the only ones used. Thus, the only real kings concerned in the battle are the Anu king (Kavaṣa) and the Druhyu king (unnamed), who are described as being drowned in the waters; the only soldiers who are described as being killed in the battle, in their thousands, are the Anus and Druhyus; and the only land and property described as being conquered by the Tṛtsus is that of the *Anus*.

Before examining the identity of some of these ten peoples ranged against the Tṛtsus, it will be necessary to examine some of the misinterpretations introduced into the matter, by the scholars who have studied these hymns, such as the unwarranted introduction of Pūrus, Yadus and

[38] HOR, Vol. 2, p. 17.

[39] *Zarathushtra and his contemporaries in the RV.*

Turvasus into the ranks of the peoples fighting against the Tṛtsus, and the attempt to black out the reference to Pṛthus and Parśus in VII.83.1:

a. *The Pūrus:* As we have already seen Sudās and the Tṛtsus were themselves a branch of the Pūrus. Hence, the attempt to suggest that Pūrus (alongwith Yadus, Turvasus, Anus and Druhyus) were among the ten peoples who fought against the Tṛtsus indicates a rather pedestrian approach to the whole subject.

The exact, and only, reference to Pūrus is in the second line of VII.18.13 (already quoted), which goes: "The goods of Anu's sons he gave to the Tṛtsus. May we in sacrifice conquer scornful Pūru." There is no indication whatsoever, here, that the Pūrus were involved in the battle against the Tṛtsus: the Pūrus are nowhere referred to either in the battle-formations or in the actual battle; they are referred to as "scornful", and the logical implication is that they refused to come to the aid of their Tṛtsu brethren in the battle against the Anu-Druhyu confederacy; and the verse talks of defeating the Pūrus *in sacrifice* after acquiring the property and land of the Anus, which logically indicates that the Tṛtsus, after winning the battle single-handedly without the aid of the scornful Pūrus, intended to perform huge sacrifices in the Anu territory, in celebration of their victory, which would put to shame similar earlier achievements of the main-line Pūrus.

The exact context is also quoted elsewhere in the Rigveda. Bhargava refers to the last great main-line Pūru king of the early period: "Śrutarvan made conquests upto the river Paruṣṇī, and having defeated the Ānavas, sacrificed in their fire...After the death of Śrutarvan, the Paurava dynasty declined and was completely eclipsed by the Tṛtsu dynasty,"[40] which, he points out earlier, was "a branch of the Paurava dynasty, descended from Ajamīdha's son Nīla. ...This was the greatest dynasty of the Rigvedic period and produced a series of noted kings."[41] This explains both the rivalry between the main-line Pūrus and the Tṛtsus, as well as the earlier model which the Tṛtsus now wanted to excel in order to shame the scornful Pūrus.

b. *The Turvasus:* The reference, which the scholars treat as evidence of Turvasu involvement in the battle against Sudās, is the first line of VII.18.6 (already quoted) which begins with: "Eager for spoil was Turvaśa Puroḍās..."

Here it is obvious that it is one particular individual named Turvaśa Puroḍās who is being referred to. He is not referred to again in the

[40] IVA, p. 217.
[41] IVA, p. 216.

hymns, and there is no evidence whatsoever that he belonged to the Turvasu/Turvasa people of the south-east who are nowhere referred to in the context of the battle. In fact, it is clear that the composer of the hymn has deliberately given his full name so as to prevent any confusion with the Turvasus. That the name of this individual was the same as the name of the founder of the Turvasu dynasty does not indicate that he belonged to that distant dynasty or people. Individuals belonging to different dynasties or peoples often did have similar names: thus, the Sudās of this battle is the 39th generation king of the Tṛtsu branch of Pūrus; and we have another Sudās who is the 59th generation king of the Ikṣvākus. Similarly, we have Daśaratha (71), father of Rāma, of the Ikṣvākus; and Daśaratha (60) of the Yadus of Vidarbha.

c. *The Yadus*: The Yadus are nowhere mentioned even once in the context of the battle, and yet scholar after scholar has firmly declared that Yadus were one of the ten peoples ranged against Sudās. Bhargava tries to introduce them into the battle through the back door: "The Turvaśa and the Yadu kings clearly survived the war, for, in a later hymn (VII.19.8), Vasiṣṭha, the priest of Sudās, prays to Indra to humiliate the Turvaśa and the Yādva kings."[42]

The verse referred to by Bhargava is as follows: "May we men, Maghavan (Indra), the friends thou lovest, near thee be joyful under thy protection. Fain to fulfil the wish of Atithigva, humble the pride of Turvaśa and Yādva."[43] Now this hymn does not deal with Sudās in the main: it refers to the deeds of various rishis and kings, including Kutsa, Purukutsa and Trasadasyu; as well as those of Indra in his atmospheric capacity. Secondly, the sixth verse of the hymn clearly states that the story of Sudās is an old one, and indicates that ages and generations have passed since the time of Sudās. Therefore, if another later king, Atithigva, expresses his desire to conquer the Turvasus and Yadus, how does this indicate that the Turvasu and Yadu kings of the Sudās period (probably long dead by the time of composition of this hymn) "survived" the war, much less that they had anything at all to do with the war?

In the last chapter, we saw similar attempts by Bhargava to introduce, out of thin air, the Ikṣvākus and Rohita, son of Harīścandra, as adversaries of Sudās in the battle. But in spite of all the different attempts of this kind, the hymns show that the ten peoples arraigned against Sudās were all different sections among the Anus and Druhyus;

[42] IVA, p. 221, footnote.
[43] HOR, Vol. 2, p. 20.

and mainly the *Anus*, on whose territory the battle was being fought.

But while the scholars try to bring in non-existent adversaries of Sudās (viz. Pūrus, Yadus, Turvasus, Ikṣvākus, etc.) into the battle, they also try, at the same time, to black out the names of certain adversaries, of Sudās, clearly mentioned in the hymns. Thus Griffith, in line with many other scholars, blacks out the reference to Pṛthus and Parśus in VII.83.1, and translates the verse as follows: "Looking to you and your alliance, O Ye Men, armed with broad axes they went forward, fain for spoil. Ye smote and slew his Dāsa and his Ārya enemies, and helped Sudās with favour, Indra-Varuṇa."[44]

In his footnote to the above, however, Griffith concedes the following: "*Armed with broad axes*: 'armed with large sickles'—Wilson. Ludwig maintains that the former meaning is perfectly impossible, and he argues that *pṛthuparśavah* must mean 'the Pṛthus and the Parśus'."[45] But that does not prevent Griffith from giving the "perfectly impossible" meaning in his translation.

But, the word *Parśu* occurs again in the Rigveda (in VIII.7.46) and here it is impossible for the scholars to try to translate it as "axe". Griffith not only translates the verse as follows: "A hundred thousand have I gained from Parśu, from Tirindira, and presents of the Yādavas"[46]; but he even makes the following comments in his footnote: "From Parśu, from Tirindira: 'From Tirindira, son of Parśu'—Wilson. Both names are Iranian (Cf. Tiridates, Persa). See Weber's *Episches im Vedischen Ritual*, pp. 36–38 (Sitzungsberichte der K.P. Akademie der Wissenschaften, 1891, XXXVIII)."[47]

The word *Pṛthu* also occurs again in the Rigveda (in VI.27.8) in circumstances where it cannot be translated as "broad". The verse refers to Abhyāvartin Cāyamāna as a Pārthava. Griffith, in his footnote, clarifies: "Of Pṛthu's seed: or 'bestowed by Pārthavas', that is, presented by Abhyāvartin, one of the descendants of Pṛthu."[48] The irony is that the Dāśarājna hymns clearly testify that one of the main adversaries of Sudās was a king or hero named Kavi Cāyamāna. Thus the Rigveda testifies in one place that Cāyamāna and his son Abhyāvartin were Pṛthus/Pārthavas, and testifies, in the context of the Dāśarājna, that another son (Kavi) of Cāyamāna was prominent among the adversaries of Sudās.

[44] HOR, Vol. 2, p. 79.
[45] HOR, Vol. 2, footnote.
[46] HOR, Vol. 2, p. 123.
[47] HOR, Vol. 2, p. 123, footnote.
[48] HOR, Vol. 1, p. 589.

Griffith translates the second line of VII.18.8 as: "Lord of the Earth, he with his might repressed them: still lay the herd and the affrighted herdsman."[49] But in his footnote, he states: "The second line of the stanza is obscure and the translation is conjectural. Wilson translates: 'but he by his greatness pervades the earth. Kavi, the son of Cāyamāna, like a falling victim, sleeps (in death).' "[50]

All these cross-references within the Rigveda provide incontrovertible proof that it is "the Pṛthus and the Parśus," and not "people armed with broad axes", who swooped down on Sudās and the Tṛtsus.

Now let us examine the names of some of the ten peoples mentioned in the hymns as constituting the Anu and Druhyu enemies of Sudās:

1. *The Pṛthus:* The Pṛthus/Pārthavas are none other than the Parthians of latter-day Iran.

The *Encyclopaedia Britannica* has the following to say about the Parthians: "Parthia: ancient land corresponding roughly to the modern Khorasan in Iran; the same is also used in reference to the Parthian empire (247 BC–AD 224). The first certain occurrence of the name is as Parthava in the Bisitun inscription (c. 520 BC) of the Achaemenian king Darius-I."[51]

2. *The Parśus:* The Parśus/Parśavas are none other than the Persians of latter-day Iran.

As already quoted before: "the first allusion to the Parsua or Persians, then localized in the mountains of Kurdistan, and to the Madai or Medes, already established on the plain, occurs in 837 BC, in connection with an expedition of the Assyrian king, Shalmaneser III..."[52]

The Madai or Medes are the only major Iranian group who do not figure in the battle. And the reason for this is clear from the Puranic accounts: one branch of the Anus had already migrated southwards and westwards into the western parts of the Saptasindhu: the Madras were an Anu people located there, far from the scene of this battle.

3. *The Pakthas:* The Pakthas can be none other than the Pakhtoons/Pashtus/Pathans. The name is so peculiar and unique that the identity is unmistakable, and even Bhargava[53] is compelled to admit the fact.

Once the key to the identification is known (i.e. that the ten peoples were, most of them, the ancestors of different sections of Irani-

[49] HOR, Vol. 2, p. 18.
[50] HOR, Vol. 2, p. 18, footnote.
[51] EB, Micropaedia, Vol. 7, p. 774.
[52] LEM, p. 321.
[53] IVA, p. 220.

ans), it is easy to identify three more of them:

4. *The Bhalānas:* The Bhalānas were the ancestors of the Baluchi people (Cf. the Bolan Pass in Baluchistan).

5. *The Viṣānins:* The Viṣānins were the ancestors of the Piśāca (Dardic) people. The original name, Viṣāṇin, was obviously mutilated into Piśāca by the later Pūrus. (In the Rigveda itself, the word Piśāci occurs only once, and means "banshee".)

6. *The Śivas:* The Śivas were the ancestors of the Khivs.

And a seventh people, of the ten, are also clearly identifiable with another group of people who were not exactly Iranians (they belonged to what, in modern classification, is a different Satem branch of Indo-European languages, the Thraco-Phrygian branch, of which Armenian is the sole living representative), but who were situated to the north-west of the Iranians, and were culturally so Iranianized as to be considered, by many scholars, to be Iranians (like the present-day Armenians, who are also often branded as Iranians).

7. *The Bhṛgus*: The Bhṛgus were the ancestors of the Phrygians. According to the *Encyclopaedia Americana*: "The Phryges or Phrygians—ethnologically the Phrygians seem to have been closely related to the Armenians. Both were of Indo-Germanic stock, as has been proved by recent studies on the Phrygian language, which is known to us only from the scanty remains of widely-scattered inscriptions and a few glosses... Like Armenian, the language seems to be Iranian in its affinities."[54]

The evidence is so clear, and so overwhelming, that it just simply cannot be denied. Eight groups of Anus mentioned in the Rigveda and the Purāṇas (seven of these being seven of the ten peoples named in a single historical incident in the Rigveda) prove to be unmistakably identifiable with a range of ancient and modern Iranian peoples, covering practically all the major ones: the Medes, the Persians, the Parthians, the Phrygians, the Khivs, the Dards (Piśācas), the Baluchis and the Pakhtoons. The names given to these groups of people in the Rigveda (one of them, the Madras, only in the Purāṇas) correspond most closely with the earliest recorded names of these eight Iranian peoples. These peoples are today found stretched out westwards from Kashmir right upto Asia Minor, but the Rigveda locates them all in Kashmir. The Rigveda is dated, even by the most invasionist of scholars, as not later than 1000 BC at the latest; and it is acknowledged that the Dāśarājña hymns are very old ones (Bhargava places the battle in 2250 BC); and

[54] *Encyclopaedia Americana*, 1966 Edition, Vol. 22, pp. 22–23.

the earliest references to these Iranian peoples outside India occur long after 1000 BC, and these references, moreover, show these Iranian peoples to be moving westwards from the east.

The Iranian texts do not appear to have retained the details of this historical battle. They do not retain the name of their great enemy Sudās , nor any memories of the great Anu king Kavaṣa who lost to Sudās (although the name Cawas, or Cawasha, is even today a common one among the Parsees). However, it is possible that they may have retained the memories of another, and later, battle, which took place as a sequel to this one. The scene of this later battle may have been the western Punjab and the north-west frontiers extending into Afghanistan, into which area a section of the defeated Anus may have retired after their defeat in Kashmir.

S.K. Hodiwala, in his book *Zarathushtra and His Contemporaries in the Rigveda*, describes a battle which took place in the time of Zoroastrian history between an army of Zoroastrians led by Vishtaspa (incidentally not known to the dynastic histories of Iran), and an army of Deva-worshippers led by Arjaspa. This battle took place in the region of Afghanistan (which constitutes the eastern part of the Iranian plateau), which is also believed to be the land in which Zarathushtra actually lived. As in the case of Vishtaspa, so also in the case of Zarathushtra, there are no contemporary historical records outside of the religious texts of Zoroastrianism; and the very first historical records which pertain to the Iranian kings of the 6th century BC show Zarathushtra and Vishtaspa to be already ancient. Hence, Hodiwala rightly deduces that Zarathushtra could not himself have also been living in the 6th century BC, as alleged by scholars, and must have been a much more ancient historical figure.

Hodiwala identifies Vishtaspa with Iṣṭāśva mentioned in the Rigveda (I.122.13; another of the blacked-out names in most scholarly translations), and Arjaspa with Ṛjrāśva, referred to in the Rigveda (I.100) as a slayer of Dasyus, and identifies the great battle of Zoroastrian history as a kind of final great battle between the followers of Zarathushtra and the worshippers of the Devas.

What is significant is that Hodiwala identifies, in the Zoroastrian textual references to this battle, the names of two kings who are mentioned in both the Puranic lists as well as the Rigveda. The Deva-worshipping kings Hushdiv (mentioned in the *Shahnamah*) and Humayaka (mentioned in the Aban Yashta, 116-117) are identified by him with the kings Sahadeva and Somaka. And these two kings are none other than the son and grandson, respectively, of Sudās of the Dāśarājña hymns.

The battle described in the Zoroastrian texts is therefore, obviously, a sequel to the great historical battle of the Paruṣṇī. However, only a minor section of the original Anu confederacy appears to have taken part in this second battle.

THE DRUHYUS: THE WESTERN INDO-EUROPEANS

The evidence for the Pūrus being the Vedic Aryans and the Anus being the Iranians is so overwhelming that it should be obvious that the Druhyus could be none other than the Western (i.e. European) Indo-Europeans. The Pūrus are located in the Punjab, and the Anus to their north in Kashmir. The Druhyus, however are located much further to the west (northwest frontiers, Afghanistan upto the north of Kashmir).

That the Druhyus were distinct from the Vedic Aryans and the Iranians is clear from the cognate words in Sanskrit and Iranian: in Sanskrit, *druh* means "enemy" (whence *droha*, "enmity"), and in Iranian *druj* refers to an evil spirit. The Druhyus were, therefore, clearly a third category among the Indo-Europeans of northwest India, not really close to either the Pūrus or the Anus (although, in the Dāśarājña battle, sections of Druhyus appeared on the side of the Anus).

The major reference in the Purāṇas is in the time of Māndhātṛ, when the Druhyus had occupied the Punjab and were driven out from there by Māndhātṛ for the sake of his maternal relations (the Pūrus). The Druhyu king of the time was Aṅgāra, and "the next Druhyu king Gandhāra retired to the northwest and gave his name to the Gāndhāra country."[55]

Thus, the main section of Druhyus were then settled in Afghanistan. The Purāṇas then mention only four or five kings after Gandhāra. Bhargava, in his collated table of dynastic lists, unwarrantedly shows the last kings as ruling in the time of Sudās and his son, by showing many gaps in the dynastic list; although he has no further synchronism to show as justification for his contention.

And then the Purāṇas make the most amazing and clear declaration of the emigration of major sections of these Druhyus from Afghanistan to strange and distant lands in the north. The evidence provided by this unique statement is so absolute that no honest scholar can deny that it constitutes evidence of the migration of Indo-Europeans from India to Europe via Central Asia.

Even Bhargava accepts this: "Five Purāṇas add that Pracetas' de-

[55] AIHT, p. 262.

scendants spread out into the *mleccha* countries to the north beyond India and founded kingdoms there."[56] The particular statement (occurring in Vāyu-99.11-12; Brahmāṇḍa III.74-11-12; Matsya-48.9; Viṣṇu-IV.17.5; Bhāgavata IX.23.15-16) is quoted by Pargiter: *"Pracetasaḥ putra-śatam rājānāḥ sarva eva te, mleccha-rāṣṭradhipāḥ sarve hyudīcīm diśam āśritaḥ."*[57]

The Purāṇas refer to "hundreds of sons" of Pracetas, the last king named in most of the Purāṇas, thus indicating that it is not the conquests of a king that are being referred to, but a large-scale emigration. Some Purāṇas name one more king Sucetas as a successor of Pracetas, but fail to give any further details about the Druhyus. In short, the evidence of the Purāṇas shows that a major section of Druhyus spread out northwards from Afghanistan, thence moving out into strange and distant lands; but that sections of Druhyus still remained behind, as for example those who took part in the confederacy against Sudās.

Now, let us examine the case to see whether the records give any further, and more specific, evidence about the identity of the Druhyus.

As we saw, the Pūrus (who, within themselves, were differentiated into different related peoples: the main-line Purus, the Tṛtsus, the Kāśīs, the Jāhnavas, etc) are identifiable with the Vedic Aryans. Likewise, the Anus (who within themselves were different related peoples: the Pṛthus, the Parsus, the Madras, the Pakthas, the Bhalānas, the Bhṛgus, etc) are identifiable with the Iranians and related peoples. The Druhyus (who must have been similarly differentiated into different related peoples) must now be identified.

We identified the names of seven of the peoples ranged against Sudās, and of one more people enumerated in the Purāṇas, as the names of eight Iranian peoples who later spread out and occupied the entire belt from Kashmir to Asia Minor. Those who choose to contend that this overwhelming evidence consists of misidentifications, based on coincidental similarity of names, may now prepare for some more such identifications.

The eight peoples, already named, form a continuous belt stretching from Kashmir to Asia Minor, practically touching the borders of Europe. If this belt were to be extended further, into Europe, which are the Indo-European branches that we would encounter? The first is the Greek (Hellenic) branch in Cyprus and Greece, followed by the Albanian (Illyrian) branch in Albania.

[56] IVA, p. 99.
[57] AIHT, p. 108.

These two constitute the easternmost European branches, but in ancient times there was another branch which was spoken even further to the east, straddling southeastern Europe and Asia Minor. The Celtic branch is today the westernmost branch of Indo-European languages, but "Celtic was spoken in the last centuries before the Christian Era over a wide area of Europe from Spain and Britain to the Balkans, with a group (the Galatians) even in Asia Minor".[58]

Thus, the three historically easternmost European branches are the Celtic, the Greek and the Albanian.

The only three peoples, among the adversaries of Sudās, remaining to be identified are the Druhyus, the Alinas and the Śimyus.

And on comparing the two groups, we find that:

1. *The Druhyus* are identifiable with the *Druids* (the ancient Celts).
2. *The Alinas* are identifiable with the *Hellenes* (the ancient Greeks).
3. *The Śimyus* are identifiable with the *Sirmios/Srems* (the ancient Albanians).

Just as the name Pūru was later applied to only one of the many peoples who constituted the Pūrus, while the other constituent peoples came to be known by other names (Tṛtsus, Kurus, Pañcālas, etc.); so also the original name Druhyu became restricted, in Rigvedic times itself, to only one of the many peoples who constituted the Druhyus (i.e. to the Celts), and in fact soon became restricted to only the priestly class among them.

Our identification of the main-line Druhyus (or, at any rate, of the Druhyu group which retained the original name) with the Celts is corroborated by the fact that these Druhyus are mentioned, in the Dāśarājña hymns, in combination with the Bhṛgus: "the Bhṛgus and the Druhyus quickly listened: friend rescued friend mid the two distant peoples."[59] Now we notice that:

1. The Bhṛgus were a community of Vedic rishis. But a major section of them were basically Anus. Griffith also recognizes this point: "Anus: probably meaning Bhṛgus, who belonged to that tribe."[60] The Bhṛgus were, at any rate, aligned with the Anus, as the Aṅgiras rishis were aligned with the Pūrus.

The Bhṛgus were also known as Atharvans (the Atharvaveda is also known as the Atharvāṅgiras or the Bhṛgvāṅgiras, thus confirming

[58] EB, Vol. 9, p. 431.
[59] Rigveda VII.18.6; HOR, Vol. 2, p. 17.
[60] Rigveda V.31.4; HOR Vol. 2, p. 492, footnote.

that Bhṛgu is synonymous with Atharvan).

The Bhṛgus undoubtedly functioned as the priestly class for all the different Anu peoples (just as the Biblical tribe of Levi functioned as the priestly class for all the other tribes). After the Anus by and large migrated westwards, the Bhṛgus retained the name (Phryge=the Phrygians), but certain sections of them who remained with the other Anu peoples retained the other name—the priestly class of ancient Iran were known as Athravans.

Now the fact that the Celtic priests retained the name Druid indicates that the main-line Druhyus probably functioned as the priestly class for the different Druhyu peoples.

Thus, it is appropriate that the priestly class of the Anus and the priestly class of the Druhyus are mentioned together, as "friends... mid the two distant peoples", at the outset of the great war between the Tṛtsus and the Anu-Druhyu confederacy.

2. And in later historical (and definitely post-Rigvedic) times, we find these same two peoples, the Phrygians (i.e. the Phryge=the Bhṛgus) and the Celts (i.e. the Druids=the Druhyus) located together in Asia Minor, at the conjunction of the Anu (Iranian) area in West Asia and the Druhyu (western Indo-European) area in Europe.

Both these points corroborate our identification. Now it can hardly be a coincidence that the names of all the ten peoples who formed the confederacy against the Tṛtsus in the Rigvedic period, and who were defeated and dispossessed by the Tṛtsus, should be so unmistakably identifiable with the names of ten peoples who are located, in post-Rigvedic times, in a continuous belt stretching from Kashmir through Asia Minor into southeastern Europe.

There can be no doubt, therefore, that what we find in the Rigveda and the Purāṇas is the actual recorded narration of the events leading to the dispersal of the Indo-Europeans from their Original Homeland in northern India.

THE SATEM AND KENTUM BRANCHES

As we know, the Indo-European languages, in the Original Homeland itself, had split into Satem and Kentum dialects which later developed into the present-day Satem and Kentum branches.

The Purāṇas, however, classify the Indo-European peoples to the north and west of the Vedic Aryans (the Pūrus) into only two categories: Anus and Druhyus. The facts therefore, suggest the following logical hypothesis: the Anus were probably the speakers of Satem dialects (and not just the Iranians), and the Druhyus were probably the speakers of Kentum dialects.

The present-day Indo-European languages are divided into nine branches of which four are Kentum: Germanic (or Teutonic), Italic, Celtic and Hellenic; and five are Satem: Indo-Iranian, Baltic, Slavonic, Thraco-Phrygian and Illyrian. But, as we have seen, the classification suggested by the Purāṇas is slightly different: while we may roughly identify the early speakers of Kentum dialects with the Druhyus, and the early speakers of Satem dialects with the Anus, the Indo-Iranians do not fall into the Anu category in toto. While the Iranians were Anus, the Vedic Aryans were Pūrus, and the speakers of the ancestral forms of the Inner-Indo-European dialects were variously Yadus, Turvasus, Ikṣvākus, Prāṁśus, etc. Keeping this in mind, we must count only Iranian, and not *Indo*-Iranian, as a branch of the Satem category.

Now, let us examine the various branches to see if our identification of some of them, in the Purāṇas and the Rigveda, is corroborated by any other factors.

Of the nine non-Indian branches, we find five branches clearly and distinctly named in the Dāśarājna hymns. They are the Iranian, the Thraco-Phrygian (Armenian), the Illyrian (Albanian), the Hellenic (Greek), and the Celtic. Most linguists agree that the Italic branch is very close to the Celtic, and many even postulate an original Italo-Celtic branch from which the Italic and Celtic branches later branched out. On this basis, we may presume the Italic branch also to have been among those present, although it is not expressly mentioned in the hymns.

Thus, we get only three branches which are emphatically not present on the scene. They are the Baltic, the Slavonic and the Germanic.

We may, therefore, postulate a two-fold division of the ancient Indo-Europeans: one group consisting of the speakers of the Baltic, Slavonic and Germanic proto-languages, whom we may term as "earlier emigrants", since there is no mention of them in the Dāśarajna hymns or anywhere else, and who may be regarded as the people whose emigration to the north of Afghanistan and beyond to distant areas is specifically described in the Purāṇas; and the second group consisting of the speakers of the other proto-languages, whom we may term as the "later emigrants", whose presence in India at the time of Sudās is clearly recorded in the Dāśarājna hymns.

This division, it may be noted, is different from the Satem-Kentum one, since both the groups contain both Satem and Kentum peoples.

And this interpretation of the Dāśarājna hymns, on the basis of which we have proved India to be the Original Homeland, stands confirmed by the fact that this twofold division agrees with certain basic geographical, historical and linguistic factors:

1. The Baltic, Slavonic and Germanic branches can be geographically designated as the "northern branches", while all the others constitute a long belt of "southern branches".
2. These three branches are the only ones (outside India) which appear to have been present in their historical habitats for so long a period that there is no actual record of their arrival there. The other branches (outside India) are known, on the basis of their own express traditions or of the records of other peoples, to have arrived into their historical habitats from outside. Hence also, scholars have tended to postulate the location of the Original Homeland in the areas of these three branches (i.e. northern and central Europe, or South Russia).
3. Linguistically also, these three branches fall into one category, while all the other branches fall into a second category. Thus, the *Encyclopaedia Britannica* describes the division into Satem and Kentum branches, and immediately qualifies it by describing a second division which cuts across the first one: "*Characteristic Developments of Indo-European Languages:* As proto-Indo-European was splitting into the dialects that became the first generations of daughter languages, different innovations spread over different territories. Indo-Iranian, Balto-Slavic, Armenian and Albanian agree in changing the palatal stops **k*, **g* and **gh* into spirants (s, ś, th) or affricates...... Of the languages that share this change, however, Balto-Slavic shares with Germanic (including English) an *m* in certain case-endings where other Indo-European languages, including Indo-Iranian, Armenian and Albanian, have *bh* or a sound regularly developed from *bh*."[61]

All this confirms the validity of our interpretation of the Puranic and Vedic evidence.

This story of the dispersion of the different branches of Indo-European languages from India is, in fact, the only theory which accounts for every single factor:

1. According to the Purāṇas, the ancestors of the Pūrus, Anus and Druhyus originally lived in southeastern Uttar Pradesh. This accounts for similarities in many basic words of proto-Indo-European and proto-

[61] EB, vol. 9, p. 437.

Austronesian (already explained in an earlier chapter).

2. The Indian linguistic situation (as we saw at various points in this book) suggests the theory of Inner, Central and Outer Indo-European dialects or languages in ancient times, spanning northern India and the northwest; and the Purāṇas provide actual recorded evidence of this. According to the Purāṇas, the people who migrated to the west divided into (five?) groups, of which the three relevant peoples (the Pūrus, Anus and Druhyus) occupied the northwestern parts of India: Punjab, Kashmir, and the area to the northwest of Punjab and Kashmir. This accounts for the following facts:

a. The most archaic Indo-European language, Rigvedic, was spoken in this area.
b. The oldest characteristically Indo-European literature (the Rigveda) shows itself to be fully indigenous to this area (i.e. the Punjab).
c. The only ancient Indo-European literature (the Iranian) which harks back to the ancient homeland proves to be referring to this area (Kashmir, Punjab and the north-west).
d. The ancient Indo-European intruders in West Asia (Hittites, etc.), who speak "the oldest attested (from about 1900 BC) Indo-European language" can be shown to have emigrated from this area.
e. The Tocharian language, which "has been characterized as a distinct dialect even before the Satem-Centum split had taken place"[62], is spoken in the vicinity (i.e. to the north of Kashmir).
f. Many minor linguistic points (such as the Burushaski words *hin/hik* for "one", already referred to) show that the original homeland was in this area.
g. The fact that many linguists consider only those words to be proto-Indo-European, which are found in "Indo-Iranian" on the one hand and in any European language on the other, is also a pointer to this area.

3. The area and the time range suggested by the Puranic account do not even clash with the arbitrary postulations of the scholars:

a. According to them, by using a method of "dead reckoning", the original language should have started splitting into its daughter dialects around 3000 BC, give or take a few hundred years. By calculating 93 generations back from the time of the Mahābhārata war to the time of Pūru, Anu and Druhyu, at 18 years per

[62] HCIP, p. 207.

generations, we get a date around 3100 BC.

b. The descriptions of the homeland postulated by the scholars, on the basis of linguistic paleontology, could very well fit Kashmir and the northwestern regions.

4. The speakers of the proto-Germanic language are identifiable with the early Druhyus whose emigration to lands outside India, to the north of Afghanistan and beyond, is clearly stated in the Purāṇas; and this explains the following facts:

a. The Germanic branch represents a "violent variation of the original Indo-European"[63], and it occupies, geographically, the most distant area from India.

b. Germanic Mythology (as we shall see in the next chapter) has retained certain older concepts of proto-Indo-European mythology (such as Varuṇa being the king of the Gods, known as Asuras; and the Paṇis being a divine race, practically a second rival race of Gods) which are found in the older level of the Rigveda, but are lost in all the other Indo-European mythologies.

The evidence of the Purāṇas and the Rigveda thus stands confirmed on all counts.

On the face of it, there is a very fundamental difference between the mutual relationship of the different Indo-European languages as suggested in this book, and the relationship suggested in the generally accepted classification of Indo-European languages. This fundamental difference relates to the position of the Rigvedic language, as we see in the charts at the end of this chapter. They show the family tree of Indo-European languages as per the traditional classification as well as according to the evidence of the Purāṇas.

The position of Vedic, with regard to the other branches, is radically different in the two versions. According to the generally accepted theory, Vedic is the oldest representative of one of the two sections of one branch of Indo-European languages, the other section being Iranian; and the other eight language groups are parallel branches. Thus, the Vedic language occupies a junior position in the international family tree, but a senior position in the Indian family tree.

But according to us, Vedic constitutes one of three branches, while the other nine language-groups (including Iranian) together constitute nine sections of the other two branches. And all these three branches together constitute one out of many Indo-European groups originally spread out over the whole of northern India. Thus the Vedic language

[63] Ibid, p. 208.

occupies a very senior position in the international family tree, (being an uncle of sorts to the Iranian and European languages), but a junior position in the Indian family tree.

Of the two, it is the second version which must be accepted as the correct one, since

1. The other version is based on constructed theories, but this version is based on actual recorded reports in the Purāṇas, confirmed by the Rigveda.
2. The other version, and its accompanying theory of Aryan origins, is unable to account for most of the linguistic and other factors. The Purāṇic version is supported by all the linguistic and other factors.
3. A study of the comparative mythology of the different Indo-European cultures shows (as will be demonstrated in the next chapter) that the Rigvedic culture stands, if not in an absolutely paternal position to the other cultures, then at least in something very much like it. It leaves us with the definite conclusion that the Rigvedic culture is either paternal to the other Indo-European cultures, or else in a very senior avuncular position to them.

In any case, the cold hard fact is that the Purāṇas provide incontrovertible evidence that the Ultimate Indo-European Homeland lay spread out over the expanse of northern India, and that the Original Homeland of the Vedic Aryans, the Iranians and the Western Indo-Europeans (i.e. the place where a migrant branch of the original Indo-Europeans, from the east, split into these various peoples) lay in northwestern India: in the Punjab, Kashmir and the northwest.

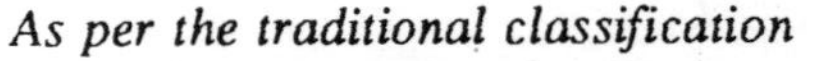
As per the traditional classification

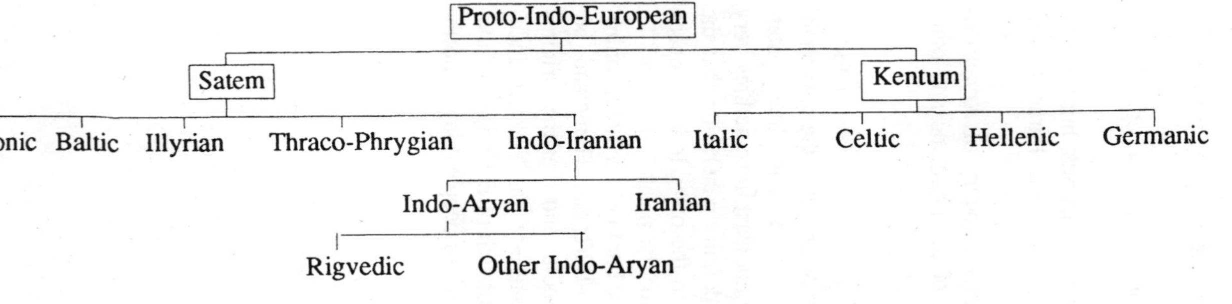

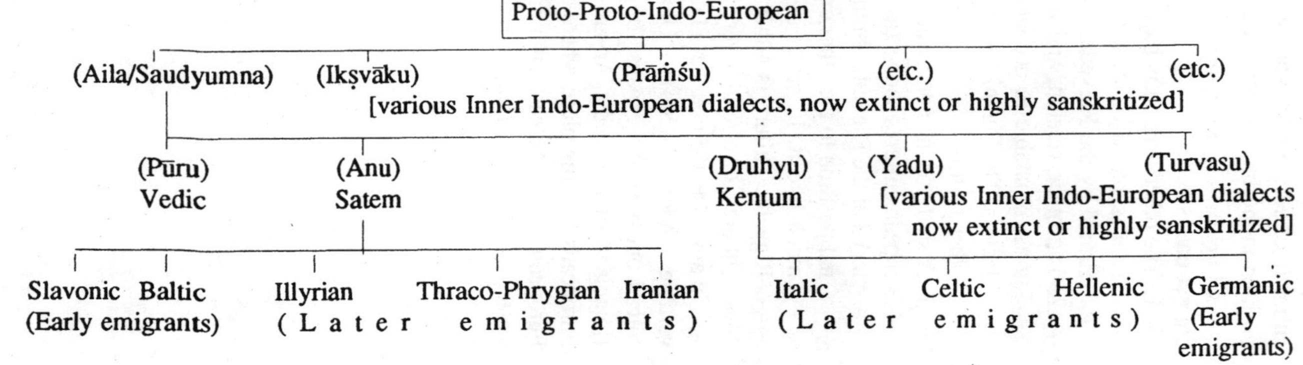

TWENTY TWO

POSITIVE EVIDENCE IN THE RIGVEDA

The Rigveda is not a historical treatise, but a collection of hymns. Hence, although it is an invaluable source for confirming and corroborating the historical evidence in the Purāṇas, the proper province of the Rigveda is the religious content of the hymns: the philosophy, the spiritual values, and the mythology. And when it comes to analysing the contents of the Rigveda for comparative purposes, it is the mythology with which we will have to concern ourselves.

In the chapter on the Kurgan culture, we saw the attempts by Marija Gimbutas to show that the Kurgan remains yielded information about Kurgan mythology, and that "the data available splendidly agree with the ancient elements of Indo-European mythology reconstructed on the basis of comparative mythology and linguistics."[1] And yet, we saw that beyond speculating that a stone figure carved on the top of some of the graves could be a "thunder God", and contending that the Kurgan people primarily worshipped a male God and that this proved them to be Indo-Europeans, Gimbutas neither managed, nor tried, to elaborate on this "splendid agreement" of the data.

However, an actual study of the comparative mythology of the different Indo-European peoples proves to be devastating for the invasion theory: it proves Vedic mythology to be practically identical with "proto-Indo-European" mythology. The only meeting point for the different mythologies is in the mythology of the Vedas.

The various Indo-European mythologies may be classified as follows:

1. Vedic Mythology.
2. Iranian Mythology.
3. West Asian Mythology.
4. North European (Teutonic) Mythology.
5. South European (Graeco-Roman) Mythology.
6. East European (Balto-Slavonic) Mythology.
7. West European (Celtic) Mythology.

These mythologies have developed in very different areas and more or less in isolation. Each of them is a mythological world by itself. Obviously, therefore, each of these mythologies must be presumed, at the very outset, to be having many elements which are pecu-

[1] IE & IE, p. 191.

liarly its own, and not part of proto-Indo-European mythology. So how do we determine which elements constitute the residual elements of the Original Indo-European mythology?

The logical method is to pick out, as elements of proto-Indo-European mythology, only those elements which are found in common (without being specifically demonstrable as having been borrowed from one of them by the others) in two or more of the mythologies. The other elements, which are found in only *one* of the mythologies, may or may not be elements of proto-Indo-European mythology: we are in no position to decide, and hence those elements must be ignored in our reconstruction. (We will also not count those elements which are found only in Vedic and Iranian, since that would be unfair from the invasionist point of view which regards "Indo-Iranian" as one group anyway; so that it would be tantamount, in their eyes, to reconstructing proto-Indo-Iranian mythology and branding it as proto-Indo-European.)

The one startling fact that comes to our notice is that each of the mythologies bears a relationship to Vedic mythology, but not to any of the others. The common elements in any mythology are common with Vedic mythology; sometimes *also* with some other mythology in addition to the Vedic, but nowhere to the exclusion of the Vedic.

Let us examine the mythologies.

IRANIAN MYTHOLOGY

The oldest elements of Iranian mythology are derived from Vedic mythology. This is so generally known and accepted that it need not even be elaborated in detail here. The major difference is that some of the Vedic Gods are the Iranian demons.

Thus, the Iranian *Ahura*=Vedic *Asura* (in the Rigveda, a term for God, later a term for demon), *Mithra=Mitra, Naonhaithya* (a demon)= *Nāsatya, Thrita* and *Athvya=Tṛta Āptya, Aspina=Aśvina, Yima =Yama, Vivanhant=Vivasvat, Indra* (a demon)= *Indra*, etc.

Even the ancient Iranian rituals were identical with the Vedic (with certain fundamental differences, such as the Iranian opposition to animal sacrifice and, originally, meat-eating): Iranian *Yašna*=Vedic *Yajña, Athravan* (a priest)=*Atharvan* (a priest), *Haoma=Soma*, etc., and the thread ceremony was common to both.

The only significant thing to be noted is that not only does Iranian mythology not have anything exclusively (i.e. to the exclusion of Vedic mythology) in common with other Indo-European mythologies, but even the elements which Vedic has in common with other mythologies are absent or different in Iranian mythology.

Thus Iranian mythology has links only with Vedic mythology. That it should have close links with Vedic mythology is not contrary to the invasion theory (which links Indo-Iranians as one group); but that it should have similarities only with Vedic, and should not be sharing the similarities which Vedic has with the other Indo-European mythologies is certainly something which the invasion-theorists cannot logically explain.

WEST ASIAN MYTHOLOGY

West Asian mythology (i.e. that of the Mitanni, the Kassites and the Hittites) is imperfectly known to us since it is known only from some inscriptions and incidental references, and because these ancient Indo-Europeans soon became completely submerged in the local religions and cultures of West Asia. What we do know is the names of some of their Indo-European Gods.

The Mitanni Gods known to us are *Indara* (Vedic *Indra), Uruwna* (Vedic *Varuṇa), Mi-itra* (Vedic *Mitra*) and *Naša-attiya* (Vedic *Nāsatya);* the Kassite Gods known are *Indaš* (Vedic *Indra) Šuriaš* (Vedic *Sūrya)* and *Maruttaš* (Vedic *Maruts);* and the Hittite God known to us is *Inar* (Vedic *Indra).*

Every single one of these Gods is Vedic; and outside the Rigveda, they are found scattered among the other mythologies: Mitra is found in Iranian mythology as well; Varuṇa is found in Teutonic and Greek mythology; the Maruts are found in Graeco-Roman mythology; Indra and Nāsatya are found also in Iranian mythology (but as demons); and the Kassite word *Bugaš*, for God, is found also in Slavonic and Iranian (Slavonic *Bog*, Iranian *Baga*, Vedic *Bhaga*).

Not only are all the Gods Vedic, but even their groupings are as in the Vedas. Most significantly, the *only* God common to the three West Asian groups is *Indra*, who is the major Vedic God and who is not found by that name in any other mythology (except the Iranian, where he is a demon).

Other than the names of these Gods, no mythology as such has survived, except for one Hittite myth about *Inar*.

The *Larousse Encyclopaedia of Mythology*[2] names only two of the Hittite myths: "that of the Great Serpent and that of Telepinu", and of these, "the myth of Telepinu is the equivalent of the agricultural myths of Dumuzi in Sumeria, Tammuz in Babylonia and of Aleyin-Môt and

[2] LEM, p. 85.

Adonis in Syria". The myth of the Great Serpent, however, is about *Inar*; and it is an Indo-European one: "The Great Serpent had dared to attack the weather-God. The God demanded that he be brought to justice. *Inar*, a God who had come from India with the Indo-European Hittites, prepared a great feast and invited the serpent with his family to eat and drink. The serpent and his children, having drunk to satiety, were unable to go back into their hole, and were exterminated."

At this point, we may go into this myth (of the killing of the Great Serpent) in some detail. This is a myth which is found in at least five Indo-European mythologies: Vedic, Iranian (by implication), Hittite, Teutonic and Greek; and a study of the myth in its different forms provides us with a perfect example of how the Vedic myth is the original one, and how it has undergone different changes in the different mythologies.

To begin with, the God Indra (derived from the same root as the word *indu*, "drop") is the main Vedic God. He represents the life-giving rain, as the God of rain and thunder. Armed with his thunderbolt, he attacks the clouds, and various demons of drought who are believed to be living in the clouds and refusing to part with the rain, and forces them to shed their rain. Representing, as he does, the all-important rainfall, Indra the Thunder-God is the predominant God of the Rigveda; and it is only natural that he should be found in most of the other Indo-European cultures as well. And we do find him in the other mythologies; and, in every case, the reference point seems to be the Rigveda.

Thus, in West Asian mythology, we find Indra still known by his name (*Indara, Indaš, Inar*). In East European mythology, the Thunder-God is known by another name of Indra: *Parjanya (Perkaunas, Pyerun*, etc.). In South European mythology, he is known by the name of another Vedic God who is often identified with Indra: *Dyaus Pitar* (*Zeus Pater, Jupiter*). The names in the three mythologies bear no relation to each other at all, and their only common meeting-ground is that they are all found in the Rigveda. In Iranian also, we find *Indra*, converted into a demon. In the other two mythologies, the name of the Thunder-God has been so totally forgotten that he is literally named after the words for thunder (Teutonic *Donar/Thor*) and lightning (Celtic *Taran)*. A comparison of the names thus proves the Vedic version to be the original.

Likewise, the myth of the killing of the Great Serpent (Ahi) Vṛtra by the Thunder-God Indra, as depicted in the Rigveda, proves to be the original version, of which the other versions represent later developments with different missing aspects.

In Iranian mythology, Indra has been converted into a demon. But his killing of the Great Serpent was obviously still remembered with reverence; hence, we find his epithet *Vṛtrahan* ("killer of *Vṛtra*", commonly applied to Indra in the Rigveda) treated as the name of a separate God of Victory, *Verethraghna*. The Iranian myth thus remembers only the name of the demon Vṛtra; it retains neither the name (Indra) nor the nature (Thunder-God) of the God who kills this demon, nor does it retain the original nature of the myth (the killing of the demon of drought for the purpose of releasing the rain-waters from the clouds).

In Hittite mythology, on the other hand, we find that the name of the God has been retained. The original purpose of the killing has also been remembered in a garbled way: "the Great Serpent had dared to attack the weather-God" (i.e. to interfere with the weather). But the nature of the God who does the killing has been forgotten: *Inar* is not depicted as a Thunder-God; he seems to have no specific characteristic, and is vaguely shown as performing the deed on behalf of another "weather-God" (who is described as the "God who presided over tempests and beneficial rainfall", and whose name is "still unknown"[3]). The thunder and fury of the battle (representing the celestial drama before the first violent rainstorm) is also forgotten, and we get a childish version of *Inar* killing the Serpent by plying him with food and drink.

The two great European mythologies (the Greek and the Teutonic) remember exactly the opposite details: they both retain the nature of the God who does the killing (*Zeus* and *Donar/Thor* are both Thunder-Gods), as well as the full fire and fury of the battle, with the liberal use of the thunderbolt by the Thunder-God. But they retain neither the name of the God (Indra), nor the original purpose of the killing (the release of the rain-waters from the clouds): in both the mythologies the Great Serpent is merely a monster killed by the God.

Thus we see that the original myth is found, in its entirety, in the Rigveda, whereas only fragments of the original myth are found scattered among the other mythologies. Moreover, every stage of development of the myth is represented in the Rigveda and its subsequent literature, from the original naturalistic stage to the later developed mythical and literalistic stage.

In the Rigveda, the Serpent Vṛtra (the demon of drought) is depicted as "lying on the mountain" (i.e. the cloud) and "covering the

[3] LEM, p. 85.

waters" (i.e. preventing the rainfall). It is this repeated description which has prompted some scholars to make the ridiculous claim that Indra represents the "invading Aryans" and Vṛtra represents the native "non-Aryans", and that the "mountain" represents a dam built on the river waters, by the natives, which was destroyed by the invaders after a general slaughter.

However, although the Teutonic and Greek mythologies have forgotten the original naturalistic character of the myth, they seem to have remembered, separately, that the Serpent had something to do with the waters (in Teutonic mythology) and with a mountain (in Greek mythology). Thus, the Great *Serpent of Midgard,* killed by the Teutonic *Donar/Thor,* is described as one "whose innumerable coils caused such violent tempests in the ocean"[4], and the Great Serpent *Typhoeus* is killed by the Greek *Zeus* by crushing him under a mountain.

While the Hittite myth retains no memory of these, it retains one more element of the original myth: the Greek and Teutonic myths have a single serpent; but the Hittite myth has *Inar* killing "the serpent and his children", just as Indra is depicted as killing Vṛtra and the Vṛtrāṇi (the minor serpents).

The Greek myth retains one more element of the literalistic depiction of the myth in the Vedic literature: the Great Serpent *Typhoeus* is in fact a creation of the Mother Goddess *Gaea,* created specifically for the purpose of fighting and killing *Zeus*. The Greek poems depict *Gaea* mourning and bewailing the defeat of her children by *Zeus,* and therefore creating the *Typhoeus* in order to avenge their defeat.

The Great Serpent Vṛtra is likewise depicted as a son of Danu (who, being a wife of Kaśyapa, like Aditi the mother of the Gods, also ranks as a Mother-Goddess), and in one place mentioned as her creation. The Rigveda (I.32.9) also depicts a forlorn Danu mourning the defeat of her children by Indra, but this takes place after the defeat and destruction of Vṛtra and the Vṛtrāṇi. Later tradition depicts Vṛtra as a creation of the God Tvaṣṭṛ, created in order to avenge the killing of his son by Indra.

Thus, a study of the Hittite, Greek and Teutonic myths (and the name of the Iranian God of Victory) proves beyond any doubt that the Vedic myth is the original one. All the mythologies are unanimous in declaring this to be the greatest deed of the God concerned; and this fact alone proves that the Vedic myth is the original one, since what could naturally be the greatest deed of a Thunder-God than the produc-

[4] LEM, p. 265.

tion of a thunderstorm?

EAST EUROPEAN MYTHOLOGY

We have already seen how Iranian mythology as well as West Asian mythology each shows direct links only with Vedic mythology and with none of the others.

In the case of East European mythology, the *Larousse Encyclopaedia of Mythology* states: "We have very few precise data on the Slavonic world in the days of Paganism."[5] However, of whatever little data is available, any parallels outside the East European circle are traceable only in Vedic mythology.

To begin with, the one God common to both the sections of the East European mythological world (Baltic and Slavonic) is the Thunder-God *Pyerun (Pyerun* in Russian, *Piorun* in Polish, *Perun* in Czech, etc.) who is known in Baltic (Lithuanian) mythology as *Perkunas/ Perkaunas*. This name has no parallel in any other mythology except the Vedic. As the *Encyclopaedia* points out: "the origin of this name goes back to remotest Aryan times. Among the Hindus, the God Indra was surnamed Parjanya, a name which has the same root as *Pyerun*."[6] Parjanya was the God of rain in the Rigveda, or, as Monier-Williams puts it: "rain personified or the God of rain (often identified with Indra)."[7]

Slavonic

The very word for God in the Slavonic languages, *Bog*, harks back to the Rigveda. *Bhaga* is the name of a Rigvedic God identified with the sun. One of the epithets of *Bhaga* is *Bhagavān* (Rigveda VII. 41), which even today is the word for God in many Indian languages (cf. Hindi); and *bhaga* is the root for many words indicating divinity (*bhāgavata, bhagavatī, bhagavad*, etc.). The Slavonic word has no parallel in any other European culture, and is found elsewhere only in the Kassite word *Bugaš* for God and the Iranian word *Baga*.

The basic God of Slavonic mythology was the Sky-God. According to the *Larousse Encyclopaedia of Mythology*, "they personified the sky as the God *Svarog*. The root of this name (*svar* means bright, clear) is related to the Sanskrit. The sky gave birth to two children, the Sun, called *Dazhbog*, and fire, which was called *Svarogich*, meaning 'son of

[5] LEM, p. 294.
[6] LEM, p. 304
[7] SED, p. 606.

Svarog'...or *Ogon* (which can be compared to the Sanskrit *Agni*)".[8]

All these show direct connections with the Vedic culture. The names *Svarog, Dazhbog* and *Ogon* have no parallels in any European mythology (the Latin *ignis,* for fire, is not the name of a God). However, all three names have their closest affiliations in Vedic mythology: *Svarog* is directly affiliated to Sanskrit *svar* (sky) and *svarga* (heaven); *Dazhbog* is obviously derived from the Sanskrit root *daṁś-* "to shine", (like the words *Dāsa, Dasyu, dasma, dasra)* and means "the shining God", and *Ogon* is *Agni.*

None of the other Slavonic Gods can be affiliated to any other God from any other Indo-European mythology, and are therefore probably Slavonic rather than proto-Indo-European Gods.

Baltic

Among the Baltics, however, we find a pair of twin Gods, twin sons of the Lettish God, who are identical with the Aśvins, and these twins are also found in South European (Greek) mythology.

Donald J. Ward, in his paper "An Indo-European mythological theme in Germanic tradition" (wherein he tries, without any success, to locate these twins in Teutonic mythology), points out the similarities in these three traditions, and calls it "one of the most striking single justifications for the comparative study of Indo-European mythology."[9]

In all the three traditions, the twins are the young and handsome twin sons of the Sky-God, and are called "sons of God" (Sanskrit *Divo napātā,* Lithuanian *Dievo Suneliai,* Greek *Dios Koûroi);* all three pairs have a sister who is the "daughter of the Sun" (Sanskrit *duhitā Sūryasya,* Lithuanian *Saules dukterys,* Greek *Helen,* daughter of *Helios,* the Sun), and the twins are her husbands as well as her brothers; and all three traditions depict the three riding together in a chariot or a boat.

In addition, Ward points out: "In each of the Indo-European traditions, the association of the Divine Twins with the horse represents the most striking characteristic of the twin brethren.... There are countless other traits and functions which the various pairs of divinities share. They are saviours at sea, they are associated with stars, they are divinities of fertility and of abundance, they are divinities of warfare, they are magic healers, and they are associated with the swan."[10]

Thus, except for this one element which it shares in common with

[8] LEM, p. 295.
[9] IE & IE, p. 405.
[10] IE & IE, p. 406.

both Vedic as well as Greek mythology, East European mythology has common elements exclusively with Vedic mythology.

NORTH EUROPEAN MYTHOLOGY

The two great mythologies of Europe are the North European (Teutonic) and South European (Graeco-Roman, but primarily Greek). There is almost nothing in common between the two, except for a few very minor points: they share in common a Thunder-God, slayer of the Great Serpent; they have in common the names of the Teutonic God *Woden/Odin* and the Greek God *Uranus*, and there is a connection in the names of the Teutonic God *Tiw/Ziu* and the Greek God *Zeus*. But in each of these cases, they share these elements in common with Vedic mythology as well, and, in fact, each of the two mythologies shares each of these elements more closely with Vedic than with each other. The similarities of *Donar/Thor* and *Zeus* with Indra are more striking than their similarities with each other, and the similarities of *Woden/Odin* and *Uranus* with *Varuṇa* are more striking than their similarities with each other. *Tiw/Ziu* (equivalent to the Vedic Mitra) and *Zeus* (equivalent to the Vedic Indra) have both borrowed their names from a third Vedic God: Dyaus.

And, in fact, there are many basic elements which each of these two mythologies, separately, has in common with Vedic mythology, extending beyond mere similarity in names.

Woden/Odin and Varuṇa

1. *Woden/Odin* (*Woden* in Scandinavia, *Odin* in Germany), is the king of the Gods, who are collectively known as the *Aesir*. *Varuṇa* (in the Rigveda) is the king of the Gods, who are collectively known as *Asuras*.

This very important feature of Teutonic mythology is not found in any other mythology except in that of the Rigveda: in Greek mythology, neither are the Gods called by any name similar to *Aesir/Asura*, nor is *Uranus* their king; and in no other mythology do we find the equivalent name of *Varuṇa*, while the Iranian *Ahura* (directly derivable from Vedic *Asura)* and the obscure *Aesus* of the Celts and *Aesun* of the Umbrians are the only other traces of the Vedic *Asura*.

2. "Like *Varuṇa*, *Woden* rules principally by magic and notably takes an interest in the wider universe, not only in the world of living men."[11]

[11] LEM, p. 258.

"It was *Odin* who ordained the laws which ruled human society."[12] "*Varuṇa* is the moral governor of the universe and the preserver of *ṛta* (cosmic order). His ordinances are fixed and he is pre-eminently called *dhṛtavrata*, whose laws are established."[13]

The chief characteristic of both *Woden/Odin* and *Varuṇa* is the rule of law, by means of magic. Both are the rulers of both the cosmic universe as well as the world of men.

3. "The representation of the first function by two divinities is a feature which the Teutons share with the Indian peoples, and which derives from the double aspect of the sovereignty as conceived by primitive peoples; firstly, there is the ruler who is the priest king, who works by the incalculable and terrifying means of magic, and secondly, the king who reflects the order of the world and of society, the constitutional monarch as it were, who incarnates the Law. The Indian *Varuṇa* and the Germanic *Woden* represent the first type, *Mitra* and *Tiw* the other."[14]

Woden is always conceived as part of a pair with another God, *Tiw/Tyr/Ziu,* who is the God of contracts.

Varuṇa is also always conceived in combination with his alter-ego (*Mitra*), who is the God of contracts.

4. *Woden/Odin* is always conceived of in royal attire, "armed with a shining breast-plate and a golden helmet"[15] and "decked in a flowing mantle."[16] He "held court in a vast hall glittering with gold which was called Valhalla....there were five hundred and forty doors."[17]

Varuṇa is likewise attired (Rigveda I.25.13) in a golden mantle and a flowing robe, and he sits in his mansion (described in Rigveda V. 67.2 as made of gold: *hiraṇyam yonim)* observing the universe and the deeds of men. His mansion has a "thousand columns" (Rigveda II.41.4) and a "thousand doors" (Rigveda VII.88.5).

Thus, there is unmistakable, and close, identification between *Woden/Odin* and *Varuṇa.*

Donar/Thor and Indra

1. *Donar/Thor* is the Thunder-God of the Teutons. He is also the God of war armed with a thunderbolt. "*Donar* was not only the God of

[12] LEM, p. 259.
[13] IVA, p. 289.
[14] LEM, p. 257.
[15] LEM, p. 259.
[16] LEM, p. 258.
[17] LEM, p. 259.

thunder. He was to a certain extent the God of war, since—according to Tacitus—the Germans invoked him and chanted his glory when marching into battle."[18]

Indra, likewise, is also the Thunder-God of the Rigveda, as well as the God of war armed with a thunderbolt. "Indra is...primarily the Thunder-God... Secondarily, Indra is the God of battle."[19] The Rigveda is full of hymns in which the Vedic Aryans invoked him and chanted his glory when marching into battle.

This dual function of the Thunder-God is found in the East European mythology also, where *Pyerun* is also a God of War. However, it has been lost in South European mythology, where *Zeus/Jupiter* is only a Thunder-God, and there is a separate God of War.

2. While *Woden* was the king of the Gods, *Donar/Thor* was "revered by all the Teutonic tribes. Some of them even considered him as the most powerful of all the Gods, and Roman authors often identified him with *Jupiter*."[20] (*Jupiter=Indra*, both are Kings of the Gods). "In one of the poems of the Edda, he confronts *Odin*"[21], and "in certain northern countries, and particularly in Norway, *Thor*—the German *Donar*—finally prevailed over all the other Gods."[22]

In the Rigveda, Varuṇa was the king of the Gods. However, Indra was (as Macdonell puts it) "the favourite national God of the Vedic Indians."[23] In one of the hymns (X.124), Indra takes over from Varuṇa. In fact the Gods, collectively known as Asuras or Devas, came to be exclusively referred to as Devas (by converting the term *Asura* into a term for demon), so that Indra became the king of the Gods=Devas. Thus, the Vedic mythology has two parallel traditions of Varuṇa as King of the Gods=Asuras (including Indra); and Indra as king of the Gods=Devas (including Varuṇa).

This parallel situation of more or less rival kings is found only in the Teutonic and Vedic mythologies.

3. *Donar/Thor* was "the very apotheosis of the warrior... a tireless adversary of giants and demons."[24]

Likewise, Indra is also, in the Rigveda, the adversary of an endless number of demons. In the Rigveda, moreover, the naturalistic origin of

[18] LEM, p. 263.
[19] VM, p. 54.
[20] LEM, p. 262.
[21] LEM, p. 263.
[22] Ibid.
[23] VM, p. 54.
[24] LEM, p. 263.

these battles is apparent, since the demons killed by Indra are almost invariably and demonstrably demons of drought.

4. One of the greatest characteristics of *Donar/Thor* is his ability to drink more than anyone else. In the legend about the giant *Utgardaloki*, who tests the skills of the Gods, "at last it was *Thor's* turn to show his skill. No one, he declared with complete assurance, could drink as much or as quickly as he."[25]

Likewise, one of the greatest characteristics of Indra is also his ability to drink more than anyone else. The Rigveda abounds in verses describing him drinking Soma, and Vedic ritual repeatedly stresses this aspect. In one place (Rigveda V.29.7), Indra is said to have drunk three lakes of Soma in one shot. Indra's first act on being born is said to have been the stealing and drinking of Soma (Rigveda III.48.2), and "the epithet *Somapā* (Soma-drinker) is therefore characteristic of him."[26]

Thus, we have unmistakable identity between *Donar/Thor* and *Indra*.

The Vanir and the Paṇis

The *Paṇis* in the Rigveda have been frequently identified as "non-Aryan" enemies of the "Aryan" composers of the Vedas. As pointed out in an earlier chapter, this is the most classic case of blinkered scholarship. Not a single scholar appears to have recognized the fact that the *Paṇis* are absolutely identical with the *Vanir* of Teutonic mythology.

1. The word *Vanir* is obviously cognate to the word *Paṇi*. In fact *Paṇi* becomes *Vaṇi* in later Sanskrit: Yāska (in Nirukta II.17) clearly states: "*Paṇih vaṇig bhavati.*" The root *vaṇ-* is, in later Sanskrit, the source for many words pertaining to trade and commercial activities.

2. The *Vanir* have basically two kinds of functions: "They provided the fields and pastures and forests with sunlight and life-giving rain... From them came the harvests, game, and all kinds of riches in general. The *Vanir* were also the protectors of commerce and navigation."[27]

The Paṇis in the Rigveda have identical attributes, but in a peculiarly contrasting way. The Rigveda in fact depicts the Paṇis as withholding sunlight (Rigveda I.182.3) from humanity, as well as withholding the cows (in the Rigveda, the cows are a symbol for rain-water, or for wealth in general). Thus, the Paṇis, far from providing sunlight and

[25] LEM, p. 267.
[26] IVA, p. 283.
[27] LEM, p. 275.

life-giving rain, are supposed to be hiding them both in the mountains (i.e. in the clouds) until Indra, the Thunder-God, wrests these from them. Further anthropomorphization of this concept converts them into miserly traders hoarding and hiding essential commodities from the public: hence, the Paṇis are intimately associated with trade and commerce, and with navigation. This, in fact, is what inspires the invasionist scholars to associate the Paṇis with the Phoenicians or with the presumed trading and maritime communities of the Indus Valley.

3. The *Vanir* were considered by some sections of Teutons as a secondary race of Gods: "Besides the *Aesir*, the Teutons—or at least the Scandinavians—considered that there was a second race of Gods, the *Vanir*."[28] The *Vanir*, however, are not given their due status of divinity by the Teutons, or by the Gods, and hence are constantly hankering for recognition as Gods. In the great war that takes place between the *Aesir* and the *Vanir*, the *Vanirs*' condition for peace is "that either a large sum of money should be paid in reparation or else that their rank should be recognized as equal to that of the *Aesir* so that they henceforward would receive an equal right to the sacrifices made by the faithful."[29]

Likewise, the Rigveda (I.151.9) also refers to the Paṇis hankering for a status equal to that of Mitra and Varuṇa.

4. The *Aesir* are depicted as being ever covetous of the wealth of the *Vanir*.

Likewise, the concept of Indra desiring the cows (originally the rain, but also wealth in general) of the Paṇis is also interpreted in the same manner: "There are more than one instances in which Indra is said to have deprived them of their wealth and the cows."[30]

5. Both the traditions depict a great war taking place between the Gods and the *Vanir* (in Teutonic mythology) and between Indra and the Paṇis (in the Rigveda). By itself, this would not constitute a similarity between the two, but for the fact that in each of the two traditions the war is preceded by a momentous incident involving a female messenger between the Gods and their adversaries.

"One Nordic tradition represents that war broke out one day between the belligerent *Aesir* and the peace-loving *Vanir*... One day the *Vanir* sent to the *Aesir*—on a mission which is not explained—a Goddess by the name of *Gullveig*. This Goddess was highly skilled in all

[28] LEM, p. 257.
[29] LEM, p. 275.
[30] CDHR, p. 37.

the practices of sorcery, and by her art had acquired much gold. When, alone, she reached the *Aesir*, they were, it is supposed, tempted by her riches. They seized her and submitted her to torture..."[31] The *Vanir* were incensed by this, and this incident ultimately led to the war.

The Rigveda portrays a different kind of messenger. The major hymn (X.108) which features the Paṇis is in the form of a dialogue between Saramā and the Paṇis. Saramā, a bitch sent by the Gods to the Paṇis, advises them to release, as demanded by Indra, the cows held captive by them in the mountains, and tauntingly warns them of dire consequences, and specifically of a battle with Indra, if they fail to release the cows. The Paṇis are shown refusing to accept her advice, thus paving the way for the great battle between Indra and the Paṇis.

Thus, the battles, in both the traditions, are preceded by an incident involving a female messenger. Now, it may appear that there is a qualitative difference in the two incidents, since in the Rigveda the female messenger is on the side of the Gods rather than of their adversaries. However, the incident, as it is shown in the Bṛhaddevatā, may be noted.

Malati Shendge points out: "The version of the Bṛhaddevatā differs.... Bṛhaddevatā (viii.24-36) narrates the story of Saramā, where she is stated to have drunk the milk of the Paṇi's cows which were hidden on the other bank of Rasā. When she refuses to disclose the hideout, she is kicked by Indra. Having vomitted the milk, she goes back trembling to the Paṇis."[32]

Here, we find the unmistakable identification: the female messenger is on the side of the Paṇis, and she is kicked by Indra (=tortured by the *Aesir)* until she vomits out the milk of the Paṇi's cows (=parts with, or "coughs up" in English idiom, the gold of the *Vanir).*

The *Vanir/Paṇis* are not found in any other mythology. It is not, as we have seen, merely a similarity in names (else we could have tried to identify the Greek *Pan* with the *Paṇis* due to the chance resemblance of the names), but in identity and incidents.

Thus, the only definite parallels, for Teutonic mythological figures, are found in Vedic mythology.

SOUTH EUROPEAN MYTHOLOGY

The mythology of South Europe (Graeco-Roman, but primarily Greek) is the most famous of the mythologies of Europe, and is second only to Hindu mythology in its detail and complexity. What is signifi-

[31] LEM, p. 275.
[32] CDHR, p. 42.

cant is that it closely resembles Indian mythology in many respects. Unlike Teutonic mythology (which practically deals only with the activities of Gods, giants and the like), both Indian and Greek mythology deal with the activities both of Gods and demons as well as of human heroes. There is, for example, a striking resemblance in the ethos of the Iliad and that of the Mahābhārata: not only do they show a similarity in the state of civilization (with a similar system of organised warfare and war ethics), but even similarity in mythological ideas (the story of Achilles' mother making his whole body invulnerable, with the fatal exception of his heel, is like the story of Duryodhana's mother making his entire body invulnerable with the fatal exception of his thighs).

The following specific correspondences among the Gods may be noted:

Zeus and Indra

Zeus is the Thunder-God armed with a thunderbolt, and he is also the king of the Gods (and so is his Roman counterpart *Jupiter). Indra* is also the Thunder-God armed with a thunderbolt who is king of the Gods.

The identity between *Zeus/Jupiter* and Indra has already been discussed earlier. Of the two, it is clear that Indra is the original name of the Thunder-God. This is proved by the earliest recorded Indo-European inscriptions of West Asia (*Inar, Indas, Indara)*, and by the different names (both traceable in the Rigveda as the names of two other Gods *Parjanya* and *Dyaus Pitar)* in East European mythology (*Pyerun, Perkunas, etc.)* and Graeco-Roman mythology *(Zeus Pater, Jupiter). Indra* is derived from the same root as *indu (*drop) and is hence the natural name for a God of thunder and rain. *Dyaus (Zeus)* is derived from "light" and is the natural name for a Sky-God, which he is in the Rigveda.

We have already seen the similarity in the Greek and Indian versions of the killing of the Great Serpent, where, in both the mythologies, the Serpent is depicted as the vengeful creation of a divine parent, mourning the death or defeat of his/her children at the hands of the Thunder-God, created with the specific purpose of fighting the Thunder-God.

Another peculiar similarity between the two mythologies is that in both of them, the Thunder-God is depicted as vanquishing or killing his own father. One of the very first acts of *Zeus* is supposed to be the vanquishing of his own father *Cronus*, whom he casts to the depths of the universe. The Rigveda (IV.18.12) also speaks of Indra seizing his father by the foot and crushing him, thereby making his mother a widow.

This story probably has its origin in a rather crude literal depiction of a natural phenomenon. The Thunder-God makes his appearance in the form of a thunderbolt: i.e. Indra is "born"; and he is born in the sky, which makes the sky his father (hymn IV.17, the hymn previous to the one which speaks of Indra killing his father, refers to Dyaus, the sky, as Indra's father). As soon as he is "born" the thunderbolt rends the sky into two, thereby "killing" his father. This immediately releases the waters of the sky onto the face of the earth (i.e. the face of Pṛthivī Mātā, the spouse of Dyaus Pitar, is bedewed with tears on being made a widow).

The identity of the Graeco-Roman Thunder-God with Indra is closer than with any other Thunder-God of the other mythologies. In the case of mythologies other than the Teutonic, very few mythological details are known about the Thunder-Gods beyond their names and/or functions. In the case of Teutonic mythology, *Donar/Thor* is not yet a king of the Gods; and there is, moreover, a simplicity about him which contrasts sharply with the shrewder Thunder-Gods of India and Greece.

The Dios Koûroi and the Aśvins

The identity among the divine twins of the Rigveda and of Greek and Baltic mythology has already been discussed earlier.

Ares/Mars and Rudra/Maruts

Here we come across a blanket identity between the Gods of South Europe and of the Rigveda. *Ares (Mars* to the Romans) is the Greek God of war. In the Rigveda, we find *Rudra* and the *Maruts* (who are also known as *Rudriyas,* or the minor *Rudras),* who are associated with the darker and more destructive aspects of a thunderstorm (while Indra is, perhaps, associated with the more beneficial aspects): the Maruts are later identified with the wind, but in the Rigveda they are identified as "storm-divinities".

1. There is a perfect identity between the name. The names *Mars* is derived by Max Müller from the same root as the name *Marut.* In respect of the name *Ares*, the *Larousse Encyclopaedia of Mythology* seems slightly less certain: "Should we, with Max Müller, connect the name *Ares*—like *Mars*—with the Sanskrit root *mar*—from which derive the Vedic *Maruts,* storm divinities?"[33]

[33] LEM, p. 137.

The name *Rudra* confirms the identification. *Rudra* is derived from the Indo-European root **reudh-*, "red", and therefore indicates a red God; and the Vājasaneyī Saṁhitā (16.7) describes Rudra as being red in colour. *Mars* is also considered to be red in colour, and has given his name to the red planet.

2. *Ares/Mars* is the God of War. The Rigveda provides the obvious context: Indra, the God associated with the beneficial aspects of a thunderstorm, is also the God of war. Rudra and the Maruts, associated with the more destructive aspects of a thunderstorm, also share the characteristics of Gods of war. In South European mythology, the functions have become slightly more sharply etched out; hence *Zeus* is properly a Thunder-God, and *Ares* (*Mars*) is properly a God of war.

In the Rigveda, Rudra is very obviously a God of war. Macdonell points out: "The Rigveda often mentions Rudra's weapons of offence. He is once said to hold the thunderbolt in his arm (II.33.3). He is usually said to be armed with a bow and arrows (II.33.10-11; V.42.11; X.125.6; VII.46.1)... In the Atharvaveda he is called an archer (I.28.1; VI.93.1; 15.5.1-7). In that and other later Vedic texts, his bow, arrow, weapon, bolt or club are frequently referred to (Atharvaveda I.28.5, etc.; Śatapatha Brāhmaṇa 9.1.1.6)."[34] Hence, Shendge brands Rudra, in her fanciful classification of many of the Vedic Gods as "non-Aryan Asuras", as the "commander of the Asura army."[35]

The Maruts (i.e. the Rudriyas or minor Rudras) are Indra's most frequent companions in his battles against the atmospheric demons.

3. In spite of *Ares* being the God of war, he is rarely shown as being successful in battle: "Indeed, the impetuous *Ares*, contrary to what one might expect, rarely emerged victorious from battle."[36]

Likewise, Rudra, for all his great stock of terrible weapons, is never shown engaged in battle in the manner of Indra. Shendge points out that Rudra "is never the partner of Indra in his armed conflicts."[37] Macdonell also remarks that "Rudra is never associated, as Indra is, with the warlike exploits of the Maruts, for he does not engage in conflict with the demons."[38] This failure to do battle with the demons probably developed, in the case of *Ares*, into a general failure to battle well; while the Roman *Mars* retained the martial abilities of the Maruts.

[34] VM, p. 74.
[35] CDHR, p. 306, etc.
[36] LEM, p. 138.
[37] CDHR, p. 303.
[38] VM, p. 74.

The reason for Rudra's reticence in battling with demons is probably connected with the fact that Rudra, the terrible, represents only one of the two aspects of the God whose other aspect is Śiva, the auspicious. The Rigveda concentrates on the Rudra aspect, although it mentions Śiva (in X.92.9) as one of the names of Rudra, and also refers to this auspicious aspect (in I.114.3; II.33.6; II.1.6; VI.49.10; VII.10.4; etc). Śiva, on the other hand, was, and still is, the aspect preferred by his worshippers, especially among the Inner Indo-Europeans. *Śiva*, the auspicious, is so innocent and pliable that anyone, even the worst demon in Indian mythology, is able to take advantage of him. Hence his value as an adversary of demons is nil.

Incidentally, Greek mythology[39] depicts an incident where Ares is humbled and defeated by the warrior-Goddess *Athene* and laid prostrate on the ground. We find a parallel theme in Indian mythology: the warrior-Goddess *Durgā* (whether or not *Athene* can be identified with her) is often depicted, in one of her terrible forms, with her foot implanted on the chest of a prostrate Śiva.

4. *Mars* was "in ancient times, the God of vegetation and fertility"[40]; and there are, in the case of the Greek *Ares* also, "hypotheses which would make him primarily a fertility-God."[41]

Rudra/Śiva is also primarily a fertility-God. The worship of the lingam is the very basic form of Śiva-worship.

5. The functions of *Mars* "were at first rustic...under the name of *Silvanus*, who later became a distinct divinity, he presided over the prosperity of cattle."[42]

In the Vājasaneyī Saṁhitā, Atharvaveda, and later, Rudra is also the God of cattle, and "unhoused cattle were...especially consigned to his care."[43] The bull is the sacred animal of Śiva.

6. *Mars* "lived in forests and in the mountains...several animals were sacred to him."[44]

Rudra, according to the Vājasaneyī Saṁhitā (16.2-4), dwells in the mountains. Śiva lives on Mount Kailāśa. Moreover, as *Paśupati* (Lord of the animals), Rudra/Śiva also dwells in the forests.

7. The wolf was an animal especially sacred to *Ares/Mars*. In the case of *Mars*, it was "the wolf whose image frequently appeared in the

[39] LEM, p. 138.
[40] LEM, p. 215.
[41] LEM, p. 137.
[42] LEM, p. 215.
[43] VM, p. 75.
[44] LEM, pp. 215-16.

sanctuaries of the God"[45], and in the case of *Ares*, "his two squires, *Deimos* (fear) and *Phobos* (fright)—sometimes said to be his sons—accompanied him."[46] They are also believed to be wolves.

In the Rigveda, Rudra was always accompanied by his "wide-mouthed, howling dogs, who swallow their prey unchewed."[47] Bhava and Śarva, which, in the Rigveda, are two of the names of Rudra also occur in the Atharvaveda, "but they seem here to have been regarded as deities distinct from one another and from Bhava and Śarva are, in a Sūtra passage, spoken of as sons of Rudra and are compared with wolves eager for prey."[48]

8. The companions of *Ares* are all kinds of ghouls and ghosts like the *Keres*, "sombre divinities eager to drink the black blood of the dying."[49]

Rudra/Śiva is likewise depicted in Indian mythology as living in the company of ghouls and ghosts.

9. *Ares*, in Greek mythology, is considered to be "a furious God, by nature wicked and fickle, who in the immortal society of Olympus found, it seems, very little sympathy... He was always thought of by the Greeks with more terror than sympathy. He was the God of war, of blind, brutal courage, of bloody rage and carnage."[50] He is treated with aversion both by the Greeks as well as by their other Gods: " 'Of all the Gods who live on Olympus,' says *Zeus* in the Iliad to *Ares*, 'thou art the most odious to me.' "[51]

Likewise, Rudra in the Rigveda is also depicted as a God isolated from the others due to his malevolent nature, and feared alike by Gods and men: "He is described in the Rigveda as fierce...and destructive like a wild beast... Malevolence is frequently attributed to Rudra in the Rigveda, for the hymns addressed to him chiefly express fear of his terrible shafts and deprecation of his wrath... Even the Gods were afraid of the strung bow and the arrows of Rudra lest he should destroy them... He is said to have been formed of a compound of all the most terrible substances... It is probably owing to his formidable characteristics that in the Brāhmaṇas and the Sūtras Rudra is regarded as isolated from the other Gods."[52] Of the three Gods of the Hindu Trinity, Śiva is

[45] LEM, p. 216.
[46] LEM, pp. 137-38.
[47] VM, p. 75.
[48] Ibid.
[49] LEM, p. 138.
[50] LEM, p. 137.
[51] Ibid.
[52] VM, pp. 75-76.

the 'Destroyer'.

The evidence for the identity of *Ares/Mars* with *Rudra/Śiva* and the *Rudriyas/Maruts* is too overwhelming to be denied.

And the total evidence, connecting South European mythology with Vedic mythology, but with none of the other Indo-European mythologies, is quite unambiguous.

WEST EUROPEAN MYTHOLOGY

Finally, we come to West European (Celtic) mythology, which is the least Indo-European of the seven. This is not to say that Celtic mythology has borrowed from "non-Indo-European" mythological sources, but that Celtic mythology has hardly any elements in common with any other Indo-European mythology, and hence it is more definitely "Celtic" than "Indo-European".

There is almost a total lack of proto-Indo-European elements. As the *Larousse Encyclopaedia of Mythology* puts it: "The most important deities were skilled in many spheres and *attempts made by scholars to equate them with the specialized Gods of other pantheons have been unsuccessful.*"[53]

These attempts include the works of Dorothea Chaplin (*Mythological Bonds between East and West*, Einar Munksgaard, Copenhagen, 1938; and *Matter, Myth and Spirit or Keltic and Hindu Links*, Rider and Company, London, 1935). However, none of these attempts make much sense, since they are based on very vague generalisations and philosophical musings, and on attempts to equate Gods *purely* on the basis of some perceived (and often implausibly perceived) "similarity" in names. Dorothea Chaplin's works serve only to show that Celtic mythology and religion were very "pagan" indeed, in which respect it certainly resembles Hinduism as much as many other pre-Semitic religions.

The *Larousse Encyclopaedia of Mythology* can point only to "the concept of the Mother-Goddess which had evolved in much earlier times and which persisted throughout and beyond the Celtic period. Whereas the Celtic Gods were specifically Celtic...the Goddesses were restatements of an old theme."[54] However, the Goddesses *Danu, Anu* and *Brigid* cannot really be identified with any Goddess in any other mythology, except *Danu*, the major Goddess, who is considered so important that all the Gods are collectively known as the "People of the

[53] LEM, p. 237.
[54] LEM, p. 239.

Goddess *Danu*". In her case, we can postulate a parallel in Indian mythology where we find *Danu*, one of the wives of Kaśyapa, who is on par with Aditi, the mother of the Gods.

T.W. Rolleston (in *Myths of the Celtic Race*, George and Harrap and Co. Ltd., London, 1911) reiterates the point about the obscurity of the Gods of the earliest Celts when he says: "What were the names and attributes of the Celtic deities? Here we are very much in the dark"(p. 86).

However, he points out that an ancient Roman writer, Lucan, "mentions a triad of deities, *Aesus*, *Teutates* and *Taranus*", and claims that "in these names, we seem to be in the presence of a true Celtic, i.e. Aryan tradition". But, here, we have only the names of three Gods. While the first of these can be compared with Vedic *Asura*, Teutonic *Aesir* and Iranian *Ahura*; the second of these seems to bear no similarity even in name with any other Indo-European God, but the name means "valiant" or "warlike", and on this basis Rolleston decides that *Teutates* is "a deity equivalent to *Mars*". The third name, *Taranus* is derived from the Welsh-Cornish-Breton word *taran* (thunderbolt) and is therefore, obviously, a name for the Thunder-God. (The word *taraṇ* in Sanskrit means "sky" or "heaven", and it may be speculated that like the name *Dyaus*, "sky", which became the name of the Thunder-God in Southern Europe, the word *taraṇ*, "sky", may have become the name of the Thunder-God in Western Europe, and later came to mean also "thunderbolt", with which the Thunder-God is identified.)

In any case, except for speculations of this kind, we have nothing concrete in respect of Celtic mythology. It has practically nothing in common with any other Indo-European mythology, and a study of Celtic mythology therefore provides no new information about proto-Indo-European mythology.

THE ORIGINAL MYTHOLOGY

Thus, we see that a study of the common mythological elements, found in two or more of the different streams of Indo-European mythology (and hence taken as common elements), provides us with a picture of a section—the reconstructable section—of the original Indo-European mythology.

And we see that this reconstructed section of proto-Indo-European mythology fits perfectly into Vedic mythology. Every single common element is found in the Rigveda; but the various common elements are found distributed, often in fragments and in later developed forms, among the other mythologies.

Two very fundamental aspects of Vedic religion and ritual are the worship of fire in elaborate *yajñas* and the ritual use of Soma. It appears that these do not form important religious elements in the other Indo-European cultures, so much so that Malati Shendge[55] argues that fire-worship and the ritual use of Soma were adopted by the "Aryan invaders" from the local "non-Aryans".

But a study of the different Indo-European cultures shows that these elements must have been present in proto-Indo-European religion and ritual, since garbled memories and traces of them were retained in the different Indo-European mythologies and rituals.

1. About fire-worship, Macdonell points out: "The sacrificial fire seems to have been an Indo-European institution also, since the Italians and Greeks, as well as the Iranians and Indians had the custom of offering gifts to the Gods in fire."[56]

The Teutons also had the custom of offering sacrifices to the Gods in fire; and in fact, as we saw, the *Vanir* are supposed to demand from the Gods a share in the sacrifices as a precondition for peace.

The Slavonic people also worshipped fire. According to the *Larousse Encyclopaedia of Mythology*, "a very ancient author said of the Pagan Slavs: 'they also address prayers to fire, calling him *Svarogich...*' "[57] And, in fact, the Slavs worshipped fire under the same name: *Ogon (=Agni)*

2. Soma in the Rigveda is distinctly the juice of a plant growing in the mountains of northernmost West Punjab and the adjoining areas of Kashmir. The identity of the plant is not known now; and in fact it was lost even to the ancient Sanskrit commentators of the Rigveda. But the plant forms a very essential element in Vedic ritual, as per the testimony of the Rigveda. However, the later Sanskrit commentators had at least retained the knowledge that Soma was a plant found on certain mountains.

In Europe, however, we find that the nature as well as the name of the Soma plant has been forgotten, but the concept of Soma (as a kind of *amrita* or nectar) has been retained; and the same importance is given to it in mythological memory (rather than in living ritual as in the Rigveda), where it is confused with honey-mead.

Macdonell points out: "The belief in an intoxicating divine bever-

[55] CDHR, pp. 88, 268, 377, etc., and pp. 109-13.
[56] VM, p. 99.
[57] LEM, p. 295.

age, the home of which was heaven, may be Indo-European. If so, it must have been regarded as a kind of honey-mead...brought down to earth from its guardian demon by an eagle (the Soma-bringing eagle of Indra agreeing with the nectar-bringing eagle of *Zeus*, and with the eagle which, as a metamorphosis of *Odhin*, carried off the mead)."[58]

Macdonell, as an ardent advocate of the invasion theory, tries to suggest that the original concept was that of honey-mead, which later became Soma in the Rigveda; but the facts speak otherwise. The ritual of Soma was a living one in the Rigveda, and both the Rigveda and the Avesta clearly describe the plant and the ritual, and the myth of its being brought by an eagle from the mountain, in similar terms; but the Teutons and the Greeks, after they had moved off into Europe, far from the source of Soma, clearly forgot the name and nature of Soma, and only retained a garbled mythological memory of "an intoxicating divine beverage" which was often confused with honey-mead.

Thus, we see that the Original Indo-European mythology, constructed out of common elements, proves to be more or less identical with Vedic mythology. This clashes sharply with the generally accepted concept of the Vedic language (and its culture) being merely the oldest representative of one of the two sub-branches of one out of nine living branches of Indo-European languages, and proves that the Vedic language and culture stood in a somewhat ancestral position in respect of the Iranian, West Asian and European languages and cultures. The exact nature of this ancestral position has been discussed in the previous chapter, in the context of the positive evidence in the Purāṇas.

[58] VM, p. 114.

Twenty Three

THE INDUS VALLEY CIVILIZATION

The Rigveda and the Purāṇas, as we saw, provide conclusive evidence that India was the Original Homeland of the Indo-European family of languages.

Not only do the Purāṇas give the earlier history of the Vedic Aryans (i.e. the Pūrus), who were the authors of the Rigveda (the oldest, hoariest and, linguistically and culturally, the most archaic Indo-European text in the world), showing them to have originated in south-eastern Uttar Pradesh before their ancestors went and settled down in the Punjab; but they also name two other groups of Indo-Europeans (the Anus and the Druhyus), with a similar origin in south-eastern Uttar Pradesh, and show them to have settled down in areas to the north and northwest of the Vedic Aryans, and even specifically record their migration northwards and away from these areas. The Rigveda, in its Dāśarājña hymns, names the historically closest five branches of the present-day Indo-European languages (Iranian, Thraco-Phrygian, Celtic, Hellenic, and Illyrian) as having been branches of the Anus and Druhyus, while its mythology proves to be practically identical with the parent mythology of all the later branch mythologies.

In this context, any theory that the Indus Civilization was a "non-Aryan" civilization (specifically "Dravidian", or even "Austric") destroyed by "Aryan invaders" stands exposed as a gross misconception or a motivated fabrication. The facts scream out that the Indus Civilization was an Indo-European one.

Practically the only general ground on which it had been branded as "non-Aryan" and "Dravidian" was that the scholars, long before the discovery of the civilization, had already formulated a theory of an Aryan invasion of a Dravidian India. The fact that they had to (as unwittingly admitted by Malati Shendge) quickly and radically reassess the Aryan vs. non-Aryan equation from a view that "the Aryan invaders of India encountered only a rabble of aboriginal savages" to a view that "the Aryan advent in India was in fact the arrival of barbarians into a region already highly organised into an empire based on a long-established tradition of literate urban culture" was, of course, only a minor detail!

However, the evidence in the Rigveda and the Purāṇas proves conclusively and finally that there was no "Aryan invasion" of India but in fact an outflow of groups of "Aryans" from India who carried the speech-family to its present habitats. This knocks out the very basis of the characterization of the Indus Civilization as "pre-Aryan" and "non-Aryan".

The *only* specific ground on which the civilization was branded as a "non-Aryan" one was that the major God depicted on the seals was Rudra/Śiva in his aspect of Paśupati (Lord of the Animals) with many of the characteristic features of Rudra/Śiva as described in the texts. This God had been, even earlier, branded as a "Dravidian God" borrowed by the "Aryans", and his sole presence on the seals clinched (in their opinion) the Dravidian character of the civilization. However, as we saw, Rudra/Śiva/Paśupati has his perfect counterpart in Graeco-Roman mythology. Moreover, those very aspects of the literary description of Rudra/Śiva in the Sanskrit texts (such as his being a nomadic mountain-and-forest dweller, his being associated with ghouls and spirits, and his being a feared, isolated and even reviled God), which had led to his being branded as a "non-Aryan" God, as well as that very aspect most prominently depicted in the Indus seals (the Paśupati aspect), are all found in Graeco-Roman mythology.

The words *Śiva* and *Śambhu* are not derived from the Tamil words *civa* (to redden, to become angry) and *cembu* (copper, the red metal), but from the Sanskrit roots *śī* (therefore meaning "auspicious, gracious, favourable, benign, kind"[1], etc.) and *śam* (therefore meaning "being or existing for happiness or welfare, granting or causing happiness, benevolent, helpful, kind"[2], etc.), and the words are used in this sense only, right from their very first occurrence.

Thus the identification of Rudra/Śiva in the Indus seals is in fact evidence that the civilization was an Indo-European one.

And then we have the decipherment of the Indus seals by Dr. S.R. Rao, already described in an earlier chapter. This decipherment, although still the subject of "controversy" in an invasionist-controlled establishment, proves conclusively that the Indus people were Indo-Europeans. But those who would like to treat his decipherment as unproved, and the linguistic identity of the Indus people as still a mystery, may note the following facts:

1. There is no tradition whatsoever among the Dravidian speaking populace of the South that they originally lived in the Northwest, or that their language and civilization extended to the Northwest, or that

[1] SED, p. 1074.
[2] SED, p. 1055.

they had a sister "Dravidian" civilization in the Northwest. The oldest Dravidian traditions speak of ancient prehistoric kingdoms in the South itself, extending, in fact, even further south into a land now sunk under the seas. There is no trace of Dravidian place-names in the Indus region even in the very ancient past. "Excavation in the South has hitherto revealed no trace of the Indus Valley Civilization."[3] There is no Dravidian tradition of any conflict with the speakers of Indo-European languages in ancient times. That Tamil has the names *Vaḍamoḷī* (northern language) for Sanskrit and *Tēnmoḷī* (southern language) for ancient Tamil is also significant.

2. Excavations at the Harappan sites have yielded many fire-altars, terracotta ladles as were used in *yajñas*, and (in some cases) pieces of bangles, pottery and animal bones in these altars (as in certain Vedic sacrifices). The book *Lothal and the Indus Civilization* by Dr. S.R. Rao shows photographs of these altars (Plates XXXVI A–D and XXXVII A–B).

3. Anthropological study of the cephalic index of the skulls found on the sites at Harappa, Mohenjodaro and Lothal (situated in Punjab, Sind and Gujarat respectively) reveals that the racial composition of each of these regions in Harappan times was more or less the same as it is now. Dr. S.R. Rao points out: "So far as cephalic index is concerned, the Harappan people of Mohenjodaro have similarities with the present day people of Sind, those of Harappa with the people of Punjab and those of Lothal with the people of Gujarat."[4]

The same has been described in detail by P. Gupta, P.C. Datta and A. Basu in *Human Skeletal Remains from Harappa* (Memoirs of the Anthropological Survey of India No. 9, Calcutta, 1962), and they conclude that "the population of the widespread region (Punjab to Gujarat) has remained more or less stable since Harappan times". This disproves the idea of displacement of an originally different "non-Aryan" Harappan population by the present-day "Aryan" inhabitants of this region.

So it is clear that the Harappans were Indo-Europeans. But what exactly is their position in the ancient texts?

THE HARAPPANS IN THE ANCIENT TEXTS

The heyday of the Indus Civilization was after the composition of the major bulk of the Rigvedic hymns. Hence, there is no mention of any people in the Rigveda who may be identified as the Harappans.

[3] HCIP, p. 193.
[4] *Lothal and the Indus Civilization*, p. 173.

According to the Purāṇas, the Pūrus (i.e. the Vedic Aryans) were in the Punjab region, but the centre of their culture soon shifted eastwards to the region later known as the Kuru-Pañcāla region and then they also expanded further east towards the south of the Ikṣvāku region and to the region of the erstwhile Prāṁśus. This, as any invasionist scholar will agree, is also demonstrated by the Vedic texts.

The Anus, on the other hand, originally lived in Kashmir, but they migrated southwards and established kingdoms in the Punjab. Continuing conflicts with the Pūrus probably led to their movement westwards.

The exact identity of the Indus people is, therefore, probably a mixture of Pūrus and Anus with perhaps also an element of Yadus. That they were not wholly Anus is proved by the fact that Rudra/Śiva/Paśupati, the only known God, and obviously the most prominent one, of the Indus people, is not prominent in any Iranian culture; and the present-day languages of Punjab and Sind are not Iranian, but "Indo-Aryan". That they were not wholly Pūrus is proved by the fact that the Pūru-based Vedic texts do not give much importance to them.

Their exact chronological position vis-a-vis the Vedic culture is shown by a comparison of the Indian texts, which refer to these people, with the Sumerian texts which also refer to them. The Sumerians are known to have had trade relations with the Indus people, and the Sumerian texts have been reliably dated; hence this cross-reference enables us to date the Vedic texts as well.

We have already described (in an earlier chapter) the evidence furnished by K.D. Sethna whereby he dates the Rigveda prior to the Indus Civilization on the basis of two factors: the mention of cotton (*karpāsa*) in the Vedic texts; and the mention of *Melukkha* (which proves to be the Indus Civilization) in the Sumerian texts collated with the mention of *Mlecchadeśa* in the earliest Sūtras.

The evidence is too strong to be denied. But what makes it irresistible is the fact that even a determinedly invasionist scholar like Malati Shendge unwittingly corroborates K.D. Sethna's line of argument.

The very name of Malati Shendge's book, *The Civilized Demons—Harappans in the Rigveda*, indicates that she places the Rigvedic Age at the fag-end of the heyday of the Indus Civilization. We have already seen, in a previous chapter, her desperate attempts to show that the Harappans were the "non-Aryan" enemies mentioned in the Rigveda. However, she totally fails in her attempt to locate the Harappans in the Rigveda, and ends up with the ridiculous proposition that most of the

Vedic Gods (who have their counterparts in European mythologies) were the "non-Aryan" Harappans.

However, at one point in the book, Shendge makes an attempt to identify the names of the Indus Civilization in the Sanskrit texts. She rejects the name *Melukkha/Mleccha* as the name of the Indus empire (She has not read K.D. Sethna's book, which was published after hers; but the identification of the Sumerian *Melukkha* with the Sanskrit *Mleccha* is an unavoidable one, and many Western scholars have been compelled to note this connection, "but, putting the Rigveda after the Harappa culture and thus dating the Śatapatha Brāhamaṇa to c. 600 BC, had to leave the value of this correspondence undecided"[5]), but she ›cates, instead, the name *Āraṭṭa*.

Let us examine the case put forward by her.

She cites a Sumerian text, the cuneiform *Epic of Enmerker*. This .c "is placed about 1700 BC... although not all the details of the epic can be treated as authentic facts, the geographical details seem to be realistic enough."[6] The epic describes the land of Āraṭṭa as lying "to the east beyond seven mountains"[7] and refers to a big river in Āraṭṭa "which could cause immense destruction". There is also a reference to the people of Āraṭṭa being asked to build a temple of "gold, silver and lapis lazuli and timber."[8]

She also points out that the Mahābhārata refers to *Āraṭṭa*, and in the Karṇa Parva (Mahābhārata, VIII.30.35–74) detailed descriptions are given. She gives the three verses which describe the location of Āraṭṭa:

1. "Where these five rivers, Śatadru, Vipāśā, the third Irāvatī, Candrabhāgā and Vitastā flow and where there are *pīlū*-forests and (where) Sindhu is the sixth to flow out, this country is called Āraṭṭa."[9]
2. "That (region) where these five rivers, emerging from the mountains flow, this Āraṭṭa (country) is called *Bālhīka* where the Arya should not stay even for two days."[10]
3. "Āraṭṭa is the name of the country, Bālhīka is the name of the people who are generally abused as *Vāsatis, Sindhus* and *Sauvīras*."[11]

[5] Karpāsa, p. 71.
[6] CDHR, p. 393.
[7] CDHR, p. 392.
[8] Ibid.
[9] CDHR, p. 393.
[10] CDHR, pp. 393-94.
[11] CDHR, p. 394.

She concludes: "All the three verses clearly define the geographical area which was called by the name Āraṭṭa. Only six rivers are named here, omitting the name of Sarasvatī the seventh, which together are referred to in the Rigveda as the *Saptasindhavah*, obviously because Sarasvatī became sacred to the Aryans as the saviour of Indra's life."[12]

The passage "gives the impression that amongst the Bālhīkas, the Aryan social structure, which became a rule in the later days, was not enforced or observed strictly. Thus it was not considered obligatory by the people to hold on to a single occupation. A brahmin who visited this region found to his dismay that 'having become a brahmin once, a Bālhīka becomes kṣatriya, then vaiśya, śūdra and even a barber. Having become a barber, he again becomes a brahmin, and having become a twice-born, he becomes a *Dāsa*. In the same family, one becomes a brahmin and the rest follow other professions', and he concluded that Gāndhāras, Madrakas and Bālhīkas are utterly thoughtless."[13]

And finally, determined to squeeze this into her theory of the Harappans being "non-Aryan Asuras", she concludes: "It is tempting not to see in this what was probably a custom of long standing and perhaps a part of the ancient way of life inherited from the Asuras"[14]; and adds that the Bālhīkas were "non-Aryans" who "did not accept the (Aryan) religious beliefs"[15], and hence "the religion of the people of Āraṭṭa is described as *naṣṭadharma*, destroyed religion..."[16]

Shendge's reasoning as usual, suffers from some fundamental flaws: in this case, it is a totally confused chronological sense. On the one hand, her whole book seeks to prove that the Harappan Civilization was a pre-Rigvedic one, which met its end during the early Rigvedic Age, and on the other, the references given by her prove that the heyday of the Indus Civilization (the period when it carried on trade with the Sumerians) was very much later to the Rigvedic Age.

What seems to escape her attention, but which has been grasped by K.D. Sethna in his analysis, is that the land which is proved by Sumerian records to be the Indus Civilization is not found described, or even mentioned, in the Rigveda or any other Veda Saṁhitā or in the Brāhmaṇas or Āraṇyakas, but in some much later texts. The Mahābhārata names and describes the land; Sethna[17] also points out

[12] Ibid.
[13] Ibid.
[14] CDHR, p. 395.
[15] Ibid.
[16] Ibid.
[17] Karpāsa, p. 65.

that "the pretty early Baudhāyana Dharmasūtra (I.1.2,14-15)" refers "in 1400 BC to countries that are *of mixed origin* and insisting that one who visits them needs purification", and "we know that it is dealing with *Mlecchadeśa*. Among these countries it mentions Āraṭṭa (Punjab), Sindhu (Sind), Sauvīra (round about Multan), Saurāṣhṭra (southern Kathiawar): all the past Harappa culture sites outside the Ganges Valley are covered."

And there is one very significant aspect in the description of the land: only five rivers and the Sindhu are named. It is obvious that the Sarasvatī, the river par excellence of the Rigveda, had already dried up at the time of the Indus Valley culture. Shendge's explanation that the Sarasvatī is not named "because Sarasvatī became sacred to the Aryans as the saviour of Indra's life" (whatever that means) is so senseless that it does not even deserve comment.

The Baudhāyana Dharmasūtra refers to this civilization as being "of mixed origin" (i.e. Pūrus, Anus, and perhaps some Yadus as well), and refers to its religion as *naṣṭadharma*, destroyed religion (i.e. the "pure" Vedic religion of the Pūrus "destroyed" by intermixing with the religion of the Anus and others). Among the peoples named, it must be noted, are the Sauvīras and Madrakas (two peoples specifically described in the Purāṇas as Anus — or even more properly, the Anus who migrated southwards from Kashmir to the Punjab and established kingdoms there among the originally Pūru population). The situation is clearly a very post-Rigvedic one; Shendge unwittingly points out that "the Aryan social structure which became a rule in *the later days*" (i.e. the days later to the Rigvedic age) had already become so rigid at the time of this description of Āraṭṭa (thus squarely placing Āraṭṭa, i.e. Harappan Punjab, in the "later", i.e. post-Rigvedic days) that a brahmin from the east (thereby indicating that the Vedic people of the time were already established far to the east of the Saptasindhu) who visited this land was shocked at what he considered to be a "thoughtless" disregard of rigid professionalism.

The name *Āraṭṭa*, incidentally, may well be derived from the same source as *Āryāvarta* and *Airyana*.

Thus, any logical comparison of Sanskrit texts with the dated Sumerian texts, for the purpose of locating common references to the Indus Civilization, inevitably brings the Sumerian texts and the Indus civilization in line with the post-Vedic Sanskrit texts. This automatically places the age of the Rigveda well before the age of the Indus civilization.

THE ORIGINAL HOMELAND

The history of the Indo-European family of languages may thus be summarized as follows:

In ancient, prehistoric times, the distribution of the languages in India may have been roughly the same as it is today: viz. the Dravidian languages being spoken in the south, the Austric languages in the east, the Andamanese languages in the Andaman Islands, the Burushaski language in a part of Kashmir, the Sino-Tibetan languages in the Himalayan and far eastern border areas, and the Indo-European languages certainly in more or less their present habitat in most of northern India.

Among the speakers of Indo-European languages, a great historical occurrence took place when a major part of the Indo-Europeans of south-eastern Uttar Pradesh migrated to the west and settled down in the northwestern areas — Punjab, Kashmir and the further north-west , where they differentiated into three groups: the Pūrus (in the Punjab), the Anus (in Kashmir) and the Druhyus (in the northwest and Afghanistan). Meanwhile, there remained various Indo-Europeans still in the interior of India: the Yadus in northern Maharashtra, Gujarat and western Madhya Pradesh; the Turvasus in the region to the east of the Yadus (not specified); groups of Sudyumnas/Ailas in central and southern Uttar Pradesh; Ikṣvākus in northeastern Uttar Pradesh (and perhaps also in Dakshina Kosala in eastern Madhya Pradesh); and Prāṁśus in Bihar, to name only those of them clearly mentioned and described in the Purāṇas.

The Pūrus developed the Vedic culture of the Punjab, while the other groups of Inner Indo-Europeans (alongwith the Austric and Dravidian language speakers) developed other religious and cultural elements integral to Hinduism and Indian culture. Later, the Vedic culture of the Pūrus spread all over India and became the elite culture of Hinduism, while the Vedic language, and the Classical Sanskrit created from it (in combination with some Inner dialects) by the grammarians, strongly influenced all the Inner languages (Inner Indo-European, Austric and Dravidian).

Meanwhile, major sections of Anus spread out all over Western Asia and developed into the various Iranian cultures. The Druhyus spread out into Europe in two instalments: the speakers of the proto-Germanic dialect first migrated northwards and then westwards, and then later the speakers of the proto-Hellenic and proto-Italo-Celtic dialects moved into Europe by a different, more southern, route.

It is possible that the speakers of proto-Baltic and proto-Slavonic (or proto-Balto-Slavonic) (who left earlier, perhaps in the first wave of migration alongwith the speakers of proto-Germanic), and the speakers of proto-Illyrian and proto-Thraco-Phrygian (who left later alongwith the later Druhyu groups and the Iranians) were Anus and not Druhyus —the Anus and Druhyus thus being, respectively, the speakers of proto-Satem and proto-Kentum.

The Indus Valley culture was a mixed culture of Pūrus and Anus; the Hittites and the Tocharians were probably different mixed groups of Pūrus, Anus and Druhyus. The Mitanni and Kassites were certainly groups of Vedic Pūrus.

This whole description is based on the most logical, and in many respects the *only possible*, interpretation of the facts, which have already been described and analysed in detail throughout this book and need not be recapitulated here.

Any further research, and any new material discovered on the subject, can only confirm this description. There may be minor points on which rectifications may become necessary, such as on the exact identities and interrelationships of the various Indo-European groups, past and present; but there is no possible way in which the location of the Original Homeland in the interior of northern India, so faithfully recorded in the Purāṇas and confirmed in the Rigveda, can ever be disproved.